Contents

Music, Thought, and Feeling

Understanding the Psychology of Music

William Forde Thompson

Macquarie University

New York   Oxford

OXFORD UNIVERSITY PRESS

2009

Oxford University Press, Inc., publishes works that further Oxford University's
objective of excellence in research, scholarship, and education.

Oxford New York
Auckland   Cape Town   Dar es Salaam   Hong Kong   Karachi
Kuala Lumpur   Madrid   Melbourne   Mexico City   Nairobi
New Delhi   Shanghai   Taipei   Toronto

With offices in
Argentina   Austria   Brazil   Chile   Czech Republic   France   Greece
Guatemala   Hungary   Italy   Japan   Poland   Portugal   Singapore
South Korea   Switzerland   Thailand   Turkey   Ukraine   Vietnam

Copyright © 2009 by Oxford University Press, Inc.

Published by Oxford University Press, Inc.
198 Madison Avenue, New York, New York 10016
http://www.oup.com

Oxford is a registered trademark of Oxford University Press

Library of Congress Cataloging-in-Publication Data

Thompson, William Forde.
Music, thought, and feeling: understanding the psychology of music/
by William Forde Thompson.
    p. cm.
Includes bibliographical references and index.
ISBN 978-0-19-537707-1 — ISBN 978-0-19-514085-9
1. Music—Psychological aspects.   2. Musical perception.   3. Cognition.
I. Title.
ML3830.T496   2008
781'.11—dc22   2008017657

Loughborough
COLLEGE est 1909

Printing number: 9 8 7 6 5 4 3 2

Printed in the United States of America
on acid-free paper

Preface

This book provides a review and critical assessment of a vast body of research and theory that is collectively known as the field of music cognition. It brings together the work of a growing number of researchers who, with varying background and expertise, have dedicated their careers to the goal of understanding the psychology of music. It provides a critical assessment of current understandings of music cognition and the emotional basis of music. The book has pedagogical aims but also posits novel ideas about many research questions and thereby represents a specific perspective that students, researchers, and instructors can critically assess and challenge.

Writing this book has been an 8-year project. As one friend pointed out, it commenced last century. When I began the process I did not fully appreciate the challenge of summarizing such a rapidly evolving area of study. More than once I worried that any overview would contain alarming gaps, both in the established literature and recent work. New findings are published each week, rendering the process of summarizing the endless output of research like taking snapshots of individuals on a passing train. Nevertheless, my hope is that this book will provide readers with a rich understanding of the central questions, experimental strategies, and theories in the field, allowing them to pursue their interests through more focused reading or investigation.

The organization of the book was influenced by my experiences as an instructor for more than a dozen courses on the psychology of music, and the significant challenges that I experienced. My approach to teaching the course was continuously refined over a decade, coinciding with my evolving views on the discipline. Unlike early textbooks on the psychology of music, this book does not begin by describing the auditory system and the physics of sound. Although it may seem logical to build on these foundations, they are typically of little or no interest to the majority of students and new researchers unless they are motivated by the broader questions that tend to capture the imagination and draw people toward the field. In my experience, beginning a course on the psychology of music with dull diagrams of a sine wave is the most efficient way to reduce enrollment quickly. Presenting such information without a broader context is also confusing to students, who may mistakenly conclude that the field has little to do with music per se. Chapter 1 contains additional discussions of the contents and organization of the book.

Some sections were adapted or excerpted from my published articles, especially Thompson and Schellenberg (2006) and Thompson and Cuddy (1997). I thank my coauthors for their contributions and support. Some of the glossary entries were adapted by permission from an unpublished glossary by David Huron. Paolo Ammirante, Tracey Morrison, Stevie Yap, and Dmitri Tcherbadji provided valuable technical assistance.

The contributions by Paolo Ammirante and Frank Russo were particularly valuable to the development and completion of this book. Paolo Ammirante edited early versions of the book and coordinated the layout design for drafts that were trialed in university courses. Paolo also conceived and wrote most the sidebars, located images, and assisted with copyright access. He also provided editorial assistance at all stages of production. Quite simply, the contributions of Paolo have been profound and professional. Frank Russo provided critical feedback on early versions of the book, and worked with me in trialing the book for undergraduate courses. Significantly, Frank also conceived and created most of the audio examples that accompany the text, and he provided the descriptions and credits for them. I am deeply grateful to Frank and Paolo for their critical role in the development of this book. To the extent that the book has limitations, however, I take full responsibility.

Many colleagues and friends provided helpful comments and suggestions on the book, in many cases using drafts in courses and providing detailed feedback from students. They include Paolo Ammirante, Lincoln Colling, Lola Cuddy, Pat Diamond, Laurie Heller, David Huron, Patrik Juslin, Frank Russo, Carol Krumhansl, Edward Large, Daniel Levitin, Steven Livingstone, Caroline Palmer, Aniruddh Patel, Glenn Schellenberg, Siu-Lan Tan, Laurel Trainor, Lena Quinto, and many others, including anonymous reviewers. In vetting the penultimate draft, the following colleagues generously shared their expertise in teaching the psychology of music course, resulting in a better pedagogical device: Karen Burland, School of Music, University of Leeds; Frederick Burrack, Kansas State University; Patricia Shehan Campbell, University of Washington; Laurie Heller, Brown University; Gary McPherson, University of Illinois at Urbana-Champaign; Andrew J. Oxenham, University of Minnesota; Zehra Peynircioglu, American University; Patricia S. Poulter, Eastern Illinois University; and Sui-Lan Tan, Kalamazoo College. I am also grateful to the many students who provided feedback on early drafts of the book. Mark Antliff and Pat Leighten provided advice on the cover design and encouragement on the project.

I would like to thank my family for their support, including my partner Pat Diamond, my sister Judith Thompson, my mother Mary and late father Bob, and more than a dozen extended family members. I would also like to thank Oxford University Press, with special thanks to Catherine Carlin and Patrick Lynch of its editorial staff for their encouragement and advice.

CHAPTER 1
Introduction

LEARNING OUTCOMES

By the end of this chapter you should be able to:

1. Identify the major subdisciplines in the field and provide examples of the issues that are addressed in each.

2. Explain three broad and long-standing controversies.

3. Analyze opposing arguments for each controversy.

4. Identify three areas of accelerated research activity and the reasons for the recent growth in these areas.

Music is an important yet puzzling part of our lives. We turn on the radio while driving our car, we hear music while at parties, bars, and restaurants, we dance to music, shop to music, sing in the shower, and attend concerts. We play music to create a mood or atmosphere. After a hectic day, we might listen to calming music. With a group of friends at a party, we might listen to energetic music. Music can manipulate our feelings and thoughts in film and television, where it is used to establish an atmosphere, foreshadow an event, or suggest an interpretation of ambiguous visual or verbal material.

How can we understand the role of music in our lives, and its relation to language, feelings, and ideas? How and why did music evolve as a human cognitive capacity? Musical activities seem very different from other human activities. It has little in common with eating, driving, talking, reading, or planning, and does not greatly interfere with our ability to engage in these activities.

Some activities are strongly associated with music. Dancing is almost always accompanied by music. Religious ceremonies frequently involve music, and parties and other special events typically involve music. Speech and music are coupled in song, and words that are sung to music seem more poetic, memorable, and insightful than the same words spoken outside of a musical context. Music frames and highlights the words, implying to listeners that they have special significance.

We can gain a general understanding of music by thinking critically about our personal experiences with music, its role in our lives, and its relation to other aspects of human experience. This exercise gives us only a very general understanding of music, however, leaving many of the details of our musical experiences unexplained. For this reason, researchers and scholars have developed and refined a range of strategies for studying music and musical experience. These research tools provide a means for understanding some of the most subtle and complex aspects of the relation among music, thought, and feeling, yielding a growing body of knowledge that we call the psychology of music.

Overview of Book Contents

Researchers from many different fields contribute to this area, and they ask many different questions. One important question is how the brain is organized to handle the many aspects of music, such as rhythm, melody, harmony, dynamics, and timbre. Another question is whether each musical quality such as rhythm and melody has a unique effect on us, or whether the various qualities of music combine to produce "emergent" experiences. Other areas of investigation include the relation between music and emotion, the origins of musical behaviors in human evolution, and links between music and other human abilities such as speech, dance, and mathematics.

This book outlines some of the major issues being investigated by leading scientists and the experimental approaches that they have used to address such issues. Chapter 2 describes some of the major theories of how and when music became a widespread part of human behavior. What is the possible origin of music in human evolution? All known cultures engage in some form of musical behavior, suggesting that it is a basic part of human life, such as eating, drinking, and communicating. Are musical activities fundamental to what it means to be human, or is music merely a popular invention used for its entertainment value, like amusement parks, ice cream cones, and wakeboarding? Many researchers maintain that musical behaviors likely came into being through processes of evolution, such that they are now inscribed in our genetic makeup as an essential human behavior. This view rests on the assumption that at some point in our evolutionary history, musical behaviors conferred crucial survival benefits, such as the capacity to attract mates or create social bonds.

A number of scholars have proposed models of why music exists in human life. There is a wide range of views on the matter, including the possibility that music is a human invention that has entertainment value but performs no biological function. Other models outline possible evolutionary contexts in which musical behaviors might have functioned to enhance reproduction. For example, although styles and genres of music vary considerably, music across all cultures seems to share an underlying affective nature, and it often performs similar social functions (in ceremonies and rituals, or to nurture group bonds). These similarities could indicate a deep and common biological basis for all musical styles in evolution, even if the surface details of musical behavior are learned.

Constructing a theory of the evolutionary origins of music presents many intellectual challenges, but one such challenge stands out. Any theory of musical origins must provide a definition of music, but there are few common features of music across cultures and historical periods. The music of Australian Aborigines bears little resemblance to Mozart piano sonatas, hip-hop, Broadway musicals, or Hindustani ragas. The striking differences between various musical genres imply that at least some salient features of musical behavior are specific to particular cultures and even subcultures, and are probably learned and appreciated through experience with such genres.

Having asked one of the "big" questions about music, chapter 3 places music under the microscope and explores its ingredients. What are the elements of sound, and why do we hear certain sounds as a "melody" and other sounds as a cough or a spoken word? By breaking down the sounds in music into elementary constituents, we can gain considerable insight into some of the most intriguing qualities of music, such as the nature of consonance and dissonance. In particular, understanding the physical nature of sound can shed light on why certain combinations of musical sounds seem to blend together and sound harmonious, whereas others clash with each other. These perceptual consequences seem unique to music. Most people would not reflect on whether the sound of a passing car "blends well" with other environmental sounds, such as birds, wind, or rain. However, these aesthetic experiences of sound combinations lie at the very heart of music perception and cognition. Certain sounds seem to "fuse" with one another and others seem mutually repellant, as though magnetic forces were involved. The key to such effects lies in the ingredients of sound, called *partials* because they are each a part of the sound. Although we cannot generally hear individual partials of sound, these molecular attributes profoundly affect our experience of music, and they can even have cascade effects on the way we compose and perform music.

Chapter 4 reviews the developmental implications of music. It is remarkable that even young infants are highly responsive to music. Careful research indicates that they are surprisingly sensitive to its structural features. On the other hand, the ability to create and produce musical sounds well (composition and performance) does not seem to emerge naturally in development but requires quite a lot of formal training. Language, in contrast, emerges in development without formal training. In Western societies, only a small proportion of the population is capable of composing and performing musical pieces that have a level of complexity comparable to grammatical structures used routinely in normal speech.

Parents of children who excel at music often proudly attribute their child's success to inherent ability or talent. It is interesting to ask why such parents are reluctant to give credit to hard work and parental support. In fact, the concept of innate musical ability or talent has been called into question because musical skill is overwhelmingly correlated with the amount of training and practice. Invariably, people who are described as talented have spent several years refining their skills. Extensive training can even lead to enlarged cortical areas associated with an acquired skill.

Chapter 5 addresses one of the most basic questions in the psychology of music: How do we actually make sense of music? If a team of anthropologists from another planet were to study the behavior of musicians on planet earth, they might describe music as sequences of sounded events (tones, chords, percussive sounds) that have no clear biological function. They would also discover, however, that earthlings are highly attuned to the temporal structure of these sound sequences.

Individual sequences of tones are perceived as "melodies," simultaneous combinations of tones are perceived as "chords," temporal patterns of events create distinctive "rhythms," and all of these structures are further shaped by a cyclical pattern of stress and relaxation, giving rise to the sense of "beat" and ultimately to "meter." Music teachers and theorists use such terms to describe the objective properties of music, but the qualities may also be viewed as psychological phenomena, reflecting complex perceptual and cognitive processes by which the human brain makes sense of music.

Merely being able to perceive the structural qualities of music is unlikely to maintain our interest for very long. Unless those structural properties provide us with something that is useful or desirable to us, they will soon be ignored. Chapter 6 describes one of the apparent benefits of music: its source of emotional information and its capacity to alter our moods and energy levels. Music both communicates and induces emotions through various cues such as tempo (pace), loudness, pitch, and timbre (sound quality). Emotional experiences are further intensified through the use of contrast effects, which are accomplished by shifting between consonance and dissonance, anticipation and resolution, stability and instability, and urgency and relaxation. The temporal patterns created by such shifts mirror our emotional lives. We have all experienced a gradual intensification of anticipation and tension as we await an important outcome, followed by disappointment and sadness if the outcome is not the one for which we had hoped. Conversely, we all know what it feels like to experience sensations of dread and worry followed by the joy associated with a highly positive outcome. Like music, our emotional lives are dynamic and nuanced, and our interpretations and experiences of any one emotion are shaped by their position within a larger emotional narrative.

The neurological source of emotions has often been linked with deep (subcortical) brain structures, but it is important to recognize that there is no single emotion "faculty" in the brain. Rather, emotional experiences are associated with cortical and subcortical activity across many regions of the brain. Similarly, our experiences of music are not associated with just one brain area. In chapter 7 we examine recent research on the complex relationship between music and the brain. Early research suggested that the right hemisphere was responsible for music, but we now know that music can elicit brain responses in both left and right hemispheres, as well as in cortical and subcortical areas. Different brain areas appear to handle different dimensions or attributes of music so that there is no single music area in the brain. Examining brain responses to music is no easy task, but researchers have discovered a number of ingenious techniques for seeing how the brain operates during a musical experience or activity.

Two techniques, electroencephalography (EEG) and magnetoencephalography (MEG), involve monitoring electromagnetic energy patterns. Electromagnetic energy is produced by neural activity and can be monitored from outside the scalp. Inferences about brain processes can then be made from these energy patterns. Brain activity not only generates electromagnetic energy; it also influences blood flow, blood volume, and oxygen consumption. Two other techniques, positron emission tomography (PET) and functional magnetic resonance imaging (fMRI), work by monitoring the flow of blood and levels of blood-oxygen at specific locations in the brain.

Cases of brain damage that lead to musical impairments can also provide insight into the neural basis of music. In particular, the presence of highly selective deficits suggests that music is not processed in a unified manner, but that different attributes of music are handled in separate parts of the brain. Cases of impaired melody (pitch) perception with no impairment in rhythm perception, and vice versa, suggest that pitch and rhythm are handled by distinct areas of the brain. Conversely, if some music impairments are consistently accompanied by language impairments, the question arises as to whether the damaged brain area was responsible for processing both music and language.

Chapter 8 outlines a growing body of research on the cognitive basis of music performance. In comparison with passive music listening, the performance of music places tremendous demands on neural resources. Virtually everyone listens to music, but only a much smaller percentage of the population engages in music performance. One of the reasons relates to the tremendous expertise expected of music performers. The brain resources that allow people to perform music at rudimentary levels must be developed and refined extensively through 10 or more years of intensive training. For performers of Western classical music, the stakes are especially high. Critical listeners are quick to point out when a performer fumbles and plays a single incorrect note, and even when a musician gives a note-perfect performance, critics may question his or her choice of expressive actions. Were changes in loudness introduced in a way that optimally conveyed phrase structure and emotional nuance? Was the performer's use of timing and pace consistent with that expected for the musical genre? No wonder so few people pursue a career in music performance.

By identifying and analyzing the many expressive actions involved in performance, including the mistakes that performers tend to make, it is possible for scientists to draw inferences about cognitive processing and motor planning. Just as investigators can draw conclusions by scrutinizing the responses of participants in carefully designed experiments (e.g., judgments of music), the expressive actions of any performance can be interpreted as a complex "response" to music, and this response sheds light on how the performer perceives, remembers, and responds to music.

Why do we still listen to music that was composed over 300 years ago? Great music, like great literature and art, can remain influential for hundreds of years. Outstanding composers such as Bach, Beethoven, Mozart, and Haydn are widely revered for their artistic skills, but what exactly does the skill of composition entail? At a general level, composition is really just a way of organizing sounds over time. What are the cognitive processes involved in this activity? Do such cognitive processes partly shape the kind of music that is composed? Chapter 9 examines the cognitive implications of music composition. Most composers create music with possible listeners in mind, and they usually want their compositions to be appreciated by these listeners. At the same time, composers frequently attempt to push the boundaries of their craft so that they are not creating predictable or conventional music. Thus, good composers must have a deep understanding of the perceptual abilities of their listeners, and their potential to make sense of novel or even shocking forms of composition.

There has been enormous speculation about the minds of musicians. In the mid-1990s there was a rash of claims that music had the capacity to make developing children "smarter" and expectant parents were even encouraged to play classical music to their unborn babies to stimulate them and enhance development. Best-selling books on the cognitive and emotional benefits of music could be found at airports across the globe (e.g., the "Mozart effect"), and music CDs were available that promised all the various outcomes that anyone might desire. Chapter 10 surveys the vast body of research on the benefits of musical engagement.

Two types of effects are considered. The first concerns the short-term effects of intensive music listening, and can be largely explained by temporary shifts in mood and energy levels produced by the music. The second concerns the possible long-term benefits of intensive training in music. Much of the research on such benefits is difficult to interpret, but there is an emerging realization that both short-term exposure to music and long-term training in music can have reliable and quite specific effects on nonmusical cognitive function.

Abiding Controversies

Not surprisingly, researchers vary in their approaches to the study of music cognition. Traditionally, there have been differing opinions on issues such as these:

1. The kinds of stimuli and methods that are most valuable for gaining an understanding of music psychology.

2. Whether music psychology is best explained in terms of brain structures and processes or by more abstract psychological laws, principles, and models.

3. The relative importance of innate structures and learning to the development of music.

What is the most appropriate level at which to investigate and explain psychological phenomena related to music? Are listening, performing, and composing music best understood in terms of neurons and networks, or mental schemata and prototypes, or moods and feelings? Studies directed at different analytic levels often pose different questions, use different methods, and promote different theories. Reductionism holds that explanations based on psychological constructs such as schemata and prototypes are reducible with the help of yet-to-be-discovered bridging laws to neurological events in the brain. In this view, theories of cognition should be reducible to neural models.

What is the most appropriate level at which to investigate and explain psychological phenomena related to music? **Figures 1.1.1–1.1.4** represent a variety of levels, each more reductionist in its approach than the previous.

The opposing position holds that psychological explanations are not always reducible to neural states, or that they may be realized in multiple configurations. It would therefore be impossible to identify systematic bridging laws that connect psychological states (e.g., beliefs, desires) to specific brain states. Rather, psychology would need to construct its own autonomous generalizations using a specialized language of thought. In this view, theories of music cognition can be developed somewhat independently of advances in neuroscience. One danger with this strategy, however, is that when psychological principles are not linked to plausible physiological mechanisms, it can be difficult to assess their validity.

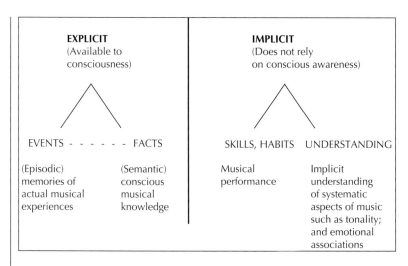

Figure 1.1.1

An example of a cognitive model. This particular model represents a role for long-term memory in music processing. Note that no specific brain structures are mentioned.

Adapted from Snyder, B. (2000). *Music and memory*. Cambridge, MA: MIT Press, p. 76. Used by permission.

Sound Examples 1.1–1.2

Sound example 1.1 is a short excerpt from Beethoven's *Symphony no. 9 "Ode to Joy."* Suppose, as an experimenter, you wanted to use this orchestral example as a stimulus to test some aspect of a listener's response to the melody. How could you be sure that the listener is able to extract the melody from the dense orchestral texture? How could you be sure that the listener has reacted to the melody itself, and has not been distracted by other factors?

In **Sound example 1.2**, the same excerpt has been electronically manipulated. The melody has been extracted from the orchestral context. Any subtle fluctuations in tempo, volume, or intensity that might have been present from tone to tone have been eliminated. The tones of the melody were produced as sine waves to control for the influence of overtones.

Although the second example is far more successful at eliminating extraneous factors that may influence a listener's response to the melody, you might also find that it doesn't sound as "musical" as the orchestral example. It sounds somewhat dull and mechanical. The music we listen to doesn't normally sound like this—the second example lacks *ecological validity*. How can we be sure that we are capturing a listener's typical response to the musical stimulus? How can we be sure that this response is not influenced by the artificiality of the stimulus?

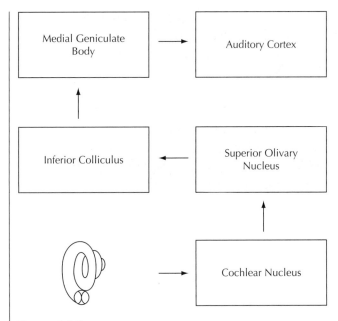

Figure 1.1.2

An example of a neural circuit diagram, in this case indicating the transmission of an auditory signal from the cochlea to the auditory cortex. The specific brain structures along the path of an auditory signal are charted; however, the role of each brain structure is not specified.

A second area of disagreement involves balancing concerns for experimental control with concerns for ecological validity. Can scientific studies using stimuli comprised of a few pure tones tell us about the cognitive processes that are activated when one listens to a symphony played by an orchestra? Can the responses of Western listeners to Western music provide insight into cognitive mechanisms that operate independently of cultural knowledge? In general, concerns about the use of artificial (nonmusical) stimuli versus real pieces of music raise empirical questions about whether a psychological process, mechanism, or neural resource generalizes to a wider range of stimuli than those used in a particular experiment. In cases where general auditory or cognitive mechanisms are at issue, concerns about ecological or cross-cultural validity may be unnecessary. For example, the neural resources involved in segregating multiple auditory sources (i.e., *auditory stream segregation*) are almost certainly the same when listening to nonmusical

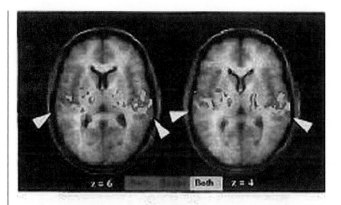

PLATE 7

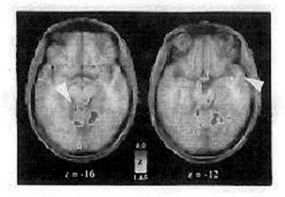

PLATE 8

Figure 1.1.3

An MRI scan of a human brain during an auditory processing task. Lit areas indicate regional brain activity. Through this technique, the roles of specific brain structures in specific auditory processes can be teased apart.

From Zatorre, R., and Peretz, I. (Eds.). (2001). *The biological foundations of music.* New York: New York Academy of Sciences, vol. 930, colour plate 8. Reprinted by permission.

tone sequences, Western music, non-Western music, speech signals, and environmental sounds.

It is also likely that the mechanisms engaged to process pitch contour (upward, downward, or lateral pitch movement) for short sequences of pure tones are the same as those engaged for long musical phrases. Such mechanisms may even be involved in the processing of speech intonation. Music and speech intonation may even share a common ancestry as temporal-spatial patterns of emotional

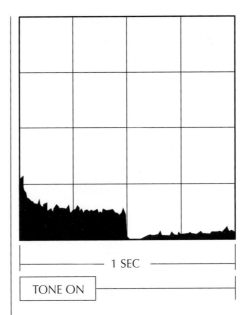

1 SEC

TONE ON

Figure 1.1.4

A histogram of the electrical activity of a single auditory nerve fiber
in response to an auditory stimulus. Auditory signal information is
transmitted via auditory nerves—each nerve is composed of approximately 30,000 nerve fibers. The single auditory nerve is pierced with
an extremely fine electrode. A tone 500 msec in duration has been presented; there is a sharp response, followed by a stable firing rate. Once
the stimulus has been removed (second half of the histogram), a spontaneous firing rate is recovered.

Adapted from Kiang, N. Y. S, et al. (1965). *Discharge patterns of single nerve fibres in the cat's
auditory nerve.* Cambridge: MIT Press, p. 69. Used by permission.

communication, which are particularly adaptive for promoting
attachment between mothers and infants. If so, then the same neural resources may be responsible for processing contour in music and
in speech.

Some auditory processes are automatically invoked for all possible acoustic stimuli, including music, and therefore operate regardless of the style of the music or the cultural context in which it is
heard. Many researchers, especially those with a strong background
in cognition, are interested in precisely these basic processes. Because
research on general auditory mechanisms and their connection to
musical experience requires careful experimental control, the use of

Modularity and the Mind

The idea that the brain can be divided into separate functional compartments has a checkered history. In the 18th century, Franz Josef Gall (1758–1828) and other phrenologists believed that the brain could be divided into a number of "organs," such as benevolence and combatitiveness, with each responsible for a specific character trait (see **Figure 1.2**). Gall believed that bumps or depressions on the skull reflected, respectively, a well-developed or underdeveloped propensity for a given trait. Hence, an individual's personality could be gleaned through careful tactile examination of his or her skull. Although initially popular, the study of *phrenology* was quickly dismissed owing to its unsound methodology. One of many examples of fallacious reasoning behind the theory was the notion that the shape of the outer skull reflected the surface of the brain underneath.

Interestingly, the basic idea of localization of brain function was soon dramatically vindicated, this time using more scientific methods. In 1861, Paul Broca's examination of the brain lesions of aphasic patients postmortem showed that a small area on the left side of the frontal lobe (now termed Broca's area) was responsible for speech production.

Steven Pinker (1997) argued that modular brain organization might have arisen throught evolutionary pressures, giving rise to "a system of organs of computation, designed by natural selection to solve the kinds of problems our ancestors faced in their foraging way of life" (p. 21).

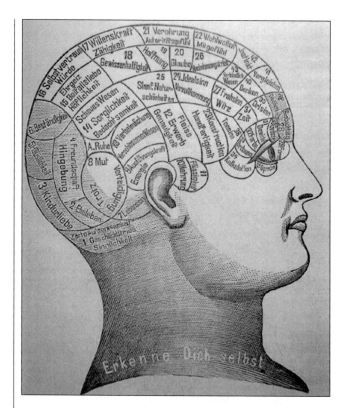

Figure 1.2

An example of a nineteenth-century phrenology chart.

From Bilz, F. E. (1894). *Das neue Naturheilver fahren.*

naturalized music listening conditions is not always advantageous. Naturalized conditions introduce uncontrolled influences (leading to highly variable observations) related to personal, social, cultural, or historical knowledge, which can mask or distort the cognitive processes under investigation.

In other cases, when cognitive processes depend on musical context, it is necessary to use more naturalized conditions. For example, some of my own research concerns the psychology of musical performance. What does the expressive use of loudness and timing in a musical performance tell us about the performer's musical knowledge, and how does a performer's use of expression influence the listener's perception of the music? Furthering our understanding of such issues requires an examination of actual music performances. In short, a complete understanding of music cognition requires the convergence of data obtained using varying approaches and methods. We need well-controlled studies involving simplified stimuli (isolated tones or tone sequences) as well as studies involving more naturalized musical stimuli.

A third issue of contention relates to the relative importance of innate and environmental influences on our perceptions and preferences for music. Are we predisposed to appreciate certain kinds of music and to perceive music in a certain way, or does our upbringing within a particular environment determine our perceptions, abilities, and tastes for music? Many scholars are skeptical of all nativist constructs such as musical talent, and prefer to emphasize social learning, education, and enculturation. They point out that different cultures and historic periods are associated with different musical styles, skills, preferences, and perceptions. Other scholars disagree, arguing that our experiences of music are constrained in subtle ways by innate cognitive principles.

Three types of evidence suggest that some aspects of music experience are innate. First, even young infants are remarkably responsive to various aspects of musical structure, such as consonance and dissonance, suggesting that these abilities are present at birth. Second, skills are often domain specific (e.g., language skills, spatial skills, music skills), implicating specialized cognitive modules. Third, it seems impossible to describe the environment in a way that adequately explains the richness and complexity of our thoughts and actions, suggesting that we must be born with the advantage of perceptual and cognitive predispositions.

Recent Areas of Research Growth

Aside from such traditional questions, the past decade has witnessed a surge of interest in a number of topic areas. First, following a neo-Darwinian movement across a number of fields, there has been a renewed interest in evolutionary perspectives on music. This interest has led to a series of major international conferences on the evolution of music, and plans for several books and special journal issues (e.g., in the European journal *Musica Scientiae*) dedicated to the topic.

A second shift has been to investigate how music can communicate and induce emotions, mirroring attempts by researchers in psychology and neuroscience to understand the role of emotion in memory, reasoning, and problem solving. Emotions are especially difficult to examine because the mental states associated with our feelings are highly variegated and cannot easily be treated as a unified phenomenon. Following the highly influential publication of *Music and Emotion* (2001), researchers Juslin and Sloboda prepared a second major collection of invited chapters by leading investigators of music and emotion (*Handbook of Music and Emotion*, in press). Another major contribution is Huron's (2006) *Sweet Anticipation*, which offers a remarkable theory that explains a wide range of emotional responses to music.

Nativism

Nativism evolved in response to the behaviorism movement in the first half of the 20th century. Behaviorists claimed that all organisms start life with a blank slate and that all animal behavior is learned—the so-called nurture view. Nativists have successfully challenged this assumption, proving that some behaviors cannot adequately be explained by learning alone, and that certain innate or "hard-wired" behaviors must exist—the nature view. Most researchers studying animal and human behavior today acknowledge the contribution of both nature and nurture.

An example of a current field of research that is nativist in its approach is *behavioral genetics*—the study of how genes influence behavior. If a given behavioral trait is genetically based, it should occur more frequently among genetically related individuals.

An important tool available to behavioral geneticists is the *twin study*. Genetically based behaviors are expected to be more concordant in identical twins (as they share 100% of their genes) than fraternal twins (50% genetic relatedness). Identical twins reared apart provide a particularly fruitful data source because a shared environmental influence can be ruled out as a behavioral factor. Twin studies have yielded promising concordances for many behaviors, most notably schizophrenia.

Despite the phenomenon of musical families such as the Bachs and the Mozarts, evidence from behavioral genetic research on the heritability of musical ability has been scarce. One recent study has found significant concordances between individuals possessing absolute pitch and their relatives (Baharloo, Service, Risch, Gitschier, & Freimer, 2000). The completion in 2003 of the Human Genome Project—a systematic mapping of the entire human genetic sequence—may greatly enhance our ability to pinpoint the roles of specific genes.

Perhaps most striking is the renewed interest in studies of brain function, following developments in neuroimaging techniques and insights gained from studies of patients with brain damage. Not surprisingly, research on the brain has been influenced by the study of music and emotion, giving rise to an emerging body of research on the neurosciences of emotional responses to music. When elderly people listen to music that has deep emotional significance in their lives, there is increased brain activity in the right temporal lobe. However, music with different emotional connotations also activates different brain areas across the cerebral cortex and subcortex of the brain. For example, unpleasant music is associated with relatively greater activation in subcortical areas such as the amygdala and hippocampus, whereas pleasant music is associated with relatively greater activation in areas in the frontal lobe and the primary auditory cortex.

Several developments have acted to amplify the excitement surrounding the study of music and the brain. The publication of Patel's (2008) book *Music, Language, and the Brain* provides compelling evidence that certain aspects of music and language are handled by the same brain areas. Major centers of research on the neurosciences of music have also been established, such as the International Laboratory for Brain, Music and Sound (BRAMS) in Montréal, co-directed by Isabelle Peretz and Robert Zatorre. Finally, several international conferences dedicated to the neurosciences of music have helped to crystallize the field and attract new researchers. The Mariani Foundation has played a critical role by sponsoring landmark conferences in New York (2000), Venice (2002), Leipzig (2005), and Montréal (2008).

A central goal of this book is to provide a review and critical analysis of traditional and emerging issues in the area. Over the past three decades, the psychology of music has moved from a highly specialized research topic to a fully established interdisciplinary field. Landmark studies in the 1960s and 1970s by researchers such as Lola Cuddy, Diana Deutsch, Jay Dowling, Alf Gabrielsson, Mari Jones, Carol Krumhansl, Sandra Trehub, and Johan Sundberg laid much of the groundwork for this highly dynamic field, and enormous progress has been made in responding to a range of scientific questions. A growing number of young and midcareer researchers—many trained by pioneers in the field—are producing influential scholarly and scientific work at a pace that is nothing short of startling. This book examines many of the major contributors to the field of music cognition, but it must be acknowledged that there are many other researchers not represented in this volume who have made important and influential contributions, and new publications appear with every passing week. Thus, this book provides a broad analysis of the field, but many exciting discoveries clearly lie ahead.

Additional Readings

Cross, I. (1998). Music and science: Three views. *Revue Belge de Musicologie, 52,* 207–214.

Gjerdingen, R. (2002). The psychology of music. In T. Christensen (Ed.), *The Cambridge history of Western music theory* (pp. 956–981). Cambridge, UK: Cambridge University Press.

CHAPTER 2
Origins of Music

LEARNING OUTCOMES

By the end of this chapter you should be able to:

1. Define the major sources of human evolution.

2. Describe and critique five adaptationist accounts of musical origins.

3. Identify conditions that give rise to nonadaptive evolution and discuss their relevance to musical origins.

4. Explain what is meant by a "theory of mind" (ToM).

5. Summarize and evaluate theories of musical precursors.

6. Appraise the idea that music is a human invention that functions to induce pleasure.

Prehistoric Music

**Charles Darwin
(1809–1882)**

"As neither the enjoyment nor the capacity of producing musical notes are faculties of the least use to man in reference to his daily habits of life, they must be ranked amongst the most mysterious with which he is endowed."

—from *Descent of Man* **(1871)**

The human mind consists of many different skills and forms of intelligence, including those relating to vision, audition, speech communication, planning, problem solving, and feeling. Many human traits evolved because they solved problems of survival or reproduction encountered by ancestral populations. Such traits are called *adaptations* because they emerged in response to evolutionary pressures. Adaptations improve the degree to which organisms can cope with challenging environmental pressures, such as predators, lack of water, extreme weather conditions, or competition for mates.

The various challenges associated with the evolution of human traits are difficult to appreciate because the time scale is unimaginably vast. The first *bipedal* members of the hominid lineages were the *Australopithecines* (about 2–5 million years ago), followed by *Homo habilis* (about 2.3 million years ago). *Homo habilis* had much larger brains than *Australopithecines* and could probably make primitive stone tools. More sophisticated tools emerged with *Homo erectus* (about 1.8 million years ago). From the *Homo heidelbergensis* line (0.8 million years ago) evolved both *Homo neanderthalensis* (about 350,000 years ago) and our current line, *Homo sapiens sapiens* (200,000 years ago).

Anatomical properties of sight and hearing evolved because they enhanced survival and reproduction, allowing animals to avoid predators and find food and mates. Can comparable adaptive benefits be attributed to musical traits? Listening to and playing music seem irrelevant to issues of survival and reproduction, so it is difficult to conceive of why such behaviors ever evolved. We enjoy music, but survival does not depend on it the way that survival depends on visual or auditory acuity, digestion, predator avoidance, or the ability to breathe. What, then, might be the origin of music?

It is possible that music evolved because it enhanced survival or reproduction a very long time ago in ways that do not apply today. Survival and reproduction are not currently dependent on music, but when early forms of music emerged over 50,000 years ago, the environment was different in ways that are now almost unimaginable. In that environment, music might have had a very important adaptive function. On the other hand, the set of activities that we call music might have evolved not from any activity that relates to the music of today, but from a confluence of separate activities and processing capacities adapted for purposes that originally had nothing to do with music. These capacities might have been coordinated and developed into musical behaviors through cultural processes, with no accompanying change in the human genome (Justus & Hutsler, 2005; McDermott & Hauser, 2005).

Before considering the possible origins of music, we review the primary mechanisms by which all physical and mental traits come into being. Traits may develop either as adaptations or as a result of other evolutionary or cultural processes (nonadaptations). Adaptations can evolve through one of two processes: sexual selection or natural selection. Sexual selection occurs when there exists a range of traits, some that promote reproduction and others that interfere with reproduction. Traits that promote reproduction are "selected" in that animals carrying them are more likely to reproduce and pass on genes that encode that trait. Traits that interfere with reproduction are extinguished because animals carrying them tend not to reproduce. There are reproductive benefits to the ability to attract mates (mate choice) and repel rivals (aggressive rivalry). Traits selected for mate choice include peacock display features, birdsongs, and musky smells. Traits selected for aggressive rivalry include sharp teeth, horns, and strong muscles.

Natural selection occurs when there exists a range of traits in an animal population, such that some traits promote survival and others interfere with it. Traits that promote survival are selected in that animals carrying them tend to survive long enough to pass on the genes that encode the trait. Traits that interfere with survival tend to extinguish because animals carrying them do not tend to survive long enough to reproduce. Traits with survival benefits include the ability to acquire food, avoid predators, overcome parasites, develop or maintain physical or mental agility used for survival, or cope with extreme cold or heat.

Both sexual selection and natural selection contribute to the evolution of physical and mental traits. For the genes of an animal to be passed on, the animal must not only be capable of reproducing; it must also survive for long enough to be able to reproduce. The importance of reproduction gives rise to the process of sexual selection; the importance of survival gives rise to the process of natural selection.

Adaptationist Accounts

The process of adaptation refers to structures with modern functions that are equivalent to those that were originally selected because they

Sexual Selection—The Peacock's Tail

The peacock uses the elaborate ornamentation on his sizable tail to attract a peahen. A peacock displays the feathers of his tail with remarkable symmetry and precision (this action even emits an audible hum).

At the same time, the weight of his tail feathers can be a liability to a peacock (e.g., a disadvantage to the mobility needed against predators or the energy resources needed to search for food). Darwin understood that this was a problem that needed to be explained by a mechanism beyond natural selection: If natural selection weeds out traits that are detrimental to survival, why would peacocks continue to have such elaborate tails? His solution was that the long tails are *sexually selected*—for a peacock, the costs incurred to survival can potentially be more than compensated for by a tail that attracts mates and ultimately produces more offspring.

Sexually selected traits are not restricted to morphological features—behavioral traits can also be sexually selected. Birdsongs are a primary example. Miller (2000), as well as Darwin (1871) himself, argue that human music making is a sexually selected behavioral trait.

Source: Original photography: Aaron Logan. Made available under Creative Commons 2.5 Attribution-Generic License.

conferred a survival or reproductive advantage (Gould & Vrba, 1982). So what is the evidence that music is an evolutionary adaptation, whether through sexual selection or natural selection, rather than a nonadaptive technology or gimmick such as ice cream, cigarettes, beer, or theme parks?

First, developmental evidence suggests that music is innate: Infants are sensitive to musical relationships without the benefit of formal instruction. Second, music is highly complex, and the degree of complexity in music is not obviously culturally determined. The musical grammars of Western and Eastern societies have similar levels of complexity, as do those of different ages. The music of Messiaen, a 20th-century French composer fascinated by birdsong, is no more complex than that of J. S. Bach, a prolific 18th-century German composer who used mathematically inspired forms such as the fugue. Third, music is recognized as having modular structure, and is considered a distinct type of intelligence. Some brain injury can render people with impaired speech perception but with normal musical abilities, or they can render people musically impaired but with otherwise normal intelligence. Fourth, music is not a recent cultural phenomenon, but has been part of human behavior for thousands of years, perhaps as long as language. The discovery in Germany of an ancient bone flute, analyzed by electron spin dating, suggests that music making must have occurred at least 37,000 years ago (D'Errico et al., 2003). It is also likely that singing preceded the use of such bone flutes, which implies an even older origin for music making, perhaps even up to 250,000 years old (Huron, 2001a).

These observations are consistent with the view that music is an adaptive response to evolutionary pressures. What were some possible survival benefits of music for our ancestors? The fact remains that no one can be certain how or even if music emerged as an evolutionary adaptation. However, two classes of adaptationist theories have been proposed: those based on direct reproductive benefits and those based on survival benefits. Both classes of theories need to explain how musical behaviors enhanced reproduction. However, whereas theories based on direct reproductive benefits assume that music functioned in the attraction of mates for reproduction, those based on survival benefits assume that musical behaviors allowed individuals to survive in the environment long enough to reproduce.

Theories Based on Reproductive Benefits

Darwin (1872) argued that music, like birdsong and peacock feathers, has its origin in the evolutionary process of sexual selection. In this view, the original function of music was to attract sexual mates, which, in turn, enhanced reproductive success. To support his position, Darwin first pointed out that enjoying and producing music are not useful to survival. He then noted that music evokes strong emotions, and love is the most typical theme in songs: "All you need is love." Finally, he observed that sounds tend to evolve for reproductive purposes. Male animals vocalize most frequently in the breeding season, and these vocalizations are used to display anger, attraction, and jealousy (cf. Miller, 2000).

"Music and impassioned speech become intelligible to a certain extent, if we may assume that musical tones and rhythm were used by our half-human ancestors, during the season of courtship, when animals of all kinds are excited not only by love, but by the strong passions of jealousy, rivalry, and triumph."

—From Darwin's *Descent of Man* (1871)

A European starling singing.

Birdsongs, peacock plumes, lyrebird mimicry, and other sexually selected traits have one feature that is not characteristic of music, however: They are sexually dimorphic traits, which means that they are disproportionately evident in one sex. Peacocks, but not peahens, have colorful feathers, and only male birds produce songs. In contrast, musical ability seems to be fairly equally represented in men and women. Male students do not dominate the classrooms of music conservatories, and the most successful female opera singers are valued in society just as much as we value our outstanding tenors. By all accounts, Madonna, Britney Spears, and Celine Dion appear to have their finances in order. In short, musicality in humans does not seem to be sexually dimorphic, which casts some doubt on the possibility that musical ability is a sexually selected trait.

Nonetheless, Darwin's ideas cannot be dismissed easily. First, not all examples of mating calls are sexually dimorphic. Second, as Miller (2000) argued, music not only evokes passion, but is also associated with many other features that are attractive to mates. Singing implies self-confidence and extraversion, rhythmic skills suggest a superior ability to sequence physical movements, dancing indicates aerobic fitness, and musical novelty attracts attention by violating expectancies. Third, music may be more sexually dimorphic than one might suspect. Analyzing random samples of jazz, rock, and classical albums (over 7,000 works), Miller (2000) observed that popular male songwriters produce about 10 times as much music as popular female songwriters, and their productivity levels peak at about age 30, when mating effort and activity are also at a peak (see also Simonton, 1993). Although such statistics are probably biased by a male-dominated music industry, they underscore the importance of distinguishing between the ability to produce music and the inclination or opportunity to do so.

Finally, many human traits that are attractive to potential mates are not sexually dimorphic. Exceptional athletic skill, for example, is observed in both men and women. A superior ability to run, jump, fight, swim, and score goals certainly implies good health, and is widely perceived to be an attractive quality in men and women. Thus, athletic skill might be a sexually selected trait, even though it is not sexually dimorphic. Interestingly, musical and athletic skills are alike in compelling ways. Expert skill among both musicians and athletes takes a decade or more to acquire and is possessed by only a fraction of the population. Such experts display their skill in either individual or group performances. The skills that are developed in both domains demand exceptional motor control, anticipation, timing, and planning. Moreover, the capacity to enjoy sports and music is widespread in the population, and audiences of both activities experience enhanced group cohesion and a strengthened sense of personal identity. Skill in both domains also involves balancing strong feelings of emotion with other objectives, such as articulating voices in polyphonic music or scoring goals and winning gold medals.

One notable difference is that emotional meaning is more nuanced in music than in sport. Music has the capacity to evoke various shades of joy, sadness, fear, anger, and peacefulness that can shift from moment to moment. Most athletic activities elicit generic and predictable patterns of emotion such as excitement and anticipation followed by elation or disappointment. Nonetheless, the two activities are congruent in many respects, suggesting the possibility of overlapping origins as sexually selected traits. The difficulty in drawing a strong conclusion about Darwin's hypothesis is not that it is seriously flawed, but that equally plausible arguments can be made for many other theories of the origin of music.

Theories Based on Survival Benefits

Many theorists have argued that musical activities evolved because they directly conferred a survival benefit to our ancestors. Such benefits might have been quite significant in prehistoric environments, but in ways that are largely irrelevant to contemporary life. Music enthusiasts may well declare that they "would simply die" without their treasured iPod, but the truth of the matter is that if we woke up one morning to a world without music, life would carry on pretty much as before.

NURTURING SOCIAL BONDS

One hypothesis is that music evolved because of its capacity to promote group cohesion and cooperation. Music can influence arousal and mood states, and sharing these affective experiences may enhance social bonds (Huron, 2001a). Group cohesion and cooperation are critical to survival in several species because groups are more effective than individual animals at detecting and defending against predators. Alliances are also

Music, Social Bonding, and the Influence of Hormones

Oxytocin is a hormone released into the brain during significant emotional moments. Where oxytocin release occurs during interaction between individuals, such as breastfeeding or orgasm during sex, the effect is to facilitate bonding. Indeed, oxytocin has sometimes been touted in the popular press as the neurochemical basis of love itself.

Neurobiologist Walter J. Freeman (2000) sees music and dance as a *technology* for the establishment of "mutual understanding and trust." He proposes that music (as evidenced by our strong emotional reactions to it) may result in the release of oxytocin.

The scope of oxytocin's bonding effect through music can extend well beyond that of a mother and child through lullaby or lovers through a serenade, to encompass large groups. Freeman cites anthropological evidence from the music and dance rituals of preliterate tribal communities in which participants enter a trance state by singing and dancing to the point of exhaustion. Raves, with the induction of oxytocin release through the artificial drug MDMA (ecstasy), might be considered an extension of this practice.

important because of the potential of threats even from members of the same species. Is it possible that music evolved to secure these social bonds?

To evaluate this possibility, it is useful to consider behaviors that secure social bonds in animals that are phylogenetically close to humans. In primates, social bonds are formed primarily through individual grooming. Grooming involves one animal manually cleaning another and accounts for up to 20% of daytime activities. Although grooming promotes cleanliness, its primary role in establishing and maintaining social bonds is widely recognized. Importantly, grooming behavior can maintain alliances only for relatively small groups of animals. To maintain alliances for large groups, the amount of time spent on grooming would interfere with other activities that are critical to survival, such as mating, foraging, and feeding.

According to Dunbar (1996), the emergence of *Homo erectus* was associated with social groups that were too large to maintain by manual grooming alone. This pressure required the evolution of new behaviors for maintaining social bonds that could replace individual grooming. Dunbar argued that language evolved to perform this function. Vocalizations (or vocal grooming) were able to replace individual grooming because they were capable of nurturing bonds with many individuals at the same time.

The earliest vocalizations were probably rewarding but not semantically meaningful. Thus, they may have combined structural and expressive properties of both language and music. Dunbar (1996) proposed that certain kinds of vocalizations started to acquire meaning with the appearance of *Homo sapiens* in Africa, about 400,000 years ago. Such vocalizations could communicate social information, but did not yet have the capacity to signify abstract concepts.

Although Dunbar (1996) did not comment on the origins of music and song, it is possible that music evolved from these early forms of vocal grooming. After reviewing the available evidence, Huron (2001a) concluded that such a possibility "holds the greatest promise as a plausible evolutionary origin for music" (p. 54). If so, then language and music have a common origin in these early vocalizations. Only over a period of millions of years would they have diverged into two distinct systems for maintaining social bonds.

During this period of divergence, the bonding capacity of music would have been distinct but complementary to that of language, making it a valuable adaptation in its own right. Singing is louder than speaking and can reach a large number of listeners. Music can also coordinate moods, which can, in turn, nurture social coherence and prepare a group to act in unison. Love songs seem to speak to everyone who listens to them, as though we were the recipient or giver of love. Joyful music played at ceremonies can generate positive moods and nurture goodwill toward others in the group. Energetic music like war cries can increase alertness and coordination, which would be useful for groups of hunters. Musical rituals, such as a rock concert or rave, cement social obligations by reinforcing a sense of group identity, whether that identity is the local opera guild, or devotees of the Grateful Dead. The common use of music in superstitious practices, religious ceremonies, sexual rites, political campaigns, and military contexts suggests that music has a powerful ability to rally and generate group cohesion in large masses of people (Roederer, 1984).

Sound Example 2.1

This example is a Calabrian tuna fishing song entitled "U Leva Leva" (Heave, Heave). The strong rhythmic drive of the music helps coordinate the movements of the fishermen as they raise the fishing net.

Sound example 2.1 is available via the *Music, Thought, and Feeling* iMix on iTunes.

TRAINING COORDINATED MOVEMENT

A related possibility is that music evolved as a means of coordinating movement. Rhythmic elements of music engage skills of regulated movement, which could benefit group tasks such as hunting and herding. Religious and social ceremonies in some cultures are characterized by coordinated rhythmic activities that continue to the point of physical collapse. Drumming, chanting, clapping, and singing may continue for several hours. The sheer amount of time and energy spent on this synchronized activity suggests that music might have evolved as a means for developing skills of coordinated movement.

One limitation of this hypothesis is that it emphasizes the rhythmic elements of music, and other features of music (e.g., melody, harmony, instrumentation) are left unexplained. Moreover, many other activities could perform the same function, suggesting that the hypothesis lacks specificity. Other activities that require coordinated movement include chanting, dancing, competitive sports, and any other activity that demands accurately timed movement among groups of individuals.

ENHANCING COGNITIVE AND SOCIAL SKILL

Cross (2003a, 2003b) proposed that protomusical behaviors provide low-risk media for the gestation of cognitive and social flexibility. Noting the enormous diversity of musical behaviors within and across cultures, he argued that music has an inherent heterogeneity of meaning that makes it highly flexible in its use and significance across different cultural contexts. According to Cross, music may be defined as any activity that is rooted in sound and movement and that is intentionally transposable. Whereas birds make use of complex patterns of sound, their songs are tied to specific functions and hence nontransposable.

Human music, in contrast, has a kind of free-floating meaning that allows it to function effectively in a wide range of contexts. A consequence of this property is that the contexts, sounds, and actions associated with musical activities are highly diverse within and across cultures. For the infant, this property makes music an extremely valuable developmental tool, allowing it to function at a stage when a range of social and cognitive skills can be explored, tested, and developed. These skills may include the ability to cooperate and coordinate with others; the capacity for sustained and focused attention; pattern detection and recognition; sensitivity of correlations between auditory, visual, and kinesthetic patterns; and the ability to anticipate and respond to significant events. In this way, protomusical behaviors may help to refine a wide range of social and cognitive skills that are beneficial for successful development into adulthood.

PROMOTING EMOTIONAL CONJOINMENT

Dissanayake (2000) proposed a variant of the social bonding hypothesis. She argued that music, along with dance, originated as part of a multimodal system of parent–offspring communication. Affiliative interactions between parents and children are thought to have occurred initially through vocalizations, body movements, and facial expressions. These interactions were not merely social, but promoted powerful emotional connections, or emotional conjoinment.

What prompted the evolution of a system for promoting such powerful connections? The emergence of hominids is associated with enlarged brains and an upright posture. Large brains require a long period of gestation to allow adequate time for fetal encephalization (brain growth). Upright postures and bipedal locomotion, however, do not permit wide birth passages. These two factors present a problem: Fetuses are relatively helpless until their large brains are developed, but they cannot remain in the womb until their brains are fully developed because maternal birth canals are too constricted. The result is that human infants are born prematurely and require extended care for their survival. Neonates in many other species are also *altricial* (i.e., dependent on a period of postnatal care for survival), but humans are unique in the duration and extent of their dependency on care. According to Dissanayake, this pressure led to the evolution of affiliative mechanisms for securing emotional bonds between parents and offspring. Strong emotional bonds were needed to ensure longer and better parental care of infants.

Parental care not only protects infants from physical harm, it provides important psychological and emotional benefits. For example, parents can familiarize infants with important affective states by alerting, soothing, praising, and pleasing them. Parents also manipulate and respond to expectations, conveying surprise at unexpected behaviors and praising anticipated behaviors. Infants also become familiarized with vocal, bodily, and facial expressions that communicate information about a person's age, mood, sex, and intentions. These expressions, like music and dance, convey affective meaning through the use of speed, duration, intensity (stress, accent), and rhythmic regularity or variety. Vocal expressions make additional use of variation in pitch (melody) and timbre. These features of sound and action may provide the foundation for creating and responding to the temporal arts of music and dance.

Along similar lines, Trevarthen (1999) emphasized the developmental significance of protomusical behaviors in infant–caregiver interactions. *Protomusical behaviors* involve appreciating, producing, and actively moving with patterns of sound. The infant engages in a synchronization of vocal and kinesthetic patterns that integrate multimodal sensory information arising from auditory, tactile, kinesthetic, and visual systems. These multisensory patterns allow the infant and caregiver to share emotional and attentional states, which aids in social and personal development.

AFFECTIVE ENGAGEMENT

Livingstone and Thompson (2006, in press) proposed a theory of musical origins in which music is conceived as an instance of a more general capacity for affective engagement—the ability and motivation to attune to and influence the affective states of other humans. Affective engagement is not unique to music. It is also observed across many nonmusical and nonauditory domains, including tone of voice, facial expressions, gestures and body language, dance, theatre, and visual arts. The theory of affective engagement is based on the assumption that these seemingly distinct domains all share a common ancestry. In other words, music emerged in evolution not because of its unique characteristics, but as one of many powerful affective systems.

The capacity for affective engagement is thought to have emerged with the appearance of *Homo sapiens* 150,000 to 100,000 years ago. This period marked a significant shift in human evolution in which there was a rapid growth in cultural phenomena. According to some theorists, these cultural activities were enabled and supported by the evolution within *Homo sapiens* of a powerful new cognitive capacity, called theory of mind (ToM; Baron-Cohen, 1999; J. K. Burns, 2004).

ToM refers to the capacity to "[understand] people as mental beings who have beliefs, desires, emotions, and intentions and whose actions and interactions can be interpreted and explained by taking account of these mental states" (Astington & Baird, 2005, p. 3). In other words, ToM allows us to take the perspective of another individual, such that we can more effectively understand, predict, and even influence the behaviors of others. ToM is thought to be strongly associated with linguistic abilities (Astington & Jenkins, 1999) and parent–child social interactions (Tomasello, 2003). Most important, a ToM also provides a means for understanding other people as beings whose actions and interactions are strongly guided by their affective states.

One consequence of a ToM is the ability to construct and employ symbols: abstractions or metarepresentations of objects, people, social constructs, and their interrelations. This capacity may have led to the development of symbolic language as well as a diverse range of nonlinguistic abstract systems that include cultural activities such as visual art, language, dance, religion, and music. According to Livingstone and Thompson (2006, in press), music and other arts emerged during this evolutionary period as powerful systems of affective interaction. Taken from this perspective, our experience with artworks can be understood as a form of affective exploration—a means of investigating affective communication within a safe environment (Davies, 2001). The affective engagement and exploration that are involved in musical behaviors both reflect and develop our ability to influence or attune to the affective states of others.

The evidence for a strong association between music and affect is compelling (Juslin & Sloboda, 2001). It should be noted, however, that not everyone agrees on the significance of emotional communication in musical activity. Cross (2003a, 2003b) persuasively questioned conceptions of music that identify it exclusively with affect, arguing that its uses are far from restricted to the mere communication or induction of emotion. However, although not all musical behaviors transmit emotional messages in a literal sense, all music experiences do involve a core affective dimension, and it is this dimension that allows music to function flexibly over a wide range of contexts (courting rituals, funerals and religious ceremonies, sporting events, social gatherings, courting rituals).

If affect is pivotal to the various uses of music, then we might expect to observe a correlation between musicality and emotional intelligence. Emotional intelligence has been described as a set of abilities for perceiving, using, understanding, and managing emotions (Mayer & Salovey, 1997; Salovey & Grewal, 2005). Perceiving emotions, the most basic component of emotional intelligence, relates to the detection and decoding of emotion in faces, voices, and cultural artifacts. Using emotions involves the ability to utilize emotions to assist in general cognitive tasks and problem solving. Understanding emotions is the ability to conceptualize emotions and understand differences or connections between them (like sadness and grief). Managing emotions refers to the regulation of emotions in oneself and others.

Resnicow, Salovey, and Repp (2004) found evidence for an association between musicality and emotional intelligence. They administered an emotional intelligence test to 24 listeners, who also identified the intended emotions of piano performances. The researchers observed a significant correlation between emotional intelligence and identification of intended emotions ($r = .54$). In another study, Thompson, Schellenberg, and Husain (2004) examined the effects of music lessons on the ability to decode affective connotations of speech prosody. Six-year-old children were assigned to music lessons, drama lessons, or no lessons for one year, and assessed for their ability to decode emotional connotations of vocal utterances. Children assigned to the keyboard condition outperformed other children, suggesting that some forms of music lessons lead to enhanced emotional sensitivity. In the same study, musically trained and untrained adults identified emotions conveyed in tone sequences that mimicked utterance prosody. Trained adults ($M = 45\%$) were better than untrained adults ($M = 29\%$) at discerning the emotional connotations of the prosodic patterns.

Affective engagement is not unique to music; it is relevant to many expressive forms, including visual arts, dance, and prosody. Auditory experiences of music are often inextricably linked with visual and kinesthetic experiences. In Western and non-Western cultures, performers and listeners experience music in an integrated, multimodal way (Thompson, Graham, & Russo, 2005). Several studies have examined cross-modal commonalities in the communication of affect. Krumhansl and Schenck (1997) exposed groups of participants to different dimensions of a choreographed work: dance only, music only, and dance and music. Judgments of emotion were highly similar in the three conditions. In another study, Thompson et al. (2005) observed that judgments of the affective quality of music were influenced by the facial expressions of performers, and recent evidence suggests that auditory and visual cues to affect are integrated preattentively and unconsciously (Thompson, Russo, & Quinto, 2008). Each of these studies points to a multimodal conception of music that is strongly connected with affect.

Nonadaptationist Accounts

In the preceding theories, music is assumed to have evolved because of direct reproductive or survival benefits. It is also possible, however, that nonadaptationist mechanisms led to the evolution of music. Evolutionary biologists urge consideration of such mechanisms to avoid the error of naive adaptationism—the use of adaptive theorizing to explain traits that emerged for nonadaptive reasons. Nonadaptationist mechanisms include genetic drift, laws of growth and form (such as general relations between brain and body size), direct induction of form by environmental forces such as water currents or gravity, and exaptation (when new uses are made of parts that were adapted for some other function).

Whereas an adaptation is a trait that was selected to perform at least one of its current functions, an exaptation performs a completely different function from that for which it evolved. Feathers were initially selected for insulation and not for flight; insect wings were initially selected as fanlike structures for cooling; legs evolved from lobed fins, used for swimming. Exaptations involve putting old structures to new uses. The *phenotype* (observable structures and behaviors) is modified with no corresponding change in the *genotype* (the genetic code).

A spandrel is the space where two arches intersect. It is an architectural by-product that is aesthetically pleasing.

Some functional traits were even exapted from features that originally performed no function, but emerged because of constraints of growth and form. The latter case is often described using the metaphor of a spandrel, an architectural feature that refers to the triangular space formed by the intersection of two arches. They are merely architectural by-products, but they are also visually appealing. Similarly, the evolution of cognitive and physical traits has left numerous vestiges or by-products that are sometimes of value to us.

Is it possible that music is an exaptation of previously adaptive traits, a squatter in the brain that opportunistically makes use of old structures for new purposes? To address that question, it is important to recognize that music is not an indivisible whole, but an interaction of several distinct qualities including rhythm, tempo, grouping, melody, harmony, and timbre. Many of these qualities are processed in discrete neural areas (e.g., Peretz & Zatorre, 2001), raising the possibility that the various components of music such as melody and rhythm may have different origins. Quite possibly, some components of music may be adaptations, whereas others may be exaptations. Certainly, some of the most significant features of music have parallels in other domains, including rhythm (important in sports and other skilled motor activities), pitch contour (used in speech prosody or "tone of voice"), and grouping (important for visual pattern recognition). Such parallels make it impossible to conclude that the features were originally adapted for purposes related to music, because they might have been adapted for purposes that relate to the other domains that share those features. Some features might have been adapted because of their musical function, and others might have been adapted because of their function within another domain. Music may represent a confluence of skills adapted or exapted from a range of different traits.

For example, melody and harmony might build on processes used to analyze and interpret the acoustic environment, called auditory scene analysis. Rhythm might build on different traits, such as timing mechanisms used to coordinate physical motion. Along these lines, Pinker (1997) proposed that music is a human technology designed to induce pleasure by activating and challenging several distinct cognitive functions. First, music activates basic processes of auditory scene analysis, which disentangle various musical textures into distinct tones, groups of tones, and instruments. Normally, these processes are engaged to sort out the conglomerate of sounds arriving at the ear, including wind, water, speech, animal calls, and traffic noise. Music activates and challenges these basic auditory processes: We distinguish melodies from their harmonic accompaniment, and we perceive multiple instruments within orchestral arrangements. Following this stage of analysis, various properties of music are thought to activate neural processes associated with the perception of speech prosody (tone of voice), emotional vocalizations (sighing, whimpering, laughing, crying), and environmental sounds (thunder, wind gusts, waves). At the same time, the rhythmic component of music is thought to stimulate the system of motor control (used for walking, running, digging, etc.).

Pinker surmised that activating and challenging these processes is inherently pleasurable. That is, music induces pleasure merely by stimulating processes that have important adaptive functions. Such a technology is comparable to the invention of drugs, which are nonadaptive but induce pleasure by interacting with neurochemical systems. In this view, music is "a cocktail of recreational drugs that we ingest through the ear to stimulate a mass of pleasure circuits at once" (Pinker, 1997, p. 528).

There are merits to this hypothesis. Like drugs and alcohol, music is used for mood manipulation and can give rise to pleasurable physiological responses such as tingles down the spine or goosebumps. Songwriters search for musical "hooks" because they understand that such devices (usually melodic or rhythmic) trigger intensely positive experiences in much of the population. The songwriter's quest to discover a great hook is similar to a chemist searching for an arresting mixture of ingredients.

When something catches our ear, we like it to be repeated endlessly in the song because, quite simply, we cannot get enough of a good hook. The degree of repetition in music often borders on the ridiculous, and suggests that our desire to hear musical hooks over and over is somewhat like an addict desperate for another fix, or an alcoholic frantic for another drink.

In this view, music was "invented" because we find it inherently pleasurable to engage processes involved in the perception of vocal patterns, sounds in the environment, and animal calls. In support of this idea, Mâche (2001) noted intriguing similarities between music and the qualities of many animal signals. Mâche's demonstrations include a variety of different traditions in human music, each one followed by a strikingly similar effect produced by a bird, mammal, or amphibian. Such similarities are compatible with the notion that music is merely derivative of the sounds in our environment, but also consistent with theories of musical origins based on the principle of continuism, discussed in the next section. Continuism holds that music and other animal signals have common origins.

Pinker's hypothesis raises a few questions, however (see also Huron, 2001a). First, it is unlikely that the pleasure of music is entirely related to its capacity to engage cognitive processes such as auditory scene analysis. Pinker surmises that music acts to "exaggerate the experience of being in an environment that contains strong, clear, analyzable signals" (p. 536), but it seems doubtful that music has this effect. A hallmark of romantic music, for example, is its melodic and harmonic ambiguity. Given that such music is aesthetically pleasing, it seems that "clear, analyzable signals" are by no means all that is required to enjoy music. It is extremely difficult for most listeners to perceive and track all of the voices in a Bach fugue or every note in a Jimi Hendrix guitar solo, but these forms of music are among the most valued by Western listeners.

Second, even if music draws from vocal (intonation) patterns, emotional calls, or environmental sounds, it is unclear why such extramusical associations in themselves should have aesthetic value. Even the notion that music is merely used for pleasure may have limited historic and cultural validity (Cross, 2003b). It seems more likely that extramusical associations—to the extent that they exist—point to communicative functions of music for ancestral populations, such as conveying emotional states or environmental and cultural information. Over time, music might have been ritualized into an aesthetic art form where its

Musical Hooks

Some famous examples of the extensive repetition of a musical hook include the line "Na na na nananana nananana, hey Jude" from the Beatles' "Hey Jude" (1968), which is repeated 19 times, lasting over 4 minutes, and the snare drum phrase in Ravel's *Bolero* (1928), is repeated 169 times, lasting over 15 minutes.

capacity to induce pleasure was nurtured. The use of music to induce aesthetic pleasure, however, may have little relevance to the origins of music.

As Huron (2001a) argued, nonadaptive pleasure-seeking behaviors (overindulgence in food, drugs, and alcohol) are generally associated with maladjustment (e.g., addicts and alcoholics dropping out on "skid row"). For example, drug dealers are among the most reviled members of society. In contrast, connoisseurs of music are usually quite well adjusted, and trained musicians and composers are among the most esteemed members of our society. There are few cultures in which avid musicians are perceived as overindulgent pleasure seekers because of their music making. We might disapprove of the recreational drugs taken by our favorite musician, especially if the drugs interfere with a concert tour for which we have expensive tickets, but it would make little sense to complain that they were "using way too much music." Conversely, there are quite compelling reasons for suspecting that music emerged because of its adaptive value, whether as courtship behavior, as one of many systems of affective engagement, to nurture social bonds, or to engage and develop physical and cognitive skills that were once useful for survival or reproduction.

Precursors to Music

The preceding hypotheses concern the evolutionary and historical processes that led to the emergence of music as an important cultural art form. Some theorists believe that music evolved as an adaptive response to pressures of reproduction or survival, and others argue that music is merely a nonadaptive invention or technology that draws on nonmusical adaptive processes. Related to these ideas are speculations about possible precursors to music. Musical styles change significantly from century to century (e.g., baroque, romantic, atonal), so it is exceedingly difficult to imagine what music sounded like 50,000 years ago, or the nature of its precursors. Music leaves no bones that can fossilize, and hence the study of musical origins is highly speculative. Did music originate from animal calls or birdsongs? Do music and speech have a common origin?

Some theorists hold that the origins of music overlap with those of other animal signals. Just as chimpanzees like to make sounds called pant hooting, humans like to sing. Is such a comparison credible? It could be, given that chimpanzees and humans are highly related in evolutionary

Among primates, gibbons are relatively monogamous, as are humans. Gibbons are also atypical among primates in that they participate in musical duetting behavior. Geissmann (2000) describes a series of stereotyped interactions between the "great calls" of the female and the male's vocalizations. The function of gibbon duetting is not yet clearly understood. Although territorial advertisement has been suggested, duetting behavior can take place in the absence of rival gibbons.

Investigating the relationship between gibbon duetting and pair bond strength, Geissmann has found correlations between the extent of duetting and measures of pair bond strength such as interindividual distance between mates. Given the urge that human couples tend to have to share love songs—whether as listeners or duetters or dancing partners—it seems plausible that these traits might also be associated in humans.

Source: Original photography: KevBow. Made available under Creative Commons 2.0 Attribution-Generic License.

terms, having only diverged from the great ape line as distinct species about 6 million years ago. Even today chimpanzees and humans share close to 99% of their genetic material, and are as closely related to each other as lions are to tigers, and rats to mice.

Chimpanzee calls involve some obvious musiclike features. Pant hooting, for example, is a rhythmic activity that continues for about 10 seconds in a continuous crescendo that explodes in a climax (Tarzan did a good imitation). It can be analyzed into sections such as the introduction, buildup, climax, and closure. In most circumstances, these calls reflect the animal's affective state and are used to achieve and modulate social contact.

In the same way, music conveys emotional information, can be analyzed into sections, and performs social functions. Thus, just as chimpanzees and humans have a common origin as species, their distinctive calls—pant hooting and music—might also have a common origin. More generally, if traits are observed in both human and nonhuman animals, they are said to be homologous, that is, inherited from a common ancestor that expressed that trait. This view, known as *continuism*, suggests that music developed directly out of an early primate signal system (Bickerton, 2001). The mating calls of our distant ancestors, for example, might have developed into what we now call singing. Because musical behaviors and mating calls are distinct phenomena, this explanation suggests that there were no adaptive pressures for music per se. Rather, adaptive pressures gave rise to mating calls, the vestiges of which have merely been coopted for use in music (McDermott & Hauser, 2005, p. 32).

As discussed, one property that distinguishes human music from most animal calls is intentional transposability. Animal sounds such as birdsongs tend to be locked into specific functions, whereas human music is distinguished by its flexibility of function. A more modest claim is that, even if music and animal calls do not have the same origin, it is still informative to examine structural similarities between them. Such similarities might reveal, for example, similar evolutionary pressures, constraints of neural organization (or production), or interactions between hominids and other animals that might have shaped the development of music. The composer Mâche (2001) identified many similarities between music and animal sounds that, in his view, are compelling enough to justify an entire discipline called *zoomusicology*. As examples, he noted that the songs of certain kingfishers involve moving up and down in small melodic intervals along a scale, and the songs of certain robins repeatedly end with a kind of key note (akin to *doh* in music).

There is a critical feature of music, however, that is not shared by the calls of chimpanzees and other animal signals: Humans produce a vast repertoire of complex musical patterns out of the building blocks of pitch, duration, loudness, timbre, and tempo. As a result, music is characterized by an almost infinite variety, creativity, and novelty. The vocal signals observed in birds, monkeys, and apes, in contrast, are hard-wired and have limited variability.

Music making is exceptionally creative because it operates according to what is called the *particulate principle*. This principle describes how, in physics, chemistry, and language, discrete units from a finite set of elements (e.g., atoms, chemical bases, phonemes) are combined and permuted to give rise to higher level structures such as molecules, genes, and words (Abler, 1989; Humboldt, 1836/1972; Studdert-Kennedy, 2000). Music also adheres to this principle in that discrete units of pitch and duration are combined to form higher level units such as melody and rhythm. That is, music making is highly creative because humans have the capacity to combine and permute discrete acoustic features to generate an infinite number of possible novel combinations. This property of music may also be a prerequisite for its intentional transposability, the significance of which has been emphasized by Cross (2003a, 2003b).

It has been suggested that once our hominid ancestors developed the cognitive ability to make use of the particulate principle, they applied it to vocalizations, giving rise to new signal systems with vast combinatorial potential (Abler, 1989; Studdert-Kennedy, 2000). One such signal system was language, but that same cognitive ability also might have led to the emergence of music. Language and music might have emerged at the same time as two distinct signal systems, or one system might have developed as an outgrowth of the other system, or a precursor to both systems—a "musilanguage"—might have developed and then later diverged into two separate systems (Brown, 2000).

In any case, the ability to apply the particulate principle to vocalizations is very likely to have occurred well after the evolutionary divergence between hominids and other great apes. Hominids made use of the particulate principle in language and music, but other apes did not. Thus, animal calls remain limited in terms of creative potential, making them categorically different from either language or music. In this view, music and language are not continuous with animal calls because they are characterized by the particulate principle. Rather, they are distinctive capacities that are unique to the hominid line.

Both language and music adhere to the particulate principle, and precursors to these domains may well have evolved at the same time or from a common signal system. There are several similarities between these two systems that support this conjecture. In particular, both domains convey emotional meaning using similar acoustic features. In speech, emotion is conveyed through tone of voice or speech prosody. For example, when we are feeling sad we tend to speak more softly, more slowly, and with less pitch variation than when we are feeling happy. These very same acoustic variables—loudness, pace, and pitch—are also used to convey emotions in music.

This similarity at the level of emotional communication raises the possibility that both language and music originated from a single emotion-based system of communication. There may have been an ancestral precursor to language and music that functioned to convey emotional meaning. Once our hominid ancestors began to make use of the particulate principle, they applied it to this emotive system, giving rise to a powerful signal system with enormous potential to communicate complex messages.

Brown (2000) proposed a similar view. He argued for a single precursor to both language and music, which he called *musilanguage*. In his view, musilanguage might have begun as a simple system of referential emotive vocalizations (REVs). A REV is an emotive response to a specific object, but one that also indicates to other animals the class of object causing the emotive response. As an example, East African vervet monkeys have emotive vocalizations that also signal snakes, leopards, and eagles. REVs have both emotive and referential meaning, providing the essential ingredients for language and music.

Brown proposed two basic stages in the evolution of musilanguage. In the earliest stage, musilanguage was characterized only by the use of lexical tone. Lexical tone refers to the use of pitch to convey semantic (lexical) meaning. For example, increases in pitch height might have signaled higher spatial positions or heightened emotional states such as surprise or anger. As language and music split into two systems, the significance of pitch differences in the two systems diverged. Pitch differences in music eventually became important for structural properties such as melody and harmony. Pitch differences in language eventually gave rise to tonal languages such as Chinese Mandarin. In tonal languages, pitch partially determines the meaning of speech sounds. Although not all languages are tonal, Brown suggested that nontonal (intonational) languages such as English might have evolved from earlier tonal forms.

The second stage was characterized by two properties: combinatorial phrase formation and expressive phrasing. Combinatorial phrase formation refers to the combining of lexical tonal units to make simple phrases that have higher order meanings. Presumably, this property emerged once hominids applied the particulate principle to the earliest forms of musilanguage. The resultant combinations of lexical tonal units (i.e., phrases) could then be further manipulated by expressive phrasing. Expressive phrasing involves modulating sequences of vocalizations in amplitude, tempo, and pitch register. As observed in speech and music today, positive emotional states might have been characterized by loud, fast, high-pitched vocalizations, whereas negative emotional states might have been characterized by soft, slow, low-pitched vocalizations. As language and music diverged into separate systems, distinctive features were added to their shared ancestral properties. Language developed into a specialized system for communicating semantic meaning, and music developed as a ritualized activity that included distinctive features such as harmony.

An example of lexical tone from Thai (Fromkin, 2001, p. 211). The five different meanings of *naa* are distinguished by intonation alone.

[naa] [__] low tone
'a nickname'

[naa] [⌐\ ] falling tone
'face'

[naa] [__/] rising tone
'thick'

[naa] [—] mid tone
'rice paddy'

[naa] [‾] high tone
'young maternal uncle or aunt'

Whatever its origins, the music of our ancestors was undoubtedly nothing like the diverse and complex musical systems found around the world today. Indeed, although cognitive capacities to perceive and produce music may have evolved as adaptations, natural selection cannot account for the sheer variety of today's musical styles. Rather, the complexity and diversity of music is more easily explained through cumulative cultural evolution, the process by which humans build on existing knowledge and skills through the combined strategies of cultural transmission and creative invention. Cultural transmission is the process by which we acquire existing knowledge and skills, for example, through imitation or direct instruction. Creative invention is the process by which we continuously modify our existing knowledge and skills, increasing or altering their complexity. These new forms are then again transmitted to other generations through cultural transmission, working as a "ratchet" to prevent slippage backward to earlier forms of knowledge and skills. In this way, cultural practices such as music composition and performance can jumpstart into variegated and complex forms over only a few generations, circumventing the glacially slow process of biological evolution.

Additional Readings

Cross, I. (2007). Music and cognitive evolution. In R. Dunbar & L. Barrett (Eds.), *OUP handbook of evolutionary psychology* (pp. 649–667). Oxford, UK: Oxford University Press.

McDermott, J., & Hauser, M. (2005). The origins of music: Innateness, uniqueness, and evolution. *Music Perception, 23,* 29–59.

CHAPTER 3

Musical Building Blocks

LEARNING OUTCOMES

By the end of this chapter you should be able to:

1. Describe how vibrating objects give rise to sound, and how sound is detected by the auditory system.

2. Explain the physical basis of periodic and nonperiodic sounds.

3. Discuss the connection between music and the acoustic structure of sound.

4. Identify the psychoacoustic effects of combining musical tones and outline the implications of these effects for music.

5. Contrast and evaluate psychological models of pitch.

6. Describe properties of sound that influence our perception of timbre.

The Elements of Sound

We are so accustomed to the soundscape of our environment that we rarely stop to contemplate how extraordinary it is that we have the capacity to detect actions and collisions of molecules that are so small as to be invisible. Not only can we sense such molecular motions, we can identify and respond to an astronomical number of different types of motion. When we hear someone sing, we are actually sensing minuscule movements of air molecules emanating from the movements of vocal cords, and interpreting these invisible movements as meaningful attributes of the song, including various qualities of the melody as well as the linguistic information in the lyrics. How is this accomplished?

The answer to this question requires some technical explanations and a few assumptions. The vibration of vocal cords causes movement in surrounding air molecules, which we ultimately perceive as sound. Jumping into a swimming pool creates a similar kind of wave, but on a larger scale. This movement of air molecules emanates outward from a vibrating source and eventually collides with the *eardrum* (outer ear). The movements detected by the ear are infinitesimal but powerful, for they are ultimately responsible for our auditory world, including our most meaningful music experiences.

When the eardrum responds to the movements of air molecules, a complex chain of events is initiated that implicates physiological and neural activity at many levels of processing. Vibrations of the eardrum lead to movement of the *basilar membrane*, a resonant structure that resides within the *cochlea* of the inner ear. The basilar membrane is not unlike the string of a guitar, in that it varies in width and stiffness and vibrates in conjunction with sound. Unlike any musical instrument, though, it is surrounded by liquid and vibrates within that medium. The actual motion of the basilar membrane is described as a *traveling wave* or progressive wave. Other examples of traveling waves include ocean waves, the movement that occurs when a whip is cracked, and audience waves at sporting events. Each point along the basilar membrane has a *characteristic frequency* (CF), which is the frequency for which it is most resonant. Thus, although any sound will cause a traveling wave along the basilar membrane, the maximum amount of movement in that wave will occur at different points depending on the frequencies involved in the sound. The basilar membrane is the base for the sensory receptors of hearing:

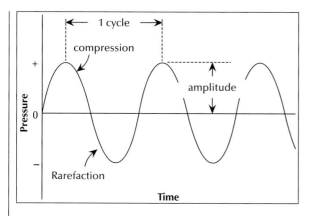

The Physics of Sound: Sine Waves

Air has mass and elasticity so any source of energy will cause fluctuations in air pressure in the form of waves. At a given point along the wave, the air molecules will either be bunched up (*compression*) or spread apart (*rarefaction*).

Shown here is a graphic illustration of the alternating pattern of compression and rarefaction of the simplest type of sound wave called a *sinusoidal* or *sine* wave. The x-axis indicates the unfolding of time, and the y-axis indicates the increase (+) and decrease (−) in sound pressure taking place.

A *period* is the amount of time that it takes for a complete cycle of the waveform. In the diagram, it is demarcated as the "1 cycle" area from one compression peak to the next.

Amplitude refers the intensity of the fluctuation in air pressure, illustrated in the diagram by the arrow indicating the maximum point of compression. It is most commonly measured in decibels and its psychological correlate is loudness. A louder sound is produced by waves with greater amplitude.

Repetition rate is measured in hertz: the number of cycles completed in 1 second. A period equals the reciprocal of the repetition rate. If the repetition rate is 100 hertz (100 cycles/1 second), then the period is 1/100 second.

Two sine waves equal in period will interact in different ways depending on their *phase*. If they are 180° out of phase (the compression peak of one wave coincides with the rarefaction peak of the other), they will tend to cancel each other out. If they are 180° out of phase and of equal amplitude, silence will result.

Source: Reproduced from Schiffman, H.R. (2000) *Sensation and Perception: An Integrated Approach*. New York: John Wiley and Sons, p.316. Used by permission.

the *hair cells*. Movement of the basilar membrane causes movement of hair cells, leading to electrical signals that are relayed from the auditory nerve to the auditory brain stem and eventually the cortex. This extraordinary mechanism for detecting the movement of air molecules allows human listeners to distinguish roughly 1,500 frequencies.

Why do certain types of movements give rise to rich experiences of music, and others give rise to experiences of speech, traffic noise, or laughter? The answer lies in an examination of the sensory attributes of sound. When sound stimulates the auditory system, it is subject to a kind of physiological interpretation or analysis, whereby vibrating molecules are converted into various forms of neural activity that represent that sound in terms of a range of sensory attributes, a process called *sensory transduction*. These sensory attributes form the building blocks of music.

Periodic Motion

A lot of the movement that occurs in our environment, including that of vocal cords when we talk or sing, is called *periodic motion*. Periodic motion occurs when an object such as a plucked guitar string rapidly moves back and forth in a repetitive manner. This type of motion, in turn, causes a periodic sound wave. When a periodic sound wave reaches the eardrum, it gives rise to a distinctive quality that is highly relevant to music: the sensation of *pitch*.

Any naturally occurring sound, such as that of a footstep, a sneeze, breaking glass, or a note played on the flute or piano, can be described as a combination of many simple periodic waves (i.e., sine waves) or *partials*, each with its own frequency of vibration, amplitude, and phase. *Fourier analysis* is the technique that allows us to analyze a complex sound into its sine-wave components. The various sine-wave components of a complex sound are collectively referred to as the *spectrum* of frequency components, or simply, the *sound spectrum*.

We do not normally perceive the individual partials of a complex sound because cognitive mechanisms operate to fuse them together, leading us to experience a unitary sound. According to *Ohm's acoustical law*, however, under certain listening conditions we do have a limited ability to hear some of the individual partials of a complex sound. For example, when a single piano note is played, under certain conditions it is actually possible to hear some of the many different pitches (i.e., partials) that make up that note.

Sounds with a discernable pitch all have a *periodic waveform*, in that the waveform continuously repeats itself over time. For example, playing an individual note on a flute, piano, violin, or any other "pitched" instrument will generate a periodic waveform. The *period* is the time taken for one complete cycle of the waveform, and is the reciprocal of the repetition rate. The *repetition rate* usually determines the perceived pitch (exceptions include circular tones, discussed later), and is measured in cycles per second, or hertz (1 Hz = 1 cycle/sec). In other words, when a periodic waveform impinges on the auditory system, it is ultimately converted into a sensation of pitch. In general, when the repetition rate of a periodic sound is increased, the perceived pitch increases.

The partials of any periodic waveform tend to occur in a predictable pattern of frequencies that is known as the *harmonic series*. Partials that fall along the harmonic series are also called *harmonics*. If the lowest frequency component of a periodic sound is n, then the other harmonics—called overtones—are members of the set $2n$, $3n$, $4n$, $5n$, and so on. That is, each overtone has a frequency that is an integer multiple of the lowest or fundamental frequency of the complex. An important property of the harmonic series is that additional harmonic overtones do not alter the overall repetition rate of the waveform (which is determined by the fundamental frequency) and therefore do not change the perceived pitch of the complex.

The Discovery of Music Within Sound

The mathematical precision of the harmonic series is actually an idealized description of complex periodic sounds, and naturally produced sounds typically include inharmonic components. Moreover, depending on the source of the sound (e.g., voice, piano, violin) and the manner and context in which that sound is produced (intensity and room acoustics), different harmonics will be more or less prominent. Nevertheless, the frequency relationships that are represented in periodic sounds are remarkably musical. Helmholtz (1863/1954) observed that several aspects of music, such as scales and harmony, have compelling parallels in the acoustical structure of sound. He noted that music from several cultures involves important scale notes that map onto the harmonics of complex tones. In the major scale, the fifth scale degree (sol) is equivalent (i.e., in note name, or *tone chroma*) to the third harmonic of a complex periodic tone built on the first note of the scale (doh), and the third scale degree (mi) is equivalent to the fifth harmonic.

Remarkably, the most important musical intervals that are used in Western music can be found within the harmonic content of a single note. The first and second harmonics of a complex tone are separated by an *octave*, the second and third harmonics are separated by a *perfect fifth*, the third and fourth harmonics are separated by a *perfect fourth*, the fourth and fifth harmonics are separated by a *major third*, and the fifth and sixth harmonics are separated by a *minor third*. How could such a mapping occur? In spite of Ohm's acoustical law, it is not easy or typical

Sound Example 3.1

Sound example 3.1 is an illustration of the harmonic series using a guitar string. The fundamental pitch of the open plucked fifth string is an A at 110 Hz. If the string is lightly fretted at the 12th fret and plucked, the second harmonic—an A an octave above and twice the frequency of the fundamental (220 Hz), is heard. The third harmonic, an E a perfect fifth above the second harmonic and three times the frequency of the fundamental (330 Hz), is found at the seventh fret. The fourth, fifth, and sixth harmonics can be found at the fifth, fourth, and third frets, respectively.

When fretting a harmonic, the physical division of the string reflects the frequency ratio of harmonic to fundamental. For example, the second harmonic forms a ratio of 2:1 and is found at the exact midpoint of the length of the string (the 12th fret). The third harmonic forms a 3:1 ratio with the fundamental and is fretted at a point that is exactly a third of the length of the string (the seventh fret).

Source: © 2008. Richard Yates.

to hear the individual frequencies contained within an individual note. Rather, the auditory system seems to fuse all of them together, giving rise to a single and unified perceptual experience of that note.

In spite of almost 150 years of scholarship on musical acoustics, it remains an intriguing mystery as to how or why the harmonic spectra contained within individual tones are mirrored in the many pitch relationships that can be found in our melodies and harmonies. The predominance of musical relationships that seem to echo the very frequency relationships contained within individual complex tones implies that, at some level, the brain must register frequency relationships within individual sounds. At a conscious level, however, we do not usually perceive frequency relationships within individual tones. If we play a single key on a piano, we hear a single note, not an array of frequency relationships. Rather than generating individual pitch sensations, the spectral content of individual tones is fused, and contributes to another attribute of sound that seems to have little to do with musical relationships: the quality of timbre. That is, notes with different spectral contents are perceived as having different sound qualities, tone colors, or timbres.

Our perceptions of sound, it seems, are deceptively oblique, and it is only through careful investigation that we have any chance of fully understanding the connection between the physics of sound and the nature of music experience. Pythagoras (6th century BC) laid much of the groundwork for this quest with his discoveries on the nature of sound, but it is only in the past 100 years following many advances in the study of human physiology that we have been able to move significantly beyond these insights to gain an understanding of the perceptual and cognitive basis of music.

Sensory Consonance and Dissonance

The spectrum of harmonic overtones not only influences our perception of timbre; it also affects the degree of sensory consonance and dissonance that we perceive when multiple tones are presented simultaneously. Long-term knowledge of music also affects perceptions of consonance and dissonance, and these qualities of music are referred to as *musical consonance* and *musical dissonance*. Sensory and musical forms of consonance and dissonance are often overlapping. However, whereas sensory consonance and dissonance result from psychoacoustic factors and arise independent of learning and enculturation, musical consonance and dissonance are dependent on musical experience, and can change throughout the life span.

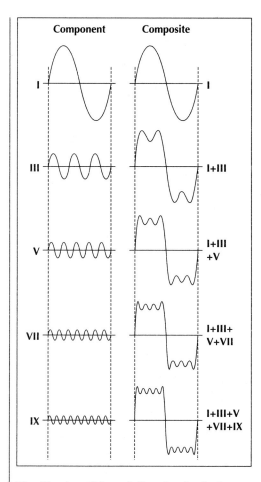

The Physics of Sound: Fourier Analysis

Any complex sound can be broken down into a set of component sine waves called partials using a mathematical procedure called Fourier analysis, named after its discoverer, French mathematician Jean Baptiste Fourier (1768–1830). The process can also be reversed: complex sound can be artificially constructed from a set of sine waves (partials) and the process is termed *Fourier synthesis*.

This figure illustrates a synthesized periodic waveform called a square wave produced by adding only the odd-numbered partials in the harmonic series to a fundamental frequency. For example, if a fundamental frequency (1) is 100 hertz, (3) is 300 hertz, (5) is 500 hertz, and so on. The amplitudes of the partials are also proportional to the fundamental frequency. That is, (3) is 1/3 the amplitude of (1), and (5) is 1/5 the amplitude of (1). The left column lists each component harmonic separately, and the right column illustrates the effect on the composite wave as each harmonic is added.

Source: Reproduced from Boring, E., Langfeld, H., and Weld, H. (1948) *Foundations of Psychology.* New York: John Wiley, p.316. Used by permission.

Intervals that give rise to sensory consonance are comprised of tones with fundamental frequencies that stand in small integer ratios. The most consonant interval—the octave—consists of pitches with fundamental frequencies that are related to each other by a ratio of 2:1. Another highly consonant interval—the perfect fifth—consists of pitches with fundamental frequencies that are related to each other by a ratio of 3:2. In contrast, intervals that give rise to sensory dissonance are comprised of tones with fundamental frequencies that stand in more complex ratios. For example, the fundamental frequencies associated with the dissonant "tritone" interval are related to each other by a ratio of 32:45.

Tone combinations with fundamental frequencies that are related to each other by small integer ratios, such as the octave (2:1) and the perfect fifth (3:2), have many overtones that either align with each other or are separated from each other in frequency by a distance that is greater than a *critical band*. The concept of a critical band originated from psychoacoustic research and refers to the range of frequencies within which so-called *sensory interactions* occur. Across the pitches that are typically used in music, the critical band corresponds to about one third of an octave. Consonant intervals do not give rise to many such sensory interactions, and the basilar membrane can largely "resolve" the many frequency components associated with such pitch combinations.

In contrast, combinations of pitches that are related to each other by complex ratios contain many overtones that are not aligned with each other but that are too close in frequency for the basilar membrane to resolve optimally. Such combinations contain a lot of harmonic frequencies that fall within a critical band, resulting in sensory interactions that include rapid amplitude fluctuations. These amplitude fluctuations seem to give rise to a sensation of roughness and beating, and the perception of dissonance. Dissonant intervals give rise to a lot of sensory interactions, and the basilar membrane is not able to "resolve" all of the frequency components associated with these pitch combinations.

Because the frequency components of dissonant intervals are poorly resolved by the basilar membrane, dissonant intervals are also discriminated poorly by infants and even by adults. Just as it is difficult to recognize a face in a blurry photograph, people are not very good at judging dissonant sounds. Moreover, the marked differences in responses by peripheral auditory mechanisms to consonance and dissonance, and hence in the sensation of roughness, provide a simple means for humans and various nonhuman species to discriminate consonance and dissonance. Interestingly, preferences for consonance appear to be uniquely human.

Sound Example 3.2

An illustration of the critical band. Two sine tones are played at the same frequency—one remains constant and the other slowly increases in frequency. As the difference between the tones passes through the critical band (one third of an octave) an interference effect known as *beats* occurs. This is followed by a roughness or dissonance that slowly dissipates. The rising tone stabilizes at a simple integer ratio of 3:2 (perfect fifth) from the constant tone and the roughness disappears.

Tuning Systems

If sensitivity to sensory consonance is a basic property of the auditory system, one might ask how this property affects scale structures and tuning systems. In most scales from around the world, consonant intervals (e.g., octaves, perfect fifths and fourths) are structurally important. For example, tones separated by octaves are considered to be similar in virtually all musical cultures. In North Indian scales, tones separated by a fifth (the sa and pa) are structurally important and are typically sounded continuously throughout a piece. The most common pentatonic scale (exemplified by the black notes on the piano), which is found in Chinese and Celtic music, can be formed by choosing any pitch as an arbitrary starting tone, adding a second tone a fifth higher, another tone a fifth higher than the second tone, and so on, until a collection of five pitches is obtained. The scale is formed by octave-transposing the collection of tones so that they fall within a single octave.

In Western music, two similarly natural tuning systems for the chromatic scale have been used historically (for a review, see E. M. Burns, 1999). One, called Pythagorean tuning, extends the pentatonic scale already described with additional tones that continue the cycle of fifths. In the other, called just intonation, the scale is formed by tuning notes so that their fundamental frequencies form small integer ratios with the fundamental frequency of the first note of the scale (doh). Both of these scales limit the possibility of transpositions between keys, because some instances of particular intervals (e.g., the perfect fifth between C and G) are tuned differently than other instances (e.g., C# and G#).

Equal temperament represents a compromise solution. It guarantees that all intervals (e.g., all perfect fifths, or all major thirds) are tuned identically, and that important intervals do not deviate greatly from small integer frequency ratios: fifths and fourths deviate from exact small integer ratios by 2% of a semitone; major and minor thirds are slightly more mistuned. These minor deviations, although discriminable in some cases, are no greater than the typical tuning deviations observed in the performances of singers or stringed-instrument players. Moreover, such small departures from exact small integer ratios have little effect on the perceived consonance of these intervals, which may explain why equal temperament has endured for many years.

Sound Example 3.3

The sa and pa in the Indian classical tradition are the equivalent of do and sol in Western nomenclature. They are sounded continuously (drones) on the *tambura* during a performance.

Source: Martin Quibell. Made available under Creative Commons Sampling-Plus License 1.0.

Sound Example 3.4

A major third interval is presented melodically in three tunings: equal temperament (most commonly used today), Pythagorean, and just intonations.

J.S. Bach and Equal Temperament

J. S. Bach's (1685–1750) pioneering endorsement of equal temperament was initiated to "expand the harmonic universe." The problem with both just and Pythagorean tuning systems is that, of the 24 major and minor scales commonly used by Western musicians at the time, only a limited number remained viable. For some scales, certain intervals would sound noticeably out of tune. As a consequence, some musicians would be entirely confined to a few scales; others would have to retune their instrument to be able to play using other scales. Equal temperament, the division of the octave into 12 equal parts, allowed musicians to borrow from any scale at any time without having to retune. Bach's *Well Tempered Clavier* was a set of 48 keyboard pieces, two in each major and minor key, designed to illustrate the virtues of equal temperament.

Sensitivity to Pitch

People are remarkably sensitive to pitch, but this sensitivity relates primarily to pitch relations. Sensitivity to pitch relations, often called *relative pitch*, refers to the ability to produce, recognize, or identify pitch relations, such as those that define a musical interval or a melody. To illustrate, "Happy Birthday" can be sung in a high or a low voice, or performed on a tuba or a piccolo. As long as the pitch relations conform to those of the melody, it is recognizable. People are much less sensitive to isolated pitches. Anyone can appreciate the quality of an isolated timbre (e.g., flute, cello, oboe, trumpet), but an isolated pitch leaves us cold. Only in exceptional cases do individuals form rich associations with isolated pitches.

In a case study reported by Luria, Tsvetkova, and Futer (1965), a person referred to as S formed detailed visual images on hearing individual pitches. When presented with a 64-dB tone pitched at 250 hertz, he saw a velvet cord with fibers jutting out on all sides. When presented with a 100-dB tone pitched at 500 hertz, he saw a streak of lightning that split the sky in two. Other cases of synesthetic experiences of pitch have also been reported, but the vast majority of people have simpler experiences. We might be able to assert that an isolated pitch sounds high or low, but the most interesting psychological qualities of pitch emerge from the relationships that are formed when we hear multiple pitches.

Musical Schemata

What schemata do we use to place music into categories? Some categories such as rap and opera seem obvious. Others seem to defy classification. What is the difference between pop and rock, or rock and heavy metal, or heavy metal and punk?

A recent music marketing trend may provide some empirical data on this question. In an attempt to appeal to as many radio station formats as possible, record companies are releasing multiple "mixes" of songs. Shania Twain's entire CD *Up!* was released in two mixes—a country version and a pop version. Examining the differences between mixes might provide some clues as to what constitutes our mental representations of these various categories.

Pitch is implicated at multiple levels of musical structure, forming the basis for melody, harmony, and key. As we listen to music, we experience pitch on all of these levels, giving us a multidimensional understanding of structure. Our understanding of music is stored in the brain as a mental representation. Mental representations of music are partly built up from experience. Through passive or active exposure, listeners gradually internalize regularities in the music of their own culture, forming long-term knowledge schemata into which novel music stimuli are assimilated. Nonetheless, mental representations of pitch may also be constrained by processing limits and biases. For example, the limits of working memory may constrain our ability to encode brief but unfamiliar melodies with accurate detail. Because of such limits, mental representations of unfamiliar melodies are sketchy, often containing little more than pitch contour information.

Models of Pitch Perception

Pitch height is the most basic dimension along which pitches are perceived to vary; it refers to the continuum that extends from low to high pitches (which corresponds to a logarithmic function of frequency, or cycles per second). The psychological relevance of this continuum is evident in similarity judgments for pairs of pitches: Tones closer in pitch are considered more similar than tones separated by greater pitch distance. The pitch-height continuum is also evident in neural activity in the cochlea. High frequencies stimulate the basal portions of the basilar membrane, low frequencies stimulate the apical portions, and intermediate frequencies affect intermediate portions.

In constructing a model of pitch perception, one may start with the basic dimension of pitch height, and then consider additional dimensions along which pitch seems to vary. Most models of pitch perception consider the special status of the octave among intervals. As noted, tones with fundamental frequencies separated by an octave are perceived to be similar in virtually all cultures. Pitch chroma refers to the quality of pitch that is independent of the octave register in which it occurs. In Western music, tones separated by an octave are given the same name (e.g., A, B, C), implicating their equivalence in some sense. Further evidence for this view comes from listeners with musical training, who perceive similarities between tones that are separated by an octave (Allen, 1967; Kallman, 1982).

If pitch chroma and pitch height are basic dimensions of pitch perception, we should expect to find similar evidence among naive listeners. When musically untrained adults or children judge the similarity between pure tones, however, they tend to focus exclusively on the dimension of pitch height (Allen, 1967; Kallman, 1982; Sergeant, 1983). For example, C4 and C#4 (notes separated by a semitone) are perceived to be highly similar, but C4 and C5 (notes separated by an octave) are perceived to be no more similar than C4 and B4 (notes separated by a major seventh). These findings do not rule out the possibility that sensitivity to the chroma dimension could be uncovered with tasks that measure implicit rather than explicit knowledge of musical associations. However, the findings make it clear that music educators should not assume that naive listeners will have an explicit understanding of octave equivalence.

An early psychological model of pitch perception incorporated the two dimensions of pitch height and pitch chroma. As shown in Figure 3.1, these two dimensions are depicted as orthogonal dimensions of a geometrically regular helix—a monotonic dimension of pitch height and a circular dimension of pitch chroma. Shepard (1964) reported evidence that these dimensions are psychologically relevant and orthogonal. He created tones with well-defined chroma but ambiguous height. Such circular tones were constructed by combining 10 pure-tone components spaced at octave intervals, and imposing a fixed amplitude envelope over the frequency range such that components at the low and high ends of the range approach hearing threshold.

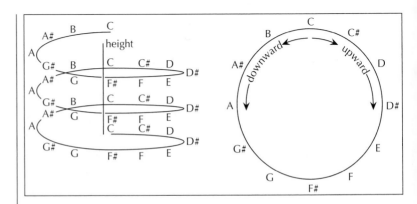

Figure 3.1

An early model of pitch perception. Two psychological dimensions are represented in the model: height and chroma.

Although the overall pitch height of any circular tone is somewhat indeterminate, listeners experience certain circular tones as higher or lower than others. In particular, listeners tend to perceive the relative height of these tones so as to maximize their pitch proximity. For example, when presented the circular tones C followed by D, one can perceive the second tone as either higher or lower than the first tone (C up to D, or C down to D). Both interpretations are possible because their individual pitch heights are ambiguous. Nonetheless, listeners typically perceive the second tone (D) as higher than the first tone (C), because this interpretation implicates a pitch distance of only two semitones. Listeners almost never perceive the second tone as lower than the first tone, because that interpretation would implicate a pitch distance of 10 semitones.

Shepard created fascinating patterns of circular tones in which chroma varied continuously around a chroma circle (see Figure 3.1). For ascending patterns, he shifted all of the octave spaced components up in frequency (adding new components at the low end of the amplitude envelope) until the complex returned to the initial configuration. When chroma was shifted continuously in a clockwise direction around the chroma circle (C, C#, D, D#, etc.), the pattern was perceived as ascending endlessly. When chroma was shifted continuously in a counterclockwise direction (C, B, A#, A, etc.), the pattern was perceived as descending endlessly. That is, listeners perceived changes in pitch chroma but not in overall pitch height. Most important, these effects were perceived by musically trained and untrained listeners alike. By making pitch height indeterminate, Shepard demonstrated that pitch chroma has perceptual significance, even for untrained listeners. Thus, although untrained listeners may lack explicit knowledge of the similarity between tones with the same chroma, they nonetheless demonstrate sensitivity to chroma.

If pitch class and pitch height are orthogonal, then the relative height of circular tones that are directly opposite on the circle, such as C and F#, should be ambiguous or indeterminate. Deutsch (1999) addressed this prediction in a series of experiments. She reported that, for a given individual, certain circular tones (i.e., chromas) are reliably and consistently judged as being higher than the circular tone that is opposite on the circle, suggesting that the perceived height of a tone is systematically related to its pitch chroma. For example, some listeners perceive a successive presentation of two particular circular tones separated by a tritone (e.g., C and F#) as upward pitch movement, whereas others perceive the same two tones as downward pitch movement. In

Sound Example 3.5

Sound example 3.5 is a scale comprised of Shepard tones. Most listeners perceive the scale as ascending because it implies smaller pitch distances from tone to tone, even though pitch height has been rendered ambiguous. Because pitch ascension is illusory, this excerpt could conceivably be looped to create the illusion of a scale endlessly rising in pitch, without the pitch ever reaching a frequency beyond human detection. A visual analogy can be made with M. C. Escher's "Ascending and Descending" (below); because the relative height of any one stair in the staircase is ambiguous, an illusion of an endlessly ascending (or descending) staircase is created.

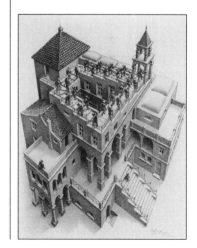

another investigation, Repp and Knoblich (2007) showed that performing a simple hand movement can affect whether sequential circular tones separated by a tritone are perceived as ascending or descending.

To date, no researcher has been able to construct a complex tone such that changes in pitch chroma do not generate corresponding changes in pitch height. For circular tones, perceived changes in pitch height are dependent on context but they are never completely absent. In fact, some listeners report that sequences of circular tones give rise to *multiple* sensations of changing pitch height—some ascending and others simultaneously descending. That is, tones constructed to have an ambiguous pitch height may sometimes break apart into individual pitch sensations, but they will always generate one or more sensations of pitch height.

Shepard (1982, 1999) and others have proposed models of pitch perception with additional dimensions besides those based on height and chroma. These models account for affinities between tones separated by perfect fifths and fourths, which are said to be relevant for musically trained listeners tested with harmonically rich tones presented in musical contexts. Even more elaborate models have been proposed to account for affinities between tones separated by thirds. The establishment of a musical key also shapes pitch judgments. For example, in the context of the key of C major, C and G are more strongly associated with each other than E and B, even though both tone pairs represent a perfect fifth interval (Krumhansl, 1979).

The effects of musical context on judgments of pitch were examined in a series of investigations conducted by Krumhansl and her colleagues (see Krumhansl, 1990). They used the probe tone technique in a variety of musical contexts. The method involves presentation of a musical stimulus that clearly defines a musical key (e.g., scale, cadence, chord sequence) followed by a probe tone. Listeners rate (usually on a scale from 1–7) how well each probe tone in the chromatic scale fits with the established key.

When musically trained listeners are tested with this method, probe tone ratings are quite consistent across listeners. As we might expect, their ratings mirror predictions from music theory. When a major key is established, a probe tone corresponding to the tonic of the key has the highest rating, followed by the dominant and mediant, then the other tones in the key (diatonic or scale tones), and finally the nondiatonic (i.e., nonscale) tones. This tonal hierarchy is more easily uncovered with musically trained than untrained participants, illustrating the influence of learning. School-age children's implicit knowledge of the hierarchy improves dramatically from 6 to 11 years of age (Krumhansl

Sound Examples 3.6.1 and 3.6.2

Sound examples 3.6.1 and 3.6.2 are demonstrations of the probe tone technique. A sequence of chords (called a cadence) is presented. Rate from 1 to 7 how well the final probe tone fits contextually, 1 being an excellent fit and 7 being a poor fit. Krumhansl derived the tonal hierarchy from the responses of a large sample with a wide range of musical experience.

& Keil, 1982), although 6-year-olds know that different tones vary in goodness once a musical context is established (Cuddy & Badertscher, 1987). Thus, although sensory dissonance is perceived by infants and musically untrained adults, judgments of pitch relations are also influenced by musical training, suggesting that our perceptions of pitch and pitch relations result from a combination of innate and learned factors.

Evidence of sensitivity to the tonal hierarchy early in development can be explained—in part—by psychoacoustic influences (Schellenberg & Trehub, 1994): Probe tones with high stability values (doh, mi, sol, fa) have the largest degree of sensory consonance with the established tonic. Alternatively, because the frequency of occurrence of tones in real pieces of music closely mirrors the tonal hierarchy, children may learn implicitly that tones heard more often in a musical piece are particularly stable. Indeed, we know that listeners are highly sensitive to pitch distributional information in music. Oram and Cuddy (1995) presented listeners with atonal sequences in which one tone occurred eight times, another tone occurred four times, and four other tones occurred once each. Following each sequence, listeners rated the extent to which various probe tones fit with the sequence in a musical sense. Ratings reflected the frequency with which each pitch occurred in the context. Thus, when listening to unfamiliar music, listeners readily construct a hierarchy of pitch importance using frequency-of-occurrence information.

Absolute Pitch

It is often asserted that listeners are largely insensitive to *absolute pitch*. Absolute pitch refers to the ability to produce, recognize, or identify an individual pitch (e.g., middle C) without reference to any other pitch. Whereas relative pitch is the norm among trained and untrained listeners, absolute pitch is rare, occurring in about 1 in 10,000 people (Levitin & Rogers, 2005; Takeuchi & Hulse, 1993). Absolute pitch can be a valuable skill for musicians, but it can also interfere with the ability to perceive pitch relations (Miyazaki, 1993, 2004). Because melodies are defined by pitch and duration relations rather than with reference to any absolute pitch, relative pitch is arguably a more musical mode of pitch processing.

Nonetheless, some forms of long-term memory for pitch level may be quite common. Halpern (1989) asked participants to sing familiar tunes on different occasions (e.g., "Happy Birthday"), and Bergeson and Trehub

(2002) asked mothers to sing the same song to their infant on two occasions. In both studies, singers varied minimally in pitch level across their different performances. In another study (Levitin, 1994), undergraduates were asked to sing the first few words of their favorite rock song. Their renditions were very close to the pitch level of the original recording (see also Terhardt & Seewann, 1983). Listeners also exhibit accurate memory for other surface (nonrelational) features of recordings, such as tempo (Levitin & Cook, 1996) and overall sound quality (Schellenberg, Iverson, & McKinnon, 1999). These results confirm that memory for absolute aspects of musical recordings, which do not change from presentation to presentation, are more prevalent than previously assumed.

Schellenberg and Trehub (2003) devised a purely perceptual task in which they presented listeners with two versions of a 5-second excerpt from an instrumental TV theme song. One version was at the original pitch and the other version was shifted upward or downward by one or two semitones. Listeners were better than chance at identifying the original, even in the one-semitone condition. A control experiment confirmed that successful performance was not due to electronic artifacts of the pitch-shifting process.

The discovery of good memory for pitch level in adults is pertinent to claims of a developmental shift in pitch processing. The traditional view (e.g., Takeuchi & Hulse, 1993) is that everyone is born with absolute pitch, although this ability typically disappears unless one receives musical training early in childhood (i.e., by age 6 or 7). Those without such early training are thought to shift to relative pitch processing, presumably as a consequence of hearing the same pitch relations (i.e., the same tunes, such as "Happy Birthday" or "Twinkle, Twinkle, Little Star") at multiple different pitch levels (e.g., sung by a man or a woman). Findings indicating that young infants attend more to absolute than to relative pitch information are consistent with this perspective (Saffran, 2003; Saffran & Griepentrog, 2001).

Nonetheless, in some instances, infants remember pitch relations rather than pitch level (Plantinga & Trainor, 2005). Moreover, an abundance of evidence confirms that infants are sensitive to relational pitch properties (contour, interval structure, or both) of melodies (for review see Trehub, Schellenberg, & Hill, 1997). When considered as a whole, the available findings indicate that both absolute and relative pitch processing are evident across the life span. Although relative pitch is easily encoded and accessed from long-term memory, sensitivity to absolute pitch also plays a role in musical experience. In particular, memory for absolute pitch is likely to be evident for brief periods of time, and for stimuli that are heard repeatedly at an identical pitch.

Timbre

Timbre is often described as the attribute distinguishing sounds that are equivalent in pitch, duration, and loudness. Timbre is influenced by the pattern of partials that are present in complex waveforms, and how those partials change over time (i.e., transient or dynamic attributes). A sawtooth waveform, which contains all harmonics, has a timbre that is distinct from a square waveform, which contains only odd-numbered harmonics. The sound of a plucked instrument such as a harp has a relatively rapid amplitude onset, whereas the sound of a bowed instrument such as a violin has a more gradual onset. In naturally occurring sounds, inharmonic partials (i.e., partials with a frequency equal to a noninteger multiple of the fundamental) also affect timbre. When inharmonic partials are removed from a piano note, for example, the note sounds artificial and unfamiliar.

For many instruments, the fundamental frequency has the greatest intensity of all harmonics in the frequency spectrum. Intensity typically

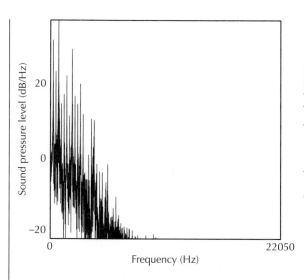
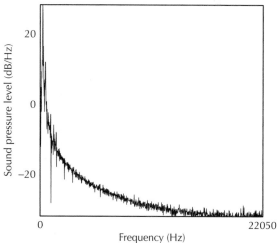

The frequency spectra for a piano (left) and violin (right); for each, the tone is middle C (261.4 Hz), and the spectrum sample is taken 0.7 seconds after tone onset. The x-axis represents frequency components (starting with the fundamental at the far left), and the y-axis represents intensity. Although intensity peaks at the fundamental for both instruments, the violin's pattern retains more spectral energy at higher frequencies.

decreases for higher frequency components. An inverse relationship between harmonic number and intensity (called *spectral roll-off*) does not hold for all instruments, however. For some instruments, certain harmonics may be disproportionately intense, giving that instrument its unique timbral character. A "bright"-sounding tone, such as that produced by a clarinet, typically contains high-frequency harmonics sounded at relatively high amplitudes.

When other aspects of a tone are held constant, differences in the frequency spectrum are associated with differences in timbre. We know, however, that the frequency spectrum is not entirely responsible for timbre, because tones with very different spectra can be perceived as having the same timbre. For example, examination of the frequency spectrum for a note played very softly on a trumpet reveals that most of the partials associated with trumpet sounds are absent. Nonetheless, the note is still perceived as emanating from a trumpet. More generally, the frequency spectrum associated with a given instrument may be quite different for soft and loud sounds despite their perceptual invariance.

Figure 3.2 provides an illustration of the dimensions of a musical instrument associated with its perceived timbre. The figure shows the

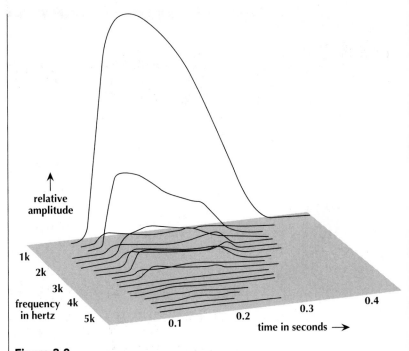

Figure 3.2

Frequency components of a clarinet.

partials that are present, their relative intensity, and how their intensity changes over time. For this particular instrument—a clarinet—the constituent frequency components vary in intensity at a similar rate. For other instruments, such as a piano, different partials change intensity at very different rates. In many instances, onset or "attack" cues (i.e., transient cues during the initial portion of the spectrum) are important for perceiving timbre.

Formants are also thought to influence the perception of timbre. A formant is a range of frequencies with high amplitude relative to other frequencies, which is a consequence of the resonant properties of the sound source (e.g., the body of a piano or an acoustic guitar). Formants correspond to local peaks in a frequency spectrum. Fixed-frequency formants

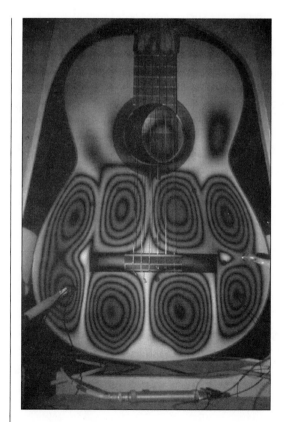 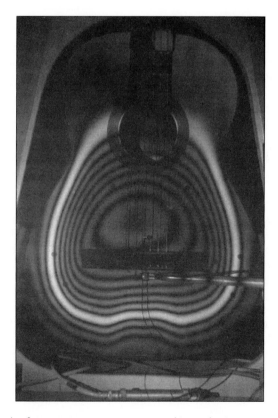

Through the use of an advanced imaging process, the fixed frequency formants of the body of the guitar can be seen as a series of concentric circles; the formant patterns represented in each picture are for two different frequencies.

Source: Photos courtesy of Bernard Richardson, Cardiff University.

are particularly interesting because they remain relatively constant across the *tessitura* (pitch range) of an instrument. Whereas individual partials of a sound provide information about timbre by their relation to each other and to the fundamental frequency, fixed-frequency formants are resonant frequencies that do not change in proportion with changes in overall pitch. The harmonics that fall within the formant region resonate louder than other frequencies, giving the sound (e.g., a musical instrument) its particular timbral character.

Hajda, Kendall, Carterette, & Harshberger (1997) described various methods that have been used to identify the acoustic properties that influence the perception of timbre. These include identification tasks (name that timbre), grouping and classification tasks (match similar sounding timbres), semantic rating scales (rate how bright or dull a timbre sounds), discrimination tasks (are two timbres the same or different?), and various types of similarity ratings (rate how similar two timbres sound). In a classic experiment, J. M. Grey (1977) asked musically trained listeners to provide similarity ratings for pairs of notes that came from a set of nine different instrumental timbres. Notes were presented with the same fundamental frequency, intensity, and duration so that they varied only in timbre. His analysis revealed that three distinct dimensions could account for a good portion of the variance in similarity ratings.

Various follow-up studies have yielded different results regarding the underlying dimensions that influence the perception of timbre. In almost all cases, brightness appears to be a significant perceptual dimension. Instruments with a wide range of spectral energy (e.g., oboe) are perceived as having a brighter timbral character than instruments with a more restricted range of spectral energy (e.g., French horn). The influence of onsets (attacks) and other temporal properties—important in some studies but not in others—depends on the specific timbres used in the stimulus set and the duration of the stimuli (see Hajda et al., 1997).

Another way to identify acoustic attributes that are essential to instrument identification is to examine how readily tone sequences involving different timbres form separate auditory streams. Iverson (1995) presented listeners with sequences consisting of two different orchestral tones and asked them to rate the extent to which one or two sequences were being played. Auditory stream segregation was influenced by differences in both static spectra (the pattern of partials present) and dynamic attributes. Moreover, the results converged with similarity judgments obtained by Iverson and Krumhansl (1993) on the same tones. That is,

Sound Example 3.7

Bob Dylan's controversial 1965 concert at the Royal Albert Hall featured electric guitars, and by some accounts was met with boos and catcalls by many of his diehard folk fans. These fans had been familiar with his use of a traditional acoustic guitar. **Sound example 3.7** is an excerpt from the concert version of "Like a Rolling Stone." The fact that what ultimately amounts to a change of timbre was met with such hostility suggests a prominent role for timbre in both our musical preferences and our perception of musical styles.

Sound example 3.7 is available via the *Music, Thought, and Feeling* iMix on iTunes.

similarity judgments predicted the extent to which timbres segregated into separate auditory streams, with similar timbres less likely than dissimilar timbres to split into separate streams.

How rapidly do listeners register timbre? Robinson and Patterson (1995) tested the limits of listeners' ability to identify the timbre and pitch of tones that varied in duration. Whereas identification of pitch proved to be a function of duration, identification of timbre was independent of duration. Listeners required several complete cycles of a periodic signal to identify pitch accurately, but only one or two cycles (i.e., milliseconds) to identify timbre. These results make intuitive sense when we consider that pitch is determined by frequency (number of cycles per second). A listener needs to hear several cycles to determine how rapidly a cycle repeats. By contrast, one or two cycles of a tone contain information about the components present in the frequency spectrum, which allows for identification of timbre.

In a related investigation, researchers tested the limits of listeners' ability to identify recordings (Schellenberg et al., 1999). In an experimental version of *Name That Tune* (the song-identification game played on TV and radio), listeners matched extremely brief excerpts (100 or 200 msec) from recordings of popular songs with the song titles and artists. Listeners' performance was better than chance with excerpts of 1/5 of a second. Performance deteriorated with shorter excerpts (1/10 of a second) but was still better than chance. Other manipulations involved low-pass and high-pass filtering, and playing the excerpts backward. Performance fell to chance levels for the low-pass filtered and backward excerpts, but was unaffected by high-pass filtering.

In short, successful identification of the recordings required the presence of dynamic, high-frequency spectral information. Note that the excerpts were too brief to convey any relational information (e.g., pitch and duration), and that the absolute pitch of the excerpts would be identical whether they were played backward or forward. Thus, successful performance presumably stemmed from accurate and detailed memory of the recordings' timbres, which consisted of many complex tones from many different instruments.

By definition, timbre and pitch are different. Nonetheless, some studies suggest that timbre and pitch are not perceived independently. For example, it is easier to judge whether two tones (Crowder, 1989), two chords (Beal, 1985), or two melodies (Radvansky, Fleming, & Simmons, 1995) are the same when standard and comparison stimuli are played on identical rather than different musical instruments. This finding suggests

Sound Example 3.8
Sound example 3.8 is an excerpt of Miles Davis playing a muted trumpet on "Round Midnight." A muted trumpet is an example of high-pass filtering. The mute absorbs many of the lower frequency components, resulting in a tinnier sound.

Telephones and radios are examples of band-pass filtering. In band-pass filtering, lower and higher frequencies are filtered out and a band of frequencies is allowed to pass. Telephones only allow frequencies of between 300 and 3,400 Hz. This is a reasonable frequency range for the transmission of speech sounds, because timbral fidelity is not as important in this context as it is in a musical one.

Sound example 3.8 is available via the *Music, Thought, and Feeling* iMix on iTunes.

that despite our experience of pitch and timbre as distinct musical qualities, they interact with each other in music processing.

Krumhansl and Iverson (1992) used another approach to study interactions between pitch and timbre. Participants were asked to classify stimulus items into two groups as quickly as possible based on a specified target attribute (e.g., pitch). Not only did the target attribute vary; an irrelevant attribute (e.g., timbre) also varied from trial to trial. Performance on the categorization task was relatively good when variation in the irrelevant attribute was correlated with variation in the target attribute, but relatively poor when variation in the irrelevant attribute was uncorrelated with variation in the target attribute. That is, participants were unable to attend to the pitch of a tone without being affected by its timbre, or vice versa. This finding provides converging evidence that pitch and timbre are not perceptually separable from each other.

Although pitch and timbre may be integrated successfully at some points in the information processing system, listeners can also become confused about the ways in which pitches and timbres are combined. In one experiment, participants listened for particular combinations of pitch and timbre in arrays of tones that were presented simultaneously but emanated from different locations in the auditory field (Hall, Pastore, Acker, & Huang, 2000). An examination of errors indicated that participants often perceived an illusory conjunction of pitch and timbre. That is, participants often heard the timbre of one tone combined with the pitch of another tone. Estimates of illusory conjunction rate ranged from 23% to 40%. The findings provide evidence that after an initial stage in which individual features of musical tones are registered (e.g., pitch, timbre), there is a stage in which these separately registered features are integrated (feature integration). Illusory conjunctions arise when errors occur at the feature integration stage of processing.

What is the relation between timbre and harmony? The principle of *harmonicity*, outlined by Bregman (1990), suggests that partials that fall along the harmonic series of a single note are fused together, such that listeners perceive the distinct timbral qualities of each note holistically. When two instruments play the same note, or two different notes with many harmonics in common, there may be some confusion in this process. Such fusion effects actually contribute to our perception of harmony. For example, if one plays two piano notes separated by a fifth, those two notes have several partials in common. Perceptual mechanisms will tend to fuse or "confuse" some of the components of the two different

Sound Example 3.9

Sound example 3.9 is Debussy's "La Cathédrale Engloutie" (The Sunken Cathedral). The section from 2:27 to 3:13 is an example of the timbral effect of tonal fusion. It is difficult to pick out a prominent melody—the constituent tones of each chord are perceptually fused. Sound example 3.9 is available via the *Music, Thought, and Feeling* iMix on iTunes.

notes, giving rise to emergent timbral effects. Compositions by French impressionist composer Claude Debussy exemplify the varied timbral effects of combining tones.

Although pitch and rhythmic relations are usually considered to define musical structure, some contemporary composers and theorists have considered the possibility that timbre might be used compositionally in a way that is analogous to the use of pitch (e.g., Lerdahl, 1987; Slawson, 1985). One challenge with this compositional approach is that timbre has a powerful influence on auditory stream segregation. Thus, any large shift in timbre is likely to signal a separate auditory stream, which would conflict with the goal of creating a coherent sequence analogous to a melody.

Nonetheless, changes in timbre that correspond to reductions in sensory dissonance (i.e., fewer harmonics falling within a critical band)—and increases in fusion—may be perceived as a change from tension to release, which commonly occurs at points of musical closure (Pressnitzer, McAdams, Winsberg, & Fineberg, 2000). In other words, changes from relatively dissonant to relatively consonant timbres have some of the resolving properties of a perfect cadence. Moreover, it is clear that timbre has a profound influence on our appreciation of music. For example, imagine the music of Radiohead played on accordion, or a rock song by U2 played on an oboe. Such changes in instrumentation would undoubtedly affect our experience of the music.

Sound Examples 3.10.1–3.10.2
These are two examples of "timbre for timbre's sake." In both of these compositions, one acoustic and one electronic, timbre is used as a compositional end in itself. **Sound example 3.10.1** is the second movement ("Hawthorne") from Charles Ives's *Concord Sonata* (1909–1915) for piano. At 1:22, as indicated in the musical score, the pianist depresses a two-octave span of the keys using a 14 3/4" board at various spots across the keyboard.

  Sound example 3.10.2 is "Where the Wind Meets the Sea" (1999) by Timothy Opie in which timbral elements are electronically synthesized. This piece is composed of tiny "grains" of sound that are less than 40 msec in length—a compositional technique known as granular synthesis.

  Sound example 3.10.1 is available via the *Music, Thought, and Feeling* iMix on iTunes.

Reconstructing Music

Sensory processing is initiated when the eardrum responds to the vibrations of air molecules. This sensory input is analyzed into a number of attributes or features such as pitch, timbre, and intensity. The same analysis occurs for all types of sound, whether it arises from wind, rain, music, or a barking dog. Sensory analysis, in turn, is just one link in a complex chain of neural events that ultimately give rise to a full auditory experience. Among those processes are ones that help to create a unified perception, so that the various attributes of sound are not experienced independently of one another. At some levels of processing, the pitch and temporal structure of music are processed in completely different parts of the brain, but listening to music does not generate independent experiences of pitch and rhythm. Rather, different dimensions of music seem to be merged into an integrated and unified experience. To understand these unified experiences requires examination of multiple levels of music structure and brain processing, from the sensory building blocks to our understanding of melody and rhythm, to our deepest emotional responses, to the skilled performances of experts, and to all of the various creative activities associated with music.

Additional Readings

Mathews, M. (1999). The ear and how it works. In P. R. Cook (Ed.), *Music cognition and computerized sound: An introduction to psychoacoustics* (pp. 1–10). Cambridge, MA: MIT Press.

Pierce, J. (1999). Sound waves and sine waves. In P. R. Cook (Ed.), *Music cognition and computerized sound: An introduction to psychoacoustics* (pp. 37–56). Cambridge, MA: MIT Press.

CHAPTER 4

Music Acquisition

LEARNING OUTCOMES

By the end of this chapter you should be able to:

1. Appraise claims about the effects of music on a human fetus.

2. Contrast active and passive forms of learning and discuss their role in musical development.

3. Design studies for evaluating the sensitivity of preverbal infants to various attributes of music.

4. Differentiate musical attributes for which infants show early sensitivity from musical attributes for which sensitivity emerges later in development.

5. Identify and discuss two ways in which early sensitivity to consonance and dissonance is manifested.

6. Describe the development of sensitivity to harmony and key.

Musical Infants

Anyone who has struggled to learn an instrument knows that it does not seem to come naturally. Mastering the expert skill required to perform a musical instrument can be a lifelong effort. Even those at exceptionally high levels of expertise often feel that they are continuously learning and improving. Do all musical skills require such enormous effort?

Much about musical development has yet to be understood, but research suggests that human infants begin life with a number of important skills including frequency coding mechanisms and multisensory connections that facilitate a range of musical behaviors. Infants have a remarkable ability to discriminate pitches and rhythms, which is one of the most basic prerequisites for music appreciation. They also prefer consonant intervals to dissonant intervals within months of being born, suggesting that this preference is present at birth. Infants are also attuned to the connection between rhythm and movement, implying that the two senses are naturally intertwined. Similar predispositions and skills emerge in infants across cultures and provide the foundation for universal aspects of musical structure. They also form the foundation for the development of mature forms of musical understanding.

Overlaying basic predispositions is the role of learning, which can occur both actively and passively. Through regular and repeated exposure to music, brain structures and representations eventually develop, shaping perceptions and experiences of music. Brain development and the acquisition of musical skill can occur following either active or passive forms of learning. Active learning is an effortful process that allows a person to control and optimize the effects of environmental input, leading to a range of skills that build on natural perceptual and motor competences, and often go well beyond the skills acquired through passive forms of learning. Active learning can lead to the acquisition of exceptional motor skills, which are needed for careers in music performance, or to the enhancement of auditory perception skills, which are valuable in professions such as sound engineering, music production, and music teaching. Such behavioral outcomes result from the development of both domain-specific processes that act on musical input and domain-general processes of attention and executive functioning.

Relatively few people engage in active music learning for a sustained number of years, but virtually everyone is subject to the effects of passive learning, and this process begins in infancy. Music surrounds us through-

Sound Examples 4.1.1–4.1.2

These are two examples of infant-directed speech. Note the exaggerated use of speech prosody.

out our lives, from the lullabies that our mothers sing to us, to nursery rhymes that we learn in school, to songs that we hear on the radio and iPod. These and other sources of music create a musical environment that provides us with a tacit understanding of music. Just as children gradually learn to speak the language of their culture even without formal training, children also acquire the ability to understand and appreciate the music in their environment—a process called *enculturation*.

Enculturation is responsible for some of our most basic musical abilities. Most people can tap or clap to music, detect if a musician plays a wrong note in a familiar tune, and decide whether a piece of music is joyful, sad, peaceful, or energetic. Through repeated exposure to music, infants internalize the regularities of their musical experiences in the form of implicit knowledge, and the mental representations that encode this knowledge shape our perceptions and interpretations of the music that we hear subsequently. As we gain more experience with different genres of music, our representations continuously develop. In this way, musical development occurs through a continuously evolving interaction between nature and nurture. As infants we are biologically predisposed to perceive the world in certain elementary ways, but enculturation and active music training allow us to refine our competencies and, for some individuals, achieve expert levels of skill.

It should be emphasized that the distinction between active and passive forms of learning is mainly a convenient dichotomy for describing a range of possible interactions between individuals and their environments. The act of enrolling children in music lessons clearly places them in a rich musical environment, but it does not guarantee that they will devote their full attention throughout each lesson. A disengaged child may passively endure the impact of music lessons and progress quite slowly, whereas a more engaged child may evoke a greater number of learning opportunities from this enriched environment, leading to rapid development of musical skills. Highly engaged children often attempt to shape their environment in a way that is consistent with their abilities, as for example when a child actively requests violin lessons or listens to music for the purpose of singing along. In fact, the art of practicing a musical instrument can be viewed as a set of strategies for maximizing the impact of an enriched musical environment. Personality and temperament play a large role in determining the degree to which individuals interact with their environment, with passive and active learning representing two ends in the continuum of that interaction (Gembris & Davidson, 2002).

Music in the Womb

It is often claimed that a fetus can benefit from music exposure, and there is a vast array of best-selling books and CDs targeting pregnant women with this intriguing idea. Are such claims credible? Certainly, many popular assertions about fetal abilities are overstated or false, but it is indeed the case that the prenatal infant (i.e., human fetus) is exposed to a number of sounds arising from the mother (Parncutt, 2006). Moreover, sensory learning can theoretically start at roughly 25 weeks (gestation age), when connections between peripheral sensory organs and the central nervous system begin to mature. Rhythmic sounds that originate from the mother include those associated with breathing, movements (walking, running, exercising), heartbeat, and certain speech patterns. Nonrhythmic sounds include digestion, isolated vocal sounds, and *borborygmi* (sounds associated with gas moving through the intestines). Even sounds from outside of the mother's body may impinge on the fetus, including sounds in the environment, voices of other people, and music.

How audible are such sounds? The intensity of external sounds is attenuated by approximately 30 dB by the time it reaches the uterus, and their significance for the fetus is far from clear. More generally, the mother's body and the amniotic fluid act as a low-pass filter, so all sounds in the uterus are muffled. The result is that the prenatal and postnatal acoustic environments are quite different. Speech sounds, for example, are mainly unintelligible when recorded in utero. Interestingly, however, many of the musical properties of speech are fairly well preserved, including the pitch contour of speech (intonation), the timing of phonemes, changes in loudness, and the overall pitch level.

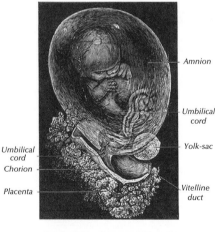

Amnion

Umbilical cord

Umbilical cord

Yolk-sac

Chorion

Placenta

Vitelline duct

A human fetus 8 weeks after conception. The amniotic fluid that surrounds the fetus acts as a low-pass filter, so all sounds in the uterus are muffled.

Source: Reprinted from Henry Gray, *Anatomy of the Human Body* (1918).

Can a fetus detect such sounds? Remarkably, it can. The fetus exhibits reliable behavioral responses to acoustic stimulation. By about 26 weeks gestation, sounds can elicit changes in the heart rate of a human fetus (Abrams, 1995). By 28 to 32 weeks, intense sounds can even elicit consistent motor responses (Lecanuet, 1996). It is also generally accepted that newborn infants are able to recognize their mother's voice (DeCasper & Prescott, 1984), especially if the high frequencies are filtered out in a way that mimics the muffled quality of the mother's voice in utero (Fifer & Moon, 1988; Querleu et al., 1984).

In short, a fetus can detect and respond to acoustic stimulation, and some of that stimulation has the potential to influence development. Sensory systems require sensory input to develop, and the muffled acoustic stimuli that are present in the prenatal environment may be optimal for training these systems. By the third trimester, the fetus can hear, process, and remember musical patterns.

On the other hand, popular claims about fetal responses to music should be treated with caution. For example, a common assertion is that fetal movements in response to music are rhythmic in nature, as though the fetus is "dancing" to music. According to Parncutt (2006), such claims are not supported by empirical evidence. The ability to synchronize to music, whether by clapping, tapping, or dancing, is seldom observed in children before their second postnatal year, so dancing in the sense of synchronizing to music is hardly likely in a fetus.

Investigating Music Perception Among Infants

Early sensitivity to music has been confirmed by showing that infants can detect subtle changes to a melody, as reflected in measures such as head-turn responses, looking times, heart rate, and differential sucking rates. Conveniently for researchers, stimuli that are perceived to be novel lead to changes in these measures, allowing researchers to devise ingenious methods of examining the perceptual and cognitive abilities of infants. In other words, it is possible to learn about an infant's ability to discriminate merely by varying the degree of novelty or familiarity of a stimulus, and then observing changes in these behaviors.

Infants orient their head toward events or objects that they perceive to be novel; they look longer at objects that sustain their interest; their heart rate decelerates when they perceive interesting and nonthreatening stimuli; their heart accelerates if those stimuli are perceived to be alarming or frightening; and they will suck more on objects that they perceive to be novel than on objects they perceive to be familiar. All of these "indirect" indicators of infant's perceptions allow researchers to evaluate sensitivity to various aspects of musical structure, even though infants cannot speak or otherwise provide direct feedback about their sensitivity to music. In fact, similar methods are used to evaluate the perceptual abilities of any nonverbal organism, such as rats, monkeys, and chimpanzees.

In the classic *habituation–dishabituation method*, two measurements are commonly recorded, corresponding to the processes of habituation and dishabituation. *Habituation* is the process by which an infant becomes familiar with a novel stimulus, and it is measured as the length of time that a response to stimulus novelty is observed (e.g., head turn, heart rate, and sucking rate). To elicit a habituation response, the researcher presents an infant with several repeated exposures to the same stimulus. Initially the stimulus will be perceived as novel and will elicit a response such as looking in the direction of the stimulus. Eventually the infant will seem to become bored with the stimulus and look away, at which point habituation is said to have occurred. The investigator can then introduce subtle changes to the repeating stimulus to see whether the infant notices any of them. For example, if the repeated stimulus is a melody, an investigator might introduce a subtle change to its pitches or to rhythm. If the infant is able to perceive the change, the stimulus will again elicit a response such as looking at the stimulus, at which point *dishabituation* is said to have occurred. When dishabituation reliably occurs for a particular stimulus change, the researcher can conclude that the infant is capable of perceiving that change.

In the head-turn procedure infants are initially "trained" to turn their head (orient) toward a loudspeaker when they hear any change in a repeating auditory stimulus. For example, a seven-note melody might be played five times in a row, after which a change to the melody is introduced, creating a novel melody. As mentioned, infants instinctively orient toward any novel auditory stimulus, so if they can perceive a change, they will naturally incline their head toward the new stimulus. Eventually, they habituate to the stimulus, at which point their interest wanes and they tend to look away. Training is used to encourage this natural process by keeping infants interested in the task, thereby increasing the reliability of the head-turning response. Training is accomplished by reinforcing head-turning behavior with a pleasant visual stimulus, such as an illuminated and activated toy animal. If infants reliably turn their head toward the speaker for certain melodic changes but not for others, the researcher can infer that the infants were more sensitive to the former changes than the latter changes. In this way, researchers can examine the ability of infants to discriminate among various aspects of musical structure.

Because changes to a repeating tonal pattern involve shifting one of the pitches, a potential challenge arises. When a single pitch is altered in the melody, that one alteration creates more than one source of novelty for the infant. First, the infant may notice the new pitch itself. Second, the infant may notice the presence of a new melodic interval defined by the relationship between the new pitch and the immediately preceding pitch. If the infant turns his or her head in response to such a change, how can the researcher determine which of the changes has been noticed? The challenge can be solved through carefully planned studies. For example, if the pitch interval C4–G4 is repeated five times, followed by the pitch interval C4–F4, a head-turning response might indicate that the infant has detected a change in interval size (a perfect fifth is changed to a perfect fourth) or a change in pitch (G4 is changed to F4). To isolate and evaluate sensitivity to relative pitch, repeated tone sequences are presented in transposition so that the infants can detect the change only by attending to pitch relations.

This type of same–different discrimination task has been used by a number of researchers to determine which melodic intervals are easy to process and remember, and which are difficult. If an interval is easily processed, then infants should show head-turning responses when changes to that interval are introduced, indicating that the infants are sensitive to the interval. By contrast, if an interval is difficult to process, infants should be unable to form a stable representation of the interval, and changes to the interval would go unnoticed, and would not generate a head-turning response.

Researchers have also established methods to evaluate infants' preference for one type of musical stimulus over another. This technique essentially involves letting infants "select" which type of music they hear. Typically, the infant is first placed between two loudspeakers. When the infant looks toward the speaker on her left, she hears one type of music, but she hears a different type of music when she looks toward the speaker on her right. Hence, the infant is controlling what she hears by the direction of her gaze. Because infants tend to have a bias to look rightward, it is important to counterbalance the stimuli presentations. That is, half of the infants hear Piece A from the speaker on their left and Piece B from the speaker on their right, whereas the other half hear Piece B from the left and Piece A from the right.

Results based on this infant preference method suggest that infants have natural preferences for certain types of musical sounds over others. As infants develop, these predispositions are overlaid with effects of learning and enculturation. The effects of learning can even run counter to initial predispositions as, for example, when a jazz musician judges a

Sound Examples 4.3.1–4.3.2

Sound example 4.3.1 is an original melody constructed from the seven tones of a major scale. One of the cognitive advantages of using scales comprised of unequal scale steps (like the major scale) is that it allows the listener to differentiate scale tones and to isolate a focal tone (or tonic). You may have experienced a sense of incompleteness to the melody— the final note in the melody (which in this case is the tonic) has been eliminated.

In **Sound example 4.3.2**, the final tone has been added. You may have experienced a greater sense of resolution on hearing the tonic. Although there is no rule indicating that melodies must end on the tonic, melodies that do end on the tonic tend to sound complete. The notation for the first part of "Twinkle, Twinkle, Little Star" is shown below. It starts on the tonic (a C on the syllable "Twin-"), moves away from the tonic, and returns to it on the word "are." Trying humming or singing the melody and stop on the penultimate tone (on the word "you"). Does it feel strange? This gravitational pull toward the tonic, as it is often described, is sometimes referred to as tonality.

Music and Williams Syndrome

Williams Syndrome (WMS) is a developmental disorder occurring in about 1 out of 20,000 births, characterized by deficits in spatial, quantitative, and reasoning abilities, and what is often described as an "elfin" physical appearance. A number of cognitive traits also tend to be spared and even heightened in WMS individuals, including displaying a rich, colorful, and creative use of vocabulary, and abilities in music perception and production. WMS individuals often exhibit an attraction to broadband noise (e.g., appliance motors, helicopters)—some parents have reported that their WMS children can identify makes

and models of cars and vacuum cleaners based on the sound of their motors.

In contrast to musical savants, whose musical ability can often be attributed to an extraordinary rote musical memory, WMS individuals may display a musical precocity that is fundamentally creative. In a recent study in which WMS individuals as well as a control group performed an echo clapping task, WMS participants were as accurate as controls. However, in contrast with controls, "errors" in reproduction in the WMS group tended to be creative elaborations that preserved the pulse and meter of the original stimulus (Levitin & Bellugi 1998).

highly dissonant chord to be more beautiful than a simple major chord. However, early preferences are quite striking, and probably have significant effects on music experiences into adulthood.

Melodic Contour

Even before the age of 1, infants are capable of perceiving and remembering melodies that they hear, but they are not very sensitive to precise changes in pitch. Rather, infants mainly notice whether a melody goes up or down in pitch, and their impressions are not much more detailed than that. That is, in early stages of development infants are primarily sensitive to *melodic contour*. Several studies have confirmed that contour changes are highly noticeable for infants, whereas changes that maintain contour but alter other musical features such as absolute pitch or interval size often go unnoticed (Trehub et al., 1997). Even very young infants are remarkably sensitive to this coarse property of music, suggesting that the perception of contour is present at birth, or *congenital*. With experience and maturation, children eventually develop the capacity to perceive and remember the precise intervals in a melody.

Why are infants more sensitive to contour than to other properties of melodies? One obvious reason is that contour is a simple description of a melody, and is therefore easy to perceive and remember. That is, the perceptual analysis of events or objects in the physical environment likely begins in development with coarse descriptions of stimuli, with more detailed descriptions such as precise pitch distances requiring more experience and maturation. In support of this view, even adults with little musical experience remember novel melodies primarily by their melodic contour. Remembering nuanced details of a melody requires either repeated exposure or an understanding of the musical genre.

There may be other reasons contour is noticed and remembered well by infants, however. It has been suggested that infants are born with a heightened sensitivity to pitch contour because it has adaptive significance in speech. It is well known that mothers speak to their infants using exaggerated intonation patterns, a mode of speaking called *infant-directed speech* or *motherese*. Such speech differs from adult-directed speech in some important ways, and infants show a clear preference for infant-directed over adult-directed speech (Cooper & Aslin, 1990; Fernald, 1985). Because infants cannot understand language, their preference for infant-directed speech implies that they are sensitive to the mother's tone of voice, or *speech prosody*.

The exaggerated use of pitch contour in infant-directed speech functions like a primitive communication system. Each pitch contour used by the mother seems to be associated with a unique communicative aim, such as giving approval, providing comfort, engaging the infant's attention, conveying an emotional message, or providing a warning (Fernald et al., 1989). The structure of infant-directed speech is remarkably similar across cultures, and early sensitivity to contour patterns in speech may have two important implications for development. First, it might enhance bonding between infants and their caregivers, because it reinforces the nature of emotional interactions. Second, it may facilitate language acquisition by providing an emotional context for semantic messages, by drawing attention to word and phrase boundaries, and by signaling points of semantic novelty or stress. Given these potential benefits, it is perhaps not surprising that infants have a heightened sensitivity to pitch contour. What is remarkable, however, is the possibility that our perceptions and experiences of music may be shaped by a predisposition that is specialized for speech.

Consonance and Dissonance

The ability to distinguish consonance and dissonance is basic to music experience. Consonant events are typically described as warm, peaceful, and harmonious. They are associated with a sense of resolution and relaxation. Dissonant events provide an aesthetic contrast and suggest tension, edginess, and discord. Composers often use consonance and dissonance, in combination with other compositional tools, to create an artful ebb and flow of tension and relaxation. This continuously shifting impression of tension and relaxation can be experienced as a kind of emotional story or narrative, and is a basic dimension of our aesthetic response to music. Infants and adults are highly sensitive to the difference between consonant and dissonant sounds. This sensitivity has been especially evident for two types of responses: discrimination and preference.

DISCRIMINATION OF CONSONANT AND DISSONANT INTERVALS

Research suggests that infants have a natural ability to discriminate combinations of tones on the basis of their consonance or dissonance. Why would this be? Many researchers believe that consonant intervals are easily discriminated from dissonant intervals merely because they are easier to process. To use an analogy, it is easy to discriminate words spoken in one's own language from words spoken in an unfamiliar language. Such a *processing advantage* for consonant intervals is seen with infants as young as 6 months of age up to adulthood.

Schellenberg and Trainor (1996) presented 7-month-old infants and adults with a background pattern of simultaneous fifths (seven semitones) presented at varying pitch levels. Listeners were tested on their ability to discriminate the intervals in the background pattern from a new interval, which was either a tritone (six semitones) or a fourth (five semitones). Fifths and fourths are consonant intervals, whereas tritones are dissonant. Both age groups used the consonance and dissonance to discriminate these intervals. Although the fifth and fourth differ more from each other in terms of interval size, the fifth and tritone were better discriminated. Presumably, the dissonance of the tritone made it stand out from the perfect fifth, whereas the relative consonance of the perfect fourth made it sound similar to the fifth.

Given the close connection between consonance and music, is the capacity to differentiate consonance and dissonance peculiar to humans, or do nonhuman animals also have this ability? The current view is that sensitivity to consonance and dissonance is not actually unique to humans. Somewhat surprisingly, nonhuman animals can readily differentiate consonant and dissonant tone combinations. This sensitivity probably arises as a natural consequence of peripheral auditory mechanisms in mammals.

On first glance, this idea might seem surprising. Surely hearing one event as warm and harmonious and another as harsh and unpleasant is a subjective experience, in the ear of the listener. As outlined in chapter 3, however, the distinction between consonance and dissonance has a psychoacoustic basis. The notes that make up consonant intervals such as an octave or fifth have many overtones in common, whereas notes that make up dissonant intervals such as the minor second are associated with numerous harmonic frequencies that are not identical but that fall within the same critical band. Dissonant intervals give rise to sensory interactions and the sensation of roughness. This sensation of roughness is not subjective or uniquely human, but merely a direct consequence of certain sound combinations impinging on the mammalian auditory system.

PREFERENCE FOR CONSONANT INTERVALS

It would not be very surprising to discover that most adults enjoy the sound of a choir singing in perfect harmony, but surely such an aesthetic judgment is too much to expect of an infant. Apparently not. Somewhat remarkably, infants reliably find consonant intervals to be more pleasant sounding than dissonant intervals. Zentner and Kagan (1996) presented 4-month-old infants with a melody accompanied by a single "harmony" line. The melody and accompaniment were separated by minor seconds in the dissonant condition, but by major and minor thirds in the consonant condition. Infants consistently preferred the consonant versions.

Trainor and Heinmiller (1998) extended these findings by examining sensitivity by infants to dissonance arising from (simultaneous) intervals that were larger than a minor second. For such intervals, dissonance results from interactions among overtones rather than interactions among fundamental frequencies. They found that 6-month-old infants preferred to listen to perfect fifths and octaves compared to tritones and minor ninths (which give rise to greater sensory interference between overtones). Infants also looked longer when a Mozart minuet was presented in its normal consonant form than when an edited version of the minuet was presented with many dissonant intervals.

Infants' responses are admittedly quite variable, and their preferences for consonance tend to be observed reliably only when there are fairly large differences in levels of dissonance. For example, Crowder, Reznick, and Rosenkrantz (1991) observed no significant preference for the major chord over the minor chord, even though the major chord is more consonant. However, the difference in consonance between major and minor chords is actually quite subtle. In short, infants do have preferences for consonant intervals over dissonant intervals, as long as these differences are fairly obvious.

It was noted earlier that the ability to differentiate consonant and dissonant intervals is not unique to humans. In contrast, preferences for consonance over dissonance do seem to be unique to humans, and it is not clear why this is so. Why would infants be born with a predisposition to prefer consonant than dissonant intervals, when nonhuman animals do not show these preferences? Are there implications of this predisposition for musical structure? Although early preferences for consonance remain somewhat mysterious, they could account for the preponderance of consonant intervals across musical cultures. Through experience, humans can and do learn to appreciate dissonance in music, but they begin life with an initial preference for consonance.

Pitch Relations

Sensitivity to consonance and dissonance allows infants and adults to differentiate musical intervals in terms of their degree of roughness. However, people are also sensitive to the precise size of intervals and can use that information as the basis for music recognition. In fact, sensitivity to the relation between pitches, relative pitch, is considered to be the foundation of our appreciation of musical structure. A familiar melody such as "Happy Birthday" retains its essential identity regardless of whether it is sung at a high pitch register by a woman or child, or at a low pitch register by a baritone. Familiar melodies are recognized not by the pitch of the starting note or the degree of consonance and dissonance that they exhibit, but by the relations among pitches in the melody.

Infants do not start out being sensitive to precise distances between pitches in a melody; they mainly notice its contour. Throughout development, however, children become increasingly sensitive to the precise size of melodic intervals, and this sensitivity forms the basis for song recognition. Interestingly, not all intervals are remembered equally well. Certain pitch relations are processed and remembered more easily than others, such as those associated with the octave and the fifth. That is, although sensitivity to relative pitch is fundamental to music perception, it does not manifest itself uniformly across all possible intervals.

Sensitivity to pitch relations can be observed for *simultaneous* tones (two notes played at the same time) or *sequential* intervals (two notes played one after the other), but the processes involved in perceiving intervals in these two forms are not identical. Simultaneous intervals generate varying levels of sensory consonance and dissonance, so listeners can differentiate simultaneous intervals by their degree of consonance. On the other hand, many people have difficulty accurately categorizing simultaneously sounded intervals. Two emergent effects of simultaneous intervals can interfere with successful classification. First, any dissonance associated with a simultaneous interval may reduce *discrimination*, as described earlier. Second, when the notes of a simultaneous interval have overlapping frequency components, they can perceptually fuse into a single sound image, making it difficult to hear the individual notes and classify the interval. Sequential intervals, in contrast, cannot generate sensory dissonance or perceptual fusion because the frequency components of the two notes are separated from each other in time.

Do dissonant simultaneous intervals also sound dissonant when played as a sequential interval? Apparently they do, but the reason for this parallel is not well understood. In a study with 6-month-old infants, Schellenberg and Trehub (1996b) observed a processing advantage for sequentially presented fifths and fourths over tritones. Infants were presented with a repeating pattern of alternating pure tones separated by one of three intervals, as shown in Figure 4.1. After eight tones (four low-pitched and four high-pitched), the pattern was shifted upward or downward in pitch. On "no-change" trials, the shift was an exact transposition, such that the interval associated with the first eight tones was repeated at a new pitch register. On "change" trials, every other high-pitched tone was displaced downward by a semitone, creating intervals that were different from that associated with the first eight tones. Infants detected these changes in interval size when the initial interval was a fifth or fourth, but not when it was a tritone.

It may be noted that fourths and fifths are consonant intervals, so the results could be interpreted as a processing advantage for consonant intervals, rather than an advantage for these intervals specifically. Again, however, consonance and dissonance refer to sensory effects of simultaneous tone combinations, not tone sequences. The stimuli used in the study described earlier were melodic sequences. Moreover, the sensory effects of dissonance arise only for combinations of complex tones, because only complex tones contain the many frequency components that are needed to generate a sensation of roughness. However,

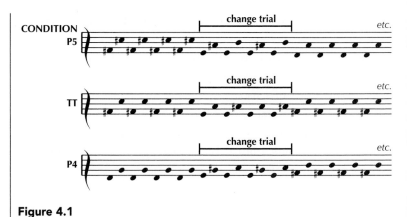

Figure 4.1

Stimuli used by Schellenberg and Trehub (1996b).

the same advantage was observed for melodic intervals presented as pure tones. That is, infants showed an advantage for some intervals over others even when the stimuli were designed to avoid sensory interactions among overtones. Because consonance and dissonance describe the sensory effects of simultaneous complex tones, the findings merit further investigation and explanation.

An advantage for processing fourths, fifths, and octaves appears to continue throughout development. Schellenberg and Trehub (1996a) asked 6-year-old children and adults to detect one-semitone changes in interval size. They were asked to discriminate two different intervals presented one after the other and in transposition: fourths (five semitones) from tritones (six semitones); fifths (seven semitones) from tritones, minor ninths (13 semitones) from octaves (12 semitones), and octaves from major sevenths (11 semitones). Each pair was presented in both orders. The discrimination task requires listeners to compare a memory representation for the standard interval (presented first) with a currently available comparison interval (presented second). If the standard interval remains stable in memory, it should be easily discriminated from the comparison interval. Performance was asymmetric in all instances. When the standard interval was a fourth, fifth, or octave, children and adults could discriminate the intervals. When the standard was dissonant, however, performance fell to chance levels. These findings suggest that listeners form relatively stable memory representations for octaves, fifths, and fourths, and relatively poor memory representations for more dissonant intervals.

Why do listeners form stable memories for these melodic intervals? As mentioned, it is difficult to interpret the results purely as a processing advantage for consonant intervals, because the effects were observed for melodic materials, and for pure-tone intervals. One possibility is that these intervals occur frequently in Western melodies, and are therefore highly familiar. It is well known that familiar input is perceived and remembered better than unfamiliar input. A related interpretation is that familiarity with octaves, fifths, and fourths in simultaneous intervals (common chords contain these intervals) influences judgments of the same intervals presented melodically. That is, processing advantages for simultaneously intervals might *generalize* to sequentially presented intervals.

Scale Structure

A rather quirky property of scales is that most have differently sized steps between consecutive tones in the scale. For example, the major scale has intervals of one and two semitones in size between adjacent scale notes, and most scales across cultures have this property of unequal steps. There are certainly exceptions, but the preponderance of scales with unequal steps in musical genres worldwide raises a basic question: Is music processed more easily when its scale consists of unequal steps?

In a test of whether the use of unequal steps confers a basic processing advantage to listeners, Trehub, Schellenberg, and Kamenetsky (1999) tested adults and 9-month-old infants on their ability to process and remember three scales (see Figure 4.2). One was the unequal-step major scale, another was an unfamiliar scale formed by dividing the octave into seven equal steps (Shepard & Jordan, 1984), and a third was a completely unfamiliar unequal-step scale. This third scale was formed by dividing the octave into 11 equal steps, and then constructing a seven-tone scale with four two-step intervals and three one-step intervals.

Both age groups were tested on their ability to detect when the sixth scale step was displaced upward slightly. Infants showed relatively good performance for the familiar (major) and the unfamiliar unequal-step scales, but poor performance for the unfamiliar equal-step scale. These results provide evidence that scales with unequal steps are inherently easier for infants to process and represent compared to equal-step scales. For infants, music composed with equal-step scales, such as whole-tone

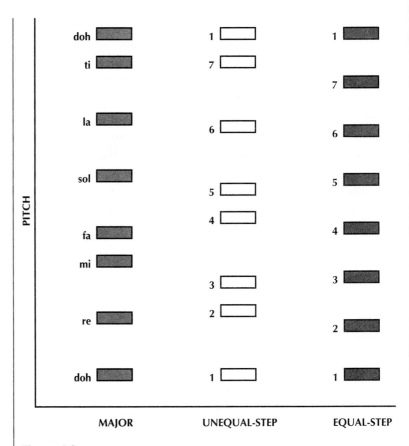

Figure 4.2

Unequal- and equal-step scales used by Trehub, Schellenberg, & Kamenetsky (1999).

(e.g., music by Debussy) or 12-tone (e.g., music by Schönberg) scales, may be more difficult to perceive and remember than music composed with unequal-step scales.

Why should infants have more trouble with equal-step scales? One possibility, discussed in chapter 5, is that the different notes in an equal-step scale are hard to differentiate from each other. They all form the very same intervals with neighboring and distant scale notes, giving rise to a kind of "sameness" about the notes contained in an equal-step scale. To appreciate this point, imagine trying to remember the position of five dots from a long row of evenly spaced dots. Now imagine performing the same task for a row of dots that are unevenly spaced. The task should be easier for the unevenly spaced dots.

Overlaying this initial advantage for unequal-step scales is the role of familiarity. Because infants are too young to benefit from familiarity with musical scales, they performed at similar levels for familiar and unfamiliar unequal-step scales. When adults were tested on the same materials, however, they showed the effects of familiarity. For the familiar major scale, adults could easily detect the upward displacement of the sixth scale step. By contrast, for both unfamiliar scales (equal or unequal-step), adults had difficulty detecting when the sixth scale step was displaced upward.

This finding suggests that with years of exposure to the scale (or scales) from one's musical culture, the initial processing advantage for scales with unequal steps is actually eliminated. When the listener is fully enculturated, she or he is familiar and comfortable with conventional scales, whereas unconventional scales of all types (including unfamiliar unequal-step scales) sound foreign and are difficult to perceive and remember.

Phrase Structure

How do listeners know when one musical phrase ends and another begins? Are infants sensitive to these phrase boundaries? Krumhansl and Jusczyk (1990) tested infants' preferences for Mozart pieces that were "correctly" or "incorrectly" segmented. Correctly segmented pieces had pauses inserted between phrases. Incorrectly segmented pieces had pauses inserted within phrases. To an adult listener, both versions sound somewhat strange, although the former version seems more musical because the pauses occur at "natural" breaks in the music. Looking times indicated that infants preferred the correctly segmented pieces, in which segments tended to end with relatively long notes and downward pitch contours. Interestingly, spoken utterances also tend to end with words of relatively long duration and downward pitch contour. This correspondence between spoken utterances and musical phrases leads to two related interpretations of the results: (a) infants might prefer the "correctly" segmented pieces because they bear structural similarities to spoken utterances, which infants have learned from being exposed to speech, or (b) downward contours and extended durations naturally mark the end of all auditory signals.

Either way, the findings indicate that listeners implicitly understand at a very early age that melodic phrases tend to end with downward pitch motion and notes of relatively long duration. Such cues allow listeners to segment melodies into melodic groups such as phrases and motifs, and to identify boundaries between larger forms such as movements and sections.

Harmony

Sound Example 4.4.1

The melody from **Figure 4.3**. Tonic harmony is implied in bars 1, 3, and 4. Dominant harmony is implied in bar 2.

Musical intervals provide the building blocks for one of the most important levels of pitch structure: harmony. The term *harmony* refers to the study of simultaneous pitches in music, which in Western music usually occur in the form of chords. At some point in development, children begin to perceive chords and chord sequences as an emergent level of structure. At this stage, chords are not merely perceived as combinations of individual pitches that happen to sound consonant or dissonant; they seem to have an emergent quality that can be appreciated and remembered in its own right, independently of the individual tones and melodies in the music. Once sensitivity to harmony develops, it helps to shape our perceptions and interpretations of music, including unaccompanied melodies, which often have an implied harmony.

Because melodies are so often heard with a harmonic accompaniment, listeners gradually learn to associate isolated melodies with plausible harmonic accompaniments, even when none is present. Consider the melody illustrated in Figure 4.3 (from Trainor & Trehub, 1992, 1994). The melody implies a shift from a tonic harmony (a chord or harmony based on doh) in the first measure to a dominant harmony (a chord or harmony based on sol) in the second measure. Musically trained listeners are highly sensitive to this *implied harmony*, and consistently identify the implied harmonic change. Are infants and untrained listeners also sensitive to these shifts in implied harmony? If so, how does sensitivity to implied harmony change over development?

Sound Example 4.4.2

The implied harmony for the melody has been realized in the form of a chord at the beginning of each bar.

Sensitivity to implied harmony has been examined by introducing a single note from a target melody in a way that does not disrupt the

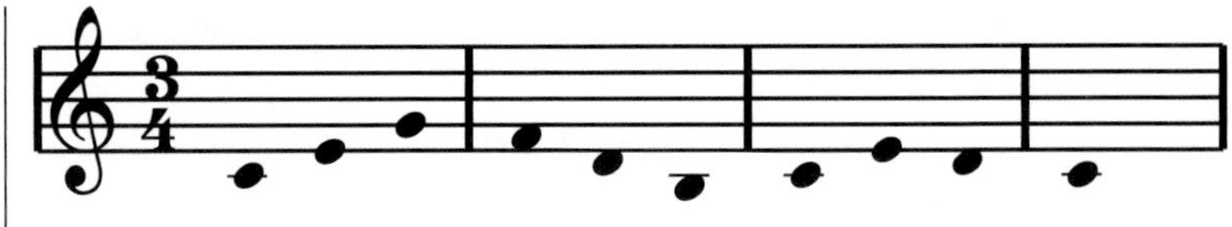

Figure 4.3
Melody used by Trainor and Trehub (1992, 1994).

implied harmony of the melody (Cuddy, Cohen, & Mewhort, 1981). For adults, such changes are very subtle and difficult to notice because adult memory for melodies includes information about implied harmony. In other words, two different melodies that have the same implied harmony sound psychologically equivalent for harmonic representations of the music, and equivalence at the harmonic level of structure actually interferes with detection of such a change to a melody. In fact, subtle changes to melodies that preserve the underlying chord sequence occur quite often in music, as when composers create "variations on a melodic theme."

A more obvious change involves altering a note from a melody in a way that is inconsistent with the implied harmony of the original melody. Although adults find the latter type of change far more obvious, 8-month-old infants are able to detect both types of changes equally well. Trainor and Trehub (1992) tested adults and 8-month-olds on their ability to discriminate alterations to the melody shown in Figure 4.3, which was presented repeatedly in varying transpositions. In each case, the alteration consisted of an upward displacement to the sixth tone in the melody. For some listeners, the displacement was a shift upward by one semitone (e.g., from G to G#), which is a small alteration in terms of interval size but inconsistent with the implied harmony. For other listeners, the displacement was a shift upward by four semitones (e.g., from G to B), which is much larger in interval size but consistent with the implied dominant harmony.

Adult listeners found the former change—which violated the implied harmony—easier to detect than the latter change—which was consistent with the implied harmony. Infant listeners performed equally well in both conditions. Interestingly, infant listeners actually outperformed adults at detecting the larger but harmonically consistent shift in pitch. In other words, adult listeners appear to have a very well developed sense of implied harmony that they acquire through years of exposure to music, such that changes in a melody that are consistent with the implied harmony are relatively unnoticeable. By contrast, infants appear to be less sensitive to implied harmony (see also Schellenberg, Bigand, Poulin, Garnier, & Stevens, 2005).

Key

The perception of key involves sensitivity to a complex set of relationships among tones and chords, and an overall tonal center or tonic. This sensitivity can be manifested in a number of ways, starting with a simple ability to distinguish scale notes from nonscale notes, to the more complex ability to detect or evaluate changes in key (tonal modulations) that occur in the music. Developmental studies have primarily focused on the first ability. One strategy has been to examine the ability of infants, children, and adults to detect changes to melodies that result in the introduction of a note that is not in the established key (a nonscale note). If such changes are more noticeable than changes that do not introduce a nonscale note, then the researcher can infer sensitivity to key (because scale notes help to define a key). Another strategy is to introduce changes to melodies that are either tonal (consistent with a key) or atonal (inconsistent with any key). Tacit knowledge of key structure should make tonal melodies more stable in memory than atonal melodies, such that changes to tonal melodies are relatively easy to detect. Thus, people who are sensitive to key should find changes to tonal melodies more noticeable than changes to atonal melodies.

In Western music, the most common key is associated with the major scale (doh-re-mi-fah-sol-la-ti). Within this scale, the first note, doh, is perceived as a point of stability and rest. It is called the tonic, or tonal center, and plays an important role in determining the syntactic structure of music. For example, an occurrence of the tonic can signal a phrase boundary or a reduction in stress or emphasis. Other pitches are less stable than the tonic and have other functions; the next most stable is the fifth note of the scale, sol, the next is the third note mi, followed by the remaining scale notes. For any given major scale, some of the tones of the chromatic scale do not appear. These tones, called nonscale or nondiatonic notes, convey a jarring sense of instability when inserted into a tonal melody. In fact, once a key is established it is rare to encounter a nonscale note, and experienced listeners do not expect them to occur.

Sensitivity to key, like sensitivity for harmony, is not evident in infants. Nine-month-olds find it just as easy to detect changes to a nontonal melody than changes to a tonal melody (Schellenberg & Trehub, 1999). Western adults find tonal melodies easier to remember than nontonal melodies, because they are highly familiar with them. Without extensive exposure to music, however, infants merely have the basic skills needed for melody discrimination, but these skills do not reflect the effects of exposure to Western tonal music.

When does sensitivity to harmony and key develop? Trainor and Trehub (1994) addressed this question by testing listeners 5 and 7 years of age. The children were required to detect the one-semitone harmony-violating change, the four-semitone harmony-consistent change, and an intermediate two-semitone shift (e.g., from G to A) that was consistent with the underlying key signature (C major) but violated the implied harmony. The 5-year-olds found the one-semitone change easier to detect than the other changes. In other words, the shift that violated both the implied harmony and the underlying key signature was more noticeable than the other shifts. For the 7-year-olds, the two-semitone shift that violated the implied harmony but not the key was easier to detect than the four-semitone harmonically consistent shift. These data, together with other research findings, indicate a systematic developmental progression. Infant listeners have a relatively poor sense of key. By 5 years of age, children are sensitive to key membership but not to harmony. By 7 years of age, children are also sensitive to harmony.

To summarize the developmental evidence on musical pitch, infants are sensitive to contour well before age 1. They exhibit a processing advantage and preference for consonant over dissonant intervals, and a processing advantage for scales that have unequal scale steps. Infants are also sensitive to phrase structure. Sensitivity to key and harmony develops relatively late in development, but by the age of 7, children are sensitive to all the basic dimensions of musical pitch.

Rhythm

One of the most natural responses to music is to move in time with it, whether by clapping, tapping, head-bopping, or dancing. Rhythmic responses to music occur in virtually all cultures and at all ages, suggesting that the temporal dimension is fundamental to musical activities. Research suggests that sensitivity to rhythm emerges very early in development, with infants as young as 2 months of age showing the capacity to discriminate rhythms. Where does this early sensitivity to rhythm come from?

One theory that has been entertained for centuries is that sensitivity to musical rhythms originates from our experience with other rhythmic phenomena, such as those associated with human locomotion (walking), heart rate, and speech patterns. Such views are compelling but difficult to prove. Rhythmic phenomena are ubiquitous, from ocean waves and bouncing balls to walking and breathing. It is therefore difficult to identify any one rhythmic phenomenon as the sole source of our sensitivity to musical rhythm. On the other hand, it is clear that the fetus is exposed to rhythmic sounds in utero, including sounds associated with the mother's breathing, walking, and heartbeat. It is entirely possible that this prenatal exposure to acoustic stimuli assists in the development of rhythmic sensitivity.

Another source of prenatal exposure to rhythm is movement itself. As a mother walks the fetus is exposed to the rhythm of human locomotion. If the sounds of her footsteps are also available, then the rhythmic movement will be correlated with rhythmic sounds. Interestingly, the word *rhythm* derives from the Latin *rhythmus*, which means movement in time. Is it possible that our sense of rhythm is interconnected with our sense of movement?

The simplest way to move in response to music is to make regular and repeated actions that match the underlying beat, such as clapping one's hands. Although infants under 2 rarely (if ever) synchronize movements to music, they are capable of perceiving a regular pulse in music. Infants as young as 7 months can categorize rhythms on the basis of meter (Hannon & Johnson, 2005), and 9-month-old infants are more sensitive to timing discrepancies if the music has a clear metric structure than if it has no obviously metric structure (Bergeson & Trehub, 2006). When infants are bounced in their parents' arms, the rhythm implied by the bouncing motion influences the infants' preference for auditory patterns that match the way they were bounced (Phillips-Silver & Trainor, 2005). In other words, movement strongly affects the way infants respond to rhythm, suggesting that our sense of rhythm originates in regularities of movement.

Like sensitivity to harmony and key, sensitivity to rhythm and meter is subject to the effects of learning and enculturation. After about 6 months of age, North American infants start to become increasingly sensitive to Western rhythm. Hannon and Trehub (2005a, 2005b) reported that 6-month-old infants detect disruptions to Western and Balkan rhythms with equal ease, but by 12 months the infants show relatively greater sensitivity to Western rhythms than to Balkan rhythms. That is, the ability of infants to process rhythm is gradually shaped by repeated exposure to typical (Western) rhythms in their environment.

Memory for Music

Not only do infants have a wide range of basic perceptual skills; they can remember specific pieces of music over significant amounts of time.

Saffran, Loman, and Robertson (2000) exposed 7-month-old infants every day for 14 days to the slow movement from two Mozart piano sonatas. Following this exposure phase, the infants did not hear the music for 2 weeks. The researchers then assessed whether the infants remembered the music. The researchers reasoned that if infants remembered the music that was presented in the exposure phase, they should also prefer that music to music of the same style that is unfamiliar to them. In other words, preference for music was interpreted as an indirect measure of musical memory. Preference was evaluated using a head-turn procedure. In the testing phase, the infants were presented with 20-second excerpts from the two Mozart sonata passages that were presented to infants in the exposure phase, or from two other Mozart sonatas that were completely novel to the infants.

The degree of preference—and hence memory for the music—was measured by the amount of time an infant looked in the direction of the musical excerpts. As predicted, the infants preferred the familiar music to the novel music, as indicated by longer looking times. Interestingly, however, this effect was only observed if the excerpts were taken from the very beginning of the sonata. That is, the infants not only remembered the Mozart sonatas; they seemed to understand that the sonatas should optimally be played from the beginning.

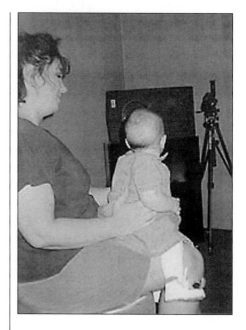

An experimental method used in studies of infant auditory perception in which head-turn responses are the dependent variable.

Source: Photo courtesy of Dr. Laurel Trainor, McMaster University.

Learning and Enculturation

Infants possess a number of basic perceptual skills that provide a foundation for the development of mature forms of musical understanding. These elementary skills include the ability to perceive and remember pitch sequences, a heightened sensitivity to melodic contour, and a preference for consonance over dissonance. By school age, Western children begin to respond to music in ways that reflect their exposure to Western music, much like the responses of adults. Four- to 6-year-old children are better able to detect changes to tonal melodies than changes to non-tonal melodies, presumably because they have already become familiar with the music of their own culture, and are attuned to melodies that are compatible with that style.

For similar reasons, 5-year-old children more easily detect changes to a tonal melody if those changes are inconsistent with the key of the melody than if they are consistent with the key of the melody. Once a key is established, any nondiatonic note that is introduced stands out perceptually, whereas a diatonic note that is introduced will generally blend in with the music, making it harder to detect. It is as though the tonal melody is able to camouflage the newly introduced diatonic note. This effect of tonality indicates that 5-year-old children have developed sensitivity to scale, and when they listen to music they expect notes that are consistent with the scale.

Seven-year-old children show an even more advanced type of sensitivity. They show a heightened sensitivity to changes that are inconsistent with the implied harmony of the original melody. Thus, a novel note that is incompatible with the implied harmony of the original melody will stand out for 7-year-old children, even if that note is compatible with the key.

All of these findings suggest that through continued exposure to music, infants gradually develop sensitivity to various structural characteristics of Western tonal music, as reflected in how they perceive and remember melodies. Different aspects of musical sensitivity develop at different developmental stages, starting with melodic contour, followed by scale, and harmony. Once established, preferences and processing advantages for the music of our cultural environment typically remain throughout the life span.

Additional Readings

Hannon, E. E., & Trainor, L. J. (2007). Music acquisition: Effects of enculturation and formal training on development. *Trends in Cognitive Sciences, 11,* 466–472.

Stewart, L., & Walsh, V. (2005). Infant learning: Music and the baby brain. *Current Biology, 15,* 882–884.

CHAPTER 5

Perceiving Music Structure

LEARNING OUTCOMES

By the end of this chapter you should be able to:

1. Identify the challenges in defining music and music structure.

2. Explain what listeners perceive and remember when they hear a melody.

3. Describe attributes of music that are also relevant to speech prosody.

4. Compare psychological models of pitch and appraise their validity.

5. Provide a psychological description of melodic expectancy.

6. Provide a psychological description of rhythm.

Arrangements of Sounds

In 1947, Random House launched its first dictionary, the *American College Dictionary*, the first in a long and successful line of college dictionaries. It defined music as an art of sound that expresses thoughts and feelings through the elements of melody, harmony, and rhythm. These ingredients were taken as the defining features of music and the main properties that we perceive when listening to music. A less specific definition was published in the 1955 edition of the *Oxford Universal Dictionary*, which construed music as the art of combining "sounds" with a view to achieving beauty of form and the expression of thought and feeling. This reluctance to identify specific music structures reflected an emerging awareness of the enormous range of sounds involved in musical activities around the world, not all of which are easily slotted into the categories of melody, harmony, and rhythm.

Even this broadened definition may be critiqued as too ethnocentric, based on Western conceptions of how music functions in society. Is the function of music universally restricted to expressions of beauty, thought, and feeling? Fans of grunge and death metal might debate this point. Across various cultural groups, music may be used for different forms: aesthetic enjoyment, emotional communication, symbolic representation, physical response, social conformity, group bonding, and as validation of social institutions and religious rituals. Music is often enjoyable and expressive of thoughts and feelings, but its scope is wider, allowing it to act as a medium for embodying and disseminating a vast array of activities and values that constitute a social matrix. Aware of such caveats, the authors of many contemporary dictionaries are reluctant to identify anything structural or functional as essential to music, preferring to define music in the most inclusive possible way as simply "arranging of sounds in time" (*American Heritage Dictionary*).

Recognizing the tremendous diversity of musical behaviors and functions around the world and at different historical periods, Cross (2003a, 2003b) characterized music as the creation of sounds and movements that have the potential to carry meaning across a wide range of contexts. Thus, music is distinguished not only by its arrangements of sound and movement, but also by a "floating intentionality" that permits it to be exploited for a variety of individual and cultural purposes. A basic prerequisite of all such purposes, however, is that its organization and structure must be tangible to the perceiver. Listeners differentiate

Sound Example 5.1

Although music can be expressive of thoughts and feelings, its function cannot be limited to this narrow range. Music can often serve a more prosaic function. **Sound example 5.1** is an excerpt from a didactic song performed in Calabrese (an Italian dialect) by a group of Calabrian women to a young child. Its function is to teach a child the names of body parts. It begins "Let's touch little Rosa's foot...," with each subsequent verse enumerating a different part of the body. Performance would most likely be accompanied by gestures. In North America, the popular children's song "Head, Shoulders, Knees, and Toes" serves the same function.

Sound example 5.1 is available via the *Music, Thought, and Feeling* iMix on iTunes.

music from noise and other nonmusical sounds because perceptual processes allow them to recognize the structure of music. In turn, musicians organize, ornament, and shape time in a manner that they and other listeners can perceive and appreciate.

Western musicians typically arrange sounds using the tools of melody, harmony, tonality, and rhythm, which interact to form complex patterns that are appreciated by listeners, but not all musical traditions revolve around these parameters. Indeed, some musical traditions emphasize movement over sound. Nonetheless, the elements of melody, harmony, tonality, and rhythm have been used in a wide range of musical traditions around the world and throughout history, whether in the form of children's lullabies or religious chants, and our sensitivity to and appreciation of them implicates a range of perceptual and cognitive processes.

This chapter focuses on the cognitive processes by which listeners appreciate these musical characteristics. What do listeners perceive and remember when they hear a melody? Are certain features of a melody more likely to be remembered than others? Melodies can be considered at different levels of analysis, including local structure (tones, intervals, contours), higher order structure (phrases, movements), and abstract structure (scales, keys). Harmony describes another level of music structure. Chords not only provide a *coloring* of the music; they also carry out specific functions in the music, and their perceived relations to other chords are meaningful in a way that is analogous to the pitch relations that constitute a melody. Sensitivity to melody and harmony develop at different ages in children, suggesting that they involve different cognitive processes. Melody and harmony often give rise to highly complex structure that is organized hierarchically, with smaller groups nested within larger music structures. Is rhythm perceived with a comparable level of complexity? How does rhythmic organization interact with melodic and harmonic organization?

Relative Pitch

Sound Examples 5.2.1–5.2.3

Some examples of famous melodies. What factors make these melodies memorable?

People are remarkably sensitive to pitch relations, so much so that they will readily provide different adjectives and elaborate metaphors to describe the distinctive qualities of pitch combinations. In an early study of the phenomenon, Edmonds and Smith (1923) presented listeners with simultaneous intervals and asked them to provide adjectives to describe them. An octave was described as "smooth, like the surface of window glass" or "like the feel of ice-cream in the mouth." A major seventh, in contrast, was described as "astringent, like the taste of a persimmon" or "a harsh, a nippy, biting effect." The perfect fifth was described as "hollow, like a hollow tree, no body to it," and the major second was described as "gritty, like the feel of small pebbles in the hand" (cf. Merriam, 1964, p. 95).

We are also highly attuned to relations between sequentially occurring pitches. When we hear a familiar song, we recognize it from the relationships that are formed between the sequential pitches of the melody and not from the absolute pitches themselves. A familiar melody such as "Happy Birthday" is immediately recognizable whether it is sung by a man, woman, or child, even though the starting notes are different. As long as pitch relations are retained, so is the identity of the melody. Transposition of familiar melodies has little effect on recognition of familiar melodies. This sensitivity to relative pitch is fundamental to the perception and cognition of tonal music, and a foundation for psychological models of tonal music.

One of the most basic descriptions of pitch relations is the distance between two notes, or *interval size*. Large melodic intervals or "leaps" form the basis for *gap-fill melodies* (Meyer, 1973), whereby a large interval is followed by pitches that fall in between that interval, thereby filling in the "gap" that it creates. Famous examples of gap-fill melodies include "My Bonny" (see Figure 5.1) and "Over the Rainbow." Large melodic intervals are also experienced as a point of accent. Conversely, melodies sound more coherent or cohesive when they consist of a sequence of small intervals (Huron, 2001b). Interval size may also influence melodic expectancy (Narmour, 1990) and grouping (Lerdahl & Jackendoff, 1983).

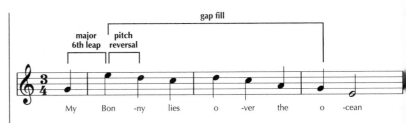

Figure 5.1

The first line of "My Bonny" illustrates the concept of a gap-fill melody. After the initial large leap of a major sixth (i.e., from "My" to "Bon-"), a pitch reversal takes place and the subsequent tones "fill in" the scale notes that were skipped over in the leap.

Sound Example 5.3

A simple rendition of the first line of "My Bonny."

Interval size is normally defined according to the number of semitones that separate the lower and upper pitch of the interval, consistent with a logarithmic relation between frequency and pitch. Recent evidence by Russo and Thompson (2005a, 2005b), however, indicates that our perceptions of interval size are influenced by a large number of factors. Participants in these studies were presented with sequences of two pitches and judged the size of the melodic interval formed by them. Estimates were larger for intervals in the high pitch register than in the low pitch register, and also varied depending on whether the interval was ascending or descending. Ascending intervals were perceived as larger than descending intervals when presented in a high pitch register, but descending intervals were perceived as larger than ascending intervals when presented in a low pitch register.

Moreover, if the upper pitch of an interval had a brighter timbre (i.e., a higher spectral centroid) than the lower pitch, the interval was judged to be significantly larger than if the timbral properties of the two pitches were reversed (Russo & Thompson, 2005a). The latter effect was so powerful that for some conditions participants judged a six-tone pitch interval to be larger than a seven-tone interval. Other evidence suggests that listeners even consider the facial expressions of performers when estimating the size of melodic intervals (Thompson et al., 2005). Presumably, the visual information related to the production of melodic intervals is integrated with auditory cues of interval size, leading to a perceptual representation that reflects the audiovisual experience.

Melodic Contour

The contour of a melody refers to its pattern of upward and downward changes in pitch over time, irrespective of the absolute pitches involved, or the specific size of the intervals between pairs of adjacent tones. In general, research indicates that listeners' mental representations of novel melodies contain contour information but relatively little information about absolute pitch or exact interval size. Memory for the absolute pitches of novel melodies tends to be poor, and memory for the exact intervals between notes also tends to be poorer than memory for contour. Findings from studies of infants are particularly compelling in this regard. Moreover, the findings for adults' memories for novel melodies converge with those from infants.

Studies with adults often adopt the same–different experimental method. On each experimental trial, listeners hear a "standard" (original) and "comparison" melody and judge whether they are the same or different. By systematically varying the ways in which the comparison differs from the standard and assessing the effects of such changes on judgment accuracy, one can determine which features are represented in memory. Listeners make errors about the interval and absolute pitch information of novel melodies relatively soon after they are presented. By contrast, they retain contour information for longer periods of time. Researchers have identified a number of implications of this heightened sensitivity to melodic contour. First, melodies with fewer changes in contour are perceived as "simpler" than melodies with more contour changes (Boltz & Jones, 1986). Second, listeners attend more to notes at points of contour change than they do to notes that are embedded within an ongoing contour (Dyson & Watkins, 1984). For example, when presented with a five-tone sequence with an up-up-down-down contour (see Figure 5.2), listeners' attention is drawn more to the middle (third) tone—the point of contour change—than to the second or fourth tones. It follows, then, that melodies with a relative abundance of contour changes contain a relatively large number of salient bits of information, and should be relatively challenging to process and remember.

A number of recent studies have examined the possible relation between contour sensitivity in melody and sensitivity to speech intonation. Speech intonation, like melody, makes use of variation in pitch, and changes to the pitch contour of speech intonation can alter the nature of the message in critical ways. For example, a rising pitch at the end of a spoken phrase indicates a question, whereas a falling pitch indicates a statement. Because contour changes are meaningful in both music and speech, the ability to make sense of contour in these domains could be associated with shared neural resources (see also chapter 10). One way to assess this finding is to test whether people who have difficulty detecting changes in melodic contour might have a similar difficulty detecting

Figure 5.2

A simple melody with an up-up-down-down contour.

changes in speech intonation. Such difficulties can arise in adulthood following brain injury or accident (e.g., stroke), or they may be present from birth as a congenital condition.

Tone deafness is used informally to refer to a lack of musical ability, but researchers reserve the label for individuals who demonstrate: (a) abnormally large thresholds for detecting pitch changes, (b) difficulty judging the direction of a pitch change, and (c) difficulty discriminating tone sequences on the basis of pitch contour. Tone deafness is also referred to as *congenital amusia*, and is thought to occur in approximately 4% to 5% of the population.

Ayotte, Peretz, and Hyde (2002) tested the ability of 11 tone-deaf individuals to discriminate spoken phrases that differed only in pitch contour. In one experiment, they presented such pairs of spoken phrases to tone-deaf individuals and asked them to indicate whether the phrases were the same or different. The contour changes altered the sense of the spoken phrase. For example, one phrase might suggest a question (he speaks French?) and the other might suggest a statement (he speaks French). Accuracy on the discrimination task was at normal performance levels, suggesting that speech intonation was not affected by the tone-deafness. Moreover, when the linguistic information was removed from the sentences and replaced by a series of musical tones that matched the pitches of each syllable (*discrete pitch analogues* of the spoken phrases), the ability to discriminate pairs of sequences was again impaired.

One explanation for this dissociation is that the neural resources involved in detecting melodic contour are different from the neural resources involved in detecting changes in contour that occur in speech. However, it is unclear whether the dissociation resulted because the spoken samples contained linguistic information, or because they contained pitch glides instead of discrete pitches. A more recent investigation by Patel, Foxton, and Griffiths (2005) addressed this complication. They presented tone-deaf individuals with nonlinguistic tone sequences derived from speech samples, but in this case they matched the pitch contour of each syllable exactly, such that tone sequences involved pitch glides that went up and down just as the pitch did in the spoken phrases. As with the discrete-pitch analogues of speech, tone-deaf individuals had difficulty discriminating these *gliding-pitch analogues* of the spoken phrases. Thus, something about the presence of linguistic information allowed the tone-deaf individuals to discriminate on the basis of contour.

The potential neural overlap between music and speech is not restricted to pitch contour. The ability to decode speech prosody might engage a range of processes that are involved in music listening, including sensitivity to contour, loudness, tempo, and rhythm (Ilie & Thompson, 2006). In support of this hypothesis, Thompson et al. (2004) reported that adults with extensive training in music were significantly better at decoding the emotional connotation of speech in an unfamiliar language. Because participants could not understand the verbal content of the speech, they relied on prosodic features such as pitch contour, loudness, and temporal properties—properties that have musical significance. In the same study, the authors found that 7-year-old children assigned to 1 year of piano lessons were better at decoding speech prosody in their own language and in a foreign language than children who did not receive such training. The findings imply that training in music engages neural resources associated with both music and speech, such that the enhanced skill acquired from music lessons transfers to an enhanced ability to decode speech prosody.

Scale Structure

A survey of the scales of various musical cultures suggests that music is constrained by basic psychological processes. For example, virtually all scales have five to seven notes per octave. There is a consensus in the literature that the limited number of notes in these scales stems from limitations in the capacity of working memory. Several decades ago, G. A. Miller (1956) demonstrated that for any continuous dimension (e.g., brightness, loudness), adults can reliably categorize instances into a maximum of seven categories, give or take about two chunks. Because this limitation of working memory capacity extends across domains and modalities, we would expect that pitch categories would be similarly limited. Hence, music composed with scales that have more than seven tones is likely to exceed the cognitive capacities of many listeners. This property may explain why many people find it challenging to listen to 12-tone (serialized) music.

A second characteristic of scales that may stem from psychological predispositions is the structural importance of intervals that closely approximate perfect consonances, such as octaves, fifths, and fourths. These structural features may reflect an innate preference for consonance, and a processing advantage for consonant over dissonant intervals.

Sound Examples 5.4.1–5.4.2

In the 20th century, a group of composers collectively referred to as the Second Viennese School felt that the tonal system that had been in place in Western music for at least 300 years had been exhausted, and began to explore atonality. One method of composition uses a 12-tone melody called a "tone row," constructed from the 12 equal steps (one semitone each) of the chromatic scale. The tone row is used as a springboard for a composition. Because the tone row is constructed from an equal-step scale, there is nothing unique or distinguishable about any given scale tone. To ensure that the listener cannot isolate a focal or tonic note from the tone row, it is constructed serially, meaning that no one tone can be repeated until the other 11 have been used. This ensures that a given tone is not given precedence on the basis of more frequent occurrence. Twelve-tone composition never achieved popularity with the general public. This may be due to the fact that the working memory demands required of the tone row far exceed Miller's magic number seven.

Sound example 5.4.1 is an example of a tone row.

Sound example 5.4.2 is an example of a 12-tone composition, Webern's Symphony Opus 21.

Sound example 5.4.2 is available via the *Music, Thought, and Feeling* iMix on iTunes.

A third property of scales, described in chapter 4, is that most have different-sized steps between consecutive tones in the scale. For example, the major scale has intervals of one and two semitones in size between adjacent scale notes. The most common pentatonic scale has steps of two and three semitones. In fact, scales from around the world (except for the whole-tone and 12-tone scales) have this property of unequal steps. One often-noted exception is a scale from Thailand, although there is doubt about its proposed equal-step structure in musical practice (D. Morton, 1976). Why would so many scales exhibit this unequal-step property?

One explanation is that unequal steps arise because consonant intervals (fifth, fourth, major third) are formed from a small number of scale notes. Balzano (1980), however, argued that unequal steps also confer a psychological benefit, because they allow tones to have different functions within the scale. In the major scale, each note has a unique set of intervals that it forms with the other notes from the scale. In C major, for example, F and B are related to each other by the interval of an augmented fourth, but C is not related to any scale note by that particular interval. This distinctive property allows listeners to differentiate scale tones from one another, and to isolate a focal or tonic tone (doh). A focal or tonic tone functions as a mental referent to which other tones can be compared. The ability to determine a focal tone and differentiate scale tones may make unequal-step scales advantageous from a psychological standpoint. Even infants are better at processing and remembering unequal-step scales than equal-step scales. Apparently, scales with unequal steps are more suited to the perceptual and cognitive processes that we possess early in development, and these psychological dispositions continue to influence the scales that are used in mature forms of musical behavior.

Large-Scale Structure

Like language, music can be segmented into a series of phrases. Each phrase is a digestible group of musical events, and we can usually hold an entire phrase in working memory. Imagine any childhood tune and its entire melody can readily be segmented into a sequence of phrases. However, music is more than a string of phrases occurring one after the other. A number of cues influence our understanding of the musical significance of different events in music. These cues include intensity, metric strength, and tonal stability. Not surprisingly, loud notes that fall on the downbeat and are tonally stable are heard as significant. Having differentiated musical events into significant and less significant ones, we tend to perceive connections between the significant events.

As an example, the song "Do-Re-Mi" from *The Sound of Music* outlines a simple ascending major scale, but the scale is perceived only by connecting the first tone of each phrase. That is, the point of the melody (teaching children the scale) cannot be perceived at the musical surface, but requires the perception of *higher level melodic structure*. Lerdahl and Jackendoff (1983) proposed a comprehensive and influential theory of melody that emphasized this hierarchic structure. They first noted that Western tonal melodies can be analyzed into essential notes and ornamental notes. Ornamental notes are notes in the melody that can be removed without altering the essential character of the melody. After ornamental notes are removed, what is left is a simplified version of that melody. With this idea as a starting point, Lerdahl and Jackendoff used the term *reductional structure* to describe how large-scale melodic structures can be analyzed into simpler and simpler skeletons. They proposed two ways in which melodies can be simplified.

In time-span reduction, certain beats and groups in a melody are designated as ornaments on other groups and beats. This simplification process is continued in an iterative manner, resulting in a tree diagram that specifies the relative dominance of each event. In prolongation reduction, primary points of tension and relaxation are differentiated from subordinate points of tension and relaxation, again resulting in a tree diagram. Both types of tree diagrams illustrate how smaller melodic units combine to form a large-scale melodic structure. Palmer and Krumhansl (1987a, 1987b) found that time-span reduction was able to predict listeners' judgments of phrase endings in music by Mozart and Bach. Other research supports the psychological validity of prolongation reduction (Bigand, 1990; Dibben, 1994).

An example of time-span reduction.

Adapted from Large, Palmer, and Pollack (1995). Reduced memory representations for music. *Cognitive Science*, 19, p. 59.

Melodic Expectancies

As a listener hears a melody, he or she continuously forms expectancies about upcoming notes he or she will hear. Sometimes we expect a particular note, but usually our expectations are not so specific. Rather, some notes seem relatively likely, whereas other ones seem less so. Learning and exposure to musical styles exert a large influence on such expectancies. Is there a role for basic cognitive processes in the formation of melodic expectancies?

According to Narmour's (1990) *implication-realization model*, expectancies are formed from a combination of bottom-up and top-down factors (Thompson, 1996). Bottom-up factors refer to innate or hard-wired cognitive and perceptual tendencies, whereas top-down factors refer to expectancies that result from experience, either with music in general, or with a particular musical piece. The true origin of these expectancies is actually unknown: the age-old nature–nurture debate. As examples, pitch proximity (expecting notes that are proximal in pitch) is thought to be an innate influence on melodic expectancy, whereas tonality (expecting notes in proportion to their importance in the scale) is thought to be based on long-term knowledge of Western music.

Two experimental methods have been used to test expectancies. In one method, listeners hear a fragment of a melody followed by a test tone. Their task is to rate how well the test tone continues the fragment. The assumption is that tones conforming to listeners' expectancies will be rated as relatively good continuations. The other method is a production task, in which participants play or sing a continuation to a stimulus provided by the experimenter. The main finding from the relevant studies is that proximity explains most of the variation in listeners' responses, regardless of experimental method, musical style, and participants' music training or cultural background. In general, tones that are proximate in pitch to the last tone heard are the most expected (for a valuable discussion of this principle, see von Hippel, 2000). This association is more or less linear, such that tones farther and farther away from the last tone heard receive lower and lower ratings, or are less likely to be sung or played.

Narmour (1990) proposed several bottom-up principles of melodic expectancy. In an examination of Narmour's theory, however, Schellenberg (1997) observed that bottom-up expectancies can be largely explained by just two basic principles. The first principle is pitch proximity (described earlier). The second principle is pitch reversal. Pitch reversal describes expectancies for an upcoming tone to be proximate to the penultimate tone heard, as well as expectancies for a change in pitch contour after a large melodic leap. Meyer (1956) called such patterns *gap-fill*, because the third note usually fills in the "gap" in pitch created by the large melodic leap (see also von Hippel & Huron, 2000). This simple model has proven to be equal or superior to Narmour's original model across listeners who vary in musical training or cultural background, across stimulus contexts (real melodies or two-tone stimuli), with both production and perceptual-rating methods, and with melodies from Western tonal, atonal, and non-Western repertoires (see Thompson & Stainton, 1998, for another simplified model). Schellenberg's (2000) model has also equaled the success of the original model in studies conducted with children.

In short, there is strong evidence that proximity is an innate cognitive principle that influences the formation of melodic expectancies. The role of proximity in melodic expectancy represents perhaps one of the clearest examples of a basic psychological process influencing music perception and cognition. Proximity is known to be a robust predictor of perceptual grouping in vision. The same holds true for audition in general (see section on "Composing with Multiple Voices" in chapter 9) and for music in particular. Tones that are proximate in pitch tend to be grouped together. Hence, a melody that contains many large leaps in pitch is difficult to perceive as a unified whole, whereas a melody with mostly stepwise motion (rather than leaps) tends to be perceived as a unified group of tones.

Implicit Memory for Music

The effects of learning that result from exposure to music are often subtle. Moreover, as the following section illustrates, they often occur without conscious awareness. It is widely acknowledged that experiences frequently affect our behavior in the absence of conscious awareness. Such effects are thought to reflect an implicit memory system that operates independently of conscious or explicit memory (Schacter, 1987). Recent advances in the understanding of implicit memory systems suggest an exciting direction for future studies of music cognition.

Implicit memory for music may explain how listeners develop an appreciation for the music of their culture. Indeed, most musical experiences are probably influenced by implicit memory. As Crowder (1993) argues, "the re-entry of a fugue theme, the occurrence of a *lietmotif*, or the developmental section of a remembered sonata-movement subject may all be examples of implicit music memory" (p. 134). Empirical

Melody and Copyright Infringement

In cases of copyright infringement, melody is considered to be the "fingerprint" of a musical work; rhythmic and harmonic elements have been deemed subordinate on the grounds that everything original has been done in these two domains—particularly within the formulaic realm of popular music.

Because it is possible to unwittingly create a melody identical to an existing melody, a prosecutor in a court of law needs to demonstrate that the defendant had reasonable access to an existing copyrighted melody (Cronin, 1998). The infringement does not have to take place consciously. In 1976, in what was probably the most famous case of melodic copyright infringement, the late George Harrison was successfully sued for "unconscious infringement." Two phrases from Harrison's "My Sweet Lord" were deemed to have been misappropriated from "He's So Fine" (a hit from the early 1960s recorded by the Chiffons). More recently, the Rolling Stones, in an effort to avoid litigation, gave a writing credit to k.d. lang when a strong similarity was observed between the melodic hook to their soon-to-be-released single "Anybody Seen My Baby" and lang's previously released "Constant Craving." In both cases, the artists denied any conscious infringement, suggesting a role for implicit memory in creativity.

studies support Crowder's suggestion. Passive exposure to music leads to implicit knowledge of tonal relations (Bharucha, Curtis, & Paroo, 2006; Tillman, Bharucha, & Bigand, 2000), musical preferences (Peretz, Gaudreau, & Bonnel, 1998), and expectancies for melodic continuations (Thompson, Balkwill, & Vernescu, 2000).

Peretz et al. (1998) presented a group of individuals with 40 melodic lines taken from the popular repertoire (study phase). In a subsequent test phase, the same 40 melodic lines were repeated along with a set of 40 new melodic fragments. Half the participants rated their liking of each melodic line and half identified those that they had heard in the study phase. Prior exposure to melodies was found to increase liking, although many were also explicitly recognized. However, in another experiment, the researchers found that changes in timbre from study to test phase significantly reduced the ability of participants to recognize melodies in the study phase, but had little influence on their liking judgments. Because of this difference, the researchers concluded that liking and recognition judgments reflected two different forms of memory: The increases in liking that followed exposure reflected an *implicit memory* system, whereas the recognition of melodies reflected *explicit memory* for the melodies.

One explanation for the mere exposure effect is that we tend to prefer music that we can predict, and music that we have heard before is generally more predictable than music that we have not heard before. Huron (2006) has gone so far as to rename the phenomenon the *prediction effect*. According to Huron, whenever we accurately predict any event, a physiological reward state is generated from the limbic system. This connection between prediction and reward is thought to have evolved in animals to reinforce successful strategies of anticipation, which are useful for survival and, hence, adaptive. Thus, our preference for familiar music is, in effect, the result of a warm and fuzzy feeling that arises simply because we are able to predict events in that music. It is as though our brains are saying "well done for predicting these musical events" and then sending out a burst of pleasant neurochemicals as our reward. However, instead of attributing our positive feelings to this biological reward system, we misattribute them to the music itself. The result is that the music "sounds nice."

Thompson et al. (2000) reported some results that are consistent with this idea. They presented listeners with atonal melodies (target melodies) as they performed a counting task or a visual task. The latter tasks reduced the depth of processing of the melodies, making it difficult for listeners to remember them explicitly. In a subsequent task, listeners heard the same melodies, as well as novel melodies that were constructed similarly. For each melody, listeners rated the extent to which they expected the final note, on a scale ranging from 1 (*unexpected*) to 7 (*expected*). Ratings were higher for the melodies that were heard previously than for novel melodies, which illustrates that mere exposure to music affects melodic expectancy. Most notably, this effect could not be explained as explicit memory for the melodies. In other words, mere exposure to melodies led to implicit memory for those melodies in the form of melodic expectancies.

The results provide insight into how listeners internalize the music of their own culture, and how they learn to appreciate unconventional music. Repeated exposure to music composed in a consistent manner leads to the development of stable expectancies for typical melodic patterns. Eventually, the music becomes somewhat predictable and "makes sense" to the listener. The mere exposure effect is strikingly powerful. Quite simply, increased exposure to an unfamiliar song invariably leads to increased preference, as night follows day. Members of the music industry are well aware of the powerful effects of mere exposure, and the practice of payola reflects their understanding of this effect. *Payola* refers to the illegal practice of paying or otherwise inducing radio stations to broadcast a particular recording, and it proved to be an extremely effective way to generate interest in a song.

Implicit memory for music is highly robust, and can often be observed even following severe impairments to explicit memory following brain damage. In one study, Tillman, Peretz, Bigand, and Gosselin

(2007) played a number of eight-chord sequences to a patient with brain damage exhibiting severe problems in music perception, a condition known as *acquired amusia*. Some of the harmonic sequences ended with a harmonically related chord (related trials) and some ended with an unrelated chord (unrelated trials). The patient was tested on implicit and explicit forms of knowledge about harmonic structure. In the explicit task, she was asked to judge the degree of *completion* of each harmonic sequence. For most people, sequences ending on a harmonically related chord sound much more complete than sequences ending on a harmonically unrelated chord, which sound unresolved. For this patient, however, completion judgments did not differ between related and unrelated trials, indicating that she lacked explicit knowledge of harmony.

To create the implicit task, the researchers manipulated the harmonic sequences such that the last chord was played on either a piano or a harp. For each trial, the patient was instructed to indicate as quickly as possible whether the last chord was played with timbre A or B. If the patient had implicit knowledge of harmony, then she should be quicker at identifying the timbre of the last chord when that chord is harmonically related than when it is harmonically unrelated. This is precisely what the researchers observed. Even though the patient had no explicit ability to perceive harmonic structure, as reflected in her judgments of completion, her judgments of timbre revealed an implicit sensitivity to harmonic structure.

Implied Harmony

Even when a melody has no accompaniment, it can imply an underlying harmony. That is, the structure of the melody itself may strongly suggest an appropriate harmony that could accompany it. In some cases, the melody may include arpeggios or "broken chords" in which the defining chords' notes (doh, mi, sol) are explicitly included as part of the melody, as in "Greensleeves." In such cases, the harmonic implications are quite obvious because the chord progression is essentially provided explicitly as a simple progression of *arpeggios*. Cuddy, Cohen, and Mewhort (1981) examined the responses of individuals with high or moderate levels of musical training, and found that their perception of tonal structure and the ease with which they recognized melodies under transposition were

Sound Example 5.5

Sound example 5.5 is Jobim's "One Note Samba." This song is an interesting inversion of the concept of implied harmony because the "melody" is a single repeated note (hence the title). Without any contextual information, there is no implied harmony. Jobim takes advantage of the fact that the single note is not burdened with the baggage of implied harmony and sets the tone in a number of shifting and disparate harmonic contexts.

Sound example 5.5 is available via the *Music, Thought, and Feeling* iMix on iTunes.

greatly influenced by implied harmony. Melodies that clearly implied a harmonic progression through the use of arpeggios were assigned very high ratings of tonal structure and were well recognized under transposition. Melodies that conveyed an ambiguous or unclear harmonic structure were assigned lower ratings of structure and were less easily recognized.

Most melodies do not provide obvious harmonic cues, including melodies that sound very simple. For example, the first two notes of the tune "Three Blind Mice" imply different chords, even though the listener has virtually no information with which to adduce an appropriate harmonic accompaniment. For such melodies, harmonic implications are subtle and can only be determined by intuition and experience about which chords would sound pleasing and interesting at each point as the melody unfolds. Because any one note can blend with several possible chords, imagining the harmonic implications can require considerable skill and experience.

One challenge is that implied harmony does not merely involve imagining chords that blend well with each note; it involves simultaneously imagining a sequence of chords that make sense musically when combined with each other as a harmonic progression. Some musicians can juggle these two aesthetic goals, allowing them to "harmonize" to a melody even after hearing it for the first time. They seem to be able to imagine the chords that blend well with each note of the melody and that also make sense as a harmonic progression.

Unless harmonic implications are quite obvious, inexperienced listeners have considerable difficulty singing in harmony with a melody, or imagining what chords might provide a pleasant accompaniment. However, evidence suggests that most people have an implicit form of sensitivity to implied harmony, even if they are incapable of harmonizing to a melody or imagining potential harmonic accompaniments. This tacit understanding of implied harmony is subtly revealed in our impressions and evaluations of melodies. For example, changing a note in a melody seems more "noticeable" if that change is inconsistent with the implied harmony of the original melody than if it is consistent with the implied harmony (Holleran, Jones, & Butler, 1995). In another study, Thompson (1993) asked listeners to rate the extent to which short melodic phrases were musically "consistent" with harmonic sequences. Ratings were higher if the melodic phrase could be harmonized to give rise to the chord progression of the harmonic sequence than if it could not be so harmonized.

Although most listeners develop an implicit understanding of implied harmony even without formal training, the ability to sing or imagine a harmonic accompaniment to a melody is an acquired skill that can take considerable musical experience. Once the ability is acquired, the perception and memory for melodies will be partially informed by the implied harmony, providing an additional source of information about the structural properties of the melody. Novices who lack the ability to perceive an implied harmony must remember melodies by encoding surface features, such as melodic contour and pitch relations.

In an investigation of the role of musical training on sensitivity to implied harmony, Schubert and Stevens (2006) asked expert musicians and novices to rate the similarity between different melodies. Melodies were composed so that they differed from each other in contour, implied harmony, or both. Both groups used contour in their evaluation of melodic similarity, but only the musical experts used implied harmony. That is, the more experienced listeners seemed to adopt a more sophisticated strategy for representing melodies in memory, such that melodies were evaluated not only by surface features such as contour, but also by the deeper structural property of implied harmony.

Musical Key

The concept of a musical key is central to Western tonal music (e.g., Piston, 1941/1962) and its cognitive implications have been the subject of extensive empirical investigations (for a review, see Krumhansl, 1990). Two representations guide the perception of key. The first references relationships among tones within a key, whereas the second references relationships among keys. Through long-term exposure to Western tonal music, listeners acquire rich mental representations of these relationships.

The establishment of key begins when music contains a collection of tones (sometimes called pitch classes) that have hierarchically organized functions. The most familiar collection outlining a musical key is the major scale—doh-re-mi-fah-sol-la-ti. Within this collection, or scale, the first note doh is perceived to be the most stable pitch. It is called the tonal center or *tonic* and often occurs at points of stability, such as the end of a piece, or on metrically strong beats. Other pitches have subordinate levels of stability to the tonic; the next most stable pitch is the fifth note of the scale, sol, followed by the third note of the scale, mi, and then the remaining scale notes.

In equal temperament tuning, the collection is a subset of the set of tones obtained by dividing the octave, or frequency ratio 2:1, into 12 equal logarithmic steps. Adjacent steps form the interval called a semitone, and a succession of 12 semitones is called the chromatic scale. For the major scale, the successive steps are two, two, one, two, two, two, and one semitones. The tonic of a major scale may be any one of the 12 chromatic tones and successive steps of this interval pattern of semitones determine the remaining scale tones. Thus, each major scale consists of a subset of the tones of the chromatic scale. Tones that are not represented in a major scale are called nonscale or nondiatonic tones, and are perceived to be least stable in the hierarchy of tone functions. They may occur in music, but they are perceived to be unstable and their presence tends to generate a sense of musical tension and harmonic dissonance. Sometimes tension and dissonance are aesthetic goals. Music by modernist composers Igor Stravinsky and Arnold Schoenberg, free jazz musician Ornette Coleman, and art musician Marilyn Manson all use tension and dissonance for their own artistic purposes.

A similar hierarchical structure applies to the minor keys in the Western idiom. In particular, the tones of both major and minor keys are organized about the tonic, which acts as a focal tone or point of reference. The role of the tonic has been likened to that of a cognitive referent point or prototype. Prototypes are representative exemplars of a category. For example, in some geographical regions a robin is a prototypical bird and an apple is a prototypical fruit, whereas penguin and avocado are less prototypical of these categories. Prototypes have been studied in several areas of cognition because they appear to be given priority in processing and are relatively stable in memory (Krumhansl, 1990). In the same way, the tonic note may be perceived as the most representative (prototypic) element of the tonal structure of the music.

Listeners also appear to be sensitive to relationships among keys. Because each of the 12 chromatic tones may function as the tonic of a major or minor key, there are 24 possible keys. A traditional description of the relationships among keys is the circle of fifths shown in Figure 5.3. The figure shows the relationships among major keys; a similar cycle represents relationships among minor keys. The note names on the cycle, C, G, D, and so on, refer to the tonic notes of the 12 major keys. The number of steps on the cycle indicates the distance between keys. Thus, the key of C is most closely related (least distant) to the neighboring keys of G and F, one step clockwise and one step counterclockwise on the cycle, respectively. It is most distant from the key of F#, six steps around the cycle. Neighboring keys share all but one scale tone of their respective major scales; the number of tones shared between keys decreases as the distance in steps between keys increases.

Figure 5.3 also shows Roman numeral codes for selected key notes with respect to the key of C. The Roman numeral code is a traditional description of the position of the key note within the scale of C. Thus the code for G is V, meaning that G is the fifth note of the scale of C; the code for D is II, meaning that D is the second note of the scale of C, and so on. The code for F# is IV#; the note F# does not occur in the scale of C, so the code indicates that the key note is a semitone above the fourth note of the scale of C.

Krumhansl and Kessler (1982) produced an empirically derived spatial map of the relationships among all 24 major and minor keys. The mapping preserved the circle of fifths but also quantified the relation between major and minor keys. Derivation of the map involved an empirical strategy

Sound Example 5.6

An interactive display of the circle of fifths. Compare two different chords by clicking on each sequentially. Chords closer together on the circle (e.g., C[I] and G[V]) tend to complement each other, whereas chords on opposite ends of the circle (e.g., C[I] and F# [IV#]) tend to clash.

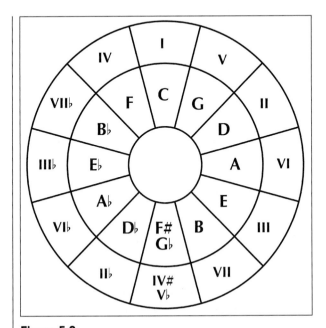

Figure 5.3
Circle of fifths.

called the probe-tone technique (Krumhansl & Shepard, 1979) adapted for use with a variety of musical contexts (Krumhansl & Kessler, 1982). The technique involved the presentation of a context followed by one of the 12 tones of the chromatic scale. The listener rated each probe tone for goodness of fit with the context. The set of 12 ratings, one for each probe tone, was called the probe-tone profile for that context.

For both major and minor keys, two types of context produced probe-tone profiles that were highly intercorrelated. These contexts were chords consisting of the first, third, and fifth tones of the scale, called tonic triads, and chord progressions. The profiles corresponded closely to the organization of the tonal hierarchy described by traditional music theory: The highest ratings were assigned to the tonic, the next highest were assigned to the other two notes of the tonic triad, the next highest to the remaining four notes of the scale, and the lowest ratings were assigned to the five nonscale notes. The profiles for the major-key contexts were averaged to form the standardized profile for the major key, and the profiles for the minor-key contexts were averaged to form the standardized profile for the minor key. These profiles are shown in Figure 5.4. The profiles illustrate the relative stability of tones for a given key, and they also provide a means for quantifying relationships between different keys. By calculating the simple correlation between the values associated with different key profiles, it is possible to quantify the theoretical distance between keys.

A number of studies attest to the psychological validity of key distance. One procedure concerns listeners' ability to discern whether an excerpt contains a single, unambiguously specified key or whether the excerpt contains movement from one key to another, called a key modulation. Thompson and Cuddy (1989, 1992; Cuddy & Thompson, 1992) demonstrated listeners' sensitivity to the direction and distance of modulation in excerpts from Bach chorales. Listeners were able to judge the direction and distance of modulations of zero, one, or two steps on the circle of fifths in both clockwise and counterclockwise directions. Thompson (1993) extended the procedure to the study of harmonized versions of melodies composed by Hindemith for modulations of zero, two, four, and six steps clockwise on the circle of fifths. Listeners' judgments of perceived key movement discriminated between nonmodulating and modulating sequences, and also showed some ability to discriminate differences in the distance of modulation for modulating sequences.

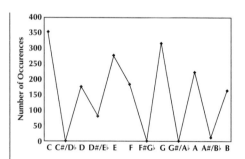

The frequency distribution of tones in Pachelbel's Canon in D (transposed to C major). It is almost identical to Krumhansl's tonal hierarchy for major keys, shown in Figure 5.4.

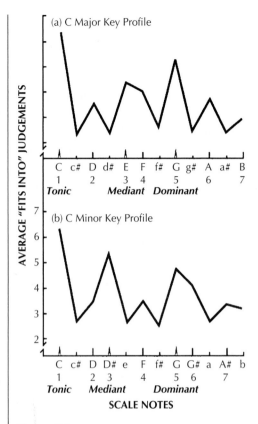

AVERAGE "FITS INTO" JUDGEMENTS

(a) C Major Key Profile

C c# D d# E F f# G g# A a# B
1   2   3 4   5   6   7
Tonic   Mediant Dominant

(b) C Minor Key Profile

C c# D D# e F f# G G# a A# b
1   2   3   4   5   6   7
Tonic   Mediant   Dominant

SCALE NOTES

Figure 5.4

The tonal hierarchy for C major (top) and C minor (bottom) scales
derived from probe tone experiments. The y-axes are the average ratings (on a scale from 1–7) of how well each probe tone "fits" with the
musical context. Diatonic notes are numbered 1 through 7. Notice that
in each case, the nondiatonic notes received the lowest ratings and that
the tonic (1), mediant (3), and dominant (5) received the highest ratings
among the diatonic notes.

Adapted from Krumhansl, C. L., and Kessler, E. J. (1982). Tracing the dynamic changes in
perceived tonal organization in a spatial representation of musical keys. *Psychological Review*,
89(4), 334–368.

Implied Key

Tonal melodies are those that suggest a musical key (C major, F minor,
etc.). Such melodies are characterized by a number of properties: (a) they
are mainly composed of scale notes, (b) tones that are stable in the key
(e.g., doh, mi, sol, fa) tend to be sounded for relatively long durations, and

(c) they often begin and end with the tonic (doh), or with another note from the tonic triad (mi or sol). Listeners rely on these types of regularities to derive the key for a particular melody.

The frequency distribution of tones in a melody and their relative durations are usually strongly and positively associated with the "tonal hierarchy" of the melody's key (Krumhansl, 1990). Krumhansl (1990, 2000) suggested that listeners match the accumulated durations of the notes they hear to mental representations of the tonal hierarchies for all possible keys. The tonal hierarchy with the strongest association is perceived as the key. Other theories have also been proposed (Auhagen & Vos, 2000; Vos, 2000). For example, listeners may rely on the presence of relatively rare intervals (e.g., the tritone) that that are associated with particular keys (Browne, 1981; Butler, 1989), or conduct relatively low-level acoustical analysis of the musical stimuli (Leman, 2000).

With music that contains simultaneously sounded notes, listeners readily derive a sense of key from isolated voices or from the harmonies that are created by combining those voices. Interestingly, the key implications in a harmonic progression (i.e., a sequence of chords) are somewhat independent of the tonal implications carried by the individual voices, which, in turn, may be somewhat different from each other (Thompson, 1993). For example, attending to a sequence of chords might suggest an abrupt change from one key to a psychologically distant key. By contrast, attending to an individual voice (e.g., the melody line) in the same polyphonic texture might suggest a smoother transition between more related keys. The use of timing and loudness in expressive performance can further influence perceived movement from one key to another (Thompson & Cuddy, 1997). These findings suggest that melodic features may implicate key and key movement somewhat independently of the harmony.

Sound Example 5.7

This example is "My Heart Will Go On" by Celine Dion. At 3:17 (the start of the lyric "You're here . . . "), there is an abrupt key change. It is highlighted by an intensification of the instrumental accompaniment as well as Dion's vocal style.

Sound example 5.7 is available via the *Music, Thought, and Feeling* iMix on iTunes.

Rhythm

Investigations of the perception and cognition of musical time include examinations of the limits of temporal discrimination, studies of temporal expectancies (e.g., when the next musical event will occur), and experiments that test listeners' experience of time in long musical passages. Most studies, however, focus on the perception of rhythm.

Rhythm perception is strongly influenced by the interonset interval (IOI), which is the time between the onset of one tone and the onset of the next tone.

Experiences of rhythm, like experiences of pitch, are partly shaped by our cognitive dispositions. For example, listeners perceive temporal organization most readily when IOIs fall within a limited range. If IOIs are much less than 100 msec (i.e., 10 notes per second), listeners tend to hear the sequence as one continuous event; if they are greater than 1,500 msec, listeners tend to hear a sequence of disconnected events. For temporal patterns involving IOIs between 100 and 1,500 msec, listeners tend to perceive rhythmic patterns of up to 5 seconds in duration, which is the approximate limit of auditory sensory memory (Darwin, Turvey, & Crowder, 1972). Thus, cognitive dispositions limit the range of IOIs within rhythmic patterns as well as the duration of rhythmic patterns.

METER AND GROUPING

Lerdahl and Jackendoff (1983) made a useful distinction between meter and grouping, which can be viewed as distinct aspects of rhythm. *Meter* refers to regular cycles of strong and weak accents. Listeners are highly sensitive to meter, and associate strong accents with phrase boundaries.

Sound Examples 5.8.1–5.8.2

Sound example 5.8.1 is an example of a regular four-beat cycle with an accented first tone (i.e., strong–weak–weak–weak).

In **Sound example 5.8.2** the accent pattern has been scrambled. Although you could probably reproduce the first example after one or two listenings, the second example would probably require many more listenings.

Figure 5.5

An illustration of the difference between grouping and meter for the first lines of "Love Me Tender" and "Amazing Grace." The braces above each stave indicate groupings and the vertical bar lines divide the music into equal metrical units.

Grouping Versus Meter

The "boundary lines" for meter are a regular cycle of strong and weak accents. With grouping, on the other hand, boundary lines are sometimes defined by more subjective criteria such as pauses, pitch proximity, temporal proximity, and breath (e.g., at what points do you feel the need to take breaths when singing "Happy Birthday"?). As a result, grouping does not necessarily coincide with meter.

Figure 5.5 illustrates a possible grouping of the first part of "Love Me Tender" by Elvis Presley. In the musical notation, the vertical lines (bar lines) divide the music into equal metrical units. Notice that the beginnings of metrical units and groupings coincide.

Figure 5.5 also shows a possible grouping for "Amazing Grace." It does not "fit" into the bar lines. Try singing or humming each individual bar in isolation. It is difficult to conceive of any type of intuitive grouping that coincides with the bar lines. "Ma-zing" and "grace, how" do not group well together lyrically or musically.

Sound Examples 5.9.1–5.9.3

Sound example 5.9.1 is an example of binary meter. A binary cycle can refer to a two-beat meter or a multiple of two (most commonly four). The distiction between a two-beat binary meter and a four-beat binary meter can sometimes be subjectively based on what one considers to be the *tactus*. "London Calling" by the Clash is an unequivocal example of a four-beat meter. The guitarist strums four times on one chord and then four times on another chord; the chord progression is then repeated.

Sound example 5.9.2 is an example of ternary meter—Strauss's "Blue Danube Waltz." The three-beat pattern can most easily be heard in the "oom-pah-pah (i.e., 1–2–3) figure in the orchestral accompaniment.

Sound example 5.9.3—"Take Five" by the Dave Brubeck Quartet—is an example of a five-beat meter. Five-beat meters are far less common than binary and ternary meters. The five-beat pattern is most noticeable in the repeated piano vamp.

Sound examples 5.9.1–5.9.3 are available via the *Music, Thought, and Feeling* iMix on iTunes.

Accent strength is determined by changes in intensity, note density, and music structure (e.g., pitch contour, tonality). Listeners show a bias to hear metrical interpretations (alternations of strong and weak beats) as binary, even when sequences are ternary (Vos, 1978). More generally, small integer ratios of durations (e.g., sequences that contain only quarter notes and eighth notes) are easier to process than more complex rhythms. Meter is hierarchically organized, with cycles at one level (e.g., groups of two beats) nested within cycles at higher levels (e.g., groups of four beats). Listeners tend to perceive one level of the metric hierarchy as more salient than others. Some models of meter identify this level as the *tactus*, or the level at which it is most natural to tap one's foot.

Metrical patterns are recognized and reproduced more accurately than nonmetrical patterns (e.g., Bharucha & Pryor, 1986; Essens, 1995). Moreover, perceptual asymmetries, similar to those noted earlier for pitch, are evident for rhythm. When listeners are asked to discriminate two patterns—one metrical and one nonmetrical—performance is better when the metrical pattern is presented first and the nonmetrical pattern second, compared to when the identical patterns are presented in the reverse order (Bharucha & Pryor, 1986). This response pattern implies that metrical frameworks facilitate the efficiency with which auditory temporal patterns are processed and represented. It is relatively easy to detect alterations to metrical patterns because they have relatively stable representations. Metrical patterns also place less demand on attentional resources compared to nonmetrical patterns, because they provide a frame of reference within which rhythmic structure can be processed and represented (Keller, 1999).

Grouping refers to perceived associations between events. As with metrical structure, temporal grouping structure is hierarchically organized, with small groups of two or three notes nested within larger groups, such as phrases. At the highest level of the hierarchy are groups corresponding to sections and movements of music. Empirical studies generally support the psychological reality of grouping structure in music (Deliege, 1987). The grouping mechanisms associated with music perception appear to be general cognitive mechanisms that may be implicated in the processing of speech and other auditory stimuli (Patel, Peretz, Tramo, & Labreque, 1998).

Although both meter and grouping are hierarchically structured, they need not coincide with each other. Rhythm is defined as the interaction between meter and grouping. Remarkably, there is little psychological work on this interaction; instead, researchers have examined these aspects of rhythm separately. Empirical studies have confirmed that listeners are sensitive to both metrical and grouping structure.

PULSE

One issue examined in studies of rhythm is the concept of the musical *pulse*, which is related to meter and can be measured in cycles per minute. Fraisse (1982) noted that three distinct temporal phenomena (walking pace, heart rate, and sucking rate in newborns) tend to have a rate of between 60 and 120 events per minute, a range that also includes the tempi of most pieces of music. The implication is that music may be linked to physiological motion. This link is manifested explicitly when listeners dance or tap to music. Early evidence for the link was provided by Gabrielsson (1973a, 1973b), who reported that judgments of the similarity between rhythmic patterns are strongly affected by a perceptual dimension related to movement. Other support for a link between music and physiological motion was provided by Kronman and Sundberg (1987), who showed that *ritardandi* in music have a close correspondence with deceleration when walking or running.

Several models of rhythm have been proposed, each designed to capture a particular aspect of rhythm perception. Some existing models consider only temporal cues to meter, such as onset times and durations, ignoring influences of pitch, phrasing, and harmony on the perception of rhythm. Parncutt's (1994) model assumes cognitive biases for certain

Sound Examples 5.10.1–5.10.3

Pulses for walking pace, heart rate, and sucking rate in newborns. Fraisse (1982) noted that these temporal phenomena tend to have a repetition rate of between 60 and 120 beats per minute, a range that includes most pieces of music.

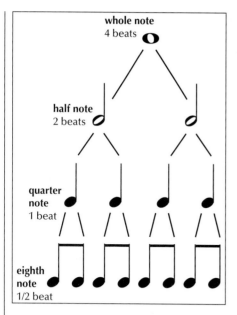

The standard Western notational system illustrates the hierarchical organization of meter. The quarter note (one beat) is often the *tactus*.

metrical experiences. In particular, certain levels in the metrical hierarchy are assumed to be more salient than others, with a bias toward the metrical level that approximates the *tactus*.

Another question concerns the kinds of neural units that might be involved in tracking the meter of complex music. It seems natural to tap our feet or clap to music. What brain mechanism allows us to synchronize our movements with the musical meter? In Large and Jones's (1999) model, meter is tracked using a small set of oscillatory neural units (neurons that fire repeatedly at a regular rate) that vary from each other in their natural resonance. Because the oscillators are able to adjust their phase and period to external periodicities, units with natural resonances closest to existing periodicities lock on and track the tempo. Related to this issue is the question of how simple patterns (i.e., small integer ratios of duration) are represented in memory when the durations and periodicities of actual performances are highly variable. To account for this *quantization problem*, Desain's (1992) connectionist model assumes that rhythmic experiences are biased toward temporal patterns defined by small integer ratios.

INTERACTIONS BETWEEN RHYTHM AND PITCH

Some researchers have examined the extent to which rhythm and pitch interact in perception and memory. This question may be relevant to music educators because pitch and rhythmic skills are often assessed separately in traditional pedagogical exercises, implying distinct cognitive mechanisms for processing these dimensions. Music theory also suggests a separation between rhythm and pitch. For example, one of the most widely used techniques for analyzing tonal music—developed by the German musicologist Heinrich Schenker (1954)—assumes that surface temporal relations operate independently of pitch structure.

Results on this issue suggest that pitch and rhythm interact at some levels of processing, but operate independently at other levels. Jones, Boltz, and Kidd (1982) reported that rhythmically accented pitches in a melody are better recognized than unaccented pitches. Similarly, if pitch and loudness patterns suggest conflicting meters, memory for melodic sequences is generally poor (Boltz & Jones, 1986;

Deutsch, 1980). Such findings imply that pitch and rhythm are integrated in memory for music. Additional evidence for the nonindependence of pitch and rhythm processing comes from a study that required listeners to rate the emotionality (i.e., happiness, sadness, scariness) of melodies (Schellenberg, Krysciak, & Campbell, 2000). The melodies' pitch and rhythmic properties proved to be interactive in their influence on listeners' ratings.

Other researchers contend, however, that pitch and rhythm are processed independently. In some experiments, pitch and rhythm have made statistically independent contributions to judgments of melodic similarity (Monahan & Carterette, 1985), and to ratings of phrase completion (Palmer & Krumhansl, 1987a, 1987b). Moreover, memory for the pitch and rhythm patterns of a short melody is far better than memory for how those features are combined. Thompson (1994) presented listeners with two test melodies followed by two comparison melodies. The task was to indicate if the two comparison melodies were identical to the two test melodies, disregarding the order in which the melodies occurred. In one condition, participants performed a distracter task as the melodies were presented. In another condition, participants listened attentively to the melodies. When the comparison melodies involved a novel pitch pattern or a rhythm that was not present in the test melodies, performance was highly accurate for participants in both conditions. When the comparison melodies were constructed by combining the pitch pattern of one test melody with the rhythm of the other test melody (or vice versa), however, distracted participants performed poorly. That is, distracted participants were relatively insensitive to the manner in which pitch and rhythm were combined.

Neuropsychological studies provide further evidence that pitch and rhythm are processed separately. Whereas some patients with brain damage exhibit normal pitch perception but impaired rhythm perception, other patients show the opposite pattern. One patient who sustained a lesion in the left temporal lobe was unable to discriminate between sequences differing in temporal structure, but he had no difficulty discriminating between sequences differing in pitch structure. By contrast, another patient with damage to the right temporal lobe showed the opposite pattern of discrimination skills. Such impairments suggest that some areas of the brain are responsible for processing pitch, whereas other neuronally distinct areas are responsible for processing rhythm (Peretz, 1996; Peretz & Kolinsky, 1993; Peretz & Morais, 1989).

Sound Examples 5.11.1–5.11.3
A ritardando is a gradual slowing down of musical tempo. It occurs most frequently at the end of a piece of music, but it may also occur at the end of any musical phrase, and can even occur within a phrase. **Sound example 5.11.1** is a phrase played without a ritardando, and **Sound example 5.11.2** is the same phrase played with a ritardando at the end. Kronman and Sundberg's (1987) study found a correlation between ritardandos and deceleration from running, suggesting a link between music and physiological motion. For comparison, **Sound example 5.11.3** is the sound of a running person coming to a stop.

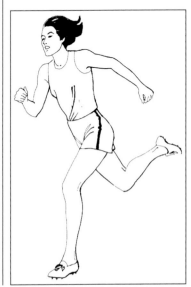

RHYTHM IN MUSIC AND SPEECH

Recent evidence suggests that rhythmic qualities of speech, which are often distinguishing characteristics of different languages, exert a "gravitational pull" on rhythmic qualities of music (Patel & Daniele, 2003; Patel, Iverson, & Rosenberg, 2004). Analyzing melodic themes from the turn of the 20th century, Patel and his colleagues made two observations. First, adjacent notes in English melodies are characterized by a greater degree of durational contrast than adjacent notes in French melodies. Second, adjacent intervals in English melodies are characterized by a greater degree of intervallic difference than adjacent intervals in French melodies. The authors argued that these rhythmic qualities in melodies arise from composers' familiarity with the rhythmic qualities of their language. As evidence for their claim, they showed that adjacent vowels in English sentences tend to differ more in duration than do adjacent vowels in French sentences, and consecutive pitch movements between syllables in English sentences tend to differ more from each other than do consecutive pitch movements between adjacent syllables in French sentences. Thus, just as melody and speech prosody use contour in similar ways, the two domains are connected by these subtle rhythmic properties. As persuasively argued by Patel (2008), these sources of overlap between music and language have profound implications for theories of musical origins, studies of brain function, and effects of music training. Indeed, progress in understanding these links will eventually shape the way that we conceptualize and define music itself.

Additional Readings

Cross, I. (1997). Pitch schemata. In I. Deliège & J. Sloboda (Eds.), *Perception and cognition of music* (pp. 353–386). Hove, UK: Psychology Press.

Krumhansl, C. L. (2000). Rhythm and pitch in music cognition. *Psychological Bulletin, 126*, 159–179.

CHAPTER 6
Music and Emotion

LEARNING OUTCOMES

By the end of this chapter you should be able to:

1. Summarize and appraise the major theories of the link between music and emotion.

2. Explain why psychological studies of music have traditionally focused on perceptual and cognitive processes.

3. Design an empirical study to assess how attributes of music communicate and induce different emotions.

4. Summarize theory and data supporting cognitivist and emotivist views on music and emotion.

5. Describe and contrast compositional and expressive cues to emotional meaning.

6. Identify five categories of expectancy responses and outline their relevance to music experience.

Emotion Work

On the Polynesian island of Futuna, the Tuamotus people use music to stimulate and express emotion in both performers and listeners. Their music includes laments that express grief, love songs that express longing and passion, and creation chants that express religious exaltation. When the Basongye people of the Congo are asked why they make music, the reason most emphasized is that they make music out of happiness, or to induce feelings of joy. The musician always experiences joy because the act of performance necessarily implicates that emotion, but they also believe that music can induce a range of other emotions in nonperforming listeners. A funeral song may induce great sadness in listeners even when it is played outside of that context. In Hindustani music of India, tones are organized into ragas, which are analogous to the modes of Western music (e.g., major, minor). Each raga may be represented with divine or human beings, placed in settings that reflect the moods that the raga is intended to evoke (Merriam, 1964).

In music therapy, sounds and music are used to support and encourage physical, mental, social, and emotional well-being (Bunt & Pavlicevic, 2001). In this type of therapy, music is sometimes used in a way that allows clients to gain insight into their own emotions. This insight, in turn, contributes to a stronger sense of self. For example, a depressed patient might experience the world as slow and dark. A music therapist might improvise music together with such a patient to stabilize and accelerate his or her sense of pulse, while expanding the range of emotions conveyed in the music so that the patient can gain better access to the complex feelings underlying the depression.

Music, it appears, is a powerful tool for *emotion work*. This was the simple conclusion of British sociologist Tia DeNora (2001), who conducted a landmark study of the uses of music by individuals from a range of backgrounds and subcultures. She observed that British women, for example, primarily use music in their everyday lives to regulate, enhance, and alter their emotional states. For these women, music is an effective device for conducting the emotional work that is required to maintain desired states of feeling and bodily energy (relaxation, excitement), or to diminish undesirable emotional states (e.g., stress, fatigue).

In spite of the extraordinary capacity of music to influence the emotional states of people, psychological studies of music have traditionally focused on perceptual and cognitive processes. One reason for this

Sound Example 6.1

The *Basongye* people of the Congo do not have a word for music per se. Instead they associate concepts like noise and music with states of mind through statements such as, "When you are content, you sing; when you are angry, you make noise. A song is tranquil; a noise is not. When one shouts he is not thinking; when one sings, he is thinking." (Merriam 1964, pp. 64–66).

Sound example 6.1 is music from the Luba of the Congo. It is being played upon return from the chief's funeral.

Source: © RMCA Tervuren (Belgium), 2008.

emphasis is that there are established and effective techniques for studying perception and cognition. Researchers may also believe that perceptual and cognitive processes are potentially universal, whereas emotional responses to music may be more subjective, or at least largely determined by social and cultural norms. Nonetheless, there is an emerging body of research suggesting a complex interaction among music, emotion, and cognition. The origins of the link between music and emotion remain unclear, but there now exist a number of promising theories.

Many theorists distinguish between basic and secondary emotions. *Basic emotions* are those that have evolved to cope with fundamental issues of survival, whereas *secondary emotions* are socially constructed and culturally dependent. There is disagreement as to which emotions are basic and which are secondary, but suggestions for basic emotions frequently include happiness, sadness, anger, and fear. Typically, emotions are considered basic if they fulfill a set of criteria; for example, if they have distinct functions that contribute to survival, if they are found in all human cultures, and if they have distinct emotional (facial) expressions (Ekman, 1992a, 1992b).

Emotion and Cognition

Before outlining specific theories of music and emotion, it is useful to consider how emotions relate to cognitive processes, such as reasoning, planning, and remembering. For the past several decades, cognition has been conceptualized within what is called the information-processing paradigm. This approach uses the computer as a metaphor for understanding perception, thought, and behavior. Visual, auditory, and other sensory stimuli are conceived as input to the system. This sensory input is then subjected to various mental processes in which critical features are extracted, transformed, classified, and interpreted. Finally, these processes lead to some mental state or physical act, described as output. How do emotions fit within this framework? Are emotions part and parcel of all cognition, or do they operate in a distinct mental system that is separate from "cold" cognition, and that underlies our emotional intelligence (Goleman, 1995)?

One view is that emotional responses depend on prior cognitive processing (Lazarus, 1982). That is, emotional responses, such as feelings of sadness or pleasure, may be the outcome of a series of cognitive processes in which features are coded, classified, and finally evaluated and appraised. According to this postcognitive conception of emotion, there is a causal chain that begins with an event, leading to an interpretation of that event, and finally to an appraisal or evaluation. The interpretation of an event is a cognitive act, whereas the appraisal or evaluation is the point at which emotion arises (see Lyons, 1980; Zajonc, 1980).

A second possibility is that emotional responses occur prior to, or independently of, cognitive processing (Zajonc, 1980). Early theorists proposed an extreme form of this view, suggesting that emotional responses correspond to activity in the peripheral (autonomic) nervous system. William James (1890) suggested that feelings of emotion are no more than the feelings associated with a physiological or behavioral state (e.g., the release of adrenaline, bodily trembling). Seeing a snake might evoke a release of adrenaline, and the sensations associated with this physiological state correspond to the feeling of fear. This view has been criticized on the basis that autonomic responses lack the specificity to define the emotion. That is, although physiological states are certainly associated with emotions, the specific emotion experienced may be determined by a cognitive evaluation of that physiological state.

Research on implicit memory suggests that preferences do not always depend on cognitive processing. Zajonc (1980, 1984) reviewed numerous experiments in which repeated exposure to stimulus patterns (e.g., novel melodies, random dot patterns) significantly influenced judgments of those patterns, even though participants had no explicit recall for the patterns to which they had been exposed. The full implications of this mere exposure effect are still being examined, but these studies certainly do demonstrate the power of experience in shaping our preferences: Even experiences that escape conscious awareness appear to influence our preferences and desires.

Neuropsychological evidence also supports an apparent dissociation between recognition and emotion. Peretz and Gagnon (1999) described a woman with right and left temporal lobe lesions who was unable to recognize familiar melodies (i.e., she suffered from a condition known as amusia), but could nonetheless discriminate music on the basis of the emotion that was conveyed. Neurologists believe that the amygdala (part of the limbic system) is an important brain structure associated with emotional responses. If the amygdala is severed from the rest of the brain, there is a specific inability to determine the emotional significance of events, a condition known as affective

Emotion and Recognition

Individuals with amusia often have impaired music perception but spared sensitivity to emotion in music. Such cases illustrate a dissociation between emotion and recognition. Is there evidence for a converse dissociation? Although there is only weak evidence to date, Temple Grandin, a high-functioning autistic, has written and spoken about her experiences as an autistic. She possesses perfect pitch and an excellent memory for melody (traits not uncommon in autistics), but admits that music does not move her. She finds Bach inventions "ingenious" but they evoke nothing deep in her (Sacks, 2007, p. 290).

blindness. Other brain structures, including cortical areas, also have been implicated in emotional responses. No one brain structure underlies all emotions. Rather, different emotional states appear to be associated with separate subsystems in the brain (J. A. Grey, 1990).

Goleman's (1995) influential book *Emotional Intelligence* also implies a clear distinction between the skills required to process emotions and those involved in other aspects of cognition. Goleman argued that there are two distinct minds: a rational mind and an emotional mind. One may know something from a rational perspective, but react differently on an emotional level. This is the difference between heart and head.

A third perspective is that emotions are highly integrated with cognitive processing from a very early stage. Damasio (1994) presented this hypothesis in his landmark book on emotion and reason. Central to Damasio's theory is the concept of a somatic marker. *Somatic markers* are affective tags that are attached to sensory images, "marking" each image with an emotional association. A dog lover may associate the image of a dog with love; others may associate that same image with fear. Damasio believes that through experience, emotions and feelings become strongly associated with certain images, including those images associated with possible outcomes of a given situation. Somatic markers may function to bias further cognitive processing of stimuli in a way that is maximally adaptive. When planning for the future, a person may reject certain courses of action if the images associated with those actions are tagged with negative emotions. In effect, somatic markers reduce the number of options under consideration, increasing the efficiency of the decision-making process.

Damasio's hypothesis underscores the possible adaptive function of emotion. Human beings are products of biological evolution, and it is reasonable to understand emotions from this perspective. According to this functionalist approach, emotions function to prepare us for biologically significant events (e.g., threatening situations, feeding and mating opportunities, etc.). In support of this idea, researchers have found that emotions may lead to a "narrowing" of attention, whereby attention is focused on critical aspects of the event, and the peripheral aspects of the event are largely ignored (Easterbrook, 1959). This narrowing of attention has been used to explain the phenomenon of "weapon focus" in eyewitness memory: When witnesses to a violent crime try to recall the event, they often remember the gun or knife vividly, but have little recollection of much else.

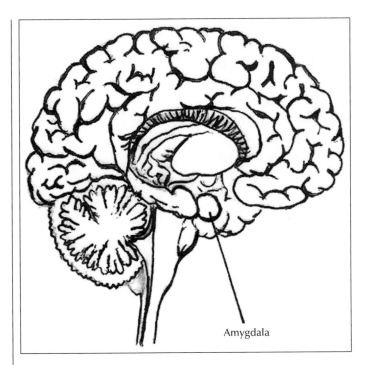

Amygdala

The amygdala is part of the limbic system and is an important brain structure associated with emotion. The limbic system is one of the oldest parts of the human brain. Many of its features can be seen in reptiles, amphibians, and other mammals. The mediation of basic emotions of fear and pleasure by structures such as the amygdala is crucial to the survival of many species, not just humans.

At first glance, there appears to be considerable confusion in the field about whether cognitive processes are involved in the connection between music and emotion. However, these contrasting perspectives can be reconciled by assuming that there are several mechanisms involved in the connection between music and emotion—some that operate automatically and without conscious awareness and others that involve a cognitive component. Changes in basic acoustic attributes such as loudness, tempo, and pitch height can give rise to dramatic changes in arousal (and hence, emotional experience) because they are potential signals of biologically significant events. Such responses are rapid, automatic, and can occur in prenatal infants. They may arise from the brain stem and bypass cognitive processing. However, there are also a number of mechanisms by which music signals emotion concurrently with or following cognitive activity. First, a highly unexpected event in music can lead to a combination of surprise (heightened arousal) and cognitive appraisal of that unexpected event. Second, music can remind us of a significant episode in our life, such as a family celebration, and this memory may lead to an emotional experience. Third, music can give rise to visual imagery that is perceived to be emotional. In short, several mechanisms are implicated in emotional experiences to music, and a number of them involve a cognitive component.

Theories of Music and Emotion

It is often observed that sound has a unique power to arouse intense feelings. Philosopher John Dewey (1934), one of the founders of functional psychology, argues the case convincingly:

> Sounds come from outside the body, but sound itself is near, intimate; it is an excitation of the organism; we feel the class of vibrations throughout the whole body....A foot-fall, the breaking of a twig, the rustling of underbrush may signify attack or even death from hostile animal or man....Vision arouses emotion in the form of interest....It is sound that makes us jump. (p. 237)

Thus, objects that we see appear wholly outside our head, detached from our sense of self. Sounds are more intimate, more "inside" our heads. It may be argued that music is the most powerful instantiation of this unique aspect of sound. What, precisely, are the properties of music associated with emotional responses, and what is the basis for this connection? Can we identify specific features of music associated with emotional messages?

MELODIC CUES

According to Cooke's (1959) influential theory the answer is yes. Cooke argued, among other things, that different melodic intervals and patterns have their own distinctive emotional quality, and that composers draw on these intervals and patterns carefully in their compositions, so as to capture precisely the nuances of emotion that they would like to express. This theoretical position implies that music is a kind of language of emotion, with its components and patterns representing different feelings or emotions.

Melodic Intervals

INTERVAL	FAMOUS SONG	COOKE'S EMOTIONAL ASSOCIATION
Major third	"Doe a Deer" (the leap from "-male" to "deer" in "a female deer")	Joy, triumph
Major sixth	"My Bonny" (the leap from "my" to "bon-")	Longing for pleasure
Augmented fourth (tritone)	"Simpsons Theme" (the leap from "The" to "Sim-")	Hostility, disruption

Intervals can occur either *melodically* (i.e., the two tones are sounded separately) or *harmonically* (i.e., the two tones are sounded simultaneously). When presented melodically, an interval can be presented in an ascending form (lower to higher pitch) or descending form (higher to lower pitch). Music students often train to be able to recognize a particular melodic interval by associating the interval with a famous song in which it is represented (usually as the first two tones in an ascending sequence). Here are some examples along with Cooke's emotional associations.

For Cooke, an ascending major third (doh–mi) suggests joy or triumph, an ascending major sixth (doh–la) suggests a longing for pleasure, the minor sixth suggests anguish, and the augmented fourth (the tritone, historically known as *diabolus in musica*) suggests hostility and disruption. Some intervals, such as the major second, are less suggestive because they function differently in different contexts. In addition, the precise emotional quality of any melodic interval depends on the scale degree of the initial note, the rhythmic placement of the interval, whether the movement is ascending or descending, and loudness.

To support his thesis, Cooke provided examples from various periods of music. Many of the musical examples have vocal accompaniment, and the words provide corroborating evidence for the adjectives he connects with each interval or pattern. Cooke pointed out that composers have switched between the minor and major intervals throughout musical history, as a way of suggesting a switch from painful to pleasurable feelings, or vice versa. Cooke proposed that these associations between musical intervals and emotions are not merely a language for Western tonal music, but are universal. In his discussion of the major triad, he argued that:

> [S]uch diverse bodies as the medieval ecclesiastics, the seventeenth- and eighteenth-century aristocrats, the nineteenth-century

late romantic composers, the contemporary avant-garde composers, the modern masses, the average concert-going public, and the official Soviet musical theorists…all concur in the principle of equating the major triad with pleasure. (Cooke 1959, p. 55)

If these associations are indeed natural, then what cognitive and perceptual mechanisms might explain them? Cooke provided no clear answer, but hinted that the emotional qualities of melodic intervals and patterns may arise through a combination of factors, including the degree of consonance and dissonance, interval size, and direction of motion.

Ancient Greeks on Music

The ancient Greek philosophers were aware of music's ability to conjure up emotions and wrote extensively on the subject. In *The Politics*, Aristotle suggests that different modes (scales), rhythms, and instruments produce different emotional effects. For example, music in the Dorian mode (from D to D on the white notes of a piano) produces a "moderate and settled temper," whereas the Phrygian mode (from E to E on the white notes of a piano) is "exciting" and suitable for "Bacchic frenzy."

Not surprisingly, while Aristotle advocated music education in an ideal democratic state, he considered Dorian music to be most appropriate for youth. He also felt that music should be taught in moderation, to discourage youth from considering taking up music professionally. Aristotle considered receiving pay for the manipulation of spectators' emotions (and even bodily movements) through music making to be a vulgar profession.

Cooke also addressed a possible criticism of his theory: If the emotional associations with particular intervals and melodic patterns are universal, then what can explain the diversity of musical styles in different cultures? His answer to this question is that each culture expresses its vitality in different ways. The "fierce minor liveliness of some of the folk music of the Spanish" is thought to reflect a cultural style or attitude. Following this logic, Cooke speculated that the influence of Western ideology on other cultures may explain certain changes in the musical styles found in those cultures:

> [W]herever Western European civilization has penetrated another culture, and set the people's thought along the road to material happiness, the [happy] tonal music of Western Europe has begun to oust the [sad] music of that culture.…This is quite definitely going on at present in India…in a recent improvisation on a raga, by one of India's leading sitar players, the normal "bare fifth" drone bass of this purely indigenous music had taken unto itself a major third. (Cooke, 1959, p. 55)

Such claims are questionable and perhaps ethnocentric, but Cooke has undoubtedly made a valuable contribution to the study of emotion and music by demonstrating that certain melodic intervals and patterns are used to convey similar emotional qualities across a wide range of styles and periods. The cognitive or psychological basis for such associations, however, remains unclear. Sloboda (1985) speculated that such associations may have developed by convention, and may have no natural basis in perceptual or cognitive mechanisms. That is, composers might associate the major third with joy simply because other composers have done so in the past, and listeners have learned those associations through repeated exposure to music.

It is important to note that Cooke's theory makes for testable predictions. To date, there is ample evidence that listeners consistently judge major thirds as more "joyful" than minor thirds (e.g., Crowder, 1984; Kastner & Crowder, 1990), but empirical tests of Cooke's more specific list of associations have provided no clear support for the theory as yet (Gabriel, 1978).

CONTOUR AND CONVENTION

Kivy (1980) proposed a related theory of emotion and music. He also argued that music has the power to be expressive of specific emotions, such as joy, sadness, and anger, but he did not restrict his discussion to musical intervals. Rather, various features of music, such as tempo, mode, and melodic patterns, display a "structural resemblance" with features of human behavior that are expressive of these emotions.

Kivy conceived the connection between music and emotions in terms of two basic categories: contour and convention. Contour refers to the "natural" connections between music and emotion. For example, a slow tempo naturally conveys sadness, because it has a structural resemblance with the slowness that we might expect in the labored gait of a sad individual.

Conventional connections between music and emotion are those for which no obvious natural connection is evident, although Kivy speculated that all conventions might ultimately evolve from natural connections. Convention is defined as "the customary association of certain musical features with certain emotive ones" (Kivy, 1980, p. 77). For example, a *plagal cadence* is associated, by convention alone, with religious ritual.

The distinction between contour and convention becomes somewhat confusing, however, when one considers other examples. For Kivy, the minor mode expresses sadness by convention, and a falling semitone has a natural connection to the emotion of a sigh (because of its acoustic resemblance). Such examples are questionable. One could equally argue that the minor mode is naturally sad because of the degree of dissonance it permits, in comparison to the major mode. Moreover, it is unclear that a sigh is naturally related to a falling half-step, as opposed to a falling third or a falling fourth.

On the other hand, it is evident that certain connections between music and emotion seem more naturally determined (and less culture-specific) than others. Contour and convention may prove to be useful concepts, but are perhaps better conceived as two endpoints of a continuum, rather than a dichotomy.

MORPHOLOGY OF FEELING

Both Cooke and Kivy believed that music can represent specific emotions. Another important theorist, Langer (1957), rejected this possibility, proposing that music is only capable of representing an undifferentiated quality of emotion, and has no specific vocabulary linking musical patterns to individual emotions. Instead, she suggested, music represents emotion in general by reflecting the "morphology of feeling." That is, there is a natural resemblance between musical patterns and the kinds

Sound Example 6.2

Sound example 6.2 is an excerpt from "When It Hurts So Bad" by Lauryn Hill (1998).

We do not like to experience negative emotions such as sadness in our daily lives, so why do we like to listen to music that expresses these emotions? In fact, songs like Lauryn Hill's, and the entire genre of the blues, go as far as to revel in negative emotions. Why?

Peter Kivy's *contour theory* presents an interesting perspective. In Kivy's view, music is emotional by virtue of resemblances between its dynamic structure (patterns of tensions and relaxation, crescendos, melodic motion, etc.) and the behaviors, movements, gaits, and comportments associated with human emotions. Sad music, like Shakespeare's tragedies, may be appreciated for its artful construction and for its ability to illuminate an emotion that is an essential part of being human. We can examine and appreciate the sadness conveyed in music while being reassured that there are no actual consequences to face.

Sound example 6.2 is available via the *Music, Thought, and Feeling* iMix on iTunes.

of affective changes that we typically experience. Music is thought to be congruent with the dynamic patterns of emotion, such that the former suggests the latter. Dynamic patterns of emotion include motion and rest, tension and release, agreement and disagreement, preparation, fulfillment, excitation, sudden change, and so on. Such patterns are also found in music.

Note that Langer's theory is consistent with the view that music is naturally meaningful. That is, music does not reference emotion merely through arbitrary signs in a culture-specific manner as in the way that words refer to objects (e.g., the word mouse is an arbitrary sign for an actual mouse; it bears no resemblance with the mammal). Rather, music acquires meaning through its natural resemblance to the dynamic forms of emotional life.

Langer's reliance on resemblance exemplifies a kind of picture theory of meaning: If two objects or events formally resemble each other, then they stand in a symbolic and semantic relationship to each other. Kivy's concept of contour reflects a similar view. Resemblance alone, however, is not a sufficient condition for expressiveness. If it were, then music could be said to represent any number of events that it clearly does not: the rise and fall of a local housing market, changes in the direction and speed of a football in flight, the acceleration and deceleration of cars in a traffic jam, and so on. Music may resemble many kinds of dynamic patterns in the world, but people tend to hear music as being expressive of emotions. The reason for this tendency is not well understood.

On the other hand, Langer's thesis is intuitively compelling. We have all experienced the gradual growth of hope and excitement, followed by disappointment or relief. There is something distinctive and recognizable about the temporal unfolding of our emotional life. It is this dynamic pattern of changing feelings to which Langer refers. Musical forms signify shifting emotions, rather than individual emotions. For this reason, Langer maintains that music does not represent individual emotions, but references a more abstract understanding of our emotional life. Music is expressive in a nonspecific, inherently ambiguous sense.

EMBODIED MEANING

The preceding theories suggest that music refers to emotions by representing their form. Meyer (1956) presented an alternative view. He began by pointing out that anything acquires meaning if it is connected with,

Sound Examples 6.3.1–6.3.2

Sound example 6.3.1 is an excerpt from Mozart's "Minuet in F major" K. 4, written at the age of 6. Mozart deviates from expectations through the use of an *appoggiatura*—at the end of the phrase, the upper note forms a dissonance with the underlying harmony; it then resolves to a consonance by shifting upward to the tonic. The arousal generated by this deviation from expectation may form the basis of our emotional response to music.

For comparison, the same phrase is played without the appogiatura in **Sound example 6.3.2**. This example conforms to expectancies and is unlikely to generate a strong arousal response.

or refers to, something beyond itself. He then distinguished between two types of meaning: designated and embodied. Designated meaning occurs when the symbol or stimulus and the referent are different in kind, as when a word refers to a nonverbal object or event. Embodied meaning occurs when the symbol and the referent are the same in kind, as when "one musical event (be it a tone, a phrase, or a whole section) has a meaning because it points to and makes us expect another musical event" (Meyer, 1956, p. 35).

According to Meyer, musical meaning is embodied (except in rare instances), and its aesthetic power lies in the expectations that it creates in the listener. If a sequence of musical events is experienced many times, listeners learn to expect that sequence. For example, most people have heard an ascending major scale many times (doh, re, mi, fa, sol, la, ti, doh). Thus, when we hear part of that scale—for example, the first seven notes—we expect the note that would complete the scale. If the event that follows does not correspond with our expectations, emotion or affect is aroused. According to Meyer, music creates a complex yet powerful experience of emotion because it continuously deviates in subtle ways from our expectations. The more unexpected the events in music, the more powerful the music. Anthropologist Levi-Strauss (1964) espoused a similar view:

> The musical emotion springs precisely from the fact that at each moment the composer withholds or adds more or less than the listener anticipates on the basis of a pattern that he thinks he can guess, but that he is incapable of wholly divining....If the composer withholds more than we anticipate, we experience a delicious falling sensation; we feel we have been torn from a stable point on the musical ladder and thrust into the void. (Levi-Strauss, 1969, p. 17)

Note that Meyer, like Langer, denied that music can refer to specific emotions. Rather, violations of expectations create undifferentiated arousal. Although an undifferentiated arousal response to unexpected events is a natural human response, the designation of specific emotion labels is, for Meyer, dependent on individual custom and tradition.

There have been numerous discussions of Meyer's seminal work on expectancy and music, including major theories proposed by Mandler (1984), Huron (2006), and Narmour (1990). As described in chapter 5, Narmour's implication-realization model focuses on the role that tone-to-tone expectancies play in our perceptions of melodic structure, rather than their relevance to the emotional side of music. However, the theories of Mandler and Huron directly confront and extend Meyer's thesis that musical expectancies are the source of emotion in music.

ADAPTIVE AROUSAL

Mandler (1984) proposed that emotional responses to music are instances of a more general adaptive biological response that occurs following all unexpected or novel events. The ability to anticipate events is a fundamental requirement for human survival, and human behavior is continuously guided and optimized by anticipatory responses. When events conflict with our expectations, the lack of congruity between expected and actual events causes an arousal response from the autonomic (sympathetic) nervous system (ANS). Arousal is a highly adaptive response, because it prepares the organism to cope with potentially dangerous changes in the environment.

Arousal alone does not result in emotion, however. ANS arousal includes increased breathing, heart rate, and blood pressure. These physiological effects may occur after climbing a flight of stairs, but the result is not an emotional response. Mandler's view, held also by Meyer (1956), is that incongruities between expected and actual events lead not only to an arousal response, but also to a cognitive reevaluation of the stimuli. It is this combination of arousal and cognitive activity that leads to an emotional experience.

The expectations that we form during music listening have no obvious implications for survival but, according to Mandler, the arousal generated by unexpected events is basic to human functioning. Such responses are automatic and unconscious, and do not depend on the type of stimuli involved. The difference between music and other stimuli is that composers are able to manipulate arousal more powerfully with music by creating a continuous stream of expectations in listeners and then violating them in subtle and interesting ways.

Listeners prefer a moderate degree of incongruity between expected and actual events. If there is no incongruity (the composer does not violate any expectations), listeners will perceive the music to be simplistic and predictable. If there is too much incongruity, listeners will perceive the music to be overly complex and unpleasant. Many listeners find the melodic patterns in serialized (12-tone) compositions very difficult to anticipate, and this style of music is generally unpopular. Repeated expo-

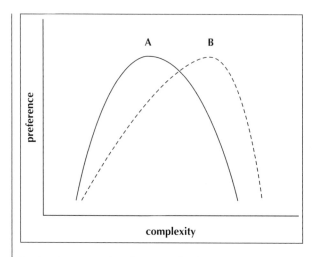

Berlyne's inverted U function for hedonic value. The x-axis represents the degree of novelty or complexity perceived in a stimulus. The y-axis represents the degree of preference. In curve A, preferences are high for intermediate levels of novelty but drop off for both low and high levels.

Perception of complexity depends, in part, on musical training and familiarity. Curve B represents preferences from a musically trained listener. In this case, preference peaks at a higher level of complexity.

sure to such music, however, may increase preference for it by refining one's mental schemata. With enough exposure, the discrepancy between expected and actual events decreases such that listeners begin to anticipate these events.

This latter aspect of Mandler's theory derives from the work of Berlyne (1970, 1971), who argued that "hedonic value" changes with arousal according to an inverted U function. That is, pieces that evoke no or little arousal, or relatively high arousal, have less hedonic value than pieces that evoke an intermediate level of arousal. Arousal, in turn, is directly determined by the degree of complexity and novelty perceived in a stimulus. Because the perception of complexity and novelty depends on the listener's musical training and familiarity with the music, it follows that training and exposure should influence the aesthetic value of a piece of music. Music that initially sounds overly complex and hence unpleasant should, with repeated exposure or musical training, begin to sound less complex and more pleasing. Music that is initially pleasing should, with repeated exposure or training, begin to sound predictable and, hence, less pleasing. Like overplayed pop music on the radio, it may even start to sound lightweight, cheesy, or trivial.

ITPRA THEORY

Like Meyer and Mandler, Huron (2006) focused on the significance of expectancy for understanding the emotional qualities of music. Huron is clear that there are several mechanisms that contribute to musically evoked emotions that do not arise from expectancy. Nonetheless, expectancy mechanisms represent a particularly powerful source of musical emotion, and they can be investigated on several levels.

Huron identified five categories of expectancy responses: *imagination, tension, prediction, reaction,* and *appraisal.* The five expectancy responses make up the core of Huron's *ITPRA theory,* where the first letter of each response category gives the theory its name. He classifies the five response systems into preoutcome and postoutcome responses. Preoutcome responses (feelings that occur prior to an expected or unexpected event) include the imagination and tension responses; postoutcome responses include the prediction, reaction, and appraisal responses.

The imagination response entails contemplating potential future states and acting in a way that makes those states more likely if they are positive, and less likely if they are negative. Imagining an outcome is a principal motivator of behavior. Musicians who imagine the experience of stage fright prior to a performance are more likely to put in extra hours of practice. Without the imagination process, individuals would fail to take steps to avoid negative outcomes. The imagination response induces an emotional state, while retaining an awareness that the event that would lead to such a state has not actually occurred.

The tension response is a more immediate physiological preparation for an imminent event and involves changes in arousal. Classic behaviors associated with the tension responses include fighting, fleeing, and freezing. The tension response is activated immediately before an anticipated moment of outcome, and adjusts the level of arousal and attention according to the degree of uncertainty surrounding the outcome, the significance of potential outcomes, and the estimated time before the outcome occurs.

Postoutcome responses include prediction, reaction, and appraisal responses. Prediction responses are transient states of reward or punishment that arise in response to the accuracy of expectation. Accurate expectations are rewarded by positively valenced emotional responses, and inaccurate expectations are punished by negatively valenced emotional responses. Both the reaction and appraisal responses are emotional states that arise from assessments of the event itself independent of whether that event was anticipated.

The reaction response is a rapid process that occurs automatically and preattentively and activates bodily actions, visceral responses, or both. Reaction responses are knee-jerk reactions but are not always instinctive reflexes; they can also be learned. Appraisal responses are more considered and conscious assessments of an outcome, and need not be compatible with the reaction response.

As with Mandler's theory, Huron's ITPRA theory not only accounts for experiences of music, but also all experiences related to expectation. Huron emphasizes that expectancy is only one source of musical emotions, but affective responses associated with expectancies are particularly salient because their biological purpose is so fundamental: to prepare an organism for the future. At a basic level, expectations are associated with feelings of anticipation and, if these expectations are violated, surprise. Through evolution, emotions have become associated with expectancies because emotions act as "motivational amplifiers" that encourage organisms to pursue behaviors that are adaptive and to avoid behaviors that are maladaptive. In other words, emotions function to reinforce accurate prediction, promote appropriate event-readiness, and increase the likelihood of future positive outcomes. Positive feelings reward states deemed to be adaptive, and negative feelings discourage states deemed to be maladaptive. Music making taps into these primordial functions to produce a wealth of compelling emotional experiences.

One of the appealing aspects of the ITPRA theory is that with five types of expectancy responses it is possible to explain a wide range of emotional responses to music. When an event is expected by one system but not another, complex emotions can result. The emotion of awe, for example, may be evoked when a tension response is highly activated, but the appraisal response indicates low tension. The sense of sustained danger generated by the tension response, combined with the broader appraisal of safety, generates a positive sense of heightened tension, which is experienced as awe. In fact, the circumstances that give rise to awe can explain why we enjoy sad music when sorrow is not a pleasant emotion (Davies, 2001). Sad music, like Shakespeare's later tragedies, often generates feelings of awe. This emotion allows us to appreciate this music for its artful narrative construction, its sense of potential, and its ability to illuminate an emotion that is an essential part of being human.

How do expectations for music develop? Many researchers believe that they are strongly shaped by experience, although some of our musical expectations may also have an innate basis (Narmour, 1990). Through experience, people internalize regularities in the world, including regularities found in music. For example, our experience teaches us that, if we drop an object, it will fall to the ground. As another example, repeated exposure to Western tonal music teaches us that the leading tone is often followed by the tonic. Such regularities are stored as mental schemata, which function to interpret new sensory input, and generate expectations for events to follow.

MULTIPLE MECHANISMS THEORY

Most researchers would agree that there are several mechanisms by which music can induce emotion, but few have attempted to identify and describe the full set of relevant mechanisms. Juslin and Västfjäll (2008) argued that six essential mechanisms jointly account for current understandings of the link between music and emotion: brain stem reflex, evaluative conditioning, emotional contagion, visual imagery, episodic memory, and expectancy. Each mechanism is thought to account for a major source of emotional responses to music.

For Juslin and Västfjäll, emotional induction involves a common set of reactions, including a cognitive appraisal (i.e., a conscious evaluation of the music), a subjective feeling of emotion, physiological responses (e.g., changes in heart rate), emotional expressions (e.g., smiling), action tendency (e.g., listening more intensely), and regulation (e.g., steadying one's breathing). Whether each of the proposed mechanisms can induce all of these reactions is unknown, but such reactions to music have certainly been observed.

The *brain stem reflex* represents the most primitive mechanism, and occurs in response to fundamental acoustic characteristics of sound. Sounds that are loud, sudden, dissonant, and fast paced generate increases in arousal, whether those attributes occur in music, speech, or elsewhere in the environment. Such responses reflect a general function of the auditory system: to scan the environment for objects or events that may have biological significance. Increases in arousal act to prepare organisms for these biologically significant events. Such signals have been defined as "psychophysical" cues (Balkwill & Thompson, 1999) and provide powerful cues for decoding emotional meaning in music and speech within and across cultural boundaries (for a review, see Thompson & Balkwill, in press).

Evaluative conditioning occurs when music that has been repeatedly associated with an emotional context (e.g., a birthday) induces an emotion through the automatic process of classical conditioning. Once a conditioned stimulus (e.g., the song "Happy Birthday") is strongly associated with an unconditioned stimulus (e.g., the birthday), the conditioned stimulus alone may evoke the same emotional state as the unconditioned stimulus (as when the song "Happy Birthday" induces positive feelings, even when it is heard in the absence of an actual birthday). This form of emotional induction can occur independently of any awareness of the association.

Emotional contagion refers to the phenomenon that perceiving an emotion can sometimes induce that same emotion. In effect, the perceiver "mimics" the expression of emotion internally by activating relevant emotional representations in the brain. As an example, a child may burst into tears at the sight of another child crying. However, subtle forms of emotional contagion frequently occur in response to music listening. Hearing a mournful cello performance may induce a genuine state of sadness in a listener. Although the processes underlying emotional contagion are not well understood, they may occur through the operation of so-called mirror neurons.

Occasionally, listening to music evokes *visual imagery*. This imagery, in turn, is sometimes emotional. Acoustic information is overwhelmingly accompanied by visual information, and powerful associations between the two modalities naturally develop through their contiguous occurrence. Visual impressions associated with birds, brooks, trains, wind, and rain are contiguous with sounds that vary in pitch, duration, rate of change, timbre, and textural density. For this reason, hearing sounds can spontaneously stimulate visual imagination. The attributes of music need only be vaguely related to the visual images to act as triggers of visual imagination, which then unfolds creatively and often induces an emotional experience. Thus, a slowly ascending passage may evoke a visual image of a beautiful sunrise, which may then induce feelings of joy and optimism.

Some music is personally meaningful because it is associated with a particular event or episode in the listener's life. When a specific memory is evoked by music, the emotion associated with that memory is also evoked, giving rise to a feeling of nostalgia. For example, a song may evoke a memory for the day a listener moved into her first apartment with a friend. This memory, in turn, may evoke strong feelings of the very excitement and optimism that the listener felt on that day. This mechanism of *episodic memory*, like that of evaluative conditioning and visual imagery, provides an indirect link between music and emotion. The emotion does not arise directly from the music itself, but it can nevertheless be quite powerful. Indeed, people frequently listen to music because it reminds them of meaningful experiences and the emotions associated with those experiences.

Musical expectancy plays a prominent role in several theories of music and emotion, as discussed earlier. It refers to the process by which an emotion is induced when a musical event violates, delays, or confirms the listener's expectation. As argued by Huron (2006), expectations can be examined on several levels and can account for a wide range of emotional responses.

According to Juslin and Västfjäll (2008), the six mechanisms just listed provide a comprehensive account for most if not all emotional responses to music. It should be emphasized, however, that research is needed to understand these mechanisms fully. For example, expectancy is conceived by Juslin and Västfjäll as one of the six mechanisms, but Huron's (2006) ITPRA theory suggests that expectancies may involve five discrete mechanisms operating at different levels of processing. Research may also help to characterize each mechanism, refining our understanding of their biological function, their developmental implications, relevant brain areas, the speed with which they operate, and their reliance on higher level cognitive processing.

Empirical Studies

The theoretical accounts already described illustrate the different ways of understanding the relationship between music and emotion. Table 6.1 provides a summary of these viewpoints. Many of these theories are strongly supported by empirical research, whereas others have less empirical support. Converging evidence from numerous studies suggests that multiple factors may underlie the connection between music and emotion, including culture-specific knowledge, expectancy mechanisms, acoustical influences, and physiological responses. We now review a number of these studies.

Do Listeners Agree on the Emotional Meaning of Music?

Empirical studies of emotion in music have demonstrated that listeners are highly sensitive to emotional meaning in music, and that there is considerable agreement among them about that meaning. One distinction that listeners make readily—often at a surprisingly young age—is between

Table 6.1

Summary of Theories of the Links Between Music and Emotion

THEORIST	BASIS OF CONNECTION	SPECIFIABLE EMOTIONS
Cooke	Melodic intervals Melodic patterns	Yes
Kivy	Contour (e.g., tempo) Convention (scale, cadence)	Yes
Langer	Dynamic form (e.g., tension and release)	No
Meyer	Expectations Evaluation of arousal	No
Mandler	Expectations Evaluation of arousal	No
Berlyne	Arousal Complexity/novelty	No
Huron	Expectations Evaluation of ITPRA	No
Justin & Västfjäll	Six core mechanisms	Depends on mechanism

"happy" and "sad" music. Hevner (1935a) presented listeners with two versions of each of 10 short musical compositions. One version of each composition was written in the major mode, and the other version was written in the minor mode. All other aspects of the two versions of each composition were identical (e.g., rhythm, tempo, etc.), so any differences in the affective quality of the two versions could be attributed only to modality. Compositions included pieces by Schumann, Beethoven, Bach, and Gluck, and were performed by the same pianist. The pianist attempted to perform the two versions of each composition in an identical manner (the same degree of dynamic range, rubato, pedaling, articulation, etc.).

Students were presented with five pieces composed in a major mode, and five different pieces composed in a minor mode. Four groups of students were tested, with each group presented a different set of major and minor compositions. Students were given a large list of adjectives and, after each composition was presented, they selected the adjectives that best described the affective character of the piece.

Table 6.2 shows the adjectives for which major and minor pieces yielded significantly different numbers of checks. The table shows two columns: In the first column are adjectives that were most often selected for pieces composed in a major mode; the second column lists the adjectives that were most often selected for pieces composed in a minor mode. These results clearly support the view that the major and minor modes have different affective characteristics.

To assess the importance of musical talent for this task, Hevner singled out the 25 students with the highest scores on the Seashore Measures of Musical Talent battery and compared their judgments to the 25 students with the lowest scores on the same tests. A similar procedure was followed to examine the importance of musical training and general intelligence. Groups with more talent and more musical training showed only slightly increased sensitivity to the differences between the major and minor modes. Students with higher intelligence scores, however, were no

Table 6.2

Adjectives Selected Reliably More Often for Pieces Written in Either the Major or Minor Mode

MAJOR MODE	MINOR MODE	
Happy	Restless	Pathetic
Light	Weird	Melancholy
Sprightly	Dramatic	Plaintive
Cheerful	Mystical	Yearning
Joyous	Serious	Mournful
Gay	Depressing	Sad
Bright	Tragic	Sober
Merry	Dreamy	Pleading
Playful	Frustrated	Mysterious
Graceful	Vague	Longing
Exhilarated	Doleful	Gloomy
Satisfying		

more sensitive to the difference between major and minor compositions than students with lower intelligence scores. Hevner concluded that sensitivity to the affective differences between the major and minor modes is not highly dependent on musical talent, training, or intelligence.

Terwogt and van Grinsven (1991, experiment 2) also found a high level of consistency in judgments of happiness and sadness in music. In their study, a professional musician first selected various excerpts of classical music that, in his view, conveyed one of four emotions: happiness, sadness, fear, and anger. The researchers then presented the excerpts to children (aged 5 and 10) and adults, and asked them to link each excerpt to one of four facial expressions corresponding to the four emotions.

Children as young as 5 years of age showed remarkable sensitivity to musically expressed emotions, and sensitivity increased with age. For all age groups, there was high agreement about the presence of happiness and sadness, but less agreement about the presence of fear and anger (these emotions were frequently confused with one another). One explanation for this finding is that the recognition of fear and anger relies to a large extent on semantic associations, which cannot be easily communicated musically. Another possibility is that the excerpts used to convey anger and fear were poorly selected. For example, an excerpt from Prokofiev's *Peter and the Wolf* was chosen to convey anger. In the accompanying text, the wolf, "feeling itself caught, began to jump wildly to get loose" (Terwogt & van Grinsven, 1991, p. 104). As it is questionable whether this circumstance is best characterized as anger, it is perhaps not surprising that anger and fear were confused with one another.

Nonetheless, the results indicated remarkable agreement among listeners for the emotions of sadness and happiness. Approximately 94% of adults linked the same excerpts to happiness and sadness. Moreover, the authors reported greater agreement among adults than children, suggesting that the perception of emotion in music is partially shaped by experience.

How Do Listeners Respond Emotionally to Music?

Listeners are clearly sensitive to emotional meaning in music. Can music actually cause an emotional response in listeners? There is considerable debate surrounding this question (see Budd, 1985; Kivy, 1980;

Krumhansl, 1997). One view, called the *cognitivist position*, holds that listeners are sensitive to the emotional meaning of music, but that they do not actually experience that emotion. Listeners may recognize great sadness in a particular melody, for example, but the experience is one of recognition: The music does not actually make them sad.

Another view, called the *emotivist position*, suggests that music can elicit an emotional response in listeners. A number of theorists, including Kivy (1980) and Meyer (1956), have questioned this view, arguing that music expresses, but does not produce, emotion. Physiological responses to music, such as increased heart rate, are dismissed as being unreliable and idiosyncratic.

Moreover, the causal connections between music and emotion are not always clear: Does music induce our emotional state, or does our emotional state simply influence the type of music we listen to? Both connections are possible. For example, a person in the mood for dancing is likely to play dance music, but on another occasion, merely hearing dance music might put that person in the mood for dancing.

It is difficult to disregard the considerable support for the emotivist position. Goldstein (1980) conducted a survey of intense emotional experiences, and observed that most of these experiences are reported in response to music. Such experiences included shudders, tingling sensations, and chills, suggesting that music can induce physiological changes.

Sloboda (1991) also conducted a survey of physical responses to music. Participants reported various physical responses, including tears, tingles down the spine, and increased heart rate. For each physical response reported, participants rated the frequency of occurrence of that response on a scale from 1 to 5. Table 6.3 shows the percentage of participants reporting various types of response to music, and the mean rating of how often they experienced that response. Table 6.3 shows that shivers down the spine were experienced more often, and by a greater percentage of participants, than any other physical response to music.

Other researchers have directly measured physiological responses to music. Thayer and Levenson (1983) observed changes in skin conductance levels (sweating) when music was added to a stressful film (see also Cohen, 2001). More recently, Krumhansl (1997) presented 38 musically trained listeners with six musical excerpts. Twelve physiological measurements were obtained, including heart rate, breathing rate, blood pressure (systolic and diastolic), respiratory depth, finger temperature, and skin conductance level. All physiological measures were significantly affected by music. On average, music caused a decrease in heart rate, skin

Table 6.3

Frequency of Occurrence of Physical Responses to Music

RESPONSE	MEAN RATING (MAX = 5)	% EXPERIENCING IN PREVIOUS YEARS
Shivers down the spine	3.08	90
Laughter	2.80	88
Lump in the throat	2.68	80
Tears	2.65	85
Goose pimples	2.40	62
Racing heart	2.31	67
Yawning	2.15	58
Pit of stomach sensation	2.11	58
Sexual arousal	1.56	38
Trembling	1.51	31
Flushing/blushing	1.46	28
Sweating	1.44	28

Note. Participants rated the frequency of occurrence of each physical response to music on a scale from 1 to 5, where 1 = never, 2 = rarely, 3 = occasionally, 4 = quite often, and 5 = very often.

conductance, finger temperature, and respiratory depth, but an increase in breathing rate and blood pressure. Interestingly, the direction of these physiological changes was the same regardless of specific emotion associated with the music: Happy, sad, and fearful music all produced the same kind of physiological changes.

A unique aspect of music is its ability to convey emotional meaning in a continuously changing manner, suggesting a kind of emotional narrative. Changing levels of loudness, for example, are associated with continuously varying levels of perceived tension (Schubert, 2001). Recognizing the dynamic quality of emotional responses to music, a number of researchers have introduced continuous measures of emotionality in music. In one study, Vines, Krumhansl, Wanderley, and Levitin (2005) presented musically trained individuals with an audiovisual recording of a clarinet performance. Participants then provided

Sound Examples 6.4.1–6.4.3

Performance practices for the expression of specific emotions in music can be observed in performance aspects such as dynamics, tempo, and accent. Fluctuations in these domains are intuitive to the performing musician, and they can be observed with relative consistency from performer to performer. **Sound examples 6.4.1 to 6.4.3** are three performances with what the performer considers to be neutral, positive, and negative affect, respectively.

continuous judgments of the degree of emotional tension in the music. Continuous judgments were made using a slider that could be increased or decreased at any time. The results confirmed that tension varied continuously as the music progressed, and both visual and auditory information contributed to the unfolding pattern of tension.

Compositional and Expressive Signals of Emotion

The emotions that we experience in music are influenced by both the structure of a music composition and by the expression used to perform that composition. By examining these two factors separately, studies have confirmed that both compositional structure and performance expression contribute in their own way to the emotional meaning of music.

Thompson and Robitaille (1992) asked several established composers to compose melodies with the specific intention of conveying each of six emotions: sadness, happiness, excitement, dullness, anger, and peacefulness. The melodies were recorded through a MIDI sequencer with no performance expression (i.e., expressive variation in timing and loudness). By eliminating the potential influence of performance expression, it was possible to determine whether emotion could be communicated in the compositional component of the music alone.

Listeners rated each of the melodies for the degree to which they conveyed each of the six emotions. The results showed that the composers were indeed capable of communicating specific emotions in their compositions. Intended emotions were assigned significantly higher ratings than unintended emotions. Some emotions, however, were easier to convey than others. In particular, composers were highly successful at conveying happiness, sadness, and excitement, but were relatively unsuccessful at conveying anger.

Other studies have shown that performers, through their use of performance expression, also play a large role in shaping a listener's understanding of emotional meaning. Kendall and Carterette (1990) evaluated the ability of performers to communicate varying levels of expressiveness. Five professional instrumentalists (one for piano, clarinet, oboe, violin, and trumpet) performed each of four melodies at each of three levels of expressiveness: no expression, appropriate expression, and exaggerated expression. The piano performances were presented to listeners as models of the three levels of expressiveness, and listeners were then asked to match each of the other performances to one of the three model performances.

The accuracy of matching performances to the corresponding model was 70% for musically trained listeners, and 64% for musically untrained listeners. Listeners found it easier to match performances involving no expression (M hits = 85%) than it was to match performances involving either appropriate or exaggerated expression (M hits = 58%). In particular, listeners had difficulty identifying the level of expression intended in violin performances. Violin performances with appropriate (intermediate) expression were most often matched to exaggerated model performances. The violin is a highly expressive instrument: Evidently, an appropriate level of expression on a violin is perceived to be far more expressive than an appropriate level of expression on a piano. Further analyses suggested that, for these performances, the expressive use of timing was more informative to expressive communication than was the expressive use of loudness.

Can the use of performance expression communicate more specific affective meanings? Senju and Ohgushi (1987) asked a violinist to play Mendelssohn's *Violin Concerto in E minor* numerous times, each time conveying one of 10 musical feelings, such as bright, powerful, and sophisticated. The responses of musically trained listeners showed only weak correspondences with the intent. On the other hand, the verbal labels of feelings may have been too subtle for listeners. More recent work has illustrated that performers are highly successful at conveying basic emotions, accomplished through a combination of expressive actions.

Gabrielsson and Juslin (1996) investigated this issue further by asking nine musicians to perform short melodies on violin, electric guitar, flute, or singing voice (see also Juslin, 1997). Performers were asked to communicate, through their use of performance expression, each of the following emotions: happiness, sadness, anger, fear, tenderness, solemnity, and no expression. Performers varied tempo, timing, dynamics, articulation, phrasing, vibrato, attack, and timbre to bring about the intended emotional expression. Using such expressive devices, performers were quite successful in communicating emotions to listeners, although certain emotions (e.g., happiness and sadness) were easier to communicate than others (e.g., solemnity).

Compositional and expressive features connote emotional meaning in a probabilistic way (Juslin, 2001). For example, fast tempi, regular rhythms, consonant intervals, and the major mode all connote a

Sound Examples 6.5.1–6.5.8

Roberto Bresin derived a set of performance rules that attempt to capture intuitive performance practices for the expression of emotions. This set of rules or *algorithm* can be fed into a computer to electronicaly alter a neutral performance of a piece into one that expresses emotion. A similar system by Steven R. Livingstone modifies both the structure (score) and performance to alter musical emotion. Algorithms were derived for the following four emotions: anger, happiness, sadness, and tenderness.

Sound examples 6.5.1 to 6.5.4 are performances based on Bresin's system for "Ekorrn satt I granen" (The squirrel sat on the fir tree) by Alice Tegner. **Sound examples 6.5.5 to 6.5.8** are performances based on Livingstone's system for Beethoven's *Piano Sonata in G major* (Op. 49 No. 2). Can you guess the emotion for each?

7 = happiness, 8 = tenderness.
5 = anger, 6 = sadness,
3 = tenderness, 4 = happiness,
1 = anger, 2 = sadness,

joyful emotion. However, fast tempi can also connote agitation, regular rhythms can connote dignity, consonant intervals can connote serenity, and the major mode can connote solemnity. That is, individual features of music have ambiguous emotional meanings, whereas combinations of features provide powerful signals of specific emotions.

What Properties of Music Lead to an Emotional Response?

The studies already mentioned implicate an association between specific aspects of performance expression and different emotional qualities. In Gabrielsson and Juslin's (1996) study, performers communicated happiness using expressive devices such as fast tempo, bright timbre, and exaggerated rhythmic contrasts. Sadness, in contrast, was conveyed using slow tempo, soft dynamic levels, and slow and deep vibrato. Performers expressed anger with rapid tempi, loud dynamic levels, and a harsh timbre. Fear, on the other hand, was expressed with irregular tempi, soft dynamic levels, and staccato articulation. In short, performers use a range of expressive devices with which to communicate emotional meaning to listeners.

Studies by Hevner (1935a, 1935b, 1936, 1937) also suggest that emotional meaning may be carried by basic properties of music, such as tempo. To examine the significance of tempo, Hevner (1937) presented listeners with fast and slow performances of eight musical compositions. For each performance, listeners had to select from a large list the adjectives that best captured the emotional quality of the music. No listener heard both versions of a given composition. Fast versions were performed at approximately double the tempi of the slow versions, but the performer attempted to play both versions equally well. The musical compositions varied in style, and included several pieces composed explicitly for the study, along with two eight-measure themes from compositions by Beethoven. Tempo greatly influenced listeners' responses.

In the same study, Hevner found that overall pitch height also influenced the emotional quality of music. She presented listeners with 13 compositions, each performed at one of two different pitch registers. For most compositions, the high and low pitch registers were one octave apart, and the performer attempted to perform both versions at the same tempo and dynamic level. Once again, for each piece, listeners checked from a list the adjectives that best described the emotional character of the music. Like tempo, pitch height greatly influenced responses.

In another study, Hevner (1936) adopted similar procedures to examine the importance of other variables, including modality, harmony, and rhythm. To estimate the relationship between each of these variables and the perceived emotional character, Hevner classified the set of adjectives into eight basic categories: happy, graceful, serene, dreamy, sad, dignified, vigorous, and exciting. For each category, she then compared the number of checks for the two versions created for each variable (e.g., slow vs. fast versions; high vs. low registers).

Summarizing the results from a series of studies, Hevner concluded that pitch and tempo were the most influential variables for determining the affective character of music. Modality (major or minor) was thought to be next in importance, followed by harmony (simple/consonant or complex/dissonant) and rhythm (firm/simple or flowing/complex). Only one of the variables assessed by Hevner—ascending versus descending melodic patterns—appeared to have little influence on affective character.

Rigg (1964) summarized the results from a number of studies, and observed remarkable consistency in the variables associated with specific affective states. More recently, Sloboda (1991) sent 500 people a questionnaire (only 83 responded) asking them to identify, with reference to a score where possible, specific phrases or moments in music that resulted in physiological responses. Table 6.4 shows the frequency of three types of responses associated with various structural properties in music. The table shows that tears were associated with movement on the circle of fifths and melodic appoggiaturas, whereas shivers were associated with new or unprepared harmony, or sudden dynamic or textural changes.

Because the preceding studies all involved Western tonal music, it is unclear whether the results reflect a universal code of emotional meaning in music, or whether they reflect culturally specific, learned associations. Opinions on this question vary, but most theorists agree that it would be naive to adopt an extreme position on this question. Most likely, music involves both culturally specific cues to emotion and basic psychophysical cues that transcend cultural boundaries.

Sound Examples 6.6.1–6.6.3

Sound examples 6.6.1 to 6.6.3 are three examples of Hindustani ragas collected by Balkwill, each conveying one of the following three rasas: anger, joy, and sadness.

Source: Hindustani ragas performed by Atul Keskar (surbahar, sitar, dilruba) and Ajit Soman (bansuri flute) recorded with their permission (and waiver of copyright) by Laura-Lee Balkwill in Pune, India, 1997.

Table 6.4

Frequency of Three Types of Responses Associated with Different Structural Properties in Music

MUSICAL FEATURE	TEARS	SHIVERS	RACING HEART
Harmony descending cycle of fifths to tonic	6	0	0
Melodic appoggiatura	18	9	0
Melodic or harmonic sequence	12	4	1
Enharmonic change	4	6	0
Harmonic or melodic acceleration or cadence	4	1	2
Delay of final cadence	3	1	0
New or unprepared harmony	3	12	1
Sudden dynamic or textural change	5	12	3
Repeated syncopation	1	1	3
Prominent event earlier than prepared for	1	4	3

Is There a Universal Link Between Music and Emotion?

Are some connections between music and emotion natural and universal, cutting across cultural boundaries? Balkwill and Thompson (1999) examined this question in a cross-cultural investigation of emotion in music. Their study examined the sensitivity of Western listeners to the emotional meaning of Hindustani music. This music is especially suitable for studying the link between music and emotion, because Hindustani classical theory explicitly outlines a connection between certain melodic forms, or ragas, and certain moods, or rasas.

On a field trip to North India, Balkwill asked expert performers of Indian music to perform a number of ragas with the intention of conveying each of four rasas, corresponding to the emotions of joy, sadness, anger, and peace. Western listeners with no training or familiarity with the raga–rasa system then judged each performance on each of the four emotions. For the emotions of joy, sadness, and peace, listeners were remarkably sensitive to the intended emotion. This sensitivity appeared to be related to their detection of basic structural aspects of the music, such as tempo and complexity. The results provide compelling evidence that at least some of the connections between music and emotion are universal.

Sources of Emotion in Music

The emotional qualities of music likely reflect the combined influence of several sources, including psychophysical cues, expectancy mechanisms, and indirect sources of musical emotion. Psychophysical cues and expectancy mechanisms have direct consequences for emotional interpretations and experience because they do not rely on extra-musical associations (as when music gives rise to visual imagery that is perceived as emotional) or learned associations (as when a song reminds someone of a specific life experience). However, emotional responses to music can also occur indirectly, as when a particular song reminds a person of a difficult period in their lives.

It is important to differentiate psychophysical cues and expectancy mechanisms, but it should also be emphasized that they are somewhat related. The very reason a psychophysical cue (such as a loud sound) seems "emotional" to us is because it signals a forthcoming event that may have biological significance. The arousal response that is experienced following a sudden loud sound is the brain's way of preparing us for a potentially significant event. That is, the emotional effects of psychophysical cues function to put us on alert. They are primitive reflexes to sound that likely arise from the brain stem and have a genetic basis. As such, their effects transcend cultural boundaries.

Expectancy mechanisms, in turn, reflect a complex interaction between our predictions of forthcoming events and the events that actually occur. Expectancies are associated with emotion for a simple reason: It is biologically advantageous to be able to predict events in the world. Thus, the experience of "surprise" following an unanticipated event reflects a failure of this most basic mechanism: The arousal response in

Candle in the Wind

Elton John's "Candle in the Wind 1997," performed at the funeral of Diana, Princess of Wales, has sold over 35 million copies and become the top-selling single of all time. Its popularity is undoubtedly related to its emotional resonance with a grieving public. What specific emotion(s), if any, does it express? Where does its emotional potency lie?

Sound Examples 6.7.1–6.7.2

How are joy and despair conveyed musically? **Sound example 6.7.1** (Verdi's "Libiamo ne'lieti calici" from *La Traviata*) and **sound example 6.7.2** (Mussorgsky's "Bydlo" from *Pictures at an Exhibition*) are Western examples of joy and despair, respectively. Contrast these Western examples to the earlier Hindustani examples.

Sound examples 6.7.1–6.7.2 are available via the *Music, Thought, and Feeling* iMix on iTunes.

a surprised individual is the brain's way of drawing attention to a breakdown in prediction, so that the individual might improve the accuracy of future predictions (Huron, 2006).

Thus, two strategies have evolved for using acoustic information to anticipate biologically significant events. One is genetic encoding: hard-wired connections between acoustic stimuli and appropriate affective responses (psychophysical cues). The other mechanism relies on an initial acquisition of knowledge about event sequences in specific environments (expectancies). The latter route functions flexibly and is best suited for coping with event sequences that vary from environment to environment, and hence must be learned.

Psychophysical cues and expectancy mechanisms are interesting from a theoretical perspective because they reflect direct links between attributes of music and emotional systems, but it should be acknowledged that emotional experiences to music also arise indirectly. As pointed out by Juslin and Västfjäll (2008), music can trigger a visual image (e.g., a stormy night) and that image, in turn, may have an emotional connotation. Similarly, music may remind an individual of a personal experience such as a romantic evening, and that memory, in turn, may generate feelings of emotion.

In short, there are several sources of musical emotion, and different types of emotional responses to music arise from different sources or combinations of sources. Direct sources of emotion in music are powerful and immediate but they are also impersonal. They do not rely on personal associations or individual memories. Indirect sources of emotion vary from individual to individual and do not always occur during music listening, but they provide music with personal and cultural significance. Listening to music that accompanied a significant life event many years ago can induce a deeply nostalgic emotional experience. When music generates both direct and indirect sources of emotion, the result can be an intensely personal and richly rewarding experience.

Additional Readings

Juslin, P. N. (2007). Emotional responses to music. In S. Hallam, I. Cross, & M. Thaut (Eds.), *Oxford handbook of music psychology*. New York: Oxford University Press.

Krumhansl, C. L. (2002). Music: A link between cognition and emotion. *Current Directions in Psychological Science, 11*, 45–50.

CHAPTER 7

Music and the Brain

LEARNING OUTCOMES

By the end of this chapter you should be able to:

1. Debate whether descriptions of brain function can provide a full explanation of thoughts, feelings, and behaviors.

2. Identify the major anatomical structures and regions that make up the brain.

3. Trace the historical development of scientific understandings of the relation between music and the brain.

4. Explain how case studies of individuals with neurological disorders can provide an understanding of how the brain operates in response to music.

5. Compare electrical/magnetic and hemodynamic/metabolic techniques of studying the brain, and provide examples of how each technique has been used to study brain responses to music.

6. Describe how brain-imaging techniques have been used to examine the relation between music and emotion.

What's in a Brain?

Why would anyone interested in music want to study the brain? It is difficult to imagine how a description of brain cells and their various connections and activity levels could possibly account for our experiences of music. How can discussions of brain states and neural connections account for the deeply personal associations that we might have between a particular tune and an old school friend? As noted in chapter 1, this question is far from simple. What is the relationship between the brain and the mind?

Philosophers and neuroscientists have debated the question of whether descriptions of brain states can ever hope to provide a complete account of psychological states such as beliefs and emotional experiences. A related question is whether neuroscientific explanations of our experiences might eventually replace nonscientific explanations, such as the kind of casual explanation we might provide to a friend as to why we like a particular style of music. Neuroscientists point out that although we normally think or talk about our experiences and behaviors without reference to neural activity, the brain is ultimately involved in the production and control of all thoughts and feelings, so there may be a way of explaining these phenomena with reference to specific brain processes (see Churchland, 1986). Of course, neuroscientists cannot yet provide a full and satisfying neurological account for our experiences of music, but given sufficient progress in the field of neuroscience, it seems possible that they may be able to do so in future.

Some scholars have gone so far as to suggest that progress in neuroscience might fundamentally change the way we understand and describe our experiences. Such progress might reveal, for example, that the casual concepts that we take for granted in everyday conversations

Encoding of Memories

How are memories encoded? Most prominent theories suggest that a given memory is distributed throughout clusters of neurons. Many researchers in computer science and artificial intelligence are working on modelling how such networks might function.

Another school of thought is that individual neurons encode highly specific information, so that a single neuron might fire, for example, when one thinks about one's grandmother (this is sometimes referred to as the "grandmother cell theory"). Although greeted with skepticism by some neuroscientists, a recent study (Quian Quiroga et al., 2005) of epileptic patients indeed found evidence of this highly specific response in single neurons. For example, a single neuron in one patient responded to images of actress Halle Berry, whether they were photographs or drawings, as the masked Catwoman, and even to an image of her name.

are actually quite flawed, just as science revealed that religious and popular descriptions of abnormal behavior in terms of demonic possession and witchcraft in past centuries was seriously misguided, and have been replaced with scientifically inspired concepts such as psychosis, epilepsy, and borderline personality. Whether or not neuroscientific research can lead to such a radical change in the way we think and talk about our behaviors and experiences, the field is rapidly expanding our understanding of the brain and music provides a unique window through which we can witness and explore some of its most intriguing capabilities.

The brain is an enormously complex and powerful biological organ that controls movement and coordination, stores memories, allows us to interpret sensory input, and gives us powers of creativity, imagination, and rational thought. The brain of a typical adult weights about 3 pounds, but within this small mass there are more than 100 billion nerve cells (neurons). Progress in understanding the brain accelerated rapidly in the 1990s, and yet remarkably little is known about the development and operation of neural circuitry, let alone questions of how the brain provides us with a sense of self, generates and controls emotions, and adapts to continuous changes in our environment. What we do know is that the brain is the product of millions of years of evolutionary adaptation and functions with unimaginable complexity. Skills and behaviors that come naturally to us such as catching a ball or walking down the street involve enormously intricate neural circuitry and processing.

What we call the brain consists of a number of anatomical structures: the *cerebrum, cerebellum* and *brain stem*. These anatomical structures, along with the *spinal cord*, make up the *central nervous system* (CNS). The CNS transmits signals to and from the rest of our body through the *peripheral nervous system* (PNS). The cerebrum is the largest part of the brain and is divided into the left and right cerebral hemispheres by the *longitudinal fissure*. The cerebral hemispheres are connected to one another by the *corpus callosum*. The cerebrum is heavily convoluted with ridges called *gyri* (singular: gyrus) and valleys called *sulci* (singular: sulcus, used interchangeably with fissure). Neuroscientists use the various gyri, sulci, and fissures as landmarks for identifying locations on the cortex, similar to the way that regions and craters are named on the moon. They are given names such as Heschel's Gyrus (the location of the primary auditory cortex), the Sylvian fissure, and the central sulcus. Many regions have two names, depending on whether the term sulcus or fissure is used. For example, the Sylvian fissure is also called the lateral sulcus.

The more pronounced sulci provide some of the boundaries between the major brain regions or lobes, as shown in Figure 7.1: the *frontal lobe* (at the front of the brain), the *temporal lobe* (at the side), the *parietal lobe* (at the top), and the *occipital lobe* (at the back). Each lobe is associated with a range of different cognitive and motor processes that have yet to be fully documented and understood. The frontal lobe is involved in many higher cognitive functions and each hemisphere contains a frontal lobe region involved in the voluntary control of muscles on the opposite (contralateral) side of the body (the primary motor cortex). On the left side of the frontal lobe is a region called *Broca's area*, which is associated with language production and has been linked to certain musical functions. The temporal lobe is most strongly associated with auditory processing and contains the primary auditory cortices (located at Heschel's Gyrus), as well as a region associated with speech perception called *Wernicke's area*. The parietal lobe is perhaps best known for its control of sensations such as pain and touch, but is also associated with other functions such as reading, arithmetic, and some musical skills. The occipital lobe is best known for its role in visual perception.

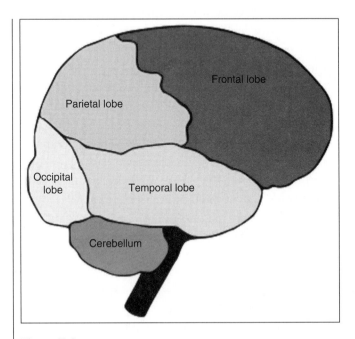

Figure 7.1

The major structures of the brain as viewed from the right side.

The outer shell of the cerebrum contains six layers of neurons and is called the *cortex*, or gray matter. Neurons are the basic units of information processing in the CNS and their operation requires energy (supplied by glucose) and oxygen. The primary mode of communication among neurons is through the transmission of bioelectric impulses called action potentials or *spikes* that propagate down fibers (axons) that link one neuron to others. Axons that combine into large fiber tracts connecting different brain regions are called *white matter*. A number of subcortical brain structures also reside beneath the cortex, such as the basal ganglia, which is involved in motor sequencing and the timing of interval durations. The cerebellum is located at the rear of the brain, below and at the base of the cerebrum. It is associated with fine motor coordination, including the rapid movements of articulation that occur when we speak.

By the 1970s many researchers believed that the brain worked in a hierarchical manner, beginning with an initial stage in which the basic features of sensory input are analyzed, followed by a secondary stage in which complex pattern perception occurs, and a tertiary stage that handles associations between multiple sensory modalities. These stages were thought to occur in brain regions called the primary sensory cortex, the secondary sensory cortex, and the association cortex. Although there is broad support for this basic progression of analysis, many researchers now believe that the brain does not operate according to such a strict sequence. In particular, a number of neuroscientists have reported neural responses to multiple sensory inputs at early stages of processing.

The Search for Music Inside the Brain

How does music get inside the brain? Sound processing begins with the inner ear (cochlea), which responds to sound waves in a manner that ultimately results in an analysis of sounds into their component frequencies (see chapter 3). The actions of the cochlea generate trains of neural discharges in separately tuned fibers of the auditory nerve, which ultimately propagate to the primary auditory cortex within the temporal lobe. Brain cells in this region respond (fire) maximally to certain frequencies and show a gradual reduction in response to neighboring frequencies. The activity of a brain cell in response to changes in frequency is described as the *tuning curve* of that brain cell. Neighboring cells are tuned to similar frequencies, resulting in a *frequency map* across the surface of the auditory cortex. This process is only the beginning, because music involves far more than individual frequencies. Brain responses to melody, harmony, tonality, rhythm, and timbre are distributed across several regions in ways that we are only beginning to understand.

By the end of the 20th century, there was considerable evidence that following the initial stage of sensory processing that handles all sound, several aspects of music processing diverge from speech processing and are handled in the right hemisphere (i.e., in right-handed individuals). Brain regions specialized for speech such as Broca's area and Wernicke's area had already been identified in the left hemisphere, so the principle of *hemispheric dominance* and *lateralization* for particular domains was widely accepted. In a landmark study conducted by Milner (1962), patients undergoing removal of their right or left temporal lobes to control severe epilepsy were administered subtests of the Seashore Measures of Musical Talent battery pre- and postoperatively. Removal of the right temporal lobe resulted in a significant drop in scores for tonal memory, sensitivity to timbre, and sensitivity to intensity. Removal of the left temporal lobe did not result in an impairment of these skills.

Kimura (1967) provided further support for the importance of the right hemisphere in music processing. She administered a melody recognition task to healthy right-handed adults in which the melodies were presented to one ear at a time, and observed a left ear advantage in recognition accuracy. Because the left ear transmits auditory signals to the right hemisphere, the results provided further evidence that the right hemisphere is dominant for music, just as the left hemisphere is dominant (in right-handed individuals) for speech.

This interpretation was especially persuasive to researchers and neuroscientists who believed that the left and right hemispheres are specialized for analytic and holistic activities, respectively. The analytic–holistic distinction also seemed to account for results reported by Bever and Chiarello (1974), who repeated Kimura's study and observed a left ear advantage for individuals with no training in music but a right ear (i.e., left hemisphere) advantage for musically trained individuals. The researchers reasoned that trained musicians tend to use an analytic strategy of recognizing melodies and hence capitalize on the skills of their left hemisphere. Nonmusicians, on the other hand, tend to use a holistic strategy of recognizing melodies because they do not have the analytic skills that are developed through music training.

```
 .88b   d88.  db      db .d8888. d888888b   .o88b.
88'YbdP`88 88  88 88'   YP     `88'   d8P  Y8
88  88  88 88      88 `8bo.          88    8P
88  88  88 88      88   `Y8b.        88    8b
88  88  88 88b   d88 db    8D   .88.   Y8b  d8
YP  YP  YP ~Y8888P' `8888Y' Y888888P   `Y88P'
```

An example of ASCII art (an image created using only the characters on a standard keyboard). We tend to view the image holistically and notice the word *music* in its entirety rather than analytically focusing on the individual characters.

Despite the appeal of this interpretation, subsequent studies of ear advantages in melody recognition have yielded mixed or contradictory results, and even studies that reveal a left ear advantage typically demonstrate the advantage in no more than two thirds of right-handed individuals, with no clear ear advantage for left-handed individuals. Indeed, results over the past several decades indicate that the neurological basis of music is not confined to the right hemisphere, even for untrained individuals. In particular, involvement of the two hemispheres is often dependent on the precise nature of the task. For example, although right hemisphere neural activity is associated with the ability to track a regular beat (meter), left hemisphere activity is associated with sensitivity to rhythmic groups and patterns (Peretz & Zatorre, 2005; Winner & von Karolyi, 1998).

In short, neuropsychological evidence has failed to reveal a rigid association between music and the right hemisphere, let alone any single music center or module in the brain. Rather, neural mechanisms underlying music appear to be distributed across regions of both hemispheres, depending on the musical properties and skills assessed. Without question, the right hemisphere is dominant for many important musical functions, including the recognition of pitch and timbre, the representation of melodies so that errors can be detected, performing music, keeping track of meter, and responding emotionally to music.

However, the left hemisphere is implicated in many aspects of music, including numerous rhythmic skills, as well as "language-like" skills such as sight-reading music or naming notes and pieces. One professional musician who suffered a left temporo-parietal stroke was left with preserved skills related to meter and melody, but was no longer able to discriminate or reproduce rhythms (Di Pietro, Laganaro, Leemann, & Schnider, 2004). Interestingly, his musical arrhythmia was only observed in the auditory modality, indicating that the stroke had damaged an area of the brain that is specialized for auditory rhythm. Finally, some musical tasks, such as interpreting a chord that is out of place for the style of music, may elicit brain activity in both hemispheres.

Much of the early work on music and the brain was based on clinical observations of patients suffering from a brain injury that left them impaired on skills related to music, speech, or both. The study of individuals with brain injuries remains a powerful strategy for understanding the connection between music and the brain. More recently, a number of brain imaging technologies have been developed that allow researchers to observe and record the brain activity that occurs while an individual is engaged in a musical task. We review these lines of research in turn.

Neurological Disorders

For most of us, the brain operates seamlessly and effectively. However, when the brain is not functioning properly, for example following a severe impact, a stroke, or a condition such as epilepsy, the effects can be devastating. Difficulties associated with improper brain function are called *neurological disorders*. Neurological disorders may occur as a result of a head injury or cerebrovascular accident (e.g., a stroke), or they may be the result of a congenital disorder. In some cases, neurological disorders give rise to problems of movement. People who have sustained damage to the right hemisphere of the brain, for example, sometimes have difficulty controlling movement on their left side. In other cases, neurological disorders give rise to difficulties with speech. People who have sustained a stroke in the left hemisphere may have difficulty speaking fluently. Still other neurological disorders have musical implications. Such disorders may result in impairments of music perception or production, or they may give rise to musical hallucinations, or they may even involve seizures that are triggered by music (Sacks, 2007).

Early research on music and the brain relied heavily on case studies of patients with neurological disorders, and the case-study approach remains a powerful strategy for investigating the brain. The knowledge gained from case studies of neurological disorders is somewhat fragmented because there is tremendous variability in the scope and location of brain injuries, and full and accurate descriptions of injuries are not always available. In general, sensory and perceptual disorders related to music tend to be associated with damage in the temporal lobe of either hemisphere. In right-handed individuals, the right hemisphere is associated with pitch discrimination tasks, whereas the left hemisphere is associated with rhythmic tasks. Timbre is also associated with the right hemisphere. Patients who have their right temporal lobe removed (i.e., a temporal lobectomy) for the treatment of severe epilepsy become quite impaired at discriminating timbre, whereas patients who have their left temporal lobe removed suffer no such impairment. Damage to either the right or left temporal lobe can also disrupt the ability to recognize familiar melodies (Ayotte, Peretz, Rousseau, Bard, & Bojanowski, 2000).

Amusia Test

You can take a 15-minute test based on a battery developed to test for amusia at:

> http://www.brams.umontreal.ca/amusia-demo/
> You will need speakers to complete the test.

Neurological disorders with musical implications can be classified by whether they are associated with positive or negative symptoms (Brust, 2003). Positive musical disorders include seizures triggered by hearing music, called musicogenic seizures, and seizures that give rise to musical hallucinations. Negative musical disorders involve some type of musical impairment or *amusia*. Amusia is defined as a difficulty in the perception of music (receptive amusia), the production of music (expressive amusia), or both. Amusia may be acquired from brain injury, for example as a consequence of brain surgery or stroke, or it may be congenital. Congenital amusia, also called tone deafness, is thought to occur in 4% to 5% of the population. It has no obvious environmental cause but appears to be present from early in development. The origin of congenital amusia is not well understood, but may arise during fetal development, from genetic factors, or from an interaction of genetic and developmental factors. Many people think that they are tone deaf (17% of university students in one study) when, in fact, their perceptual skills for music are in a normal range (Cuddy, Balkwill, Peretz, & Holden, 2005).

Acquired amusia can occur in the absence of deficits in other domains such as speech (aphasia), although amusia and aphasia may also occur together. Peretz (2002) reported several cases of amusia without aphasia. One patient, referred to as I. R., developed a musical impairment following successive surgeries to treat ruptured aneurysms. The surgeries damaged the right and left temporal lobes and the right frontal lobe, and resulted in severe impairments in music perception and memory. Her verbal skills were unaffected, however, suggesting that musical and verbal skills are associated with distinct brain regions. Interestingly, I. R. enjoyed music in spite of her severe impairment, and was even able to identify the emotional connotation of music (Peretz, 2001). Evidently, the damaged areas were involved in the perception and recognition of melody, but not emotional responses to music.

Amusia can sometimes result in *selective impairment*, whereby only one property or dimension of music is involved, such as rhythm, melody, tonality, or emotionality. One well-known case was French composer Maurice Ravel, who in 1933 began to show symptoms that suggested focal cerebral degeneration, a disorder that results in atrophy of specific areas of the brain. Ravel could still perceive and remember his compositions and could even conceptualize new compositions in his head. He even claimed that he could "hear" new musical compositions in his head. Sadly, however, he had lost his ability to convert these musical conceptions into concrete compositions.

Sound Example 7.1

Sound example 7.1 is Ravel's *Bolero*. Ravel's brain disease, thought to be focal cerebral degeneration, was progressive, gradually deteriorating until he was no longer able to compose at all by 1933. A few minor incidents suggest that his health may have begun to deteriorate as early as 1927.

Some researchers have suggested that his last works, like his famous *Bolero* composed in 1928, show stylistic changes that might be symptomatic of this early deterioration.

Bolero is unusually repetitive for Ravel—the snare drum repeats the same phrase 169 times, and essentially the same melody is repeated 18 times, but with a different orchestration or instrumentation for each repetition. Amaducci, Grassi, and Boller (2002) suggested that Ravel's marked concentration on timbre, known to be lateralized to the right hemisphere, could imply that early atrophy may have already begun in the left hemisphere. Cybulska (1997) has suggested that *Bolero*'s repetitiveness could be a sign of perseveration— or persistent repetition of an activity—symptomatic of Alzheimer's onset. The fact that Ravel retained his musical memory even after 1933 is not necessarily inconsistent with Cybulska's diagnosis of Alzheimer's, as spared musical memory has been reported in advanced cases with severe memory loss in other domains.

Sound example 7.1 is available via the *Music, Thought, and Feeling* iMix on iTunes.

Selective impairment of musical skills can also occur following a stroke (Peretz, 1993; Peretz & Morais, 1989). Two patients, G. L. and C. N., suffered bilateral strokes affecting their temporal lobes. G. L. was impaired at tasks that required sensitivity to tonality in melody, but was able to perform tasks that required sensitivity to contour. C. N. was impaired on tasks that required sensitivity to either tonality or contour. Both patients also showed tune agnosia, or the inability to name or recognize music that was once familiar. Sensitivity to rhythm, environmental sounds, or words was not impaired in either patient. From these cases it may be concluded that impairment to melodic skills can be highly selective, implicating dedicated brain regions for processing melodic information.

It is possible for musical skills to be spared when a brain injury results in serious impairments of speech. For most, this sparing of musical skills does little to compensate for the devastating effects of speech impairment. For a musician, however, the implications may be significant. One of the most famous cases was the Russian composer Vissarion Shebalin. As an adult in the 1950s, Shebalin suffered a series of vascular accidents in his left hemisphere (i.e., strokes) that left him unable to understand or produce speech, a condition known as *aphasia*. His musical abilities were spared, however, and he continued to compose some of his most brilliant works. Shebalin's case is often cited as evidence that music and speech are associated with anatomically separate brain regions.

For reasons that are not entirely understood, individuals with severe cases of Alzheimer's disease (dementia) often have spared musical memory. Anecdotally, many caregivers have observed that patients who have lost their ability to speak or recognize their own family members can still sing and recognize familiar music. Scientific research on the issue, however, has been problematic because people suffering from advanced dementia are generally unable to complete the written or oral tasks that are used in musical assessment tasks. To overcome this difficulty, Cuddy and Duffin (2005) designed a new way of testing musical memory and sensitivity. Familiar songs were played to a patient in an advanced stage of dementia and the patient was encouraged to sing along. They then stopped the music in the middle and allowed the patient to continue singing. In most cases, the patient was able to continue singing the songs quite accurately, as well or better than a group of people the same age who did not suffer from dementia. In another test, incorrect notes were unexpectedly introduced into familiar songs and the patient's reaction was observed. By noting when the patient reacted with surprise or displeasure, the researchers deduced that the patient was highly sensitive to the details of musical structure.

When a neurological disorder results in impairment for one domain such as language but no impairment for another domain such as music, the pattern of effects is said to reflect a *dissociation* of domains. One implication of dissociation is that the domains in question are not associated with shared neural resources but, rather, may be processed in separate brain areas. For if the same brain areas were involved in both domains, then damage to those areas should invariably disrupt skills in both domains, never in only one.

Amusia and aphasia quite often coexist, although it is difficult to estimate the exact association between the two disorders because researchers do not always use or report comprehensive tests for each domain. Case reports of aphasia often do not include an evaluation of musical abilities, or if they do, the evaluations are often anecdotal or incomplete. It is more typical in reports of amusia for researchers to include tests for the presence of aphasia. In a review of 87 case studies of amusia, Marin and Perry (1999) found that 22% of the amusic patients showed no signs of aphasia. This percentage may not reflect the incidence of pure amusia (i.e., a musical deficit in the absence of any other type of deficit), because case reports are variable in the scope of tests administered, the data reported, or both. At any rate, a co-occurrence of amusia with aphasia would not indicate that the domains are associated with common brain regions because injury can be spread across several brain regions; some that handle music and others that handle speech. In contrast, a single case of amusia without aphasia can be used to draw the logical conclusion that there must be a brain region at some level of processing that is dedicated to the processing of music, such that damage to that area results in selective impairment in music with no impairment in speech.

It is important to acknowledge that inferences related to dissociations are not always as clear-cut as they might initially seem. It is often difficult to use identical standards and task demands when evaluating the degree of impairment in these two domains. Skills and behaviors associated with music and speech are very different from each other. Verbal comprehension has no obvious analogy in music, and musical harmony has no clear analogy in speech. It is therefore difficult to use identical task demands when evaluating these two domains. When one skill appears to be spared relative to another skill, it is essential to assess whether this dissociation can be explained by differences in task demands. If a task used to assess speech was more demanding than a task used to assess music, performance on the speech task might seem "impaired" relative to performance on the music task. It would be a mistake, however, to conclude that the underlying skills are dissociated and processed in separate brain areas.

Double dissociations largely overcome this potential pitfall and provide more compelling evidence that two domains are neuroanatomically separable. Demonstrating double-dissociation requires at least two clinical cases: one case in which the first domain (e.g., music) is impaired and the second (e.g., speech) is spared, and another case in which the second domain is impaired and the first is spared. Double dissociations cannot easily be explained by overall difficulty of tasks, especially if similar tasks were used to clinically evaluate both cases.

Double dissociations have often been reported for music and speech. Famous cases of aphasia without amusia, such as the Russian composer Shebalin and cases of amusia without aphasia described by Peretz, suggest that music and speech are dissociable and separable neuroanatomically. In spite of such cases, however, the idiosyncratic nature of impairment resulting from brain injury leaves open the possibility that there are undiscovered areas of overlap between these domains at some stage of processing. One area of potential overlap is pitch processing. Sensitivity to pitch is crucial to our perception of melody, but it is also critical to our ability to interpret speech intonation. *Speech intonation* refers to the pitch variation that occurs in speech and contributes (along with other nonverbal qualities of speech such as loudness, timbre, and speaking rate) to speech prosody. Interestingly, the case of I. R. described earlier involved impaired sensitivity to both melodic and prosodic information (Patel et al. 1998), suggesting a possible association between melody and nonverbal aspects of speech.

In an investigation of the issue, Patel et al. (2005) tested individuals with congenital amusia (tone deafness) on their ability to discriminate pitch sequences derived from the pitch variation in spoken phrases. Being tone-deaf, these individuals were insensitive to pitch changes that occur in melodies, and the researchers wanted to know if they were similarly insensitive to pitch changes that occur in speech. Pairs of spoken phrases were created in which the two sentences were lexically identical but differed in intonation. In some cases the pitch movement used to signal emphasis was placed on different words in the two sentences (e.g., "I like BLUE ties on gentlemen" vs. "I like blue TIES on gentlemen"). Pitch was manipulated by computer editing to avoid timing and intensity differences.

Sound Examples 7.2.1–7.2.6

These are the "I like blue ties on gentlemen" stimuli used in Patel et al. (2005). **Sound examples 7.2.1** and **7.2.2** are identical except for the difference in intonation—the former contains pitch movement on "blue," the latter on "ties."

In **Sound examples 7.2.3** and **7.2.4,** the two phrases have been electronically manipulated so that each syllable from the spoken phrases has been replaced with a tone with a steady pitch.

In **Sound examples 7.2.5** and **7.2.6** glides between the pitches in the previous two examples have been inserted to make the sequences sound more speech-like.

Source: Courtesy of Aniruddh Patel.

Two sets of tonal sequences were derived from these spoken phrases. In the first set, each syllable from the spoken phrases was replaced by a tone that had a steady pitch with a fundamental frequency that was midway between the maximum and minimum fundamental frequency of the syllable. These sequences sounded somewhat like a melody, but sequential tones did not form familiar melodic intervals. In the second set, the pitch of each tone precisely mirrored the upward and downward pitch glides of the spoken syllables. These sequences sounded more speechlike than the first type of pitch sequences, but were still incomprehensible. Participants were presented with pairs of identical or different tone sequences and indicated whether the two sequences of each pair were the same or different.

Participants showed impaired performance for both types of sequences. That is, not only were these individuals insensitive to musical pitch, they also had poor sensitivity to the kinds of pitch changes that occur in speech. The results seem to suggest that a single brain region controls sensitivity to pitch pattern in music as well as sensitivity to pitch variation that occurs in speech. To complicate matters, however, when spoken phrases were presented intact, tone-deaf individuals were able to discriminate them quite well. This was true even though spoken phrases were matched in all respects other than differences in pitch. Apparently, participants were impaired at detecting pitch variation in music and speech, but they could still notice the effects that such changes had on the meaning of spoken phrases.

A second area of potential overlap is syntax. Both music and language involve discrete elements (tones, words) that are combined in meaningful and systematic ways. Linguists and music theorists have developed careful descriptions of the manner in which basic elements

---

An Example of Syntax in Language

The following is an example of syntax known as a *phrase structure rule* that occurs in the English language:

> **In a noun phrase (NP), a noun (N) can be preceeded by a determiner (Det).**

A determiner is a word that qualifies a noun, such as an article ("the" or "a") or a demonstrative ("this" or "that").

The NP "the gargoyle" follows this phrase structure rule; "gargoyle the" does not because the determiner "the" does not precede the noun "gargoyle."

This rule of syntax is descriptive (i.e., indicative of how English speakers speak) rather than prescriptive

(i.e., how English speakers should speak). Notice this phrase structure rule does not state that an NP *must* consist of a determiner plus noun, only that it *can* contain a determiner and a noun. It can also contain, for example, an adjective ("the hideous gargoyle"), or, conversely, the NP may not contain a determiner at all ("gargoyles").

As infants we tend to acquire these syntactic rules even though they may not be specifically taught to us. As adults, "gargoyle the" sounds wrong immediately.

are combined, and these descriptions are formally referred to as *syntactic principles*. Listeners seem to have an implicit understanding of these principles, because when a word is misplaced in a sentence or when an unexpected note in a melody occurs, it is highly noticeable. Patel (2003) argued that syntax in music and language might be associated with shared neural mechanisms located in an area within the frontal lobe known as Broca's area. It is well established that Broca's area is involved in language skills, but its potential role in music skills has only recently been considered.

Intriguingly, Patel's hypothesis appears in direct opposition to several case studies of patients with impaired perception of harmonic relations in music, but no corresponding impairment for speech stimuli (e.g., Griffiths et al., 1997; Peretz, 1993; Peretz et al., 1994). These clinical dissociations suggest that there is a level of processing at which skills related to music syntax are handled in brain regions that are distinct from skills related to speech syntax.

On the other hand, several neuroimaging studies suggest that linguistic and musical syntax are processed in the same brain regions. Described in some detail later, *functional neuroimaging* is a technique that allows researchers to observe brain activity while an individual is engaged in some task. It is an extension of *structural neuroimaging*, which focuses on static images of the brain and is often used for medical diagnostic purposes (e.g., CAT scans, MRI). The results from a range of functional neuroimaging studies suggest that tasks related to music syntax and language syntax elicit neural activity in the same regions of the brain, including a left hemisphere frontal lobe region known as Broca's area and its right hemisphere homologue (for reviews, see Koelsch, 2006; Patel, 2003). In short, by the end of the 1990s, the results of clinical and neuroimaging studies seemed contradictory.

Patel's solution to this contradiction was to propose that sensitivity to syntax involves a set of general processes that operate on neurologically distinct syntactic representations. The general processes may occur in frontal regions of the brain, and function to provide neural resources for syntactic connections to be made, whether those connections are made for musical or linguistic stimuli.

Syntactic processing is critically important for language comprehension. For example, in the sentences "The band played two sets" and "The band that my mother joined played two sets," the verb "played" must be connected in a meaningful way with the noun "band," but integration of the verb and noun is more difficult in the second sentence because of the intervening material. More specifically, the second sentence requires more extensive syntactic processing, and hence greater neural resources. We also make connections between musical events and preceding events. Patel believes that the provision of resources needed for integrating current and past events involves the same neural regions for music and speech.

However, these general processes operate on mental representations of the musical and linguistic events, and these representations are likely to be domain specific and neurally separable. Thus, Patel's hypothesis is that clinical dissociations reflect damage to domain-specific *representations* used for musical and linguistic syntax, whereas neuroimaging results reflected activity related to *general syntactic processing*. Whether this hypothesis is correct has yet to be determined, but the issue illustrates how brain imaging studies can complement and clarify case studies of patients with brain injury.

The technique of examining patients with brain injury to identify skills that are impaired has a long and successful history with researchers such as Wernicke and Broca, who identified brain regions associated with speech using these techniques. However, recent brain-scanning methods have allowed researchers to investigate healthy brains, and these methods have yielded a rich body of evidence that is deepening and expanding our understanding of the brain. There are now several such scanning methods, including fMRI, PET, EEG, and MEG. These techniques are reviewed in the following section, followed by a summary of neuroimaging results that bear on the relation between music and the brain.

Techniques of Neuroimaging

Early in the 1900s, the X-ray was the best technology available for looking inside the human body. Unlike bones, however, the brain consists mostly of soft tissue and is invisible to such examination. Several techniques have been developed and refined since that time for monitoring neural activity in the brain. These techniques may be divided into electrical/magnetic techniques, and hemodynamic/metabolic techniques.

ELECTRICAL/MAGNETIC TECHNIQUES

Neuroimaging can be accomplished by monitoring the electrical activity or electromagnetic fields generated by neuronal activity. Two techniques include the EEG and the MEG. The techniques work because all brain activity involves chemical changes that generate electrical charges. These electrical charges are strong enough to be detected on the outside of the scalp by measuring the amount of electricity in volts (EEG) or by measuring magnetic signals associated with electrical activity (MEG).

In electroencephalography, the voltage of electrical activity, also called electrical *potential*, is measured by placing *electrodes* directly on the scalp, typically after preparing the scalp with some light abrasion and applying a conductive gel to the target areas. The voltage of this electrical activity is miniscule to begin with, and is greatly attenuated by the time it reaches the outside of the scalp, so each electrode is connected to an amplifier that magnifies the voltage by as much as 100,000 times, and then inputs the information to a computer for analysis. To monitor the activity emanating from various locations in the brain, researchers may place up to 100 or more electrodes all around the scalp.

An electrophysiological response to an internal (cognitive) or external stimulus is called an *event-related potential* (ERP). ERPs are represented as a wave (*voltage* over time) that can have positive and negative deflections, representing the *polarity* of the electrical charge. Each deflection in the wave is described by its polarity as P (positive) and N (negative), by the number of milliseconds that elapsed between the event

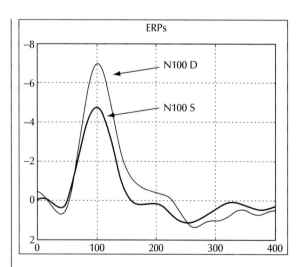

An event related potential (ERP) evoked from an auditory stimulus. The x-axis represents time in milliseconds (msec) after the presentation of the stimulus and the y-axis represents voltage. Activity below 0 on the y-axis has a positive polarity (P) and activity above has a negative polarity (N).

The thick line is the N100 for standard stimuli (N100 S) and the thin line is the N100 for deviant stimuli (N100 D).

Source: Adapted from H. Yppärilä et al. (2004). The effect of interruption to propofol sedation on auditory event-related potentials and electroencephalogram in intensive care patients. *Critical Care* 8(6), R4835.

and the deflection (e.g., P300 indicates that a positive deflection occurred 300 msec after the event), and by the number of deflections that have occurred (e.g., P3 indicates the third positive deflection).

Over the past several decades, researchers have identified patterns of electrical activity that are stable and predictable from person to person. One well-known electrical pattern is referred to as *mismatch negativity* (MMN), which is a negative deflection that occurs in the frontal lobe about 150 msec after any stimulus change. The MMN pattern reflects the detection of simple changes in acoustic input, such as a change in the pitch or timing of a musical event. MMN responses tend to be observed following any "oddball" in an otherwise predictable stimulus. Depending on which electrodes detect electrical activity, researchers can estimate the location of the brain activity. However, ERPs are distorted by the resistive properties of the skull and scalp, which makes it difficult to localize this activity precisely.

Magnetic fields are not susceptible to distortion from the scalp, so spatial resolution is much better for MEG than it is for EEG. Of course, unless other forms of brain imaging are used (e.g., MRI), localization of brain activity using either procedure requires the assumption that the individual's brain is "standard." The primary challenge with MEG is that magnetic fields arising from brain activity are so weak that measurements must be done in special research environments that shield the procedure from ambient magnetic fields that might distort the data, including the Earth's magnetic field. Without an extremely sensitive measurement device (called a superconducting quantum interference device [SQUID]), the incredibly weak electromagnetic signals arising from brain activity would be totally overwhelmed by ambient magnetic noise from the environment.

Unlike EEG, the procedures used for MEG do not involve applying electrodes to the scalp. Rather, the individual is placed inside a magnetically shielded room (to reduce contamination from environmental sources of magnetic activity) and his or her head is positioned within either a movable helmet or a helmet-shaped compartment that contains up to 300 sensors. Data from the sensors are then transferred to a computer for analysis. Magnetic activity is averaged over a very large number of trials because the data for any one trial are subject to considerable noise and contamination. Even if the individual adjusts her or his leg slightly, or blinks, or a truck moves past the building, the electromagnetic fields associated with these sources will mask the much subtler signal that is generated by a perceptual and cognitive task.

Both EEG and MEG techniques allow researchers to examine brain activity with high temporal resolution (MEG is accurate to 1 msec), but they acquire information in different ways and provide somewhat different representations of brain activity. For example, the *polarity* of ERPs is not represented in MEG signals, even though both techniques can be used to examine the MMN or "oddball" response. Not surprisingly, determining the precise location of brain activity is challenging with either EEG or MEG data because measurements are taken at the scalp and not within the brain itself.

Imagine trying to identify the location of a furnace that is inside a locked room by feeling for heat on the other side of the wall. It may be possible to infer that the furnace is somewhere behind the warmest point on the wall, but it would be difficult to pinpoint its exact position. Now imagine a room filled with hundreds of furnaces and estimating which ones are turned on by feeling for heat on the other side of a wall that has variable heat conductivity at different positions. This challenge in determining the precise location of neural activity from electrical and magnetic information outside of the scalp is addressed using sophisticated data analysis techniques, but ultimately the techniques have low spatial resolution compared with other neuroimaging techniques. On the other hand, electricity moves rapidly so researchers can determine the time of an electrical response with enormous accuracy, giving these techniques relatively high temporal resolution.

HEMODYNAMIC/METABOLIC TECHNIQUES

In the same way that intense physical activity causes our breathing and heart rate to increase, neurons in active regions of the brain require increased levels of oxygen, which are supplied by increased blood flow. Hemodynamic neuroimaging methods are designed to detect changes in blood flow and oxygen metabolism in the brain. Two hemodynamic techniques are PET and fMRI.

PET involves injecting a radioactive solution into the bloodstream. Although the levels of radiation are not considered hazardous, introducing any foreign substance into the CNS is by definition an *invasive technique*. The radioactive substance only stays in the bloodstream for a limited time but, while it is there, any increase in blood flow at a particular brain region will be detectable as increased levels of radiation emanating from that region. The technique is called *positron emission tomography* because the injected substance emits *positrons* that interact with *electrons* to produce photons of electromagnetic radiation. A photon detector (i.e., the scanner) is then placed around the participant's head to detect regions of the brain in which there is increased radioactivity. Greater levels of the radioactivity indicate greater blood flow and, hence, greater neural activity. As with any X-ray device, the scanner can identify the location of the radiation with great precision, and its spatial resolution is on the order of 4 to 6 mm. The temporal resolution (i.e., identifying precisely when the brain activity occurred), on the other hand, is quite poor because it is constrained by a lengthy image acquisition time of 90 to 120 seconds.

fMRI is a more recent technology than PET and has better spatial and temporal resolution for detecting brain activity. It also has the advantage that it does not require the researcher to inject a radioactive substance into the participant's bloodstream. fMRI capitalizes on the fact that neural activity requires increased levels of blood oxygen, and changes in the ratio of oxygenated to deoxygenated blood (oxy-hemoglobin and deoxy-hemoglobin) results in measurable changes to the electromagnetic field associated with that brain region. Thus, the scanner in fMRI is used to identify magnetic fields that reflect elevated blood oxygen levels and, hence, increased neural activity. This measure of neural activity is referred to as the *blood oxygen level dependent* (BOLD) signal. By monitoring the BOLD signal, neuronal activity can be localized to within a few millimeters, which is a better spatial resolution than all the other neuroimaging techniques described. Its temporal resolution is limited because changes in blood oxygen only occur several seconds after a stimulus.

Neuroimaging and Music

The number of neuroimaging studies that involve music is growing rapidly, with results reported from studies involving a range of techniques. Results allow researchers to identify brain regions associated with different aspects of music cognition, and they allow investigations of potential overlap in the neural circuitry associated with music and other domains such as speech. Several imaging studies using music stimuli have revealed activity in brain areas traditionally associated with other domains such as speech. Although these findings are intriguing, it must be acknowledged that the spatial resolution of all available imaging techniques is limited and convergence of brain regions associated with music and other domains

A musician receives an MRI scan while he performs a musical task.

Source: Zatorre, R., and Peretz, I. (Eds.). (2001). *Biological foundations of music.* New York: New York Academy of Sciences, vol. 930, colour plate 6. Reprinted by permission.

does not verify that these domains are associated with identical neural circuitry. Neuropsychological evidence often points to *neural resource convergence* for distinct domains such as music and speech. Whether this convergence reflects the involvement of common neural resources or merely reflects proximity of neural resources has yet to be confirmed.

There are several reasons for choosing one technique over another. One consideration is cost. The equipment required for fMRI, PET, and MEG is extremely expensive in comparison to the equipment required for EEG. Another consideration is safety. For researchers working with young children, MEG is preferable to fMRI or PET because the latter two procedures may be harmful to small children. A third factor is the focus of the research. For researchers concerned with localizing brain activity with high precision, fMRI and PET are preferable to electrical/magnetic techniques. Conversely, for researchers interested in the time course of brain responses to stimuli, MEG and EEG are preferable to the hemodynamic/metabolic techniques. A fourth factor is the nature of the task. The scanners used in PET and fMRI restrict head movement, which limits the types of tasks that can be administered, and makes it difficult to use effectively with infants and young children. In contrast, MEG may involve placing a prepared helmet on the participant, allowing somewhat more head movement. Other factors include the technical expertise required to analyze data, setup time, and machine noise. The scanner used in fMRI, for example, generates quite loud and repetitious banging sounds, which researchers must work around when conducting experiments involving auditory stimuli such as music.

ELECTRICAL/MAGNETIC STUDIES OF MUSIC

One of the most basic functions of the brain is to detect a change. This type of brain response can be measured using the electrical/magnetic techniques of EEG and MEG. When an individual is presented with a series of identical tones spaced at regular intervals (i.e., isochronous tones), a simple change in one of the tones will elicit brain activity about 150 msec after the change occurs. As previously described, the evoked potential associated with this activity is referred to as MMN because it has a negative polarity and is evoked by a change (mismatch) in an ongoing signal.

The MMN response occurs in the *auditory cortex* and reflects the detection of basic features of sound, such as pitch, duration, loudness, or timbre. The MMN response can be elicited even when participants are not attending to the change (e.g., when they are asked to perform a different task), which indicates that the brain processes that detect such basic changes do so *preattentively*, that is, without the need for conscious attention. MMN responses are not restricted to basic acoustic changes. They are also elicited by simple aspects of musical structure such as the contour and interval (pitch distance between tones) of melodies (Trainor, McDonald, & Alain, 2002).

The high temporal resolution of electrical/magnetic imaging techniques makes them especially well suited for studying properties of music related to timing, such as rhythm. Interestingly, brain activity occurs not only as a response to sound input; it also occurs when a rhythmically anticipated event is *omitted*. As this activity is not evoked by a stimulus but by the absence of a stimulus, it is referred to as an *emitted potential* (or *omitted stimulus potential*) rather than an evoked potential. The emitted potential is a positive peak about 300 msec after the expected onset time of an anticipated event that is omitted from a regular sequence (Barlow 1969; Takasaka 1985). Thus, brain activity not only monitors and interprets incoming sound; it also monitors and interprets the *omission* of an event that is expected at a particular moment in time. Research on the neural basis of rhythm is still in its infancy, but according to Large and Jones (1999) the generation of temporal expectancies is fundamental to rhythm perception. If so, then emitted potentials may prove to be a central constituent of the neural basis of rhythm.

Evoked potentials can also be used to understand how the brain processes the timbre of individual tones. Shahin, Roberts, Pantev, Aziz, and Picton (2007) presented musically trained and untrained participants with tones of varying harmonic complexity. The most complex tone had eight harmonics and the simplest tone consisted of a single frequency (i.e., a sine tone). ERPs were then collected for each type of tone. Next, ERPs for the sine tone were subtracted from ERPs for the harmonically rich tone, yielding what are called *difference waves*. Logically, the difference waves should reflect brain activity associated with the overtones of the harmonically rich tone, but not with its fundamental frequency, which was the same as the simplest tone.

Both groups showed positive difference waves at 130 msec and 300 msec. The difference wave at 130 msec was also larger (greater amplitude) in the musically trained group than the untrained group. The source of brain activity was localized in the anterior temporal cortex, with a relatively greater response in the right hemisphere. Thus, the anterior

Sound Examples 7.3.1–7.3.2

These examples demonstrate the musical syntax of the Western tonal tradition (from Maess, Koelsch, Gunter, & Friederici, 2001). Similar to the previous syntax example from the English language, even without explicit knowledge of a specific syntactic principle, the last chord in **Sound example 7.3.2** likely sounds unexpected and out of context in comparison with the last chord in **Sound example 7.3.1**.

Syntactic principles, whether for music or language, need not be invariant over place or time. **Sound example 7.3.2** would likely sound less "wrong" to a person unfamiliar with Western musical traditions or more "wrong" to a Western European born two centuries ago.

temporal cortex seems to be responsible for analyzing the timbre of tones, and a greater response is observed for musically trained than untrained participants. Why would musically trained individuals show a greater brain response to complex tones? One possibility is that training leads to increased responses to all musical sounds. However, it is also possible that individuals who naturally possess such enhanced brain responses to musical sounds are those who gravitate toward music lessons.

EEG and MEG have also been used to understand how the brain responds to harmonic structure. This research indicates that musically trained and untrained adults, as well as children 5 years old, show EEG and MEG responses to violations of Western harmonic conventions (Koelsch, 2005). Why do such brain responses vary as a function of Western harmonic conventions? Most researchers believe that these responses develop through passive music listening. That is, through long-term exposure, we internalize the conventions of the music of our own culture, and this gives us an implicit understanding of the kinds of chord progressions that make musical sense and those that do not. This feature of music—that some sequences "work" and some do not—is called *musical syntax*. Musical syntax is analogous to linguistic syntax. Just as some word combinations make sense (e.g., the boy went to the store) and others do not (e.g., the went store to the boy), some chord combinations make musical sense and other chord combinations are unmusical.

In one experiment, participants were presented with harmonic sequences that either fulfilled or violated harmonic conventions. In conditions involving a violation of harmonic expectancies, the researchers inserted an unexpected (inappropriate) chord in the middle of the sequence and measured the evoked potentials associated with that chord. Measurements taken from EEG and MEG showed an evoked potential that was labeled an *early right anterior negativity* (ERAN). The ERAN response to harmonic irregularity occurred about 200 msec after the onset of the expected chord, which is a fairly rapid (early) brain response, although not as rapid as the MMN brain response that occurs when a simpler acoustic or melodic change is introduced. As the name implies, ERAN is detected more on the right side of the scalp and toward the front (*anterior*), and has a negative electrical polarity.

Electrical activity is measured at the scalp and not in the brain itself, so statistical techniques must be used to estimate the location of brain activity that generated the scalp measurements. The term right in ERAN indicates that the evoked potential was strongest on the right side of the scalp, but the brain activity responsible for these evoked potentials is not necessarily confined to one hemisphere. Using statistical analyses and corroborated by fMRI studies, Koelsch and his colleagues localized brain activity responsible for the ERAN response in the right and left frontal lobes (some temporal lobe activity was also observed). Most significantly, brain activity was observed in the *inferior fronto-lateral cortex*. Within the left hemisphere this particular region is known as Broca's area and is strongly implicated in the processing of syntax in language.

Consistent with Patel's (2003, 2008) suggestion that there are common neural processes for handling musical and linguistic syntax, the discovery of brain responses to music in Broca's area implies that there is overlap in the neural resources for processing music and language. It should be emphasized, however, that brain activity is by no means identical for these two domains. Music syntactic processing is associated with a greater right-hemispheric bias in brain activity (hence the R in ERAN), whereas language processing is associated with a greater left-hemisphere weighting. Thus, the evoked potentials for detecting syntactic errors in language are called ELAN rather than ERAN, because they are maximal on the left side of the scalp. In spite of these overall differences in hemispheric bias, at least some of the brain regions associated with musical and linguistic syntax may be the same.

The ERAN response occurs relatively soon after a syntactic violation in music (about 150 msec) but sensitivity to music involves more than the detection of syntactic violations. Having detected an expected chord, the musical relationship between the current chord and preceding chords must be determined so that the listener can make sense of the progression. This process is called *structural integration*. Interestingly, additional bursts of brain activity from musical syntactic violations have been observed well after the initial ERAN response. Many researchers believe that this later brain activity may be responsible for integrating current and preceding musical events.

One such evoked potential is called P600, which indicates that it has a positive polarity and occurs about 600 msec after the onset of the unexpected event. The P600 is triggered by structural incongruities of both music and language, which may suggest that some aspect of structural integration is shared between music and language (Patel, 2003, 2008). In other words, music and language may share neural resources for early syntactic processing (i.e., hence the overlap between the brain activity responsible for ERAN and ELAN responses) as well as later syntactic processing (hence the P600 response that is observed for both music and speech syntactic processing).

HEMODYNAMIC/METABOLIC STUDIES OF MUSIC

Hemodynamic/metabolic techniques are unable to differentiate rapid and slower brain responses that correspond to basic and more complex analyses of sound and music, but they are vastly superior to electrical/magnetic techniques in their ability to pinpoint the location of brain activity. In general, fMRI and PET studies have confirmed that, although brain regions in the right temporal lobe are strongly associated with music, many musical tasks can generate activity in the left temporal lobe or other regions of both hemispheres. The involvement of the temporal lobe is not surprising given that it contains the primary auditory cortex (described anatomically as Heschel's Gyrus), and the involvement of other regions is gradually becoming understood.

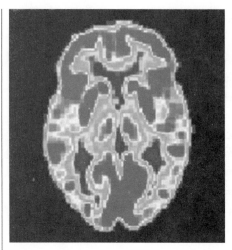

A PET scan.

Source: Alzheimer's Disease Education and Referral Center, a service of the National Institute on Aging.

Some researchers have proposed broad characterizations of the right and left hemispheres in an attempt to explain why they are differentially engaged for different skills. One popular claim (relating to the *bicameral mind*) is that the left and right hemispheres are specialized for analytic and holistic activities, respectively. In an attempt to characterize the two hemispheres in their response to sound, Zatorre and Belin (2001) proposed that the right hemisphere is generally specialized for pitch-related (*spectral*) information, whereas the left hemisphere is more specialized for timing (*temporal*) information. Using PET, they presented their participants with a number of different tone sequences, all of which included a range of different pitches. The sequences varied either in the rate of presentation (*temporal variation*) or in the number of different pitches within an octave span (*spectral variation*). Manipulations of temporal variation altered the rate at which tones were presented but did not alter the number of different pitches in the sequence; manipulations of spectral variation altered the number of different pitches in the sequence but did not alter the rate of presentation.

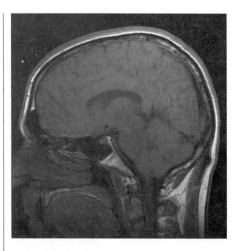

An MRI scan.

Source: Erat (Flickr). Made available under Creative Commons 2.5 Attribution-Generic License.

The PET scan indicated bilateral temporal lobe activity in response to both types of variation. However, responses to changes in presentation rate showed greater left hemisphere activity, whereas responses to changes in the number of different pitches showed greater right hemisphere activity. The researchers concluded that left hemisphere auditory cortex is specialized (*dominant*) for rapid temporal processing, whereas the right hemisphere auditory cortex is specialized for representing detailed pitch (spectral) information. In other words, brain responses to temporal and pitch processing tend to be *lateralized*. Training in music may actually increase this lateralization. In a study by Limb, Kemeny, Ortigoza, Rouhani, and Braun (2006), musicians and nonmusicians heard regular or random rhythmic patterns. As they listened passively, their brain activity was monitored using fMRI. Rhythm processing areas were taken as those regions of activity that occurred in response to regular but not random patterns. In both groups, rhythm processing occurred mainly in the left hemisphere (although there was some right hemisphere activity), and there was greater lateralization of activity in musicians compared to nonmusicians.

Why should the two hemispheres differ in this respect? Zatorre (2005) pointed out that throughout human evolution it may have been adaptive to respond to sound information in different ways depending on the circumstance, and the two hemispheres may have evolved as parallel strategies of evaluating and responding to sound. When sound energy was changing rapidly, survival may have depended on the ability to track such changes quickly even if the fine details of the sound were sacrificed. Conversely, when it was not necessary to track rapidly changing sound information, it may have been advantageous to analyze the details of sound in the form of a spectral analysis. The left and right hemispheres appear to have evolved for these two different purposes, respectively. Understanding speech requires rapid attention to changing spectral energy and therefore makes greater demands on the left hemisphere. Perceiving music involves sensitivity to detailed differences in pitch and therefore makes somewhat greater demands on the right hemisphere. Both hemispheres are implicated in each domain, but the demands placed on the two hemispheres differ for speech and music.

RESPONDING EMOTIONALLY TO MUSIC

One of the great discoveries in the film industry is the extraordinary capacity of musical soundtracks to induce visceral terror, and recent research has identified some of the brain areas that are responsive to fearful music. Much to the delight of film score composers, it turns out that music is seemingly capable of inducing fear to a greater extent than visual

Music and Marijuana

For many musicians (e.g., Bob Marley, Willie Neilson, Cypress Hill) and music lovers, music and cannabis seem to go hand in hand. Although empirical research on the effects of cannabis on music perception is scarce, cannabis users' subjective experiences are well-documented and exhibit some consistencies. Listeners, for example, often report that music enhances the euphoria induced through consumption, or conversely, that music seems more vivid when under the influence.

Many musicians have also reported that their musical performance is enhanced through cannabis consumption (Fachner, 2003). In particular, some jazz musicians have reported that marijuana facilitates improvisation. One of the most universal reactions to the marijuana high is its effect on time perception—time seems to slow down. This effect has been validated in the lab,

where participants tend to overestimate the amount of time passed in time perception tasks. Some jazz improvisers claim that this altered time perception gives them greater insight into "the space between the notes." That is, the sense that time is moving more slowly gives the improviser the impression of having more time to make spontaneous musical decisions.

There may be a partial neuropsychological explanation for this subjective experience. A marijuana high is experienced when the psychotropic compounds in cannabis (primarily THC) are metabolized by *cannabinoid receptors* in the brain. The cerebellum—long known to be implicated in time perception, particularly for the smaller time intervals important to music—is known as an area of the brain with high concentrations of cannabinoid receptors.

images. Visual images are experienced as "out there," whereas sounds are experienced both outside and inside our heads. We feel sounds in our very bones, making it difficult to distance ourselves from them. Sounds are also less easily localized than visual images, creating nervousness about their source. In industrialized society, fear of predation is largely nonexistent, replaced with a fear of our own technology: car and airplane accidents, nuclear disasters, and weapons. However, fear responses today are the result of adaptive pressures that took place thousands of years ago when predation was a constant threat, and the brain area most strongly associated with fear—the amygdala—is thought to have a long evolutionary history. It is therefore not surprising that when predators of humans are portrayed in film, as in *Jaws* or *Jurassic Park*, the experience of fear is almost unbearable.

In a study by Gosselin et al. (2005), patients with amygdala resection for the relief of medically intractable seizures rated the extent to which musical passages expressed various emotions, including fear. Compared with a control group, the patients showed normal perceptual abilities. However, whereas recognition of happy and sad music was normal, they were significantly impaired in the recognition of frightening music. Without the amygdala sounding an alarm, music that is terrifying to most people is experienced as relatively neutral and nonarousing (Gosselin, Peretz, Johnsen, & Adolphs, 2007).

Neuroimaging has revealed many other regions of the brain that are engaged when we respond emotionally to music. In a study using PET, Blood and Zatorre (2001) reported various types of brain activity associated with the experience of musical chills (often felt down the spine). Brain activity was observed in an area of the frontal lobe called the orbitofrontal cortex, as well as other regions of the brain including the brain stem. Most significantly, many of the regions showing activity are the very same as those known to show activity in response to euphoria-inducing stimuli such as sex, drugs, and eating chocolate. The researchers proposed that highly pleasurable music seems to recruit general brain regions involved in pleasure and reward. Pleasurable music may also lead to the release of neurotransmitters associated with reward, such as *dopamine* (Menon & Levitin, 2005). One wonders whether these results have any relevance to the association between drugs and music that was evident in the psychedelic 1960s.

Koelsch (2005) reviewed studies of how the brain responds to emotional music, and concluded that various limbic and cortical structures are implicated, with the region of activity dependent on the type of emotion that is expressed. Using EEG and fMRI, Flores-Gutierrez et al. (2007) found that pleasant music was associated with several areas of the left hemisphere, including regions within the temporal, parietal, and frontal lobes. In contrast, unpleasant music was more strongly associated with the right hemisphere, including regions in the frontal and temporal lobes. This lateralization for pleasant and unpleasant stimuli might arise because the left hemisphere is generally associated with *predictable* situations, whereas the right hemisphere is associated with *novel* situations.

IMAGINING AND PERFORMING MUSIC

Halpern and Zatorre (1999) used PET to compare brain activity associated with listening to or imagining music. Many of the same areas in the temporal lobes that were involved in listening to the melodies were activated when those melodies were merely imagined. Imagining music also resulted in brain activity in regions known as the premotor areas, suggesting a possible connection between imagining music and movements involved in playing music.

Meister et al. (2004) used fMRI to compare brain activity associated with performing a piece (with the right hand) and imagining that piece of music. For both tasks, there was *bilateral* brain activity (i.e., activity in both hemispheres) in the premotor area. When participants performed the piece, but not when they imagined it, there was also activity in the *contralateral* hemisphere. This activity was located in the *primary motor cortex* of the left hemisphere as well as a posterior area of the parietal lobe associated with integrating visual and motor activity.

Can brain activity also account for the difference between performing a simple scale and performing by memory a piece of music composed by J. S. Bach? Parsons (2001) used PET to compare these two conditions and found activity in a number of brain regions when participants played the Bach piece, but not when they played scales. Both tasks required movements of similar frequency, although the Bach piece with its intricate structure required more complex movements. The primary difference in brain activity was seen in the temporal lobes. Interestingly, performance of the scales resulted in relatively more left than right temporal lobe activity, whereas performance of the Bach piece resulted in more right than left temporal lobe activity. This difference may reflect the fact that certain regions in the right temporal lobe are specialized for representing and interpreting the detailed melodic patterns that are characteristic of the Bach piece but not the simple scale patterns.

BRAINS OF MUSICIANS

Not everyone is capable of performing music, which raises the question of whether the brains of skilled musicians are any different than those of people with no or little training in music. Pantev et al. (1998) used MEG to examine this very issue. They found that, when people listened to a piano performance, there was about 25% more brain activity in the left hemisphere auditory regions of musicians than nonmusicians. This effect is specific to musical tones and is enhanced when those tones are taken from the musician's own instrument. The effect was specific to musical tones, however. Musicians and nonmusicians show no difference in brain activity in response to nonmusical sounds.

Using MEG, Pantev et al. (1998) found that the younger a person began his or her music training, the greater amount of brain activity occurred in response to musical tones.

Source: Original photography: woodleywonderworks (Flickr). Made available under Creative Commons 2.0 Attribution-Generic License.

Pantev et al. (1998) also found that the younger a person began his or her music training, the greater the amount of brain activity in response to musical tones. Thus, early musical experience may facilitate brain development in regions responsible for music processing. Shahin, Roberts, and Trainor (2004) used MEG to record brain activity in 4- and 5-year-old children after they were exposed to piano, violin, and pure tones. Brain activity was greater in children who received more music exposure in their homes. Music experience may result not only in greater brain responses to musical sounds but also in more extensive development of the cortical areas responsible for processing sound. Schneider et al. (2002) found that the total volume of the auditory cortex was 130% larger in musicians than in nonmusicians. In other words, it appears that taking music lessons can actually increase the number of neurons that are dedicated to music.

A Rapidly Evolving Field

Over the past two decades our understanding of the neural basis of music has expanded and changed. Research findings have forced a revision of the traditional view that music is processed squarely in the right hemisphere, just as language is processed in the left hemisphere. Among the first clues was Bever and Chiarello's (1974) discovery that musically trained individuals use their left hemisphere when performing various musical tasks. Since that time, clinical and neuroimaging studies have pointed to a complex picture of the neural basis of music, with the right hemisphere handling some of the most salient aspects of musical behavior, the left hemisphere handling fewer but essential properties of music, and the combined operation of both hemispheres associated with a surprisingly large number of musical behaviors and skills.

Within each hemisphere, brain activity is not restricted to a particular region such as the temporal lobe. An initial analysis of sound certainly occurs in the primary auditory cortex, which is situated in the temporal lobe, but other regions including areas within the other lobes and subcortical brain structures are also implicated in most musical behaviors. The right temporal lobe plays an important role in the computation of pitch relations, including pitch height and pitch contour, and sensitivity to pitch interval is associated with the left and right temporal lobes. The ability to recognize familiar tunes can be impaired following damage to either the right or left temporal lobe, and neuroimaging studies indicate that temporal and frontal areas in the left hemisphere are involved in melody recognition (Platel et al., 1997).

Sensitivity to musical syntax, as indicated by evoked potentials to harmonic violations, is associated with the left and right frontal lobes in regions that correspond to Broca's area in the left hemisphere and its homologue in the right hemisphere. Insofar as Broca's area is strongly associated with linguistic syntactic processing, it seems plausible that music and language share neural circuitry for processing syntax. On the other hand, the brain regions observed through neuroimaging are so densely populated with neural circuitry that they could conceivably contain several distinct subregions. The *convergence* of brain activity for musical and linguistic stimuli observed in brain imaging studies might reflect shared neural resources, but it is also possible that they merely reflect proximal but distinct neural resources.

Rhythm perception is associated with neural activity in the left hemisphere, in that left hemisphere damage causes impairment in rhythm discrimination. Conversely, sensitivity to meter (e.g., tapping) appears to be a right hemisphere skill: Patients who have had their right temporal lobe surgically removed have great difficulty keeping track of meter (Peretz & Zatorre, 2005). Moreover, musical time is not only monitored by the cerebral hemispheres. Motor and perceptual timing is also associated with activity in the cerebellum and basal ganglia.

Several regions of the brain are involved in our emotional responses to music, which is not surprising given the complex nature of emotion. Somewhat more surprising is the connection between music-induced pleasure and the kind of pleasure induced by food and sex. Many musicians claim that their most intimate experiences of music occur when they are actively performing, and music performance is associated with a wide range of brain regions, including premotor areas, the primary motor cortex, the right temporal lobe, and regions of the parietal lobe associated with integrating visual and motor activity.

The picture that is emerging from this vast new body of research suggests that music engages multiple areas of the brain, some of which overlap with general auditory skills, others that may overlap with skills in related domains such as speech, and others that are domain specific. Many of these areas can be developed through extensive music experience and training, such that the brains of musicians are physically different than the brains of nonmusicians. Musical memory is also highly robust, and is preserved in cases of dementia even when most other cognitive skills are severely impaired. Although an enormous amount has yet to be discovered about the neurosciences of music, the rapid expansion of research makes this field one of the most exciting ones in the psychology of music.

Additional Readings

Koelsch, S., & Siebel, W. A. (2005). Towards a neural basis of music perception. *Trends in Cognitive Sciences, 9,* 578–584.

Peretz, I. (2006). The nature of music from a biological perspective. *Cognition, 100,* 1–32.

Zatorre, R. J., & Peretz, I. (2004). Brain organization for music processing. *Annual Review of Psychology, 56,* 89–114.

CHAPTER 8

Performing Music

Playing Music

Everyone who has taken music lessons is familiar with casual requests from friends to "play something" when their music experience is discovered. What exactly does playing something involve? Performing music requires not only playing the right notes at the right time, but also involves varying the loudness, timing, pitch, and timbre of notes in a way that sounds expressive and meaningful.

The memory demands on performers can be enormous (Aiello & Williamon, 2002), and performance also includes the use of expressive actions such as the *ritardando* (a gradual slowing down), *accelerando* (a gradual speeding up), *crescendo* (a gradual increase in loudness), and *diminuendo* (a gradual decrease in loudness), all implemented at strategic points in the music. Expressive timing is especially valuable for articulating structural properties of music (Ashley, 2002). Performers also introduce changes in loudness, accenting notes that have a significant musical function and attenuating others that have a subsidiary role. Instruments such as the violin, flute, and electric guitar allow the performer to vary timbre and pitch in expressive ways. Violinists may increase or decrease the amount of noise at the onset of a note by applying more or less force to the bow. Vocalists may nurture a raspy voice for singing the blues or a purer tonal quality for singing Italian opera. The gritty sound of Janice Joplin's voice enhances our experience of the blues just as the pure vocal quality of Kiri Te Kanawa enhances our experience of *La Boheme*. Vocal pitch may be varied through the use of *vibrato* or by playing a note slightly higher or lower than the pitch that is notated in the score. Electric guitarists may create melodic accents by bending pitches at strategic moments, and they may introduce distortion to augment the dramatic tension of a melodic line. Guitar distortion is a particularly powerful expressive device, evoking abrasiveness and emotional instability; it can even act as a kind of timbral *leitmotif* for ideas expressed in the lyrics. All such actions have striking aesthetic effects, and are collectively referred to as performance expression, or performance variation.

Certain aspects of performance expression are indicated in the score. Western composers often insert markings to indicate the overall desired loudness of sections using abbreviations such as *f* for the Italian *forte* (loud), *ff* or *fff* to indicate greater intensity levels, *p* to indicate *pianissimo* (soft), and so on. Converging lines signal the performer to gradually decrease the loudness; diverging lines to increase it. However, there

The opening bars of Brahms's *Intermezzo in A Major* (Op. 188, n. 2) for solo piano. Brahms's scores tend to contain a great deal of performance expression indications. This short excerpt contains several expressive markings, including tempo or speed (A = *andante teneramente*, which means "at a walking pace, tenderly" in Italian), dynamics (B = *piano* or quietly in Italian, E = getting louder, G = getting softer), articulation (C = with a smooth connection between notes), note onset (D = separate the onset of the two connected notes), as well as subtle details such as phrasing (F = an indication to group the notes contained within the arch), and timbre or tone (H = *dolce* or "sweetly").

are too many dimensions of music to be completely specified in a score. Thus, performance expression is sometimes used to refer to everything in the music that the score leaves partially or wholly unspecified, including variations in timing, intensity, timbre, and pitch. The written score provides the basic *structure* of the music, and performance expression is needed to fill in the details, often referred to as the *microstructure* of music. Without this microstructure, music would sound flat, fixed, and regular, and we probably would not bother to spend much time listening to it.

Some aspects of performance variation merely reflect a lack of precision related to imperfect skill, nervousness, inattention, or muscular constraints. Among skilled performers, however, most expressive actions are intentional and systematic, reflecting a desire to express and communicate emotional meaning and musical knowledge. Performers often have very specific communicative intentions as well as an individual style, so their performances of the same piece of music can be remarkably similar on different occasions (Gabrielsson, 1987; Shaffer, 1984). There are also commonalities in the expressive actions used by different musicians, suggesting that expressive actions are not entirely idiosyncratic but are partially shaped by stylistic traditions and perceptual constraints.

As listeners, we attend carefully to performance expression because it highlights the emotional, stylistic, and structural dimensions of music. It gives a sense of the personality of the composer, conveys emotion and passion, and provides an interpretation or perspective on the music. Performance expression can also help us to appreciate details of musical structure, such as phrase boundaries, melodies, and other significant musical events. Uses of expression can also tell us about the internal

Sound Examples 8.3.1–8.3.2

Performance expression can take the same piece of music in different directions. Consider **Sound example 8.3.1**, the jazz standard "Night Train" as performed by the Oscar Peterson Trio, and **Sound example 8.3.2**, as performed by the Dynamic Duo (Jimmy Smith and Wes Montgomery) and a big band orchestra. Beyond the obvious differences in orchestration, the two versions have a very different feel. How would you characterize the difference?

Sound examples 8.3.1 and 8.3.2 are available via the *Music, Thought, and Feeling* iMix on iTunes.

states of performers themselves, reflecting their mental representations of the music, the motor plans they use to convert these mental representations into a sequence of well-timed movements, and their unique personality as a musician.

Acquiring Performance Skill

The ability to make music in daily life is not rare. Most people have sung at a birthday party, a school choir, in church, or in the shower. Clapping or tapping to music is an instance of performance and requires sensitivity to musical timing. Few people develop a high level of musical proficiency, however, and those who do often do not sustain their ability to perform expertly for very long. Many primary and secondary school programs offer classes in music, but most students acquire only a modest degree of musical skill. In fact, the vast majority of adults in Western societies probably consider themselves to be musically illiterate. They may appreciate music, but they cannot read from a score, they cannot perform except in the most mundane and clumsy ways, and they typically feel they lack an adequate vocabulary for effectively describing what they are hearing in music.

A very small proportion of children excel at music performance. We celebrate their achievement at school recitals, local music competitions, and gatherings hosted by proud parents. In Western society, almost any degree of musicianship is viewed as a highly specialized skill rather than normal behavior, more equivalent to the skills of a professional gymnast than a good conversationalist. Individuals who develop an exceptional level of skill for music performance are frequently referred to as talented or gifted, but the concept of musical talent may be deeply misleading. As pointed out by Sloboda, Davidson, and Howe (1994), to label musically skilled individuals as talented implies that they possess an innate capacity for musical achievement, and ignores or underplays the crucial role of experience and training. Without question, there may be hereditary traits associated with musical ability, but the widespread application of the construct of musical talent may well exaggerate the role of genetic factors in determining musical ability, and underplay the role of learning and practice.

Although the concept of talent is applied in many domains, it appears to be applied disproportionately in the domain of music and art.

Sound Examples 8.4.1–8.4.2

Performers have been known to change their preferred interpretation of a piece over time. A well-known example is Bach's *Goldberg Variations* as performed by the famed Canadian pianist Glenn Gould. The earlier rendition (**Sound example 8.4.1**) recorded in 1955 (at age 22) is a departure from traditional interpretations of Bach. In some of the variations, Gould introduced bebop influences to create a fast-paced, swinging performance. By 1981, Gould could no longer identify with the earlier version and had changed his mind about how it should be performed. The second rendition (**Sound example 8.4.2**), recorded in 1981 (at age 48, a year before his death), is characterized by a clear, unwavering pulse and is far more traditional than the first. The two interpretations by the same performer could easily be confused as recordings of different pieces.

Sound examples 8.4.1 and 8.4.2 are available via the *Music, Thought, and Feeling* iMix on iTunes.

According to Davis (1994), over 75% of a sample of educational professionals believed that composing, singing, and playing concert instruments required natural talent. In contrast, less than 40% of the same sample believed that any natural gift or talent was required to develop skills of playing chess, performing surgery, or writing nonfiction.

Are these intuitions on the nature of musical ability warranted? Not according to a study by Ericsson, Krampe, and Tesch-Römer (1993). They examined student and professional instrument players and found that individuals with the highest levels of musical achievement undertook approximately double the amount of daily practice as moderate achievers, for many years. These findings parallel the effects of practice in other domains such as chess and sports. Sloboda et al. (1994; Sloboda, Davidson, Howe, & Moore, 1996) extended this study by examining the practicing habits of individuals within five different levels of musical skill. They found no evidence that high achievers were somehow able to "fast track" their way to high achievement. Apparently they did not possess any special qualities or talent that could account for their expert skill. Rather, high-achieving individuals practiced up to eight times more than did individuals in lower levels of achievement.

The acquisition of musical skill, it seems, takes enormous effort and dogged persistence. Why do some individuals bother to dedicate the amount of time and effort needed to reach such high levels of achievement? Sloboda and his colleagues noted two particularly important factors. The first related to parental involvement. Parents of high-achieving children were more likely to attend instrument lessons with their children and actively supervise their daily practice. Parents of lower achieving children were likely to restrict their involvement in music training to telling their children to "go and practice." The second and less understood factor involved a gradual change during adolescence in the degree of self-motivation experienced by high-achieving children. For reasons that are not entirely understood, high-achieving individuals seem to find and nurture their own motivations for honing their musical skills.

Although the importance of practice cannot be overstated, in very rare cases we encounter individuals who really do seem to have a genuine gift for music. These remarkable individuals advance in music at rates that cannot easily be explained. Their ability is often noted at an astonishingly young age, and hence they are labeled *prodigies*. Some of these prodigies or musical savants are impaired in other cognitive domains. One of the most famous cases is known

Thomas "Blind Tom" Wiggins (1849–1908).

Source: Library of Congress Prints and Photographs (Washington, DC, 1918).

as Blind Tom, a mentally retarded and blind young slave who was sold in 1850 to a Colonel Bethune (Jourdain, 1997). Bethune owned a mansion in Georgia and allowed Tom considerable freedom in his home. Tom especially enjoyed listening to the Colonel's daughters as they played the piano. The Colonel was amazed one day to discover Tom playing a Mozart sonata. He had heard the piece being played by one of the daughters but had been given no instructions. He was only 4 years old. Tom went on to become a concert pianist and performed for 40 years.

Cases such as Blind Tom appear to support the notion that we are born with or without musical talent. However, these cases are highly exceptional and very complex, and researchers who study musical savants are still not entirely sure how they manage to acquire such high levels of musical skill. Severely impaired in other domains, many savants dedicate themselves exclusively to music. It may seem as though their skills arise out of nowhere, but close examination of the behavior of prodigies and musical savants suggests that they often spend an inordinate amount of time engaging in musical activity.

Communicating Musical Structure

Performance expression is strongly related to musical structure, and this connection is reflected in the terms used in performance pedagogy and analysis such as *phrasing* and *articulation*. How should we conceptualize this connection? One of the most prevalent views is that performance expression is an act of *communication* in which performers vary timing, loudness, and other expressive qualities with the intention of clarifying and emphasizing details of the musical structure to listeners. This interpretation makes a conceptual distinction between musical structure (e.g., as reflected in the score) and the expressive actions of performers, and it implies that performance expression is implemented consciously and intentionally.

Some authors have pointed out that we never actually experience music structure as an abstract entity separate from the expressive choices made by performers. In their view, expressive actions organically reflect the performer's understanding of music but should not be conceived as a message that is consciously conveyed to listeners about musical structure. Music performance is not distinct from or supplementary to musical structure, but is the very basis of it (N. Cook, 2003). Consistent with this view, it appears that the expressive actions of performers are not entirely voluntary. When performers are asked to eliminate expression and give a flat performance, they can reduce their use of expression but cannot eliminate it entirely (Gabrielsson, 1974; Palmer, 1989).

There are merits to both conceptions of performance. Some aspects of performance expression do appear to be intentional acts of communication, whereas others seem to arise without conscious intention as a consequence of cognitive and affective processes operating within the performer. The combined effects of intentional and unconscious uses of expression by performers provide powerful cues to listeners about the structure of music, facilitating their ability to perceive and remember various musical features.

Meter is one of the most basic aspects of music structure and it greatly affects the use of timing and loudness in performance. Strong beats tend to be emphasized in performance by lengthened durations and slightly delayed onsets (Henderson, 1936; Palmer & Kelly, 1992). Other expressive actions have the perceptual effect of segmenting the music into shorter structural units called phrases (Clarke, 1982, 1985; Palmer, 1989; Todd, 1985). As a phrase boundary is approached, the performed duration of events increases beyond the notated duration, and the loudness may decrease. Once the phrase ending is reached, the performer may also introduce a slight pause before the start of the next phrase. These expressive actions emphasize melodic connections within phrases, and encourage listeners to attend to their structural function and aesthetic value.

In music that features a melody and an accompaniment, the melody line is often emphasized by playing it louder, and by introducing timing asynchronies where the musical notation indicates simultaneity (Rasch, 1979). Palmer (1989) examined performances of Mozart's *Sonata in A major*, K. 331, and found that notes of the melodic line preceded other voices by an average of 20 msec. Because each note of the melody is played slightly ahead of its accompaniment, the melody stands out from the rest of the music. Such expressive actions capitalize on processes of auditory stream segregation, which are essential under most listening conditions for disentangling the various sound sources arriving at our eardrum (Bregman, 1990).

Performance variation not only reflects an understanding of melody, it also reflects more subtle knowledge of musical pitch structure. Palmer and van de Sande (1993) devised a method to examine whether music performances reflect knowledge of harmony (the accompanying chords) and key. Their approach was to examine errors in performance, rather than intended expressive actions. Performance errors were coded in terms of the level of pitch structure implicated. Errors involving one note were coded as single-note units, and errors involving multiple simultaneous notes were coded as chord units. Errors in single-note units occurred most often for polyphonic music (containing strong within-voice associations), and errors in chord units occurred most often for homophonic music (containing strong across-voice associations). For both polyphonic and homophonic music, diatonic (same-key) errors were more common than nondiatonic (different-key) errors. These findings suggest that motor programs for music performance reflect knowledge of multiple levels of pitch structure: voices, chords, and keys.

A study by Thompson and Cuddy (1997) supported this idea. Listeners were presented with numerous segments of music, many of which contained a change in key. The musical segments were played either by a highly trained performer (performed versions) or under computer control exactly as notated with no variation in loudness or timing (mechanical versions). After each segment of music, listeners indicated whether they perceived a change in key. Measurements of timing and loudness in the performed versions revealed that expressive actions were related to key structure. For example, notes that did not fit well with the current key were emphasized through the use of loudness, as if to emphasize the drama of an unexpected musical event. Moreover, a comparison of judgments for performed and mechanical versions revealed that expressive actions strongly influenced listeners' perceptions of key. Timing and loudness can be used expressively to make a small change in key sound intense and dramatic, or they can be used to diminish the effects of a large or unexpected key change.

One of the most important structural properties of Western music is its hierarchical organization, which is characteristic of both pitch and rhythmic structure. The concept of hierarchical organization refers to the idea that certain pitches and rhythmic moments are more essential to the musical structure, whereas other pitches and rhythmic moments are perceived as elaborations, ornaments, or in some other way subsidiary to the essential musical structure. Hierarchical organization is described formally in music theory as a series of nested levels, which begin with an abstract skeleton or essence of the music, progress to increasingly detailed elaborations on this foundation, and end with a fully detailed musical surface. Events that are essential to the musical structure are represented at

A runner's deceleration phase continues well past the finish line. It has been suggested that the tendency to slow down at the end of a musical phrase alludes to the physical motion of deceleration.

deeper levels, whereas ornaments or elaborations of essential events are only represented near the musical surface.

Close analyses of timing in performance suggest that expressive actions are guided in subtle ways by sensitivity to hierarchical structure in music. It is well established that performers slow down at the end of phrases. Todd (1985) and Shaffer and Todd (1987) examined performances and found that the degree to which notes were lengthened at phrase endings corresponds to the depth of nesting. The greatest degree of expressive lengthening was observed for structurally important segments; less expressive lengthening was observed for segments that were less important structurally.

The tendency to slow down at the end of a musical phrase or section is something of a mystery. The habit is by no means universal, but it occurs in performances of music in a range of cultures and it seems naturally associated with musical endings. One theory holds that performers slow down at musical endings as an allusion to physical motion. This view has been supported by modeling the pattern of ritards in performances according to constraints of biological motion (Kronman & Sundberg, 1987; Sundberg & Verillo, 1980). Any organism that is moving rapidly must go through intermediate stages of slowing down to stop completely, and this transition of braking is constrained by biological and physical forces. A galloping horse cannot stop instantly but must go through a transition period in which the force of the forward motion is countered by an opposing force that slows the animal but does not jeopardize its stability.

Perception and production may also constrain the rate at which performers slow down in performance (Honing, 2005). First, tempo changes that occur too rapidly may interfere with accurate perception of rhythmic and melodic structure by listeners. Just as a galloping horse may slip and fall if it attempts to stop too quickly, our perceptions of music may become unstable if the tempo is slowed too abruptly. Thus, performers may introduce expressive devices to facilitate accurate perceptual segmentation by listeners. Second, motor planning by the performer involves chunking musical information into phrases, and expressive timing may partly reflect cognitive and motor processes involved in this planning. As a performer approaches the end of one phrase, a decrease in tempo may facilitate memory and motor planning for the upcoming phrase.

Executing the performance of a musical phrase requires the coordination of two mental processes—one for retrieving musical information from memory and a subsequent process of movement preparation

Sound Examples 8.5.1–8.5.4

These are synthesized examples of the implementation of the *duration contrast* rule. The melody is the theme from the first movement of a Haydn String Quartet (op. 74, no. 2). The duration contrast rule specifies that, under certain circumstances, longer durations are lengthened and shorter durations are shortened to highlight contrasts between the durations of adjacent notes.

In **Sound example 8.5.1**, the rule has not been implemented. **Sound example 8.5.2** contains medium contrast, **Sound example 8.5.3** contains exaggerated contrast, and **Sound example 8.5.4** contains inverted contrast (i.e., longer notes are shortened, shorter notes are lengthened). Notice how the latter sounds highly counterintuitive.

Source: From Friberg, A., Sundberg, J., & Fryden, L. (1994). Rules for musical performance. In Information Technology and Music, CD-ROM produced by the Royal Swedish Academy of Science.

(Palmer, 2005; Palmer & Pfordresher, 2003). Evidence supports a *cascade model* of the time course of these two mental processes, whereby retrieval and production are considered distinct processes that overlap in their time course. That is, movement preparation begins after retrieval has begun but also operates simultaneously with the retrieval process. This overlap of processes means that motor planning can actually affect retrieval.

The link between performance expression and musical structure is also assumed in rule-based systems for performing music. Sundberg and his colleagues proposed a large number of performance rules to describe expressive actions that should be applied when performing any piece of Western music (Sundberg, Askenfelt, & Frydén, 1983; Thompson, Sundberg, Friberg, & Frydén, 1989). In early stages of the development of the rule system, the rules were implemented in a computer program that generated expressive performances of melodies. The authors evaluated the musical quality of these computer-generated performances and refined their rules accordingly. This methodology is called *analysis-by-synthesis* because it is based on the strategy of investigating the nature of music performances by trying to synthesize them. The rules indicate which expressive actions should be initiated at different structural moments.

The *phrase arch* rule was developed to model the use of tempo and dynamics within melodic phrases. In general, phrases are relatively slow and soft at the beginning, fast and loud in the middle, and slow and soft at the end. That is, musicians tend to perform phrases by starting with an *accelerando* and *crescendo* and ending with a *rallentando* and *diminuendo*. For each of these two parameters, tempo and dynamics, the increasing and decreasing levels over time are graphically displayed as an arch (Juslin, Friberg, & Bresin, 2002).

Other rules act on various levels of music structure. The *final ritardando* rule indicates how to slow down at the end of a piece, and is modeled on constraints of biological motion. The *faster uphill* rule indicates that the tempo should be increased during sections of a melody that are ascending in pitch, and decreased during sections of a melody that are descending in pitch. The *punctuation rule* inserts slight pauses between melodic fragments to emphasize structural boundaries. The *duration contrast* rule specifies that under certain circumstances durations are lengthened or shortened to highlight contrasts between the durations of adjacent notes. For example, if the score indicates an eighth note followed by a quarter note, the application of this rule would result in a slight shortening of the eighth note and a slight lengthening of the quarter note, highlighting the contrast in duration between these two notes.

Two of the performance rules link performance expression to musical key. *Melodic charge* and *harmonic charge* specify appropriate adjustments to the loudness and duration of notes and chords, respectively, according to their stability within the current key. Notes and chords that are less stable in the key, such as the note F# in the key of C major, are considered to be charged and are accented through the use of loudness and duration. Research has shown that computer-delivered melodies were judged to be more musical when such principles were applied than when they were not. However, further refinements are undoubtedly needed, and it is possible that appropriate uses of expression are inherently imprecise and variable, and cannot be entirely described by a set of definitive rules (Friberg, Bresin, & Sundberg, 2006).

Communicating Emotional Meaning

One of the greatest mysteries of music is its powerful association with emotion. As discussed in other chapters, this association has led to speculations about the origins of music and the relation between music and other domains such as speech prosody. According to Langer (1957), the unfolding patterns of tension and relaxation that commonly occur in music are analogous to the changes in tension that occur when we experience strong emotions. She argued that this isomorphism is the primary basis for the connection between music and emotion.

Performances by Western and non-Western musicians are often strongly influenced by an emotional interpretation of the music or by an intention to communicate an emotional message. However, not all music functions to communicate an emotional message. For the Kaluli people of Papua New Guinea, it plays a role in communicating with the dead (Feld, 1990); in the *domba initiation* of the Venda people, it functions to establish social relations (Blacking, 1973); in Jewish *klezmer* music, it acts as a medium for defining and reinventing cultural identity (Slobin, 1993; see Cross, 2003a). On the other hand, some music is overtly about emotions and moods. The theoretical basis for Hindustani music explicitly identifies connections between traditional musical forms (ragas) and their corresponding moods (rasas). Performers of Hindustani music use expressive devices and improvisation to reinforce the intended rasa of each piece.

Western performers are also strongly guided by emotional responses to music, and individuals who have positive emotional responses to music early in life are more likely to engage in musical behavior over their life span (Sloboda, 2005, p. 216).

Researchers have identified a number of acoustic features that have strong emotional connotations, and many of these features are under the direct control of the performer. Emotionality can be conveyed through a wide range of expressive actions. Different emotions are associated with differences in tempo, loudness, timbre, articulation, and in the amount of variation in these dimensions over time. Individual features of expression, such as a fast tempo, cannot by themselves determine emotional meaning because each feature is associated with several possible emotions. Instead, emotional meaning is determined by the unique combination of expressive features in a performance.

Performances can be emotional in general and particular ways. At a general level, performances that involve relatively more expressive variation are perceived to be more emotional, whereas performances that lack expressive variation are perceived to be cold and mechanical. At a more specific level, performers from Jesse Norman to Bono to Thom Yorke all use expressive actions in specific ways to communicate particular emotional connotations such as joy, sadness, and anger. Performers can even play the same music with different emotional connotations through the expressive choices that they make during a performance, and listeners are sensitive to the emotional messages intended (Gabrielsson & Juslin, 1996). Two expressive qualities, tempo and loudness, are used in highly consistent ways to achieve specific emotional connotations. Playing louder and at a faster tempo tends to evoke energetic emotions such as anger and joy, whereas playing more softly and at a lower tempo tends to evoke less energetic emotions such as sadness.

Other expressive actions, along with structural features such as the degree of consonance and dissonance in the music, further specify the nature of the emotional connotation. For example, both anger and joy are energetic emotions that are associated with a relatively fast tempo and increased loudness, but joyful music is also associated with consonant intervals, the major mode, and relatively simple melodic, harmonic, and rhythmic structure. Evidence suggests that certain acoustic features in music communicate similar emotional messages across cultures (Balkwill & Thompson, 1999; Balkwill, Thompson, & Matsunaga, 2004). Moreover, speech prosody conveys emotional meaning largely using the same emotional cues that are found in music (Juslin & Laukka, 2003).

Such observations imply that the link between music and emotion may reflect primitive emotional responses to basic acoustic features.

Singing

The first musical behavior to emerge in human evolution was probably singing. Within prehistoric caves in France, dated from the Cro Magnon era, the chambers that have the most paintings also happen to be those that are most resonant, suggesting that they may have been used for religious purposes involving song. The first musical behavior that infants display is also singing. Indeed, the most common form of music making in the world is undoubtedly singing, even if our own contribution to this ancient and universal activity is usually performed while in the shower or driving in the car.

When we sing, the sound energy that is produced reaches our ears in two ways: from the acoustic energy that travels from the mouth to the ear canal, and directly through bone conduction to our inner ear. The acoustic contribution from bone conduction affects the frequency distribution of the sound, such that recordings of our own voices may sound quite different from what we might expect. Many people are embarrassed

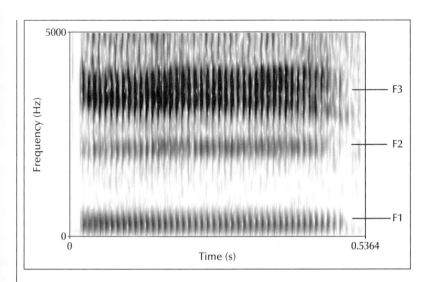

A spectrogram of an adult male pronouncing the vowel sound in the word "beat." Three formants are visible as dark colored bands (F1, F2, and F3). The y-axis indicates the frequency range for each formant. The darkness of each band indicates the amount of spectral energy.

by the sound of their own voice in a recording, which can sound higher in pitch and more nasal in timbre.

The voice works like other musical instruments. Vocal folds consist of thick membranes that vibrate when they are stretched and stimulated by a blast of air from the lungs. Changing the tension of the vocal folds alters the frequency with which they vibrate, and hence the pitch that is produced. Different positions of the larynx, jaw, tongue, and lips, called *articulators*, are associated with distinct ranges of resonant frequencies, called *formants*. A formant describes a particular range of frequencies that radiates from the lip opening at higher amplitudes than neighboring frequencies, displayed graphically as a local peak in the sound spectrum. Each position of the articulators may result in a spectrum that has several formants, and the position of these formants greatly influences the timbre of the sound produced. Vowel sounds in speech are strongly associated with the position of the lowest two formants.

For a given vowel sound, formants remain fairly stable regardless of changes in the overall pitch level (fundamental frequency) of the speaking voice. Slawson (1968) demonstrated that vowel quality is maximally similar if formant frequencies are raised by 10% for every octave (100%) increase in overall pitch level. Thus, formant frequencies move only slightly in the direction of the overall pitch; their properties are somewhat independent of the fundamental frequency.

This acoustic peculiarity means that articulation problems arise when we are singing at a pitch level that is above the formant frequencies needed to produce a vowel. If the vowel is part of a word that we need to sing, its quality will necessarily be altered. More generally, the quality of vowels in singing is often very different from the quality of vowels in speaking. This difference occurs not only for high-pitched singing, but also as an acoustic consequence of the way articulators are positioned to produce a resonant singing voice, such as a relative widening of the pharynx and lowering of the larynx. Vowels sung by male opera singers often have formant frequencies that are closer to those associated with a different (unintended) vowel (Sundberg, 1999). Yet we are usually capable of identifying the words in a song. How do we understand verbal materials in songs when the acoustic information is so distorted?

In fact, we have a limited ability to understand vowels or syllables produced at high pitches (Sundberg, 1999). We can probably understand words and phrases in songs because we draw on our knowledge of the context, much in the way we can understand someone speaking with an accent that differs from our own. When the benefits of context are removed, however, as in isolated vowels or syllables, identification accuracy drops. The ability to identify syllables sung by female singers slips to around 80% accuracy when sung at the pitch of B4 (495 Hz), and falls to 10% accuracy when sung at the pitch of C6 (1,046 Hz). Isolated vowels produced at the highest pitch levels tend to sound the same. The constraints of singing at the highest pitch levels are such that formant frequency patterns are roughly equivalent regardless of the vowel intended. In short, spectral information about vowel quality is grossly deficient at very high pitches, and listeners often must draw on their knowledge of context to perceive words accurately.

Singers are faced not only with the challenge of being understood; they also have to be audible in large concert halls when accompanied by loud orchestras. Singers tackle this challenge not merely by singing with great intensity, but also by developing a tonal quality in their voice that

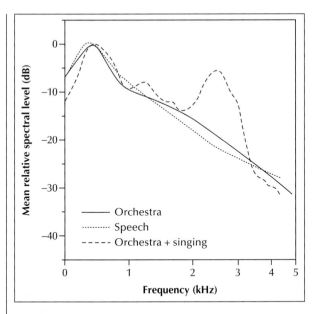

A graphical representation of the singer's formant in prominent Swedish tenor Jussi Bjorling's voice. At lower frequencies, spectral properties of the singing voice are similar to those observed in speech (dotted line). If this trend were to continue at higher frequencies, the singing voice would be drowned out by the orchestral accompaniment (solid line).

Instead, Sundberg's (1999) analysis showed that singers develop the ability to penetrate the sound of the orchestra not just by singing louder, but by developing a high amount of energy in the frequency range of 2500–3000hz.

Source: Drawing after I.R. Titze, *Principles of Voice Production* (Denver, CO: National Center for Voice and Speech, 2000).

Paul Broca (1824–1880).

contains a high amount of energy in the frequency range of 2,500 Hz to 3,000 Hz. Partials falling within this region are projected out of the singer's mouth with greater intensity, giving rise to a peak in the frequency spectrum that is known as the *singer's formant*. Apparently, it is easier to hear a singer's voice that is embedded within orchestral sounds when that voice possesses a prominent singer's formant than when it does not. Singing teachers often emphasize the importance of *projecting* the voice to be clearly audible, and the singer's formant is one of the most important acoustic consequences of this skill.

Learning to project one's voice is also important in public speaking, but there are important differences between speaking and singing. The acoustic structure of vowels has already been mentioned. Studies of individuals with brain injury also suggest that there may be distinct neural resources for controlling the production of singing and speaking. In 1861, Broca discovered the patient known as *tan*, the most famous case of expressive aphasia. Broca reported that this patient was entirely unable to speak, with one exception: He could pronounce the word "tan." Remarkably, however, he was able to produce intelligible words when singing. Some researchers have interpreted this dissociation as indicating two routes to word articulation: one that originates from the left hemisphere and is normally used when speaking, and one that originates from the right hemisphere and is used when singing (Cadalbert, Landis, Regard, & Graves, 1994). This interpretation has practical implications, such as the treatment of stuttering through singing (Healy, Mallard, & Adams, 1976), or melodic intonation therapy. In melodic intonation therapy, individuals with speech problems following strokes and other brain injuries are taught to sing their words rather than speak them (Albert, Sparks, & Helm, 1973). Not all researchers are convinced of the efficacy of this therapy, however, arguing that the same brain areas may well be involved in the production of words in speech and song (Peretz, Gagnon, Hébert, & Macoir, 2004).

Improvising

Musical improvisation may be distinguished from the performance of composed music in that it does not require the performer to remember or sight-read music, and there is no musical score that can be used as a benchmark for evaluating the degree of interpretation or expression.

During improvisations, musicians spontaneously create a musical composition as they are performing it, but quite often these compositions are not recorded in the form of a score. Some improvisers may try to minimize all musical planning prior to their improvisation and focus on spontaneous innovation. Innovation and originality is often a principal goal, and many improvisers avoid drawing from standard or hackneyed musical patterns.

Until recently, the skill of improvisation was rarely taught in music education programs, and was mostly learned through experimentation and oral tradition rather than by manuals and pedagogical materials. More recently, however, the art of improvisation is being recognized as an important skill for musicians. McPherson (1993) developed a test to measure improvisational ability, and reported a positive correlation between improvisational skill and other skills of music performance.

Drawing from his own improvisational experience, Pressing (1984, 1988) described musical improvisation as an ordered sequence of musical event clusters. Each event cluster is shaped by current goals but may also be associated with previous events. A major challenge in improvisation is deciding how it should continue. Novice improvisers have a limited repertoire of ideas and tend to rely on familiar patterns and resort to them repeatedly. Pressing outlines two typical strategies of advancing an improvisation: associative generation and interrupt generation. In associative generation, the performer continues the improvisation by introducing materials that are either similar to or contrasting with previous event clusters. In interrupt generation, the performer introduces a completely new musical idea that is unrelated (neither similar, nor contrasting) to previous events. A time-dependent tolerance level for repetition determines which of these two strategies is most likely to be used. If the current level of repetition is high, the performer is likely to use interrupt generation; if the current level of repetition is low, the performer is likely to use associative generation.

It has been argued that all performances involve some degree of improvisation because not all the parameters of music can be entirely specified in any score. To the extent that certain dimensions of any composition are left unspecified, performers must partially create the music that they are playing. However, there is a qualitative difference in the creative possibilities associated with improvisation and those entailed by the performance of an established composition. This difference may be appreciated by considering the distinction between primary and secondary parameters of music. The expressive manipulations exercised by performers are overwhelmingly limited to secondary parameters of music, such as loudness, timbre, timing, and tempo. The skill of improvisation, in contrast, emphasizes the expressive manipulation of primary parameters, such pitch, harmony, and rhythm. By expressively manipulating primary parameters, improvisers create musical works that are perceived to be unique and original, and not merely an expressive rendering of a preexisting composition.

On the other hand, our sense that improvisers create original music may be somewhat misleading. As much as improvisers attempt to produce truly original pieces of music, an improvisation cannot arise out of nothing, but must be based on knowledge of music. How composers and improvisers are able to convert their memories for past music into apparently novel compositions is little understood. As discussed in later sections, it may involve rapid processes of recombining elementary fragments of musical memories and mentally selecting those combinations that are likely to yield the most rewarding outcomes.

Gestures and Facial Expressions

Most people prefer to experience music live at a performance rather than sitting at home and merely hearing the performance. Do visual aspects of music influence its appreciation and understanding? Music is overwhelmingly conceptualized as an auditory experience, but musical activities across cultures and at different times in history are more typically multimodal, often involving significant actions that cannot be meaningfully dissociated from the music experience. Indeed, music performances were almost always experienced as integrated audiovisual events prior to the invention of the gramophone and phonograph at the turn of the 20th century. These technologies isolated the auditory component of music, filtering out visual information and thereby limiting our conceptions of music. However, live performers invariably use facial expressions and gestures in salient and meaningful ways, and audience members attend carefully to those actions. A full music experience involves watching as well as listening (Thompson & Russo, 2007).

Certain body movements used during performance are introduced intentionally for aesthetic and interpretive purposes. These gestures and facial expressions are not physical consequences of the technical demands of performance but reflect the performer's understanding of the music.

Soprano Erika Miklosa (left) and blues guitarist and singer B.B. King (right) use gesture and facial expression while making music. Both cases can be considered primary movements in that the gestures and facial expressions are not physical consequences of the technical demands of the music (i.e., secondary movements) but reflect the performer's understanding of the music.

These expressions might also be considered to be diverging examples of nonverbal behavior. Miklosa's facial expression and hand gesture might belong to the class of *affect displays* used with the intention of conveying an emotional message. King's facial expression might be considered an *illustrator*. He may be playing a particularly prominent and perhaps sharply dissonant note, and uses his facial expression to accentuate its character.

Sources: Photo of Erika Miklosa as Lucia di Lammermoor reproduced by permission. Photo of B.B. King: Roland Godefroy. Made available under Creative Commons 2.5 Attribution-Generic License.

They may be described as *primary movements* because they directly reflect the performer's interpretation of the music and are not incidental effects of some other dimension of performance. Other body movements arise merely as a result of technical demands. Movements are required to sing or play an instrument and they necessarily track the basic structural characteristics of the music. Specific postures may be adopted to cope effectively with technically difficulty passages, inadvertently providing visible cues about musical structure. Similarly, facial expressions may reflect the degree of concentration needed to perform different types of passages. Such movements arise as a consequence of the technical demands of music, and may be described as *secondary movements*.

Both primary and secondary performance movements carry important information and can greatly influence our perceptions and experiences of music. Facial expressions and gestures shape our experience of music in obvious and nonobvious ways. At a general level, it is well known that audiovisual information is more intelligible perceptually than audio information alone (e.g., as in a cocktail party or noisy environment).

More subtly, visual aspects of performance direct our attention toward the acoustic aspects of music at strategic points in time, signaling the timing of important acoustic events and highlighting rhythmic structure. They also underscore significant melodic and harmonic events, reinforcing their role in the music and increasing the likelihood that they will be remembered. The temporal patterning of gestures and expressions reflect musical grouping structure, combining with acoustic cues to convey points of closure for small structures (phrases) and large structures (sections). Unexpected musical events are often signaled acoustically by changes in loudness and timing, but they are also associated with facial expressions and gestures that underpin their aesthetic function. Even key structure is reflected in facial expressions, which often differ for tonally stable and unstable events.

The use of facial expressions in music is also critically important for communicating affective connotations of music (Di Carlo & Guaitella, 2004). When asked to evaluate the affective meaning of music, individuals without musical training will actually rely more heavily on visual cues than aural cues (Davidson & Correia, 2002). Thompson and his colleagues have reported a number of experiments in which individuals were presented with audiovisual presentations of sung intervals and were asked to rate their emotionality (Thompson et al., 2005; Thompson et al., in press). The interval was either a major third, which has a strong positive affective valence, or a minor third, which has a strong negative affective valence. Video clips were edited to create two additional conditions in which the facial expressions used to produce the major third were coupled with the sung minor third, and vice versa. These mismatch conditions pitted visual cues against auditory cues, allowing the researchers to evaluate the relative influence of each source of information. Both visual and auditory information influenced ratings. The highest ratings of joy were assigned to video clips that coupled the sung major third with facial expressions used to produce a major third. Ratings were lower if the clip showed the facial expressions used to produce the minor third, or if the clip played the sung minor third, and they were lowest when the sung minor third was coupled with facial expressions used to produce the minor third.

It is useful to consider facial expressions used in music performance as an instance of the general phenomenon of nonverbal behavior (Ekman & Friesen, 1981; Kurosawa & Davidson, 2005). Four classes of nonverbal behaviors are particularly relevant to music performance: emblems, illustrators, regulators, and affect displays. *Emblems* are visual analogues of simple words in that they can be translated into a specific verbal message. The meaning of these gestures is usually culturally determined and may change over time. By the 1960s the hand gesture indicating a peace sign became highly recognizable, borrowed from the victory sign of the 1940s. These gestures may often be quite specific. The peace sign, for example, depends critically on the position of the fingers and the orientation of the hand. *Illustrators* are used to accentuate, underscore, or clarify the content of a message. In a music performance, they may be used to emphasize a verbal message in a sung performance, or an aspect of the musical structure. In the classic song "Over the Rainbow," facial expressions might be used to illustrate the initial ascending interval by raising the eyebrows on the second note. *Regulators* are used to maintain interactions and include eye contact and head nods. These gestures are often essential between band members or an ensemble of musicians, but they also occur between performers and audience members. Such gestures personalize the musical experience for listeners, and they imply that the performance is an interaction between the musicians and the audience members. *Affect displays* convey emotional messages and affective states, and include strutting, frowning, and smiling.

Thompson et al. (2005) reported several experiments confirming that visual aspects of performance greatly influence experiences of music. Facial expressions were capable of causing lead guitar sections to sound more or less dissonant; they could cause melodic intervals to sound larger, smaller, happier, or sadder; and they greatly shaped affective judgments of music. More recent evidence suggests that auditory and visual sources of emotional information are balanced and integrated with each other automatically and unconsciously (Thompson et al., in press). Research on visual aspects of music is currently being carried out at laboratories around the world, leading to rapid progress in understanding the cognitive processes by which visual and auditory dimensions of music are integrated to form a unified musical experience.

Evaluating Performance

Performers are constantly being judged, and these judgments have a powerful influence on the expressive choices that are made. If a performance is judged to be saccharine and overwrought, chances are the performer will deploy expression more subtly in the next performance. If the

Sound Examples 8.6.1–8.6.2

Objective adjudication is a difficult task. Consider the two renditions of an excerpt from Tarrega's "Lagrima" heard in **Sound examples 8.6.1** and **8.6.2**. Is one rendition clearly better than the other? If so, can you explain why in objective terms?

same performance is judged to be cold and unemotional, the performer is likely to work on enhancing his or her use of expression. Western culture is almost obsessed with adjudicating the quality of music performances, whether such evaluations are made in a private music lesson by a teacher, in the context of a formal music program at a conservatory, in a music competition, or in newspaper and magazine reviews of a performance at a concert hall. Such judgments reflect the high value that we place on excellence in music, and they reveal some of the qualities of performance expression that are most valued. *American Idol* and the Frederic Chopin International Piano Competition may attract very different types of musicians, but the aim of both events is to select a single winner from among hundreds of aspiring contestants. Many outstanding musicians find it difficult to cope with the potential for being judged harshly, and suffer music performance anxiety or stage fright (Kenny & Osborne, 2006).

The majority of people who attend music performances have limited or no formal training in music, but performers care most about the judgments of people with high levels of musical expertise. To provide a detailed assessment of a performance requires the ability to distinguish between the music itself (as indicated by the score) and the performer's use of expression. Having made this distinction, adjudicators must then consider how the expressive actions of the performer relate to the musical structure, and stylistic conventions, and whether the music is challenging technically. Not surprisingly, there is disagreement among adjudicators about the desirability of certain expression qualities. For example, to what extent is it desirable for performers to have a distinctive and instantly recognizable performance style, as in the case of Glenn Gould? There is no correct answer, and yet this factor can have a significant effect on an adjudication outcome. Finally, all of the factors considered must be balanced and synthesized into an overall assessment.

Because the process of performance adjudication is so difficult, music performance programs may use formalized methods for evaluating expressive playing. These methods involve the establishment of criteria or recommendations for the most valued constructs in performance, such as phrasing, balance, articulation, rubato, and dynamic range (for a review, see McPherson & Thompson, 1998). Such recommendations encourage adjudicators to listen analytically to performances, breaking them into a number of distinct qualities that are evaluated separately. Several formal assessment tools have been developed. As an example, the Music Performance Assessment tool (MPA) requires the adjudicator to assign a rating to various descriptive statements listed under the headings of technical, pitch, time, interpretation, and overall (Winter, 1993). As another example, the Brass Performance Rating Scale (BPRS) requires the adjudicator to provide 27 different ratings (Bergee, 1989, 1992).

Unfortunately, breaking the adjudication process into smaller components is not always effective. A major challenge is that the recommendations listed in pedagogical documents and adjudication tools are often quite general, allowing a range of interpretations. These challenges are even more evident when expert performers are being assessed (Thompson, Diamond, & Balkwill, 1998). Indeed, studies that have scrutinized the process of assessment have yielded sobering results. Not only is the reliability among assessors low; it appears that trained performance adjudicators are highly susceptible to a number of biases. Of course, these problems do not arise when there are obvious differences in the skill level of performers, but they emerge to an alarming degree when the range of performance excellence is narrow, as in a prestigious music competition or within an elite conservatory.

Fiske (1978) presented experienced adjudicators with a large number of different performances of the same piece and asked them to rate each one on overall musical quality. What the adjudicators did not know is that each performance was presented twice, and therefore they provided two judgments for each performance. The reliability (r^2) of judgments for individual adjudicators was embarrassingly low, typically between .09 and .16. For some judges, there was a negative correlation between performance ratings after the first hearing and second hearing! These findings raise serious doubts about the consistency and reliability of performance adjudication.

In another study, Flores and Ginsburgh (1996) analyzed performance rankings in the Queen Elizabeth Music Competition, an international competition for violin and piano. Examination of rankings over a 10-year period indicated that the mere order of the performers had a significant influence on the final rankings. Performers who appeared on the last day of the competition had a much greater chance of being ranked among the top competitors. It seems possible that when adjudicators heard the same piece of music repeatedly, their appreciation of that music gradually increased, and their rankings went up accordingly. It is also possible that the adjudicators relaxed their criteria as the competition progressed, either because they realized that their initial expectations were too strict, or out of sheer exhaustion from listening to so many performances (Flores & Ginsburgh, 1996, p. 102).

Adjudicators are also affected by their expectations or beliefs about who "should" perform well. Duerksen (1972) presented listeners with two tape recordings of an identical piano performance, but labeled them misleadingly in a manner that suggested they were different performances. One was labeled the professional performance and other was labeled the student performance. Not surprisingly, the performance labeled as the student performance was assigned significantly lower ratings for both technical and musical characteristics.

Professional music organizations are well aware of such biases and have sometimes made attempts to avert them. Some band competitions and international festivals use a blind evaluation process in which the adjudicators listen to the music but cannot see the performers. Orchestras and professional ensembles may also hold blind auditions in which the performers are placed behind a screen so that the selection committee cannot see them.

Potential biases notwithstanding, some adjudicators insist on watching as well as listening to performances because they believe that appropriate gestures and facial expressions are pertinent to a comprehensive evaluation of performance excellence. This stipulation is not without merit. Research on performers' use of facial expressions and gestures indicates that visual information can powerfully affect our aesthetic and perceptual experience and is a critically important dimension of music performance (Davidson & Correia, 2002; Thompson et al., 2005). Schumann made a similar point when he remarked, "If Liszt played behind a screen, a great deal of the poetry would be lost" (cf. Davidson, 1993, p. 103). Thus, although the potential risks of bias are very real, in certain circumstances it may be valuable for adjudicators to consider both visual and auditory information when making their assessment.

The Craft of the Performer

Pursuing a career as a music performer demands a range of expert cognitive and motor skills. The acquisition of these skills requires intensive focus and years of training, and there is little evidence that outstanding musicians are able to bypass this effort by relying on innate talent. Performers use expressive actions in highly complex and systematic ways that reflect and convey musical structure and emotional meaning. Phrasing, articulation, and accenting reflect the performer's internal representation of musical structure. Our perceptions and experiences of music, in turn, are greatly influenced by the expressive actions of performers.

Performers also use expressive devices to communicate emotional meaning. Joyful music is often performed with greater articulation, faster tempo, and greater intensity, whereas sad music is often performed at a slower tempo with less intensity. The human voice is perhaps the most evocative musical instrument and singing is the first music making to occur in development. Singers face a number of challenges, such as articulating vowel sounds and projecting their voice so that they can be heard over an accompanying orchestra. Distinct brain regions for singing mean that people with brain injury may have severe language impairment but spared singing ability.

Musicians use a range of body gestures and facial expressions during performance, and these visual displays are systematically related to musical structure and emotional meaning. Audience members attend to such gestures and facial expressions because they carry important information about the music and, indeed, may be construed as integral to the music experience. Western culture places considerable emphasis on the evaluation of performance, even though performance evaluation is subject to a number of significant problems, including biases and lack of reliability.

Market forces also act to differentiate performers: Some performers attract larger audiences, sell more recordings, and enjoy prolonged performing careers. Such economic forms of evaluation, along with pedagogical ones, reflect the enormous value that is placed on excellence in music performance. Expert music performers are held in such high regard that audiences overlook almost all idiosyncrasies and foibles. Along with Glenn Gould's remarkable genius for performance came a series of unconventional behaviors. He avoided shaking hands, wrapped himself in layers of clothes in the hottest months of summer, and traveled with disinfectant spray to guard against imaginary germs. When performing he would sit hunched in a low-slung chair, eye level with the keyboard, breathing heavily, bursting into faint singing and clucking, head bobbing, feet stamping, sweating copiously, body swaying, and hands flailing. When one hand was momentarily free, it would instantly begin conducting the other hand's actions. What he gave the world, however, was a powerful vision of music as a lifelong state of wonder and serenity.

Additional Readings

Sloboda, J. A. (2000). Individual differences in music performance. *Trends in Cognitive Science, 4,* 397–403.

Thompson, W. F., Dalla Bella, S., & Keller, P. E. (2006). Music performance [Special issue]. *Advances in Cognitive Psychology, 2.*

CHAPTER 9

Composing Music

LEARNING OUTCOMES

By the end of this chapter you should be able to:

1. Discuss the relation between the perceptual abilities of listeners and the structural features of music compositions.

2. Identify possible cognitive constraints on music composition.

3. Appraise the quantitative measurement of melodic originality.

4. Summarize principles of auditory scene analysis that account for conventional rules of voice leading.

5. Compare explanations of creativity at the turn of the 20th century with behaviorist and cognitive explanations of creativity.

6. Explain why *selectionist principles* are needed to account for musical creativity and the emergence of novel ideas.

The germ of a future composition comes suddenly and unexpectedly. If the soil is ready—that is to say, if the disposition for work is
there—it takes root with extraordinary force and rapidity, shoots
up through the earth, puts forth branches, leaves and, finally,
blossoms.

—Tchaikovsky (2004, p. 274)

The Radius of Creativity

Known for his six symphonies and classic ballets such as *Swan Lake*
and *The Nutcracker*, Pyotr Ilyich Tchaikovsky held a romantic view of
his craft. Creativity was viewed as an organic process of growth that
occurs deep within a composer and almost independently of choice. A
musical composition, in turn, was understood to be a unified entity that
can be appreciated mainly as a whole. Such metaphors of growth and
unity were part of an aesthetic movement known as *organicism*. In
some circles, such conceptions of art persist. Yet cognitive theories of composition reflect a more pragmatic and prosaic view of
creativity. They do not consider music composition to be a mysterious and solipsistic process that emerges unpredictably from
deep within an individual, but the result of explicit and implicit
choices that are guided in tangible ways by perceptual, cognitive,
and social factors (Pearce, Meredith, & Wiggins, 2002; Toynbee,
2003).

In comparison with tasks such as following a recipe or a road
map, there is no clearly defined set of steps that can be taken to
complete a musical composition. Faced with an ill-defined task,
composers must search for ways of reducing the range of choices
by drawing on a number of compositional constraints. Stylistic
constraints specify the compositional type or genre; biophysical
constraints dictate what can physically be performed; acoustics
determine the effects of combining sounds; and perceptual and
cognitive systems limit and shape the structural features that can
be perceived and remembered.

Pyotr Ilyich Tchaikovsky (1840–1893).

Social conditions can also influence the compositional choices that are made. An analysis by Cerulo (1984) suggested that melodies composed during periods of war have more complex contours and involve more chromatic transitions. There are also influences internal to the composition itself, such as the degree to which musical continuations are strongly implied at various moments in the composition. These and other constraints provide an orientation for composers, reducing the number of choices they must make to complete a composition and thereby decreasing their radius of creativity (Toynbee, 2000). Individual attitudes toward constraints can influence personal approaches to composition. Pervasive attitudes toward constraints can initiate new musical genres.

Western music has witnessed many broad stylistic changes, moving through periods such as Medieval (before ~1450), Renaissance (~1450–1600), Baroque (~1600–1750), Classical (~1730–1820), Romantic (~1815–1910), Modern (~1905–1975), and contemporary. Any cognitive model of music composition must reflect its fluid and evolving nature. The 19th century represented a particularly critical period for music composition. Tonality was considered indispensable for the organization of music but it greatly constrained creative possibilities. Edward Said (1992) described the effect of tonality as analogous to a "police regime" that suppressed contravention (p. 56). At the same time, originality was increasingly valued. Earlier composers such as Haydn and Mozart had established distinctive voices within the language of tonality, but in the 19th century a musical bidding war soon emerged in which new composers established their originality by diverging further and further away from the central tendencies of tonal music, loosening and rebelling against them. Eventually, pervasive concerns among composers about the constraints of tonality led to the advent of serialism, advocated by composers such as Arnold Schöenberg and Alban Berg in the 20th century. Composing serialized music involves the use of procedures that avoid the establishment of a tonal center, while still allowing nontonal melodies (called tone rows) and variations on those melodies (e.g., inversions, retrogrades).

To create a work that is perceived to be original, composers must possess a clear understanding of the conventions of their musical idiom and devise musically acceptable ways of deviating from those conventions. Too little deviation will produce music that sounds unoriginal and predictable; too much deviation will produce music that sounds opaque

---

Sound Example 9.1

This example is an excerpt from Olivier Messiaen's *Quatuor pour la fin du temps* (Quartet for the end of time). This piece was composed in 1941 while Messiaen was being held as a prisoner of war by the Germans.

It was included for analysis in Cerulo's study as an example of a "combat" composition (i.e., a piece of music composed in a place of war during wartime). Her analysis showed that combat compositions tended to have more complex contours and involve more chromatic transitions.

Sound example 9.1 is available via the *Music, Thought, and Feeling* iMix on iTunes.

and unmusical. Composers often aspire to a middle ground that pre-serves a strategic gap between compositional structure and the capacity of listeners to appreciate that structure. For some composers and theorists, this gap not only serves aesthetic goals for individual listeners; it also promotes the development of music as an evolving art. According to Nattiez (1987), composing music merely for the benefit of a listener's full comprehension represents a failure on the part of the composer to participate in the evolution of music.

We can gain some sense of the originality of a composition just by listening to it, but some researchers have developed methods of quantifying the degree of originality in compositions more precisely. One strategy is to calculate the frequency with which different notes follow one another in a large corpus of melodies, and then check whether individual melodies contain note sequences that are more or less common. Simonton (1980, 1984) estimated two-note transitional probabilities based on an analysis of 15,618 classical themes and 477 composers spanning from the Renaissance to the 20th century. The probability of each two-note transition was calculated for the first five note transitions (i.e., six notes) in the melodies. For example, for music in the key of C major or minor, the probability that G and C will be the first two notes in the melody is .048. Given such values, a measure of any given theme's melodic originality was defined as one minus the probabilities associated with the first five two-note transitions. The value reflects originality in that it indicates the improbability of that melodic theme occurring in music, whereby highly improbable (i.e., original) themes are those that contain two-note transitions that are extremely rare.

As acknowledged by Simonton, the validity of this measure of originality is dependent on a number of assumptions. Most obviously, the measure considers only the first six tones of a melody, which may not reflect the originality of the music as a whole. Second, melodies are not the only aspect of music that can be original; other parameters such as harmonic progression, rhythm, and large-scale musical structure also determine originality. Third, the measure gives equal weight to all tone transitions considered in the analysis and does not capture the degree of originality perceived when, for example, a highly predictable melody takes an unexpected turn. Nonetheless, there are intriguing associations between the melodic originality values and other attributes of musical compositions such as their popularity, suggesting that the approach is a promising step in quantifying and understanding this important attribute of creativity.

Composers and Listeners

Western musical traditions frequently distinguish between music makers and music listeners. Put crudely, the composer creates, the performer plays, and the listener sits still and claps. Such distinctions are not meaningful for all music. The passive, detached, and motionless listeners so typical of the Anglo-European musical concert tradition are observed in few musical traditions. They are less relevant to musical traditions such as the Bebuten trance in Bali music or Pentecostal musical offerings, where the boundaries between music making and music listening are blurred (Becker, 2001). Even listeners who are accustomed to the European concert tradition often find it difficult to conform to expectations of statue-like stillness and silence throughout a formal recital, but inclinations toward greater participation are countered by the potential embarrassment of clapping or vocalizing inappropriately. In contemporary concert settings, audience interaction is largely restricted to nervous coughing between movements and endless unwrapping of hard candies. Considering the full range of musical traditions, past, present, and across cultures, the concept of detached and passive listeners whose role in musical behavior is restricted to perception is rather peculiar. Yet psychological studies of music perception overwhelmingly outnumber those concerned with processes of active music making.

Given the fidelity with which modern recording technology can reproduce a performance, why do we continue to attend concerts? Perhaps, as in many non-Western cultures, listeners are seeking more active, group participation in a music-making event.

Source: Original photography: Psylight (Flickr). Made available under Creative Commons 2.0 Attribution-Generic License.

For the most part, music is composed with listeners in mind, ensuring that it contains structures that can be appreciated by listeners. Usually, composers use their own perceptions to infer how listeners will perceive their music, but this strategy can overestimate the perceptual capacities of listeners. Most of us have the highest respect and appreciation for our own *oeuvre*, but our views may not represent the views of everyone. With these ideas in mind, Pulitzer Prize–winning composer Roger Reynolds decided to collaborate with psychologists and musicologists to determine whether his intentions as a composer were realized in the perceptions of listeners. Reynolds composed thematic materials for a piece entitled *The Angel of Death* (Reynolds, 2001). A number of researchers then presented piano and orchestral arrangements of the preliminary materials to experimental listeners, who provided judgments of their perceptions. The results were then given to Reynolds to consider when finalizing the composition. The collaboration highlighted the difficulties faced by composers of contemporary musical materials, who are often very uncertain about the perceptual and cognitive consequences of their work. By using the results of psychological experiments as feedback, Reynolds was able to evaluate whether the intended perceptual effects of his composition were largely realized. Several articles on the compositional process and the experimental work were then published in a special issue of the journal *Music Perception* (see Levitin & Cuddy, 2004; McAdams, 2004a, 2004b; Reynolds, 2004; and others).

Some theorists argue that compositions are only successful if they contain musical structures that can be perceived and mentally represented by listeners (Lerdahl, 1988). In this view, composers who produce excessively complex structures in their pursuit of originality run the risk of undermining the value of their music. If music cannot be perceived, how can it have aesthetic value? Good music is perceivable, and the best music makes full use of our cognitive resources (Lerdahl, 1988, p. 255).

Not everyone holds this view. A number of theorists argue that strategic gaps placed between compositional structure and the cognized result can generate a range of aesthetic effects that are fundamental to artistic experience and hence desirable (N. Cook, 1990; Nattiez, 1987). In this view, worthwhile compositions contain enticing structures that are slightly beyond the grasp of the listener, producing an elusive quality that invites deeper and richer contemplation. Conversely, music that is utterly transparent and leaves nothing to the imagination cannot contribute to the development of music.

What does it mean to appreciate music? Are there limits to the kinds of musical structures that can be grasped, such that certain music is inherently obtuse and inaccessible? Or can all musical forms be appreciated given sufficient experience? If composers do not have a clear road map for successful composition, there are certainly no clear criteria for music listening. People can appreciate the sounds of wind, surf, and rain, but music appreciation involves complex melodic and harmonic patterns that must be perceived. Music is not understood in the way that language is, but there is still a sense in which some music is more accessible than other music.

One way in which listeners can appreciate music is to perceive its structural characteristics. Thus, understanding music is less like verbal comprehension and more like perceiving and appreciating spatial forms and structural relationships as in architecture or painting. Familiar forms in classical music include phrases, melodies, meter, movements, chords, and large-scale form (e.g., sonata form). Appreciating these features allows listeners to form associations between different sections of the piece, such as hearing the connection between a melodic theme and variations on that theme. Such associations provide the music with coherence. If we did not perceive these musical connections, music would sound fragmented, as a series of musical *nonsequiturs*. They also provide a way of mentally reducing the total amount of sonic information into more manageable forms that can be represented in memory, adding to the general knowledge of music that allows us to evaluate and appreciate new music. When we listen to new music we generally expect to hear the musical structures with which we are familiar, and music that deviates from such forms will be perceived as aberrant, generating unsettling arousal responses. Violations of expectations can have especially strong aesthetic effects when they are used at strategic moments (e.g., a deceptive cadence).

Certain compositions are easier to perceive, remember, and appreciate than others, a property that may be termed *musical accessibility*. The degree of accessibility depends on familiarity with the musical genre, such as Western classical sonata form, Hindustani raga, serialized music, or hip-hop. Passive exposure allows listeners to develop familiarity with musical genres without conscious effort, but it would be wrong to assume that any Western listener can readily appreciate all Western music. A teenager who listens primarily to hip-hop will undoubtedly perceive, remember, and appreciate a Mozart sonata far less sensitively than an individual who is deeply immersed in classical music. Similarly, an individual who listens primarily to classical music may have difficulty appreciating hip-hop, which may sound as foreign and inaccessible as music from a different culture.

Cognitive Constraints on Composition

Musical accessibility may also depend on hard-wired cognitive constraints. Beyond the obvious differences between the many musical genres associated with various cultures and historical periods, there may be a set of basic properties to which all music must conform to be perceived and appreciated. At one extreme, hard-wired properties of the auditory system can place strict limits on what is audible or perceptible. We cannot appreciate melodies composed with extremely high or low pitches because the auditory system is not equipped for the task. Other constraints influence musical accessibility to varying degrees. Melodies composed with a relatively small number of pitches may be more memorable than melodies composed with a large number of discrete pitches, because there are fewer pitch categories to keep in mind. Music that has a simple meter may also be relatively accessible because it allows listeners to predict the timing of structurally important notes. Many other constraints have been proposed, and their significance and origin are the subject of ongoing investigations.

The ease with which we perceive certain structural characteristics of music may be influenced by enculturation (repeated exposure to those characteristics), innately determined constraints, or qualities inherent to the stimulus. Does the prevalence of meter in music indicate a unique processing bias in the auditory system, or is a regular accent structure simply informative about timing? If the latter, then there would be no need to infer enculturation or innate predispositions for metrically organized music. The nature of the stimulus accounts for the ease of processing. In the same way, we would not infer innate brain structures specialized for noticing a bright star more easily than a faint star. A simple description of the stimulus accounts for the ease of processing.

Lerdahl (1988) proposed an account of the primary perceptual and cognitive constraints that influence musical accessibility, and argued that these constraints reflect innately determined properties of the CNS. After noting that most listeners have little appreciation for serialized music, Lerdahl speculated that the strategies used to compose this type of music might overlook hard-wired limitations of perceptual and cognitive systems. That is, it may be beyond the perceptual and cognitive reach of listeners to comprehend serialized musical structure because the composers of such music are inattentive to the capacities of listeners. His claim was not that people uniformly dislike such music, but that any enjoyment experienced has little or nothing to do with the serialized nature of the music. Anyone can form associations as they listen to music, but in Lerdahl's view these are nonmusical associations of the type that might be formed while staring at clouds. To appreciate music is to perceive its complex structural properties, and this requires the successful transmission of compositional structure into perceptual and cognitive representations.

With these ideas in mind, Lerdahl proposed that certain properties should be present in music for it to be understood and appreciated by listeners. These properties were described with reference to a large number of hypothetical constraints that constitute an innate listening grammar. The set of procedures used to create a composition was defined as the compositional grammar, and may consist of a combination of artificial and natural grammars. Natural grammars are defined as those that arise spontaneously, whereas artificial grammars are defined as conscious inventions. It is through artificial grammars that composers are able to introduce strategic gaps between compositional and listening grammars.

Two important qualities that allow music to be appreciated are simplicity and memorability, and many of the constraints are related to these goals. One class of constraints dictates the properties that must be present for listeners to perceive groups of events on multiple hierarchical levels. At the most basic level, the music must consist of a sequence of discrete events. Music that does not consist of discrete events would be a continuous sound, which would preclude the perception of complex structure. Gyorgi Ligeti's *Lux Aeterna* and *Atmospheres* are examples of compositions that are not easily parsed into discrete events, making it difficult to infer structure. Grouping cues must be available at the musical surface to create perceptible boundaries between these discrete events, and salient musical transitions achieve this goal. Events should be composed in a way that allows listeners to perceive hierarchical structure. Hierarchical structure, along with regularity of phenomenal accent (meter), greatly promotes musical accessibility.

Without hierarchical structure, events would be perceived on the same structural level. There would be no deep structure and listeners would be unable to make connections between nonadjacent events. When musical events follow one another and no one event is subordinate to any other, the music sounds "like beads on a string" (Lerdahl, 1988, pp. 341–342). On the other hand, listeners' sensitivity to hierarchical structure may be limited, so its requirement as a musical property may be overstated. Listeners do not even appear to notice when music starts and ends in a different key (N. Cook, 1987), suggesting that short-term memory limits the extent to which hierarchical structure can be extracted. N. Cook (1987) proposed that theories of music that emphasize hierarchical structure are "better seen as a means of understanding the practice of tonal composers than as a means of predicting the effects of their compositions upon listeners" (p. 204).

Another class of constraints determines the kind of underlying materials that are used in compositions. These constraints suggest that music should contain a fixed collection of elements. In most music, these elements are pitches, but they could also be timbres or other qualities of sound. Once a fixed set of elements is established, listeners can infer

Sound Example 9.3

This example is an excerpt from Gyorgy Ligeti's avant garde orchestral composition *Atmospheres* (1961). In this piece, the building blocks from which hierarchical structures are usually built—melody, harmony, and rhythm—are purposefully subverted.

The piece was later used as an overture to the theatrical release of Kubrick's (1968) *2001: A Space Odyssey* with the screen completely black for the duration of the composition—an appropriate visual analogue to Ligeti's structureless-sounding music.

Sound example 9.3 is available via the *Music, Thought, and Feeling* iMix on iTunes.

levels of musical stability to the different elements. In tonal music, the first note of the scale, the tonic, has the highest level of stability. When pitch elements are used as the basis for a composition, they should recur at the octave to produce pitch classes. The composition should also use the pitch classes in a way that allows listeners to perceive pitch distances along more than one dimension. As a simple example, pitches separated by an octave are psychologically close in terms of pitch class, but psychologically distant in terms of the number of semitones separating them.

Some of the details of Lerdahl's thesis remain unconfirmed. First, the ease with which certain properties of music are processed, such as a regular beat, may reflect the inherently informative nature of those properties, rather than a cognitive predisposition. Second, the psychological significance of hierarchical structure in music has yet to be fully determined. Music theory and analysis emphasizes the hierarchical structure of tonal compositions, but empirical support for its psychological significance is not strong. N. Cook's (1987) results imply that listeners have a limited ability to appreciate deep structure, which raises questions about its relevance for listeners.

Third, the role of memory in musical appreciation is unclear. Lerdahl argued that a primary aim of composition should be the creation of music that can be represented in memory, but it is not obvious why memorability should be essential for enjoyment. It seems possible to perceive structure in a transitory way that generates enormous enjoyment yet does not lead to a stable mental representation. Indeed, memory is unreliable for some of the qualities of music that we most appreciate. In particular, Raffman (1993) emphasized the aesthetic importance of musical nuances: the expressive variation that takes place within the boundaries of musical categories, including subtle changes of pitch, intensity, and duration. We have an ongoing awareness and appreciation of such shades as we listen to music, but they do not affect the way that we represent musical structure, and they are not readily retained in memory.

Fourth, the view that compositional grammars must be closely aligned with listening grammars has been challenged. A number of theorists and composers have argued persuasively for the value of strategic gaps between compositional structures and the cognized result. If people only liked music they could easily perceive, then they would listen to children's lullabies throughout their entire life. Fifth, it is an empirical question whether the constraints associated with the listening grammar are innately determined. It is very likely that some hard-wired constraints influence the appreciation of musical structure, but the effects of enculturation on perception are often surprisingly powerful. Music of the Romantic period challenged audiences in its day because it was on the cutting edge, but most listeners today have little difficulty appreciating a waltz composed by Chopin. Throughout history, musical understanding has gradually accommodated the cognitive demands placed on listeners by new musical styles.

Composing with Multiple Voices

Walking down the street with a friend on a rainy night, we hear the sounds of our conversation, traffic, wind, rain, a barking dog, and radio music from a passing car. All of these sounds combine at the eardrum, yet we are able to hear each of them separately. Auditory scene analysis describes the set of auditory processes that allow us to differentiate these sounds. Music also involves simultaneous textures that must be differentiated, whether instruments of an orchestra or band, or voices in polyphonic music. Thus, mechanisms of auditory scene analysis are actively engaged during music listening.

Music theory describes the task of composing with multiple voices by a set of principles known as the *rules of voice-leading*. These rules describe voice-leading practices that date back hundreds of years, but their connection with auditory scene analysis has only recently been explored. Huron (2001b) identified several general principles of auditory scene analysis that seem to play a critical role in voice-leading practices. These principles reflect general properties of the auditory system and have been extensively studied using both musical and nonmusical stimuli (Bregman, 1990). According to Huron, a number of these principles are instantiated in our perceptions of individual tones and voices in polyphonic music, and culturally encoded as rules of voice-leading.

Considerable progress has been made in understanding the perceptual and cognitive constraints underlying the practice of composing with multiple voices. Individual voices are heard as melodic lines, but their combination creates harmonic effects that must be perceptually balanced with these melodies. Although mutually intertwined, melody and harmony do not necessarily work in the same way. For example, a melody may suggest tension even when the accompanying harmony suggests consonance and closure. Different levels of tension or dissonance in melodies and their harmonic accompaniments may even be a source

Sound Example 9.4

The first "Kyrie Eleison" from Bach's *Mass in B Minor* is an example of polyphonic music. In this example, each of the voices may be tracked independently. Listen to the entry of each voice on the word "Kyrie" (tenors at 2:30, altos at 2:40, sopranos at 2:59, basses at 3:35). Notice how the melodic line carried by each voice moves independently from its counterparts.

Sound example 9.4 is available via the *Music, Thought, and Feeling* iMix on iTunes.

of aesthetic interest. This is often true in the music of Brahms, where intense dissonances outlined in the melodic line may be offset by warm supporting harmonies. Melodies and their harmonic accompaniments may also differ in how they implicate key and key change. In short, melodies have psychological effects that are somewhat different from the harmonies in which they are embedded.

The composition of polyphonic music must achieve a balance between melodic and harmonic goals. This balance is guided by established conventions of Western tonal composition, which are often formalized as rules of harmonic progression and voice leading. Although these rules may be broken by composers for aesthetic purposes, a close examination reveals important insights into their perceptual and cognitive origins. In particular, several rules of voice leading are related to more general principles of auditory scene analysis (Bregman, 1990; for a detailed discussion, see Huron, 2001b). Auditory scene analysis refers to the set of general processes that allow perceivers to organize acoustic information arriving at the ear into distinct sound events or sources. These basic auditory processes allow listeners to hear an individual speaker in a crowded room or to track individual voices in polyphonic music.

Beginning with the perception of individual tones, the conditions that lead to a clear sense of pitch are linked to the pitch range conventionally used in harmonic writing. Pitch clarity varies with the fundamental frequency of tones. Pitch perception tends to be clearest in a region that corresponds roughly to the center of a piano keyboard (extending from F2 and G5 and centered at 300 Hz, which is approximately two semitones higher than middle C). By contrast, listeners' sense of pitch is much poorer for the lowest and highest notes on the piano. The distribution of pitches in both Western and non-Western music corresponds precisely with the region associated with high pitch clarity. This correspondence suggests that harmonic writing reflects a tacit goal of using tones with a clear sense of pitch.

Mechanisms of auditory scene analysis also operate to link acoustic events over time. Pitch proximity represents one of the most important cues for such temporal grouping. To reiterate an idea discussed earlier, a sequence of tones is most readily perceived as a group or stream when the pitch distance between temporally adjacent tones is small. Tones with pitches that are distant from each other tend to be perceptually segregated into separate streams. In music, this effect is exploited in pseudo-polyphony or compound melodies, where a single sequence of notes may be

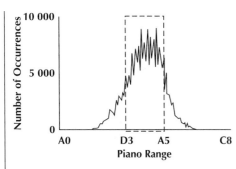

The frequency distribution of tones across the entire range of the piano for 100 pieces of music from the piano repertoire (18th–20th century). The highlighted middle section (from D3 to A5) constitutes only 34% of the piano's range but accounts for 77% of tone occurences.

written to evoke the impression of two distinct melodic lines. As the pitch distance between successive tones is increased, creating alternating high- and low-pitched tones, listeners become more and more likely to perceive two streams (two separate melodies). This effect of pitch separation is known to depend on tempo. As tempo is decreased, a larger pitch separation is needed to evoke an impression of two auditory streams (van Noorden, 1975).

Thus, the coherence of an individual voice is enhanced if temporally adjacent tones are proximate in pitch. When leaps in pitch are introduced in a voice, coherence can be maintained by reducing tempo. Consistent with these findings, rules of voice-leading restrict the use of large leaps in part writing. When wide leaps are unavoidable, composers tend to use long durations for the notes forming the leap (the first note, the second note, or both notes), a convention called leap lengthening (as used in "Somewhere Over the Rainbow"). The convention of avoiding large leaps maps directly onto listeners' sensitivity to the effects of pitch proximity on auditory stream segregation. The convention of leap lengthening mirrors an additional sensitivity to the interactive effects of proximity and tempo. Yet a third convention in voice-leading is also relevant to pitch proximity. To ensure perceptual independence of voices, the pitches of temporally adjacent tones within each voice should be more proximate than the pitches of temporally adjacent tones in different voices (soprano, alto, tenor, bass); otherwise, confusions in voice attribution may occur. Such confusions are especially probable if voices "cross" in pitch register, in which case streaming mechanisms may group part of one voice with a continuation of the other voice. Not surprisingly, part-crossing is avoided in voice-leading, especially for music with three or more voices (Huron, 1991a).

Independence of voices is also affected by *harmonicity*. This principle describes the mechanism by which the partials of periodic sounds are grouped into unified auditory events. Specifically, frequencies that fall along the harmonic series tend to be fused (DeWitt & Crowder, 1987), giving rise to a single pitch sensation and a timbre associated with the spectral composition. In harmonic writing, the same mechanism may partially fuse tones from different voices, which works in opposition to the more general goal of creating independent voices. Such fusion among different tones helps to account for our perception of chords as higher order musical units. In voice-leading practice, however, it is often desirable to avoid strong fusion effects in the interest of emphasizing the melodic component of individual voices.

Sound Example 9.5

This is an example of the Organum technique from the Medieval European chant tradition. Notice how the voices appear to blend into a unified whole. This perceptual unification is encouraged because of the consonance and parallel motion between the tones that each voice is producing.

Sound example 9.5 is available via the *Music, Thought, and Feeling* iMix on iTunes.

An example of pseudo-polyphony from the fourth movement of J. S. Bach's "Fifth Violin Sonata." The strategic use of wide spacing between notes in this single melodic line gives the illusion of three separate voices. The effect is somewhat apparent in the graphic notation itself, as illustrated.

Proximity

A visual illustration of the Gestalt Law of Proximity. We tend to perceive the five vertical bars as being divided into two groups (1 and 2, and 3, 4, and 5) because the gap between 2 and 3 is much larger than any other. This is analogous to the tendency to segregrate pitches with large distances between them into separate streams.

Gestalt psychology suggests that perception is governed by general principles, such as the Law of Proximity, that are not necessarily restricted to one modality.

The pitch intervals that most promote tonal fusion are the unison, octave, and fifth (perfect consonances). For music that is composed to emphasize independence of voices, composers appear to avoid tonally fused intervals. Huron (1991b) showed that in the polyphonic writing of J. S. Bach, tonally fused intervals are avoided in direct proportion to the strength with which each interval promotes tonal fusion. Unisons occur less often than octaves, which occur less often than perfect fifths, which occur less often than other intervals. This observation implies a tacit understanding of how tonal fusion can undermine the musical goal of separation of voices.

Like harmonicity, pitch comodulation (i.e., different voices or pure-tone components that vary similarly in contour and interval size) is used as a cue for unifying the harmonics of individual sound events. Here, tonal fusion is promoted between sounds that have positively correlated pitch motions. The mechanism described by this principle is especially important for unifying the components of sounds that involve inharmonic overtones, which would not be fused by mechanisms attuned merely to harmonicity. Tonal fusion is strongest if pitch motion is precise with respect to log frequency (i.e., exactly the same shifts in interval size), although any positively correlated pitch motion contributes to tonal fusion.

Again, voice-leading conventions reflect this cognitive principle. Similar pitch motion between two voices is avoided, especially when voices are separated by an interval that promotes tonal fusion (unison, octave, fifth). Although identical or parallel pitch motion is particularly eschewed, all cases of similar motion are avoided as a general principle. This general psychological principle is formalized in rules that discourage parallel unisons, octaves, and fifths, and in rules that encourage contrary melodic motion among voices.

The spacing of tones within chords reflects another acoustic principle, namely the association between sensory dissonance and pitch register. Briefly, there is less potential for sensory dissonance between voices in the upper pitch register than between voices in the lower pitch register. Although we often think of certain intervals as consonant (e.g., the perfect fifth) and others as dissonant (e.g., the tritone), sensory dissonance is influenced by pitch register as well as interval size. A more direct measure of sensory dissonance considers the occurrence of interactions among partials, which is related to the concept of a critical band.

As discussed in earlier chapters, a critical band is defined as the range of frequencies within which masking effects (in which the presence of one tone affects the audibility of another tone), loudness summation (in which overall loudness corresponds to the sum of the amplitude of two tones), and other interactions among frequencies occur. Such interactions are the basis for sensory dissonance. Importantly, critical bandwidth decreases (as measured in log frequency) as pitch register increases. The result is that a given musical interval (e.g., a major third) yields fewer interactive effects and is therefore associated with less sensory dissonance when that interval is played in a higher pitch register than when it is played in a lower pitch register. This effect is manifested in the spelling of chords (i.e., the exact position of the different notes of the chord). In particular, the pitch separation between lower voices is much larger on average than the pitch separation between upper voices (Plomp & Levelt, 1965; see Figure 9.1). For example, bass and tenor voices are often separated by an octave, whereas the soprano and alto voices are often separated by just four or five semitones. This aspect of polyphonic writing may function to maintain a balance of relative consonance and dissonance across pitch regions.

Interestingly, when dissonance between two voices occurs, it is possible to reduce its salience by emphasizing the melodic structure within which the dissonant tones occur. This may be accomplished by adhering more assiduously to the principles that enhance auditory stream segregation. When stream segregation is enhanced, listeners attend more to the melodic aspect of the music, which seems to inhibit effects related to the harmonic aspect of the music, such as tonal fusion and dissonance (Wright & Bregman, 1987).

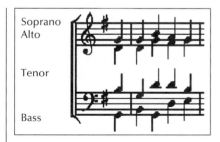

Figure 9.1

An excerpt from a chorale for soprano, alto, tenor, and bass by Martin Luther. Notice that the pitch separation between the lower voices (tenor and bass) is generally larger than the pitch separation between the upper voices (soprano and alto).

The connection between voice-leading conventions and auditory scene analysis exemplifies multiple ways in which musical practice and basic cognitive mechanisms intersect. The connection also helps to explain how listeners perceive melodies within a harmonic context. Mechanisms of auditory stream segregation allow listeners to track individual melodies and voices, whereas tonal fusion emphasizes harmonic structure and the combining of individual voices into a unitary event (a chord).

Where Do New Ideas Come From?

[I]deas rose in crowds; I felt them collide until pairs interlocked, so to speak, making a stable combination. . . . Among the great numbers of combinations blindly formed by the subliminal self, almost all are without interest and without utility . . . only certain ones are harmonious, and, consequently, at once useful and beautiful. . . . Only this disorder itself permits unexpected combination.

—*Henri Poincaré (cited in Ghiselin, 1955, p. 36)*

If cognitive or psychoacoustic constraints narrow the choices that composers must make, there is still little understanding of how a completely new idea can emerge from existing musical knowledge. Composing music by drawing on existing memories of music is not a creative act; it is an act of plagiarism. If novel musical ideas do not emerge from existing memories of music, however, then where do they come from? The inability of models to account for creativity is not limited to music cognition. According to Jerry Fodor (1980), "we simply have no idea of what it would be like to get from a conceptually impoverished to a conceptually richer system by anything like a process of learning" (p. 149).

The most widely accepted explanation of the emergence of novel forms is Darwin's theory of evolution. His arguments for natural selection form the tenets of modern biology, and are supported by research in modern genetics. The transmission of genetic information from par-

Memes

The *Oxford English Dictionary* defines a meme as "an element of culture that may be considered to be passed on by non-genetic means, esp. imitation." This term was coined by Richard Dawkins in 1976 as a cultural analogue to a gene. He also suggested that memes might be subject to many of the same kinds of selection pressures as genes.
   He wrote:

Just as genes propagate themselves in the gene pool by leaping from body to body via sperms or eggs, so memes propagate themselves in the meme pool by leaping from brain to brain via a process which, in the broad sense, can be called imitation… Examples of memes are tunes, ideas, catch phrases, clothes fashions, ways of making pots or of building arches. (1999, p. 192)

ent to offspring involves a random but essential variability. When environmental conditions change, genetic variation increases the probability that some offspring will adapt to, and reproduce in, the new conditions. Novel biological traits, created through random variation, are "selected" if they offer a reproductive advantage.

Shortly after Darwin described his theory of natural selection, there was enormous excitement about the explanatory power of these selectionist principles. If the concepts of random variation and selection could account for the emergence of novel biological structures, they might also account for novelty in other domains. William James applied selectionist principles to human creativity, suggesting that "new conceptions…are originally produced in the shape of random images, fancies, accidental outbirths of spontaneous variation in the functional activity of the excessively unstable human brain" (1880, p. 456). James believed that from this variation, "the outer environment simply confirms or refutes, preserves or destroys—selects, in short" (1880, p. 456). Ernst Mach made a similar argument, but proposed an internal selection process. According to Mach, prolific composers such as Mozart and Richard Wagner imagined innumerable melodies and harmonies, but their true skill as composers was to retain or select the best ones (Cziko, 1995).

Such views of creativity were common at the turn of the 20th century, but theories were sketchy and there was little supporting evidence (for a review, see Campbell, 1974). Campbell (1974) reintroduced these ideas, arguing that all creative processes must involve (a) mechanisms for introducing variation; (b) selection processes; and (c) mechanisms for preserving or propagating the selected variations (this mechanism is balanced with mechanisms for introducing variation). According to Campbell, cognitive models that do not include variation in output are simply unable to account for the emergence of ideas that diverge from existing memories.

Sound Examples 9.6.1–9.6.7

"Oops I Did It Again," the title of a hit song by Britney Spears, may imply more than just teenage angst. It seems that the opening phrase of this hit (**Sound example 9.6.1**) shares a great deal of similarity with openings of other pieces composed over the centuries in the Western musical tradition (see **Sound examples 9.6.2–9.6.7**). Although the exact pitches and durations differ, the underlying pitch contours are highly similar. The examples were found by executing a "refined contour" search using the melodic theme finder (www.themefinder.org) developed by David Huron and the Center for Computer Assisted Research in the Humanities at Stanford University.

Theorists have identified at least three ways that principles of variation, selection, and replication might operate at the level of human behavior or thought (see Dennett, 1995). The first, exemplified in the ideas proposed by Skinner (1969), is that random variation occurs at the level of our responses to stimuli. Only some of these responses are selected by the environment, in that they result in reinforcement. Reinforcement then acts to increase the probability that the response will be repeated. Skinner's approach, although ignoring the role of internal processes, has considerable power in explaining many aspects of novel behavior.

A second possibility is that random variation is inherent to cognitive operations, thereby providing a mechanism for generating novel ideas. This variation is thought to be followed by a preselection process that screens out inappropriate responses. Preselection is based on mental schemata that reflect knowledge of environmental regularities. The screening process may still leave considerable variation in actual responses, and only some of these responses will be reinforced. Thus, selection may occur both internally and externally.

Finally, variation may occur internally, but not in a random or blind manner. Rather, variation in thought may be constrained by innate or learned mental structures and dimensions (Gregory, 1981). In language, these "mind tools" would include semantic categories and grammatical forms. In music, they would include metric and rhythmic forms, scales, pitch intervals, and knowledge of how temporal patterns tend to continue (Jones & Boltz, 1989; Narmour, 1990). These are some of the internalized parameters that may constrain the process of generating new musical ideas.

These possibilities assume that there are cognitive processes that regularly provide variation in thought or response. Such variation may well occur in the process of analyzing and integrating sensory features. Neurophysiological and psychological evidence indicates that sensory input is analyzed into separable dimensions or features, such as edges and colors. Following this is a reintegration process in which the separate features are recombined to form a unified image. Both processes of analysis and integration are at times imperfect, resulting in a low but consistent frequency with which novel perceptions are formed (Treisman & Schmidt, 1982). Memory for features and how they are combined is even more error prone, providing another source of novel musical materials. Inattention may also increase such errors (Treisman & Gelade, 1980).

There is no clear evidence that creative imagery occurs in this manner, but there is certainly evidence for processes of feature analysis and integration. In all sensory systems, peripheral receptors transduce only specific forms of energy. As examples, cones in the retina respond to specific wavelengths of light, and hair cells on the basilar membrane respond selectively to different frequencies of vibration. At higher levels of processing, different neurons or classes of neurons respond to characteristics such as edges, line orientation, direction of movement, rising or falling pitches, and different stereoscopic disparities (Hubel & Wiesel, 1968; Treisman, 1986; Whitfield & Evans, 1965).

Research on humans with neurological lesions suggests that a comparable analysis occurs for music. Peretz and her associates (Peretz & Kolinsky, 1993; Peretz & Morais, 1989) cite double dissociations between pitch pattern and rhythm as evidence for a neural dissociation between these dimensions. One patient with a lesion in the left temporal lobe could not discriminate different rhythmic patterns, but could discriminate sequences differing in pitch pattern. Another patient with damage to the

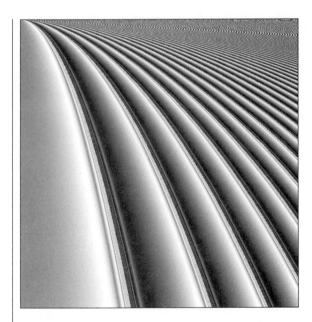

Evolutionary Art

This is a computer-generated "evolved image" from the Evolutionary Computation and Machine Learning Group at RMIT University in Melbourne.

It is an example of evolutionary art in which a computer program produces random images subjected to an array of aesthetic pressures. These pressures may come from humans who rate the images or they can be built into the program through parameters set for aesthetic variables (e.g., amount of contrast or symmetry). Random mutations can also be introduced into the program.

New generations of the images produced by the program survive if they can adapt to the selection pressures. Some theorists have proposed that human creativity may also function in this way.

Source: Photo courtesy of Vic Ciesielski.

right hemisphere showed the reverse effect: Discrimination on the basis of pitch pattern was impaired whereas discrimination on the basis of rhythm was normal. Such reports illustrate that temporal and pitch information is separated at some levels of processing.

Research with musicians provides additional evidence for a perceptual analysis of music into separate dimensions or features. Peretz and Babai (1992) found a left ear advantage for contour discrimination, but a right ear advantage for pitch-interval discrimination. The asymmetry implies that contour is processed in the right hemisphere and pitch interval is processed in the left hemisphere. Overall, it appears that melodies are neurally separated into components such as rhythm, intervallic pattern, and contour. Thus, various components of music are analyzed separately, but we eventually experience a unified piece of music.

How does this happen? One explanation is that once features are analyzed, there is a process in which the separate dimensions or features of objects are recombined. Reintegration is essential to the formation of unified mental representations of objects or events. Research on visual perception suggests that reintegration is at times imperfect (Treisman, 1986; Treisman & Gelade, 1980). Treisman argues that accurate reintegration of visual features is linked to focused attention. Without focused attention, visual features may remain perceptually free-floating, or may combine more or less at random with each other, giving rise to illusory conjunctions of features. For novel stimuli, reintegration without attention is essentially random. For familiar visual patterns, reintegration is guided by long-term knowledge of visual patterns (visual mind tools), giving rise to a kind of informed hallucination.

Similar processes may also occur for musical stimuli. Illusory conjunctions have been investigated for pitch and timbre (Hall & Weiberg, 2003), pitch and duration (Thompson, Hall & Pressing, 2001), and pitch pattern and rhythm (Thompson, 1994). In the latter study, listeners were presented with two different test melodies, followed by a pause, and then two comparison melodies. They then indicated if the test melodies differed from the comparison melodies. If the comparison melodies were constructed by combining the pitch pattern of one test melody with the rhythm of the other test melody, and vice versa, listeners could only detect this difference if they were fully attentive. Distracted listeners were poor at detecting when a new combination of melody and rhythm was presented, even though they could easily detect a new melody or a new rhythm. When these listeners were distracted, reintegration of pitch and temporal information was incomplete or inaccurate.

For complex novel stimuli, even attentive listeners may have difficulty integrating features. Krumhansl (1991) presented listeners part of a piano piece by Messiaen, and asked them to compare the segment to different comparison sequences. The pattern of responses indicated that listeners were sensitive to pitch and duration information, but quite insensitive to the manner in which those features were combined. One interpretation of her finding is that, even for these attentive listeners, the reintegration of pitch and duration was incomplete or inaccurate.

The scale illusion, reported by Deutsch (1975), represents another case of improper perception. Deutsch simultaneously presented two major scales to listeners—one ascending and one descending. As illustrated in Figure 9.2, successive tones in each scale were presented alternately to the left and right ears, such that when a tone from the ascending scale was presented to the right ear, a tone from the descending scale was presented to the left ear. Listeners did not accurately perceive the manner in which locations and pitches were combined. Rather, they perceived illusory conjunctions of pitch and location information in a way that preserved pitch proximity. That is, the perceptual tendency to group tones according to pitch proximity interfered with accurate encoding of how pitch and location were combined.

These misperceptions, along with errors in memory, are a source of novel material that may well be harnessed in the act of composition. Personal, historical, and cultural conditions then guide and constrain the musical choices made by composers. Meyer (1989), for example, linked the romantic period of music composition with a culture-specific fascination with unclosed structures. Such an understanding of composition fits nicely with the selection part of this argument: Composers ultimately make selections from the set of musical materials in their musical imagination, and these selections may be partially influenced by the cultural milieu.

Emotional states may provide another important basis for selection, but to explain musical imagination—that is, the very ability to form new compositional ideas—it is essential to identify a process that generates novel variations from existing musical memories and forms. Musical experiences include a wide range of attentional and listening conditions, many of which have been shown to result in misperceptions of musical features, and how those features are combined. Composition, then, may be understood as the process of harnessing this vast source of novel material. In some cases, a composer may select combinations of qualities that merely represent variations on an established theme. In other cases, remote combinations may be selected, giving rise to new musical phrases

Sound Example 9.7

A re-creation of Deutsch's scale illusion is provided in **Sound example 9.7**. You will need headphones to experience the illusion.

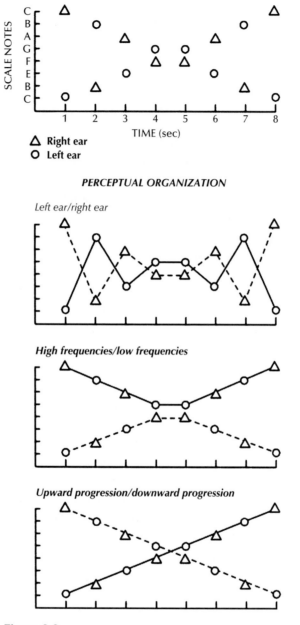

Figure 9.2

The results from Deutsch's scale illusion showed that listeners did not perceive the left and right ear inputs as separate streams (second graph from top) because of the awkward leaps in pitch that violated the principle of pitch proximity. Instead, judgments of the left and right ear input were made (as in the bottom two graphs), such that pitch proximity was preserved.

From Handel, S. (1989). *Listening*. Cambridge, MA: MIT Press, p. 201. Reprinted by permission.

and melodies that bear little resemblance to the musical images and passages from which they were derived.

The Craft of Music Composition

Research in music cognition has placed enormous emphasis on the perception and memory of musical structure. Much less is known about the ability to compose music. In Western musical traditions, composition is often a self-conscious creative endeavor (Meyer, 1956), but some type of process of composition is recognized and practiced across a wide range of other musical traditions around the world, including the Ibo, Gros Ventre, Omaha, Solomon Islands, Baoule, Mafulu, Tikopians, and Teton Sioux (Merriam, 1964). The ability to perceive and appreciate a musical composition is influenced by cognitive constraints, and composers who are in step with the capacities of listeners create music that is readily perceived and appreciated. In Western tonal traditions, voice-leading practices must be attuned to processes of auditory scene analysis so that listeners can perceive individual voices in polyphonic music. Composers may also introduce properties in their music that are not readily appreciated, providing an implication of structure that listeners cannot quite grasp. This strategy prevents listeners from forming a full and accurate mental representation of the music, encouraging deeper contemplation of its potential meaning and enriching the musical experience. Ernest Hemingway argued for a similar strategy in literature that he referred to as the principle of the iceberg. For every part of the story that is explicitly visible to the reader, there should be seven-eighths of it "underwater." By challenging full comprehension, the author is thought to be able to induce more intense feelings in the reader.

It is important to recognize that the separation of music makers (composers and performers) from music listeners is not meaningful for all musical genres. The separation is perhaps sharpest in genres where music is used as a commodity for entertainment. The distinction is less clear in many other genres such as religious trance music (e.g., Blacking, 1973; Diallo & Hall, 1989; Kartomi, 1980), or the Saami (Lapps) tradition in which each individual has a repertoire of songs or *joiks* that may be sung, for example, while herding reindeer (Blumenfeld, 1993). Even within the history of Western tonal music, the craft of music composition has been a rare occupation, and a large proportion of the tonal repertoire taught in music conservatories can be boiled down to a small number of composers, such as Bach, Beethoven, and Mozart. Listeners of this music embrace the idea of a small number of exceptional composers making up the musical canon. Just over a dozen composers account for approximately half of all music performed in concert and recital halls (Simonton, 1997).

One explanation is that learning and sharing knowledge about music is far simpler when we agree to admire a limited number of artists (Adler, 1985). Composers tend to restrict their activity to music and have been characterized as less versatile intellectually than successful figures in other disciplines (White, 1931). Many of the great composers of the classical period began making contributions to their creative productivity at a very young age, and continued composing until the end of their lives.

At the heart of music composition is creativity, a process that is poorly understood (Collins, 2005). There is an enormous body of research on perception and memory, but we still have very little understanding of the processes by which individuals are able to create novel musical ideas. Although new music compositions almost always resemble other works, at least some details of any composition seem novel. However, within our current understanding of cognition, composers only have existing mental representation of music to draw from. How are these existing memories converted into a unique creation? Processes of natural selection provide a model for understanding creative acts. This model implies that creativity requires mechanisms of random variations in thoughts followed by a cognitive selection process in which certain random combinations of ideas survive to be used in a creative act. Selection involves attending to various cognitive constraints, as outlined by Lerdahl (1988) and illustrated in the traditional rules of voice-leading. Composers may not be fully conscious of these processes, leading to the impression that, in Tchaikovsky's words, a composition emerges on its own, like a flower that takes root, puts forth branches, and blooms.

Additional Readings

Huron, D. (2001). Tone and voice: A derivation of the rules of voice-leading from perceptual principles. *Music Perception, 19,* 1–64.

McAdams, S. (2004). Problem solving strategies in music composition: A case study. *Music Perception, 21,* 391–429.

CHAPTER 10
Music and Other Abilities

LEARNING OUTCOMES

By the end of this chapter you should be able to:

1. Provide a critical evaluation of the so-called Mozart effect.

2. Explain short-term effects of music exposure.

3. Summarize and appraise research on long-term benefits of music training.

4. Identify challenges in concluding that music training leads to long-term benefits in nonmusical domains.

5. Contrast and appraise different arguments for government funding toward educational programs in arts and music.

6. Summarize evidence that musical sensitivity is related to emotional sensitivity.

233

> The purpose of art is not the release of a momentary ejection of adrenaline but rather the gradual, lifelong construction of a state of wonder and serenity.
>
> —*Glenn Gould (1962, p.11)*

Is Music Unique?

At first glance, music seems unique. It appears to share few surface qualities with other aspects of human experience. During a musical activity, one or more individuals produce a collection of sounds by banging on surfaces, plucking thin filaments of metal or nylon, scraping catgut and hair strands against one another, and blowing through openings that are sometimes so tiny that their faces turn purple. A visitor from another planet might well ask: "What is the purpose of this peculiar behavior?" Music is not used to communicate or evince specific ideas or constructs; it does not attract prey, deter predators, or heal wounds; and with a few exceptions it bears little resemblance to other sounds in our experience, such as wind, rain, speech, or breaking glass. Although we often play music with others, the act of performing in a group is distinctly different from other social activities, such as a conversation. A performance by a string quartet might be described as having a "conversational" quality, but we all know that it is not a conversation. More accurately, it is four individuals (often highly educated) simultaneously scraping dried intestine with strands of hair from a horse's tail.

Yet people are surprisingly willing to accept claims that this rather peculiar behavior is naturally and intimately related to a host of other human skills and activities. Popular media often

A jazz trio banging on surfaces, plucking filaments, and blowing into a twisted metal tube is pictured above. A visitor from another planet might well ask "For what purpose?"

Source: Original photography: antanask (Flickr). Made available under Creative Commons 2.0 Attribution-Generic License.

Priming

Poke, cloak, soak. What is the white of an egg called?

If you answered "yolk" (instead of *albumen*) it may be because, consciously or not, you had been primed by the rhyming words. That is, the target was made more readily available in memory through priming.

Priming has become one of the most important paradigms in experimental psychology, particularly in psycholinguistic research. Often the effect of priming is measured in reaction time (RT) needed to produce a given target. Faster RTs tend to indicate greater sensitivity to or awareness of a target.

make extravagant claims about the power of music, as though it were a supernatural force. It has been claimed that playing an instrument can improve a child's grades, self-esteem, mathematical ability, reading skills, emotional intelligence, and overall intelligence. We read that listening to certain types of music can energize us physically and mentally; that it can activate beta waves that enable us to work, study, think, and exercise with optimal productivity. Many researchers are usually skeptical of such claims because they are politically and economically motivated, with little attention given to the scientific basis of these assertions. Does this mean that we should reject such claims entirely? No, but we should be aware that the scientific evidence for links between musical and nonmusical phenomena is mixed, and strong claims are simply not warranted.

Music exposure may have short-term and long-term nonmusical consequences. Short-term effects of music listening on nonmusical activities are typically secondary effects of music on mood states and levels of arousal, but such effects could also arise directly through a process known as priming. Long-term benefits of music lessons on a nonmusical skill are classified as an instance of cognitive transfer. Priming and transfer, although not identical, are related phenomena. Priming occurs when prior exposure to some stimulus results in enhanced processing of a related stimulus at a later time. Transfer occurs when experience or training in one activity enhances the ability to perform a related activity. Instances of priming and transfer are well documented, but are usually observed only between highly related skills.

Ever since the aerobic dance phenomenon of the 1980s, exercise to the accompaniment of music has become an inseparable combination for many people. In many cases, music serves to coordinate repetitive movement. In other situations, it can serve as a distractor. Some studies have found that listening to music while exercising can reduce perceived exertion ratings in participants.

Source: Original photography: myself (Wikipedia Commons). Made available under Creative Commons 2.5 Attribution Share-Alike License.

A large number of researchers have examined possible connections between musical and nonmusical skills. Although many investigators report support for such associations, the evidence is inconsistent from study to study and the effects are usually modest. In fact, there is little agreement about which nonmusical skills might be enhanced by music or how such enhancement effects would arise. This lack of agreement is not surprising, because it is not at all obvious why training in music should have benefits for other skills such as mathematics, reading, and chess.

If popular media are any indication, the public is fully prepared to accept that music experiences bestow extraordinary benefits for various aspects of our lives, but researchers must be more cautious. When scientific investigations of the topic are reported, the neurological and cognitive bases for hypothetical associations are often left unstated, or are highly speculative, or are so general that they would predict associations between music and almost any human activity. Predictions of priming and transfer effects between music and nonmusical activities also sit uncomfortably with the widespread belief that distinct domains such as language and music are processed independently. This modularity thesis has dominated cognitive psychology for much of the past 20 years, and seems to contradict predictions of priming and transfer effects between musical and nonmusical domains.

Short-Term Effects of Music

There is a limited amount of psychological research on the short-term effects of music listening on nonmusical skills, but the capacity of music to influence our behavior is widely accepted in advertising and market-

Effect of Musical Genre

Some evidence suggests that music's short-term effects on behavior might not be limited to specific musical features such as tempo, but can also be elicited by manipulating broader variables such as musical genre.

In one study (Areni & Kim 1993), customers at a wine store spent more money buying more expensive wine when classical music was played than when top 40 music was played. This suggests customers made an implicit association between more expensive items and classical music.

Classical music has also proven to be a successful deterrent of unruly behavior by youths loitering outside of shopping malls and other public places after hours. A potential troublemaker might find classical music ill-suited to rebellion.

In recent years, the company Muzak—infamous for producing and distributing easy-listening versions of popular music—has begun creating playlists for clients who want to project a particular image to the public.

ing and well documented in studies of consumer behavior (Bruner, 1990). Theme music in advertisements or background music in stores and shopping centers clearly affects consumer behavior, largely because of its capacity to induce mood states and influence actions. If music can induce a positive mood in individuals, then they will be more inclined to adopt a positive attitude toward the merchandise. Along similar lines, a number of researchers have reported that music can be used to engender a compliant attitude, and that virtually any message accompanied by music is perceived to be more persuasive (e.g., Schwarz, Bless, & Bohner, 1991; Thompson & Russo, 2004). Music can also influence the pace and timing of movements that, in turn, have consequences for behavior. Milliman (1982) observed that people walk more slowly through stores when the tempo of the background music is slow; and Nkeita (1988) described how the Frafra people of Ghana use music as work songs to facilitate efficient actions when cutting grass.

THE MOZART EFFECT

One of the most striking reports of short-term effects of music was also one of the most widely publicized and misinterpreted studies in the recent history of psychology. In a study published in the prestigious journal *Nature*, Rauscher, Shaw, and Ky (1993) discovered that college students performed better on certain tests of spatial abilities after listening to 10 minutes of a Mozart sonata than after listening to relaxation instructions or sitting in silence. The results became known as the Mozart effect and received enormous attention in the popular and scientific media (e.g., Holden, 1994; NBC News, 1994). Although the authors noted that the effect was transient, lasting only about 10 to 15 minutes, the results were widely interpreted as evidence that "music makes you smarter."

A flurry of research activity on the issue ensued, and professors of music psychology have been descended on by students asking them to supervise a project or thesis on the topic. Unfortunately for these students, it turns out that replicating the Mozart effect is no small achievement. Many experienced researchers have simply been unable to replicate the effect, raising serious questions about its reliability (Steele, Bass, & Crook, 1999; Steele, Dalla Bella, et al., 1999). Others have successfully replicated the effect but could account for their results in terms of temporary changes in arousal and mood induced by the music (Husain, Thompson, & Schellenberg, 2002; Thompson, Schellenberg, & Husain,

Sound Examples 10.1.1–10.1.2

The Mozart effect has spawned a cottage industry of recordings proclaiming the music's positive intellectual effects. In 1998, the governor of Georgia even legislated that all new mothers be given a Mozart CD for their newborn child for free. However, subsequent studies have shown that the Mozart effect (increased spatial ability on a standardized test) probably arises from the positive mood and arousal response induced by the music chosen for the initial study. **Sound example 10.1.1** is an excerpt from the Mozart piece used a stimulus in the original study (1993)—*Sonata for 2 Pianos in D Major* (K. 448). The major key, lively tempo, and generally bright character of the piece may contribute to a positive mood and a high arousal response. **Sound example 10.1.2** is an excerpt from the "Lacrymosa" in Mozart's *Requiem*. The minor key, slow tempo, and somber character are unlikely to generate a positive mood or a high arousal.

Sound examples 10.1.1 and 10.1.2 are available via the *Music, Thought, and Feeling* iMix on iTunes.

2001). The latter studies suggest that the Mozart effect works not by priming other skills directly; rather, listening to certain types of music can induce positive and energetic affective states that then enhance performance in other (nonmusical) domains.

In other words, the Mozart effect is an example of enhanced performance caused by manipulation of arousal or mood, rather than an instance of priming. It is known that very high or low levels of anxiety or arousal inhibit performance on cognitive tasks, whereas moderate levels facilitate performance (Berlyne, 1967; Sarason, 1980). Moreover, negative moods and boredom can produce deficits in performance and learning (Koester & Farley, 1982; Kovacs & Beck, 1977; O'Hanlon, 1981), whereas positive moods lead to improved performance on various cognitive and problem-solving tasks (Ashby, Isen, & Turken, 1999; Isen, 1999).

Thompson, Schellenberg, and Husain (2001) compared the effects of listening to excerpts from two musical pieces: a sonata composed by Mozart and an adagio composed by Albinoni. The excerpts consisted of 10 minutes from Mozart's "Sonata for Two Pianos in D Major, K. 448" (Mozart, 1985) or 10 minutes from Albinoni's "Adagio in G minor for organ and strings" (Albinoni, 1981). The Mozart sonata is the same piece that was used in the original study of the Mozart effect. It is a relatively fast-paced piece of music written in a major key, and was expected to induce heightened arousal and positive mood. Conversely, the adagio by Albinoni is a relatively slow-paced piece of music written in a minor key, and was expected to induce low arousal and sad mood.

Participants listened attentively to one of the two excerpts, and were then assessed for spatial abilities, arousal, mood, and enjoyment. Spatial abilities were measured using the paper-folding-and-cutting (PF&C) subtest from the Stanford–Binet intelligence test, which consisted of 17 multiple-choice questions. In each question, participants are shown a rectangular piece of paper subjected to a series of folding and cutting manipulations. They are next shown five unfolded pieces of paper that represent possible outcomes of the folding and cutting manipulations. The task is to choose the correct outcome from the five options. An example of the task is shown in Figure 10.1. To succeed on the task, participants must mentally fold and cut the rectangular piece of paper in accordance with the instructions, and then mentally unfold the paper and imagine the resultant shape.

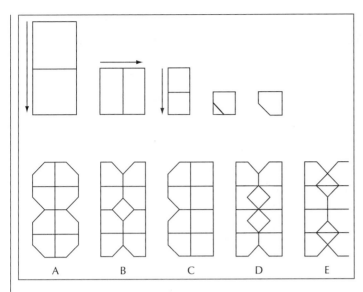

Figure 10.1

A sample question from the paper-folding-and-cutting (PF&C) subtest from the Stanford–Binet intelligence test.

Mood and arousal were assessed using the short form of the Profile of Mood States (POMS; McNair, Lorr, & Droppleman, 1992). The POMS consists of 30 adjectives describing feelings and mood. These adjectives are classified into a number of subscales that measure different dimensions of mood and arousal. The adjectives that make up the Vigor-Activity subscale (lively, active, energetic, full of pep, and vigorous) describe positive arousal; those that make up the Depression-Dejection subscale (sad, unworthy, discouraged, lonely, and gloomy) describe negative affect. For each adjective, participants indicated the degree to which the adjective described their mood using a 5-point scale (anchored by *not at all* and *extremely*). Participants also rated their level of enjoyment of the music, and provided an overall mood and arousal rating.

At the start of the experiment, all participants were assessed for mood and arousal to ensure that there were no preexisting differences between groups. Participants in the silence condition sat in silence for 10 minutes. Those in the music condition listened to music by Mozart or Albinoni for 10 minutes. All participants were then assessed once more for mood and arousal. As expected, performance on the PF&C task was better after listening to Mozart than after sitting in silence, but there was no such effect for the Albinoni group. Scores were also higher in the Mozart group than in the Albinoni group on the POMS arousal subscale, and on the subjective mood and arousal rating, and they were lower on the POMS (negative) mood subscale.

Figure 10.2 illustrates PF&C scores, POMS arousal scores, POMS mood scores, subjective mood and arousal ratings, and enjoyment ratings as a function of musical excerpt. All of the measures are converted to standard scores to facilitate comparison. Figure 10.2 shows that the different levels of arousal, mood, and enjoyment closely mirror performance differences on the PF&C task, which strongly suggests that the Mozart effect can be explained by participants' mood and arousal level.

If the Mozart effect is merely a consequence of arousal or mood, then exposure to any pleasant and engaging stimuli should lead to enhanced performance on spatial tasks. Results reported by Nantais and Schellenberg (1999) support this prediction. Interestingly, the short-term effects of increased arousal and positive mood are not identical. Performance on certain tasks, such as creative problem solving, may be facilitated by positive affect but not by arousal. According to Ashby et al. (1999), effects of positive mood are associated with increased levels of the neurotransmitter dopamine, whereas arousal is strongly associated with the neurotransmitter norepinephrine. Thus, mood and arousal rely on different neurochemical systems, but these systems have overlap-

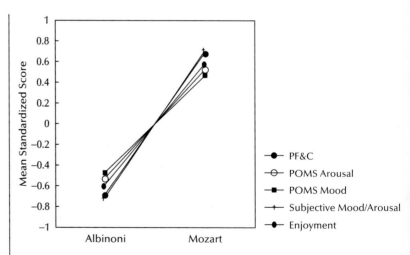

Figure 10.2

Standardized scores on five measures after listening to Mozart or to Albinoni: the paper-folding-and-cutting (PF&C) task, Profile of Mood States (POMS) arousal subscale, POMS mood subscale (reverse coded), subjective mood and arousal ratings, and enjoyment ratings.

ping neural substrates and may in some instances have similar effects on performance.

Long-Term Benefits of Music

In addition to short-term effects of listening to music, there may be nonmusical benefits of long-term musical instruction (Hetland, 2000; Schellenberg, 2000, 2005). Such benefits cannot be explained by temporary changes in mood and arousal. Unfortunately, much of the data on such benefits are inconclusive because researchers frequently adopt a correlational method of conducting their research, making it impossible to draw causal inferences. There are myriad preexisting differences between people who gravitate toward music, as well as the families who have the inclination and financial means to support such musical activities. People who become musically trained may differ from musically untrained individuals in countless ways, and associations between musical and nonmusical skills might arise because of these preexisting differences rather than as a consequence of music training per se.

Children with high levels of motivation and parental support may develop many skills, but it would be foolish to assume that the development of one skill caused the other skills; any correspondence between skills can be explained by the underlying motivation and parental support. Researchers who adopt a correlational approach typically attempt to control for obvious differences, often by matching groups for variables such as family income and school grades, or using statistical techniques. However, it is unreasonable to assume that researchers can identify and account for all possible differences between musically trained and untrained individuals, so any conclusions that are drawn from correlational studies invariably must be acknowledged as tentative.

Correlation Versus Causality

Correlational analysis can be a powerful means of discovering associations between variables. However, it is limited in its explanatory power because it provides limited insight into causality.

This limitation has been cited by tobacco companies as a primary defense against charges that cigarette smoking is harmful. To prove that smoking causes gum disease, it would be necessary to rule out any other factors that might contribute to gum disease. A controlled study would need to be implemented in which two groups are subjected to identical conditions, except that one group is made to smoke. Given the ethical problems associated with such a study, health researchers have had to rely on correlational approaches, or studying long-term effects of smoking within a population.

Experimental studies of the benefits of exposure to music allow causal inferences to be drawn with greater confidence. Such studies involve random assignment of individuals to music training groups or to control groups that receive comparable levels of training in nonmusical domains. Random assignment ensures that individual differences such as family income and levels of self-esteem are randomly distributed across the experimental and control groups, and are hence negligible. After a period of training, participants are assessed for skills, and any differences between groups can be attributed to the effects of music training. Experimental studies are not without their challenges, but they allow causal inferences to be drawn with some confidence.

Research on the potential benefits of music for nonmusical skills is not only of scientific value because of its cognitive implications; it can also have applied ramifications. Music and arts education programs are often considered subsidiary to core education programs in the curriculum such as mathematics and history, and are vulnerable to government cutbacks. Arguments for retaining government funding for music programs often involve the suggestion that music training has benefits that extend beyond music skill to a wide range of other cognitive abilities. We next examine evidence bearing on a few of the most widely cited connections between musical and nonmusical skills.

MUSIC AND MATHEMATICS

The connection between music and mathematics has a long history. Pythagoras (c. 582–497 BC) contributed to our early understanding of harmonic ratios, such as the 2:1 ratio associated with the octave and the 3:2 ratio associated with the perfect fifth. During the Middle Ages, music was taught as a science. Boethius was involved in establishing music as one of the four disciplines of the Oxford *quadrivium*, which consisted of music, arithmetic, geometry, and astronomy. At the time, music education focused on the mathematical roots of harmony. The science of harmonics was applied not only to the understanding of music but also to distances between planets and orbital speeds. The connection between music and mathematics arose because music was studied in terms of the physics of sound, and at this physical level all phenomena can be quantified and described mathematically.

This historic connection between music and mathematics may be distinguished from contemporary theories that posit a cognitive link between these two domains. According to this view, there are

Boethius (480–524 AD).

Source: Illustration from an English manuscript in the Cambridge University Library (ca. 1130).

Although the relationship between musical and mathematical ability remains unclear, music served as an inspiration and source of mathematical inquiry for many of the greatest mathematical minds (e.g., Euclid, Galileo, Euler, Kepler). Some scientists, such as Albert Einstein (1879–1955), actively take up music making as a hobby. An amateur violinist of apparently mediocre talent, Einstein said "If I were not a physicist, I would probably be a musician. I often think in music."

convergent cognitive processes associated with skills involved in music and mathematics that may have implications for priming and transfer effects. These common cognitive processes would account for alleged associations between music and mathematical abilities.

Research on the potential association between music and mathematics has been carried out with individuals across a wide range of ages. Whitehead (2001) randomly assigned middle and high school students into one of three groups: full treatment (music instruction for 50 minutes five times per week), limited treatment (50 minutes of instruction once per week), and no treatment. After 20 weeks, the full treatment group showed greater achievement gains in mathematics than the other two groups, and the no-treatment group showed the fewest gains. In another study, Gardiner, Fox, Knowles, and Jeffrey (1996) tracked the effects of an art instruction curriculum on academic achievement among children in Grade 1. At the beginning of the school year, children who participated in the arts curriculum had test scores below children who did not participate in the arts curriculum. After 7 months, students receiving arts instruction had higher scores on mathematics achievement. These students continued to have higher mathematics achievement scores after a second year of arts instruction. Because arts instruction involved both music and visual arts, it is difficult to evaluate whether the effect was related to music instruction, visual arts instruction, or their combination. Finally, Geoghegan and Mitchelmore (1996) reported that preschool children enrolled in a music program scored higher on a mathematical achievement test than children who had not been involved in the program.

A meta-analysis conducted by Vaughn (2000) suggests a modest but reliable association between musical and mathematical abilities. Her analysis considered 20 correlational and 5 experimental studies and led to three conclusions. First, individuals who voluntarily choose to study music tend to demonstrate higher mathematical achievements than those who do not choose to study music. The reasons for this correlation cannot be determined and no causal inferences are possible. It could be that children who pursue music feel somewhat more comfortable with academic pursuits that rely on nonverbal forms of representation. Second, background music heard while thinking about math problems may, in certain circumstances and to a limited extent, enhance mathematical ability. Although the origin of this benefit has yet to be determined, it may be secondary to the effects of music on affective states. Third, individuals exposed to a music curriculum in school show higher mathematical achievement as a consequence of their music instruction. It was possible to infer this causal link by considering the results of the six experimental studies, but only three of the experimental studies revealed modest effect sizes; the other three produced effects sizes of approximately zero.

The results of Vaughn's meta-analysis provide modest support for a connection between music and mathematics, implying that there may be cognitive operations that are common to the two domains. Formal instruction in both subject areas involves attention to numbers, repeating patterns and ratios. More generally, both activities require extensive engagement with and manipulation of nonverbal materials. Musical abilities such as counting to the beat and perceiving durational ratios involve a kind of mathematical thinking. Additional assumptions would be required to explain how such basic connections account for associations extending beyond elementary levels of music and mathematics. One might argue, for example, that musical activities provide an embodied and hence deeply personal understanding of numbers and ratios, and this depth of understanding at an elementary level provides a firm foundation on which more advanced mathematical constructs can be appreciated. To date, however, no such hypothesis has been examined.

MUSIC AND SPATIAL-TEMPORAL ABILITY

One of the most general properties of music that could link it to other phenomena is that it involves complex patterns that are perceived and remembered as structural units. We associate a melodic theme with variations on that theme by recognizing that, beneath the surface of the music, there is an essential melodic pattern that connects each variation with the theme. The ability to detect, appreciate, and respond to patterns is essential in many other domains, such as mathematics, chess, architecture, chemistry, physics, and language. Thus, one might argue that these domains are associated with each other because they all involve the ability to extract and respond to complex patterns.

According to Rauscher and her colleagues, perceiving certain forms of Western music involves holding mental images of tonal patterns (e.g., a melody) and using them as models with which new tonal patterns (e.g., variations on that melody) can be compared. Described more generally, music perception involves the ability to maintain and relate complex mental images. These processes are thought to exemplify a general human capacity known as spatial-temporal reasoning, which is applicable in skills such as chess and mathematics. Understanding geometry, for example, requires sensitivity to transformations of geometric images in space and time. These researchers predicted that training in music engages and refines brain processes involved in spatial-temporal reasoning, and could lead to cognitive transfer effects for other domains that involve spatial-temporal reasoning (Rauscher et al., 1997; Rauscher & Zupan, 2000).

A meta-analysis of 15 studies involving 701 children ages 3 to 12 years suggests that children provided with music instruction indeed score somewhat higher than controls on spatial temporal tasks (Hetland, 2000). Relatively larger effects have been reported for young children (Gromko & Poorman, 1998), although the duration of the effect is not entirely clear. Costa-Giomi (1999) reported that 9-year-old children provided with piano instruction scored higher than controls on a spatial-temporal task after 1 year of instruction, but not after 2 years of instruction. A number of researchers have also questioned the theoretical connection between music listening and spatial-temporal reasoning (e.g., Chabris, 1999; Thompson, Schellenberg, & Husain, 2001), even though the association has been justified on neurological grounds (Leng, Shaw, & Wright, 1990). Unfortunately, the media frenzy surrounding the Mozart effect, with its many grandiose claims, left many researchers questioning

Sound Example 10.2

Sound example 10.2 includes excerpts of the first phrase of the theme and its 12 variations in Mozart's variations on the song "Ah! vous dirai-je, Maman" (known to English speakers as "Twinkle, Twinkle, Little Star"). The theme is presented relatively plainly at the beginning and is then subjected to 12 elaborations. An appreciation of the form of this piece requires that the listener be able to recognize the essential melodic pattern of the theme in each of the 12 variations. Rauscher and her colleagues have argued that the ability to track the theme in the variations involves a general human capacity for spatial-temporal reasoning.

the scientific credibility of the original findings. Investigations of the role of spatial-temporal processing for music cognition are ongoing, but to a limited extent.

MUSIC AND VERBAL SKILLS

A number of studies have revealed a correlation between music instruction and verbal skills, particularly reading ability and memory for verbal material. Such a correlation might be expected if verbal and musical skills engage similar perceptual, cognitive, or motor processes. Certainly, both activities engage the auditory system in some way. Given sufficient overlap in the processes involved, training in music might even lead to enhancements in verbal abilities.

Reading music notation shares some of the characteristics of reading verbal material, although there are striking differences in emphasis. Music reading typically involves the conversion of visual symbols into a set of motor commands, and therefore engages visuo-motor processes. The visual input is not converted directly into action but is interpreted through perceptual and cognitive processes specialized for music. A similar process is involved when we read verbal material aloud, but reading aloud is taught mainly in early stages of reading instruction. Speaking fluency is important primarily as a gauge of a child's progress in reading ability. After elementary skills of reading have been acquired, the art of reading aloud is further developed only rarely, as in drama lessons. Advanced reading skills usually do not involve spoken accompaniment. Readers convert visual symbols (written material) into ideas through perceptual and cognitive processes specialized for language, and these ideas are not voiced. This process of interpreting visual symbols also occurs in music reading but is usually followed by implementing motor commands in the form of music performance. It is rare to read music in silence (for discussions of the psychology of music reading, see Sloboda, 2004).

Among 4- and 5-year old children, musical skills are positively correlated with skills in reading (Lamb & Gregory, 1993). Memory for spoken words (verbal memory) was also enhanced for 6- to 15-year-old boys who had music training (Ho, Cheung, & Chan, 2003) as well as for adult musicians who received musical training before the age of 12 (Chan, Ho, & Cheung, 1998). Song lyrics are also remembered better by musically trained than untrained individuals (Kilgour, Jakobson, & Cuddy, 2000). The connection between music training and verbal memory is not immediately obvious, but it could reflect enhanced function of the left temporal lobe among musicians. Auditory processing areas of the left temporal lobe are enlarged relative to musically untrained individuals (Schlaug, Janke, Huang, & Steinmetz, 1995), and musicians show greater left hemisphere activity than do nonmusicians for a range of tasks (Bever & Chiarello, 1974). The left hemisphere, in turn, is specialized for processing verbal materials.

Butzlaff (2000) conducted a meta-analysis of 24 correlational studies, some involving sample sizes of more than 500,000 high school students. He reported a strong and reliable association between music instruction and reading skills. As with all correlational studies, however, causal inferences cannot be established. Exposure to music could lead to these improved verbal skills, musical aptitude could stem from verbal ability, or a third factor such as self-esteem or general intelligence could predict verbal and musical abilities.

There are a few experimental studies involving random assignment of participants to different groups, and these studies have sometimes revealed effects of music lessons on verbal skills. Standley and Hughes (1997) observed that prekindergarten children who took 15 music lessons performed significantly better than other children on prereading and writing skills. Unfortunately, the children in the comparison condition received no additional lessons of any kind, so it is not possible to pinpoint the source of the effect. The enhanced verbal skills might have resulted from additional instruction time rather than from music training per se. The results of other experimental studies do not show a consistent pattern. Douglas and Willatts (1994) conducted an experimental study of children with reading difficulties and found that those who received music instruction ($n = 6$) performed better on reading tests than those who did not receive music instruction ($n = 6$). However, a similar study by Overy (2002) on boys with dyslexia revealed an effect of music instruction on rapid temporal processing skills, phonological skills, and spelling skills, but not on reading tests. Finally, Butzlaff (2000) reported a meta-analysis of six experimental studies and observed highly variable effect sizes.

On the whole, there is only limited support for a causal connection between music training and verbal skills, but reasonably convincing support for some kind of association between music training and verbal skills. What is the nature of this association? One possibility is that children with musical training have greater phonological awareness (Anvari, Trainor, Woodside, & Levy, 2002). Phonological awareness is the understanding that words are made up of more elementary speech sounds, called phonemes. The letters of the alphabet stand for various speech sounds, and learning to read in an alphabetic system requires an awareness that language is made up of these basic units of speech. Many researchers have argued that phonological awareness is fundamental to reading: Children who are able to hear the basic speech sounds that make up a word can readily associate these phonemes with letters. Both speech and music involve a finite number of units (phonemes, notes) that are combined according to rules (called linguistic or musical grammars) to produce an unlimited number of linguistic or musical phrases. If the skills of auditory analysis are similar for music and reading, then one would expect abilities in one domain to be positively correlated with abilities in the other domain.

A second possibility is that children with musical training have a heightened ability to determine the temporal order of acoustic input (Jakobson, Cuddy, & Kilgour, 2003). Temporal-order processing, in turn, may facilitate the ability to accurately perceive and encode verbal material. Both music and speech involve rapidly changing acoustic information, and their accurate perception depends on the ability to track these changes in real time. This possibility is consistent with clinical studies that show a link between auditory temporal processing skills, and improvements in speech discrimination and language comprehension.

MUSIC AND SPEECH PROSODY

Speech prosody refers to the overall sound contour with which a word or phrase is pronounced. Prosody supplements and modifies the semantic aspects of speech with cues about emphasis, turn taking, attitude, and emotional meaning. Several aspects of prosody appear to be universal, including declination (the association of low or falling pitch with completion), the association of high or rising pitch with questions and with nonfinality, and the presence of local pitch movements on new or informative words. Speech prosody refers to the musical aspect of speech, and includes the melody (intonation) and rhythm (stress and timing) of speech. Both music and speech prosody involve variations in rate, amplitude, pitch, timbre, and stress, and are powerful systems of communicating emotional meaning and syntactic structure. This commonality suggests that these domains engage the same mechanism for evaluating variation in acoustic information (Juslin & Laukka, 2003).

Discussions of links between music and prosody have a long history. From the Renaissance to the Baroque periods, European com-

---

Sound Examples 10.3.1–10.3.2

The following are two musical examples that blur the line between music and speech.

Sound example 10.3.1 is a *recitative* from Handel. Recitative is used in opera and oratorio, usually in particularly "wordy" sections of the libretto or text. It normally functions to advance the plot, or set the scene. Recitatives are traditionally performed with a great deal of rhythmic flexibility. Rather than conforming to any strict pulse, the performer tends instead to follow the natural rhythms of the text. Stereotyped melodic contours also exist for recitative, which mimic the natural contours of speech. Recitative is often referred to as a kind of heightened speech.

Sound example 10.3.2 is "I Ain't No Joke" by Erik B. and Rakim. Unlike recitative, the rap delivery is typically rhythmically precise. In fact, the ability to fit a phrase around a strongly delineated pulse in novel and intricate ways is one of the most valued aspects of rap performance. Although rappers tend not to use discrete pitches in their delivery (i.e., melody), there typically is a stylized and exaggerated use of speech prosody.

Sound examples 10.3.1 and 10.3.2 are available via the *Music, Thought, and Feeling* iMix on iTunes.

posers took for granted the strong connection between composition and oratory. In Greek and Roman literature on rhetoric (Aristotle, Cicero, and Quintilian), musical rhythm was conceived in terms of the rhythms of speech (Durr & Gerstenberg, 1980). Rhythm was thought to include three components: speech, singing or playing, and dance. The rhythm of speech was considered primary, and was thought to be the basis for rhythms that occur in song and dance. Quintilian (in the *Institutio Oratoria*) and Aristotle (in *Rhetoric*) had similar views on the goals of rhetoric:

> ...to instruct the orator in the means of controlling and direct-
> ing the emotional responses of his audience, or in the language
> of classical rhetoric and also later music treatises, to enable the
> orator (i.e., the composer or even the performer) to move the
> "Affections" (i.e., the emotions) of his listeners. (Buelow, 1980,
> p. 793)

The connection between music and speech prosody was also recognized by Darwin (1872) and remains widely accepted, although the origins of this connection are not entirely clear. Some people have proposed that music might be linked phylogenetically with speech prosody (e.g., see Brown, 2000). Dissanayake (2000) makes a particularly convincing argument that music, speech prosody, and facial expression are very likely to share a common ancestry as temporal-spatial patterns of emotional communication, which are particularly adaptive for affiliative interactions between mothers and infants.

Like music, speech prosody is intimately associated with emotion. According to Bolinger (1978, 1986), speech prosody probably originated from the prelinguistic use of pitch to signal emotion. High or rising pitch signals interest, arousal, and incompleteness, whereas low or falling pitch signals absence of interest and hence finality. It is not uncommon in verbal exchanges for people to confine their expressions of emotion to the vocal qualities of speech even when they communicate nothing about the underlying emotional meaning in the verbal material (semantic meaning). Emotions are often expressed in speech not by what is said, but by how it is said. Most people are experts at manipulating various acoustic features of their voices to communicate an underlying emotional message. Table 10.1 summarizes some vocal characteristics that are associated with various emotions (for a review, see Murray & Arnott, 1993).

Table 10.1

Vocal Effects Commonly Associated with Four Emotions, Relative to Neutral Speech

	EMOTION			
	ANGER	HAPPINESS	SADNESS	FEAR
Speech rate	Faster	Faster or slower	Slightly slower	Much faster
Average pitch	Very much higher	Much higher	Slightly lower	Very much higher
Pitch range	Much wider	Much wider	Slightly narrower	Very much wider
Intensity	Higher	Higher	Lower	Normal
Voice quality	Breathy	Breathy	Resonant	Irregular voicing
Pitch changes	Abrupt	Smooth upward inflections	Downward inflections	Normal

Note. Adapted from Murray and Arnott (1993).

What types of emotional messages can be conveyed in music and speech prosody? Many theories of emotion assume a core set of basic emotions, thought to be hard-wired, universal, or psychologically primitive (i.e., not interpretable as a combination of other emotions). Although there is little agreement on the precise set of basic emotions, most theories include joy, sadness, anger, and fear (Ekman, 1992a, 1992b; Ekman & Davidson, 1994). Johnson, Emde, Scherer, and Klinnert (1986) assessed the ability of listeners to identify these four emotions from speech prosody, and found that joy and sadness were easy to recognize, whereas anger and fear were more difficult. This pattern has also been observed in cross-cultural studies of speech prosody (Thompson & Balkwill, 2006) and music (Balkwill & Thompson, 1999; Balkwill et al., 2004).

The ability to recognize and interpret emotion in speech prosody may develop with age and experience. J. B. Morton and Trehub (2001) examined children's understanding of emotion in speech. Children (from 4–10 years old) and adults judged the happiness or sadness of spoken sentences. When verbal (semantic) cues conflicted with vocal (prosodic) cues, children relied mainly on verbal content, whereas adults relied on speech prosody. An implication of this finding is that children and adults use different cues to judge a speaker's emotional state. Whereas children appear to have limited appreciation of the role of vocal emotion in communication, adults interpret vocal affect as indicative of the speaker's emotional intention.

Numerous research findings suggest that music and speech prosody are associated with convergent or overlapping neural areas. PET data (images of the brain obtained through positron emission tomography) implicate right frontal circuits in the retention and comparison of pitches in melodic phrases (Zatorre, Evans & Meyer, 1994) and syllables (Zatorre, Evans, Meyer, & Gjedde, 1992). The right hemisphere is generally thought to be dominant for interpreting nuances in vocal inflection, such as stress, intensity, timbre, emotional tone, and pitch contour (Joseph, 1988; Shapiro & Danly, 1985). Moreover, the right hemisphere is superior to the left at identifying emotional meaning in music (Bryden, Lev, & Sugarman, 1982).

Van Lacker and Sidtis (1992) found that patients with right hemisphere damage relied heavily on temporal cues when judging emotion in speech prosody. In contrast, patients with left hemisphere damage relied on fundamental frequency (pitch) information when making these judgments. These results suggest that under normal conditions, emotional meaning in speech prosody is carried by a combination of rhythmic cues processed by the left hemisphere and pitch information (intonation) cues processed by the right hemisphere. The results also illustrate that, like music, both pitch (melodic) and temporal (rhythmic) aspects of speech prosody carry emotional meaning.

A study of patients with brain damage suggests that the left primary auditory cortex and right prefrontal cortex are involved in the retention and comparison of pitch and temporal patterns in musical and linguistic domains (Patel et al., 1998). Prosodic and musical discrimination abilities were evaluated in two adults with bilateral brain damage. One showed good performance on both linguistic and musical discrimination tasks, whereas the other had difficulty with both tasks. In both individuals, the level of performance was similar in both musical and linguistic tasks, implying that these two domains share the same (damaged) neural resources. Patel et al. (1998) speculated that shared neural resources are used to process melodic (contour) and rhythmic (grouping) aspects of speech and music. A decade later, Patel (2008) developed these ideas further, arguing that music and language share deep and essential connections in the brain.

Sound Examples 10.4.1–10.4.3

These are some examples from Tagalog of sentences conveying specific emotions using speech prosody. Studies tend to show that nonnative speakers, in the absence of any semantic information, are able to make accurate judgments of the emotion being conveyed. This suggests that certain elements of speech prosody may be universal. Which emotion is being conveyed in each of the following examples: happy, sad, angry, or neutral?

Other evidence suggests strong associations between prosodic and facial channels of emotion perception. Borod et al. (2000) presented normal adults with prosodic and facial stimuli, and asked them to identify or discriminate (same or different) eight emotional expressions. Measures of emotional sensitivity were highly correlated across channels of communication, even when demographic, cognitive, and nonemotional perceptual variables were statistically controlled. The results suggest that there is a general affective processor for the identification of emotional stimuli across communication channels. Although the underlying neural substrate for such a general processor is unknown, candidates include the amygdala, orbital frontal cortex, anterior cingulate, and posterior parietal cortex. Most important, however, if there is indeed a general processor for the identification of emotional stimuli across communication channels, then enhanced sensitivity to emotional meaning in one channel is likely to lead to enhanced sensitivity in other channels. That is, expert musicians may be more sensitive than nonmusicians to tone of voice.

If music and speech prosody involve overlapping neural circuitry, then the skills acquired through musical training might enhance sensitivity to speech prosody. A study by Nilsonne and Sundberg (1985) supported the prediction. Undergraduate law and music students were presented with sequences consisting of the fundamental frequencies of voice samples recorded from depressed and nondepressed individuals. Music students were significantly better than law students at judging the emotional state (depressed or not depressed) of the speakers. In addition, those law students with music training performed better on the task than their nonmusically trained classmates. Nilsonne and Sundberg concluded that, "The mastery of the expression of emotional information in music, which is a prerequisite for a competent musician, would then correspond to an enhanced ability to decode emotional information in speech" (p. 515).

More recently, Thompson et al. (2004) examined the possibility that music training among children might lead to increased sensitivity to speech prosody, a component of emotional intelligence. One hundred and forty-four 6-year-olds were randomly assigned to one of four treatment groups. One group received weekly instruction in keyboard; a second group received weekly singing lessons; a third received weekly training in drama; and a fourth received no training. Drama lessons emphasize using the voice to convey emphasis, surprise, and emotion, so children in this condition were expected to perform better than the no-lessons group at decoding prosody. The critical question was whether music lessons might confer similar benefits. After 1 year, the children who had received keyboard lessons were equivalent to children who had drama lessons and significantly better than the no-lessons children at decoding emotional meaning from prosodic patterns. The findings suggest that keyboard lessons appear to yield transfer effects that improve listeners' ability to decode prosody in speech.

MUSIC AND EMOTIONAL SENSITIVITY

Perhaps the most distinctive quality of music is its power to convey emotional meaning, and a fundamental aspect of musical understanding is the ability to interpret nuances of emotional meaning. Music experiences are strongly linked to our emotional lives. Numerous theories of music consider the interpretation of emotional meaning to be at the core of understanding music (e.g., Kivy, 1980; Langer, 1957; Meyer, 1956). An implication of these theories is that the development of musical ability is linked fundamentally to the development of emotional sensitivity. Emotional sensitivity, in turn, is a highly adaptive skill that plays a role in many cognitive tasks (Damasio, 1994), and is of paramount importance in social interactions, where emotional meaning is conveyed through tone of voice (prosody), facial expression, and body language (Goleman, 1995).

Emotional signals can be communicated in ways that have nothing to do with music. Facial expressions and words can be used unambiguously to convey an emotional message. Why would anyone communicate emotions using such an elaborate system as music when they can articulate that message far more clearly using facial expressions and language? Part of the reason may relate to the differing impact and scope of these other means of signaling emotions. A facial expression typically signals the current emotional state of an individual, and the desired emotional message may be less personal or more dynamic and complex. Language can be used to convey complex emotional signals, but it is not always possible or desirable to articulate an emotional message literally. Music may be used to convey emotional meaning when other means of expressing that emotion, such as facial expressions or speech, are unavailable, ineffective, or undesirable. The emotions felt may be confusing and difficult to articulate verbally, or they may be stifled, discouraged, or debated when presented unambiguously in a verbal message.

Sound Example 10.5

The example is the "The Host of Seraphim" by Dead Can Dance. The band is reknowned for its evocative, emotionally charged music, and has enjoyed a huge following for over two decades despite the fact that the singer, Lisa Gerrard, most often sings in a language totally incomprehensible to anyone.

Often referred to as *glossolalia*, Gerrard strings together phonemes for emotional and musical effects rather than semantic ones. The fact that the music of Dead Can Dance—and Gerrard's voice in particular—can have such emotional resonance with its audience using meaningless syllables for lyrical content suggests that the semantics of musical lyrics may sometimes play a peripheral role in conveying emotion through music.

Sound example 10.5 is available via the *Music, Thought, and Feeling* iMix on iTunes.

Thompson et al. (2004) reported that piano lessons enhance sensitivity to emotional meaning conveyed by speech prosody, which is one dimension of emotional intelligence (but see Trimmer & Cuddy, in press). It remains to be determined whether music training enhances other aspects of emotional intelligence. If so, this effect could have consequences for general cognitive functioning. It is widely acknowledged that there are powerful links between emotion and other aspects of cognition, which implies that sensitivity to emotional meaning could be a valuable life skill. Evidence reviewed by Goleman (1995) suggests that well-adjusted individuals who excel professionally are distinguished by their emotional intelligence—a heightened sensitivity to emotional meaning and expression. Although popularized views must be evaluated with caution, Goleman's arguments are difficult to dismiss.

Individuals with high emotional intelligence are not only good at interpreting and responding to emotional cues; they are also likely to pursue emotional states that optimize their ability to function effectively in work and social environments. As reviewed, emotional states greatly influence performance on cognitive tasks. Ashby et al. (1999) reviewed numerous studies indicating that positive affect improves creative problem solving. Positive affect also increases the ability to organize ideas, classify material, access multiple perspectives, and cope with negative events or information. Heightened arousal, in turn, influences task performance by enhancing speed of processing (Berlyne, 1967; Yerkes & Dodson, 1908). Do musicians capitalize on such emotional benefits? Perhaps, but there is little research on the question.

MUSIC AND GENERAL ABILITIES

As described in the preceding sections, research has revealed associations between music and several different domains. It is possible that all of these connections are instances of a more general association between music and intellectual functioning, such as those measured in standard IQ tests. Musically trained individuals might simply be "smarter" on average than people without music training, which would account for associations between musical proficiency and various nonmusical skills. Although some researchers have observed exclusive associations between music and one specific skill such as reading, many have noted associations that extend to a range of nonmusical domains. Widespread associations with nonmusical domains might emerge because of a general trait possessed by musically trained individuals such as enhanced skills of executive function. Alternatively, such associations might emerge because musical ability involves a large number of subskills such as pattern perception, acoustic analysis, memory, attention, syntactic processing, emotional processing, motor planning and skill, and transcription of visual symbols (music notation) into action. Each of these subskills may benefit nonmusical as well as musical abilities.

Many studies have reported an association between musical skill and academic achievement. Data from the National Center for Education Statistics show that in a sample of 13,327 American high school students, those who participated in music reported higher grades in English, math, history, and science than those who were not involved with music (Morrison, 1994). Unfortunately, it is unclear whether the musically active students had superior achievement prior to enrolling in music studies. Without this crucial information, it is impossible to interpret the association.

Schellenberg (2004) conducted one of the few experimental studies of the issue. He assigned 144 6-year-old children to music lessons or comparison conditions. Just before entering Grade 1, the children were assessed on a standardized IQ test (the Wechsler Intelligence Scale for Children–III [WISC–III; Wechsler, 1991]). Two groups of children received music lessons (keyboard or singing) and two groups of children participated in the control conditions (drama lessons or no lessons). Aside from the children in the no-lessons group, the children received 36 weeks of lessons in keyboard, singing, or drama. After a year, the children were retested on the WISC–III.

All four groups had reliable increases in full-scale IQ, which is a typical consequence of attending school. However, the increase in IQ was greater for the two music groups than for the two control groups. Moreover, similar increases were observed for all four areas of intellectual ability measured by the WISC–III, suggesting that the benefits of music lessons were general, and not restricted to a specific intellectual skill.

An important caveat noted by Schellenberg (2005) is that children taking music lessons differed from those in control groups merely by a few IQ points, and the practical implications of this benefit are probably minimal. Moreover, the results do not confirm that music is unique in its ability to confer this modest benefit for IQ. It merely suggests that the benefits of music lessons on this measure of intellectual ability are greater than those for certain extracurricular activities such as drama. Other types of extracurricular training, such as instruction in chess, may have comparable benefits. Finally, it should be stressed that whereas drama lessons had no effect on IQ, they conferred significant benefits on social skills. It seems possible that the long-term practical benefits of enhanced social skills might be even greater than that of a few additional IQ points.

The precise origin of the effect also cannot be determined from the data, but there are a few plausible explanations. One possibility is that music lessons encouraged children to become more attentive and engaged when confronted with challenging activities of any kind. A second possibility is that children taking music lessons developed an enhanced ability to give their full attention over extended time spans (e.g., while performing a piece of music), and the development of concentration skills made it easier for them to remain on-task when completing the WISC–III. A third possibility is that the activities and demands of music lessons overlap with those involved in other school subjects, such that the general benefits of attending school are exaggerated by the inclusion of music lessons. That is, each of the distinctive subskills developed in music training may be associated with skills required in one or more nonmusical domains. The result would be a constellation of individual enhancements, each requiring its own explanation in view of the cognitive operations involved.

The long-term benefits of music training are somewhat difficult to assess. Schellenberg (2004) reported benefits of 1 year of music lessons on IQ, but an experimental study by Costa-Giomi (1999) suggested that many cognitive benefits of music lessons evaporate after 2 years of study. Schellenberg (2004) also reported a correlation between years of music training and full-scale IQ among adults, but a study by Duke, Flowers, and Wolfe (1997) revealed no connection between piano performance ability and academic achievement.

All told, the findings imply that structured extracurricular instruction confers a range of benefits on intellectual functioning for at least a year. These benefits may extend for longer periods, but the evidence is mixed. Benefits may arise because of a general skill, such as the ability to concentrate or engage fully with challenging materials, but it seems far more probable that they arise because music training involves the acquisition of numerous subskills, each of which can be applied in nonmusical as well as musical activities.

Educational Implications

Research has revealed a number of intriguing associations between musical and nonmusical abilities, although their reliability and underlying cognitive basis remain under investigation. Such connections not only have cognitive implications; they also have applied applications for arts education. On the other hand, it may be dangerous to advocate the continuation of music education programs on the basis that they benefit skills in other domains. As Winner and Cooper (2000) pointed out, it would be unrealistic to expect music training to be as effective in teaching another subject as instruction in the subject itself. Justifying music education by its potential to influence learning in another domain may also have the unwanted effect of implying that music is not inherently valuable. Instead of justifying music on the basis of its connection with other skills, it is essential to engender an appreciation for the unique and powerful role that music plays in all of our lives.

Additional Readings

Patel, A. (2003). Language, music, syntax and the brain. *Nature Neuroscience, 6*, 674–681.

Schellenberg, E. G. (2006). Exposure to music: The truth about the consequences. In G. E. McPherson (Ed.), *The child as musician: A handbook of musical development* (pp. 111–134). Oxford, UK: Oxford University Press.

Glossary

absolute pitch Also called perfect pitch. The ability to identify the pitch of a tone accurately and without relying on an external reference pitch.

accelerando A gradual increase in musical tempo (plural accelerandi). Accelerandi are among the expressive actions that may be introduced by musicians during a music performance.

acoustical Pertaining to the objective physics of sound. Used in contrast to auditory—which pertains to the subjective experience of a sound. For example, frequency is a physical or acoustical property, whereas pitch is a subjective or auditory property.

acoustic analysis A general term referring to procedures for identifying significant physical attributes of an audio signal. One analysis relevant to music acoustics involves identifying and describing the intensity of audible component frequencies in a complex tone, but time-varying attributes of an audio signal (onset and offset characteristics) are also often identified.

acquired amusia An impairment in musical functioning that has an environmental cause, such as a brain injury.

adaptation A change in the structure or behavior of an organism that confers survival or procreative advantages.

affect A term that refers to mental states associated with emotion or mood. Although researchers vary in how they use these terms, affect is usually the most general of the three terms (a superordinate term), whereas emotion and mood refer to specific types of affective experience. *See also* emotion, mood.

affective engagement The degree of emotional connectedness between two or more individuals for the exchange of emotional state.

affiliative Connections between individuals, often emotional in nature, that often help to maintain social bonds.

agnosia A neurological disorder that causes a partial or complete loss of the ability to recognize otherwise familiar stimuli. Auditory agnosia is an inability to recognize sounds.

altricial Incapable of moving or surviving on its own after birth. An *altricial infant* is dependent on parental care for survival. The term contrasts with *precocial*. Butterflies and bees are precocial as they are able to fend for themselves almost immediately after birth.

Alzheimer's disease (dementia) A neurodegenerative disease that results in the progressive loss of nerve cells in the brain, leading to severe intellectual impairment.

amplitude The magnitude or strength of a signal. Amplitude is the degree of excursion about an average or equilibrium value exhibited by some oscillating quantity. Amplitude is commonly measured by one of three methods: (a) the difference between the maximum excursion and the equilibrium point (peak amplitude), (b) the difference between the maximum positive and maximum negative points of excursion (peak-to-peak amplitude), and (c) the standard deviation of all values (RMS amplitude). For signals of audible frequency, amplitude corresponds roughly with our perception of loudness.

amplitude modulation (AM) The varying of the amplitude of a signal, usually repetitively. For signals of audible frequency, amplitude modulations in the range of 1 Hz to ~15 Hz evoke a tremolo effect.

amusia Impaired musical functioning. The impairment can be congenital (present from birth) or acquired through an environmental factor such as a stroke. Amusias include musical alexia (impaired ability to read music), musical agraphia (impaired ability to notate music), and musical anomia (e.g., impaired ability to name works, composers, or styles).

amygdala A small, almond-shaped structure that is part of the brain's limbic system. It is involved in the generation of emotion, particularly fear.

analysis-by-synthesis Modeling or synthesizing a phenomenon to examine it. For example, expressive actions of performers may be investigated by attempting to write a computer program that outputs expressive music performances given the information contained in notated scores.

anomia A neurological disorder that causes a marked inability to name otherwise familiar stimuli. Auditory anomia is an inability to name sounds such as a doorbell. An example of musical anomia is the inability to name musical instruments from their sounds.

aphasia A complete or partial loss of language-related abilities. Loss of the ability to speak is referred to as expressive aphasia. Loss of the ability to understand spoken language is referred to as receptive aphasia.

arousal Metabolic readiness to perceive and act. Increased arousal is associated with increased heart rate, body temperature, breathing rate, oxygen consumption, glucose uptake, and other physiological changes. Sleeping is associated with low arousal, whereas running from an attacker is associated with high arousal.

arpeggio Notes of a chord played in succession to one another, rather than simultaneously.

arrhythmia Musical arrhythmia refers to impairment in perceiving, remembering, or producing musical rhythm. Not to be confused with *cardiac arrhythmia*, or irregularity in the normal heartbeat rhythm. Musical arrhythmia may result from brain injury (e.g., stroke) or exist as a congenital impairment.

articulators Anatomical structures in the mouth area responsible for speech production (tongue, jaw, palate, lips).

attentional Relating to attention. A cognitive process of selective concentration on a particular aspect of the environment.

attenuate To lessen. In acoustics the term usually means to lessen the amplitude of a signal. When audio signals are attenuated, a decrease in loudness typically occurs. Attenuation is also used for other attributes. For example, attenuating vibrato will result in lessening the "depth" of the vibrato.

audio frequency Any frequency audible to the human ear. The range of audio frequencies is usually considered to lie in the region between 20 Hz and 20,000 Hz. However, the range of audio frequencies varies from person to person, and with age.

auditory Pertaining to the subjective experience of sound. Used in contrast to acoustical, which pertains to the objective physics of a sound. For example, frequency is a physical or acoustical property, whereas pitch is a subjective or auditory property.

auditory evoked potential *See* evoked potential.

auditory streaming The subjective sense of connectedness that arises when two or more successive sounds seem to come from the same sound-generating source.

augmented Pertaining to the enlargement of a music interval (major or perfect) by one semitone.

Australopithecines Among the most famous of extinct hominids. Closely related to humans (*Homo sapien sapien*), they inhabited eastern and northern Africa between 3 and 3.9 million years ago.

autonomic nervous system (ANS) Part of the body's peripheral nervous system that acts to maintain control of vital body functions such as heartbeat, respiration, and digestion without conscious control.

basilar membrane A thin membrane within the cochlea of the inner ear in which the hair cells are embedded. It moves in response to pressure waves in the cochlea, initiating a chain of events that results in a nerve impulse to the brain. *See* cochlea.

Berlyne's theory of optimum complexity A theory promoted by Daniel Berlyne that the pleasure evoked by different kinds of stimuli is related to their degree of complexity. Those stimuli with the greatest hedonic value tend toward an optimum level of complexity. Stimuli that have too little or too much complexity have reduced hedonic value.

birdsong The characteristic songlike vocalizations produced by birds. Birdsong is often distinguished from shorter vocalizations, termed *bird calls*.

blood oxygen level dependent (BOLD) A method for observing active brain regions using the technique of functional magnetic resonance imaging (fRMI). Active neurons are differentiable from inactive neurons through perturbations in the magnetic fields produced by the supply of oxygen.

body language A form of nonverbal communication accomplished through the use of body movement and gesture.

borborygmi Sounds associated with gas moving through the intestines.

bottom-up Pertains to the upward hierarchical organization from low-level detail to high-level detail, structure, or concepts. Also used to refer to psychological phenomena that arise from peripheral (sensory) processes. Often contrasted with top-down or knowledge-driven psychological phenomena.

brain anatomical structures The major structures of the brain are the *cerebrum, cerebellum,* and *brain stem.*

Broca's area A brain region located in the frontal lobe of the left hemisphere involved in language processing, speech production, and comprehension.

cadence A sequence of notes or chords used at the end of a phrase or composition to mark an ending (relaxation of tension, point of stability or closure). Each musical style has a limited number of cadences, which change historically. In Western tonal music (e.g., Mozart), the "perfect cadence" gives the strongest sense of closure. It consists of a dominant chord (a chord built from the fifth note of the scale) followed by the tonic chord (a chord built from the first note of the scale).

camouflage A form of disguise that acts to hide an object, event, or organism through blending in with the surrounding context.

categorical perception The tendency to perceive some stimuli as falling into discrete categories rather than in terms of gradients. In categorical perception, a perceptual boundary will be evident, even though the physical phenomenon is continuous. One of the clearest examples of categorical perception may be found in the perception of color. Physics tells us that a rainbow exhibits a continuous gradient of wavelengths from longer wavelengths (seen as red) to shorter wavelengths (seen as blue). Although the rainbow is physically continuous, our perceptual experience is of discrete bands of colors, such as red, yellow, and green.

causal connection Involving or constituting a cause, wherein there exists a cause-and-effect relationship between two phenomena. For example, it is widely believed that there is a causal connection between cigarette smoking and lung cancer.

central nervous system (CNS) Representing the largest part of the body's nervous system, includes the brain, spinal cord, and spinal nerves. The CNS is fundamental in the control and functioning of the body.

characteristic frequency The frequency of a sound to which a system (e. g., a neuron) is most responsive.

chorales A hymnlike song of the Lutheran church, characterized by block chords. Chorales were popular in Germany during the Baroque period.

chord In a musical context, a chord is a collection of notes or pitches that are played simultaneously or near simultaneously. On the music staff, a chord is representative of the vertical structure of music.

circle of fifths A circular map of musical notes in which adjacent notes on the circle are separated by an interval of a fifth (e.g., the interval between doh and sol). The map illustrates that 12 successive steps around the circle (assuming octave equivalence) return to the original note. The circle of fifths has been useful in the analysis of harmony. Chord movement between adjacent points on the circle is common (in classical and popular contemporary music) and sound smooth (e.g., from C to G). The circle of fifths also explains relations between keys, in that keys based on adjacent points on the circle have all but one scale note in common, and key changes (tonal modulation) most commonly occur between adjacent points on the circle.

circular tones A complex tone that contains octave-spaced partials (i.e., adjacent frequency components are related to each other by a ratio of 2:1). For example, a circular tone might consist of pure tones at the following frequencies: 50 Hz,

100 Hz, 200 Hz, 400 Hz, 800 Hz, 1,600 Hz, 3,200 Hz, 6,400 Hz, and 12,800 Hz. The amplitudes of the partials are weighted so that the extreme high and low partials have the least energy. The position of this *amplitude envelope* is then fixed across all circular tones. Circular tones permit a variety of illusions, such as the illusion of endlessly increasing or decreasing pitch. Roger Shepard discovered them in 1964.

closure The sensation of finality or ending. Points of closure occur at the ends of works, with lesser points of closure occurring at phrase boundaries. In speech, the closure of spoken phrases is known to be influenced by five factors: (a) the presence of a silent pause at the phrase boundary, (b) lengthening of the final stressed syllable, (c) a drop in amplitude, (d) phrase-final descending pitch, and (e) reduction in pace as the phrase boundary is approached. In Western tonal music, closure is often signaled by cadences, in addition to these five factors.

cochlea A snail-shaped, fluid-filled structure within the inner ear. The cochlea receives vibrations conveyed from the tympanic membrane via the small bones of the middle ear. The last of these bones is connected to the oval window of the cochlea. Sound-induced vibrations are communicated to fluid in a tube-shaped chamber that is coiled to make two-and-one-half rotations. Motions of this fluid cause interior membranes (the tectorial and basilar membranes) to be displaced. Hair cells along the membranes are activated and resulting neural impulses are communicated to the auditory nerve.

cognition The processes of human or animal thought. The acquisition, understanding, representation, and manipulation of knowledge.

coherence A state in which a set of elements are mutually supportive and logically consistent with one another.

complex tone Tone consisting of more than one frequency component. Often the component frequencies (called partials) of a complex tone are related harmonically (complex periodic tones), but many times they are not. Virtually all naturally occurring tones are complex.

congenital Believed to have been present since birth. Congenital conditions are sometimes inherited and therefore genetically determined, but they can also be acquired by an environmental factor during development in the uterus.

consonance The subjective experience of pleasantness, euphoniousness, smoothness, fusion, or relaxedness evoked by sounds. The subject of consonance and dissonance has a long history and many psychoacoustic, cognitive, and ethnomusicological theories have been advanced. Some regard consonance as the absence of dissonance, whereas others posit consonance and dissonance as distinct phenomena. *See* dissonance.

constraint A factor that limits or shapes an outcome. The concept of a cognitive constraint implies that there are limits arising from the structure of the human mind to what we can perceive, interpret, remember, or understand.

continuism The view that any evolutionary development is a continuation of traits found in an ancestral species. Some continuists hold that language developed out of an earlier system of animal communication, with warning calls possibly developing into words. Similarly, some theorists believe that music developed out of animal sounds found in ancestral species.

contralateral Relating to the opposite side of the body. For example, the contralateral arm to the right arm is the left arm.

converging evidence Evidence that is corroborated by data from a range of scientific approaches. Hypotheses are frequently accepted or rejected not by a single scientific result but by the accumulation of converging evidence.

corpus collosum A structure in the brain that connects the left and right cerebral hemispheres. It is the largest white-matter (axonal) structure in the brain.

correlational research Research that examines and measures the strength of associations between phenomena. It is usually not possible from correlational data to determine whether a change in one variable caused a change in another variable. It is often contrasted with experimental research, which, in principle, allows researchers to draw inferences about causation.

cortex Anatomical term designating the convoluted or wrinkled surface region of the brain (from the Latin word for the bark of a tree). A living brain has a light red-brown color; after death the color changes to gray. This color continues until a depth of about an eighth of an inch, where it changes to white. The surface (historically called gray matter) constitutes the cerebral cortex. The gray matter coincides with a large mass of nerve cell bodies, and the underlying white matter coincides with long axon fibers emanating from the cell bodies in the gray matter. Much of the higher level mental functioning of the brain has been traced to cortical locations. The cortex is divided into left and right cerebral hemispheres. Four subdivisions or lobes can be identified in each hemisphere: the frontal, temporal, parietal and occipital lobes. Neural activity of the cortex can be measured using techniques such as electroencephalography.

crescendo A gradual increase in loudness. Often used by performers for dramatic emphasis, or as part of the expressive shaping of important musical groups (e.g., phrases).

critical band A frequency region within which multiple inputs give rise to sensory interactions.

There are many forms of such interactions, but the most common is masking where one sound may obscure or mask the other. A common way to define the critical band is the smallest distance beyond which masking no longer occurs. This distance corresponds to roughly 1 millimeter of distance along the basilar membrane of the cochlea.

Cro-Magnon One of the main types of *Homo sapiens*, named after the cave in southwest France where the first fossils were found. It describes the oldest modern people in Europe, estimated at between 40,000 and 10,000 years ago. Cro-Magnons may have been responsible for the extinction of the Neanderthals, with whom they coexisted. DNA studies indicate that the Cro-Magnons, but not the Neanderthals, are closely related to modern Europeans.

cross-cultural Cross-cultural research typically involves a comparison of cultures, or a close examination of a culture by a researcher who is not indigenous to that culture. Increased globalization means that cultural boundaries are usually blurred, with most cultural activities reflecting wide-ranging influences from various other cultures or subcultures. Among the many assumptions of cross-cultural research is the idea that cultural works are collective rather than individual creations. Thus, cross-cultural music research would not view a music composition as entirely unique to its composer but as a reflection of social norms and symbol systems. *See* culture.

cue A feature or attribute that a perceiver can use to identify, classify, interpret, or remember sensory input.

culture Patterns of human activity and their associated norms, ideas, artifacts, and symbol systems. Because such activities are not predictable from the physical characteristics of individuals, culture is sometimes contrasted with biology.

It is often used casually but misleadingly as a synonym of *country*, but cultural practices need not align with geographical boundaries. Indeed, many distinct cultures can coexist within the same country or city (often called *subcultures*). Cultural activities are thought to result largely from the effects of learning or enculturation such that they are not highly constrained by biological factors and can change. The term is exemplified by activities associated with music, literature, theater, visual arts, dance, and other arts, which may be contrasted with instincts such as breathing, eating, sleeping, and procreating. However, all cultural activities reflect a balance of biological constraints, early predispositions, and long-term effects of learning. *See also* cross-cultural.

cycle The action of a vibrating system such that its pattern of change passes through a complete turn of events. The elapsed time for the completion of one cycle is called the *period*. The number of cycles occurring in one second is called the *frequency*.

cycles per second The number of complete repetitions or occurrences in 1 second.

deceptive cadence A chord progression in which the dominant chord (build on the fifth scale degree) is followed by a chord other than the tonic chord (built from the first scale degree, or doh). Because dominant to tonic chord sequences suggest closure, a deceptive (or interrupted) cadence invokes a hanging or suspended feeling.

decibel A measure of the magnitude of a physical quantity, such as sound intensity. The decibel is a logarithmic unit of measurement that correlates with human perception of loudness. The thresold of hearing is assigned a sound level of 0 decibels.

declination The tendency in speech for the pitch of a speaker's voice to drop over the course of a phrase or sentence. This general pitch decline is associated with the reduction of subglottal air pressure as the lungs are exhausted. Some evidence exists showing that there is a weak tendency for musical phrases to also exhibit a slight decline in average pitch over the course of the phrase.

Deutsch tritone effect or paradox When listening to circular tones, the interval of the tritone is theoretically ambiguous as to whether it is heard ascending or descending. Diana Deutsch discovered that for many listeners, certain tritones tend to be heard as predominantly ascending and others as descending. For example, a listener might hear the D–G# tritone as ascending and the F–B tritone as descending. Such listeners can be characterized by the position on the chroma circle where the tritone is heard to switch direction.

diatonic Western tonal music involves two scales: the diatonic major scale and the diatonic minor scale. The diatonic major scale is the most well known (doh, re, mi, fa, sol, la, ti, doh). Diatonic scale notes represent a subset of the chromatic scale, which includes all 12 pitches of the octave. *See* scale.

diminuendo A gradual decrease in loudness used by composers and performers for expressive purposes at strategic points in a composition.

dissociation In neuropsychology, two skills are dissociated when a change in one skill is observed with no corresponding change in the other skill. Evidence for dissociated skills is often interpreted as an indication that different brain areas or processes are responsible for the two skills. For example, a stroke may result in a dramatic impairment of verbal skills but no corresponding impairment of musical skills. Similarly, a stroke may result in impaired pitch perception with no corresponding impairment in musical rhythm. In each case, the skills are dissociated. Dissociation may also be observed when one skill is enhanced (e.g., by caffeine) with no corresponding enhancement of another skill. A double dissociation is said to have occurred when selective changes in both skills have been reported, in each case with no corresponding change in the other skill. As an example, one stroke patient may have impaired pitch skills but normal rhythm skills whereas a second stroke patient may have impaired rhythm skills but normal pitch skills. The observations from these two cases collectively indicate that pitch and rhythm are doubly dissociated.

dissonance The subjective experience of unpleasantness, ugliness, dysphonia, roughness, or tenseness evoked by sounds. In music theory, the intervals of the major and minor second, the major and minor seventh, and the tritone are considered dissonant when played simultaneously. The subject of consonance and dissonance has a long history and there are many theories and perspectives. Most perspectives acknowledge that there are both sensory and cultural influences on the perception of dissonance. Sensory influences are primarily associated with the peripheral auditory system and can be explained psychoacoustically. Cultural influences are dependent on knowledge of musical structure. *See also* musical dissonance, sensory dissonance.

domain general A psychological process is domain general if it applies to many different psychological domains, such as language, music, mathematical reasoning, and spatial ability. Some models of attention consider it to be a domain-general process, such that the same general operation affects performance across domains. Contrasted with domain specific.

domain specific A domain-specific process is one that applies to a single domain, such as music.

dominant The fifth note of the scale, or sol. Chords based on the dominant (e.g., dominant seventh) play an important role at cadences, which signal temporary or permanent endings in the music. In a perfect cadence (which strongly suggests an endpoint), the dominant chord is followed by a tonic chord (a chord built from the first note of the scale).

dopamine One of the major neurotransmitters in the brain. It is commonly associated with the pleasure system of the brain, providing feelings of enjoyment and reinforcement to motivate a person proactively to perform certain activities. It is released by naturally rewarding experiences such as food, sex, certain drugs, possibly some music, and other stimuli that become associated with these rewarding stimuli. In the frontal lobes, dopamine controls the flow of information from other areas of the brain. There are several types of dopamine receptors.

double dissociation A double dissociation is said to have occurred when changes in two skills have been reported, but in each case the change in one skill occurred with no corresponding change in the other skill. Double dissociations are commonly considered to be strong evidence that two skills or processes are handled by distinct brain resources. *See also* dissociation.

dynamics The variations of loudness in a musical composition, traditionally expressed through the use of descriptive Italian words such as *forte*, *mezzo-piano*, *crescendo*, and *sforzando*.

early right anterior negativity (ERAN) A type of brain activity that occurs relatively soon after certain stimuli. The four terms in ERAN describe the temporal and spatial characteristics of the activity. It has an *early* onset, is localized primarily or entirely in the *right* hemisphere and toward the front (*anterior*) of the brain, and has a *negative* electrical polarity. It has been reported following violations of musical syntax and can be observed with EEG.

ecological validity The use of experimental stimuli that approximate real-world conditions. If stimuli lack ecological validity (e.g., using isolated tones to study music perception), psychological processes involved in normal conditions may not be engaged. With the use of ecologically valid stimuli, it is justifiable to generalize from experimental findings to real-world conditions. However, ecological validity may come at the expense of experimental control, in that real-world conditions usually involve unpredictable changes in many variables.

electrode An electrical conductor used to make contact with a nonmetallic part of a circuit.

electroencephalography (EEG) A technique for measuring electrical activity of the brain using electrodes placed on the scalp or subdurally in the cerebral cortex. The resulting traces, an electroencephalogram, represent a summation of postsynaptic potentials from a large number of neurons.

embodied meaning The acquisition of meaning through self-reference alone. Contrasts with *designative meaning*. Language acquires meaning by referring to objects and events outside of the system of language, and hence has designative meaning. For example, the word *desk* does not refer to another word but to a physical desk. Some theorists (e.g., Leonard Meyer) believe that the emotional power of music lies in its embodied meaning. Although some music refers to events (e.g., Tchaikovsky's *1812 Overture*), most is primarily self-referential.

emotion An affective state that arises in response to a personally significant event. An emotion is usually more transient than a mood and the individual who is experiencing the emotion is usually aware of its cause. Emotions have experiential, behavioral, and physiological components. *See* affect, mood.

emotional conjoinment Deep, significant emotional bonding between individuals, especially between caregivers and their offspring. The term *conjoinment* is used instead of bond to emphasize the significance of this type of interaction for the successful development of emotional, intellectual, psychosocial, and linguistic functioning.

emotional intelligence The ability to perceive, assess, and manage the emotions of oneself and others. The concept of emotional intelligence has evolved as more research is conducted in the area.

empirical Related to knowledge acquired from observation. Empirical research tests hypotheses through experiment or observation. An *empirical result* is an experimental observation.

encephalization In evolution, the tendency for a species toward larger brains over evolutionary time.

enculturation The acquisition of implicit or explicit knowledge about the norms, symbols, and values of the society within which one lives. Enculturation is often used in the context of child development but it is recognized to be a lifelong process.

equal temperament Any set of discrete pitches in which the interval of an octave is divided into a whole number of equal divisions. In traditional Western European practice, an equally tempered system employing 12 intervals (called semitones) is used. Although Western music has nominally adopted the use of equal temperament tuning, acoustic factors such as inharmonicity may result in slight differences between the pitches of a tuned instrument (e.g.,

piano) and the pitches that would be produced by equal temperament tuning.

event-related potential (ERP) Any electrophysiological response to an internal (cognitive) or external (physical) stimulus. These responses are thought to reflect cognitive and perceptual processes. For example, when an isolated sound is heard, thousands of neurons in the auditory cortex are activated. The near simultaneous firing of large numbers of neurons induces electrical potentials that can be measured with electrodes on the scalp. Auditory signals typically activate regions of the temporal lobes. *See also* P300.

evoked potential Any electrophysiological response (brain activity) that is elicited by the presentation of a stimulus, as contrasted with spontaneous brain activity.

evolution The change in the inherited traits of a population from one generation to the next. These traits are the expression of genes that are copied and passed on to offspring during reproduction. The theory of evolution by natural selection was mainly proposed by Charles Darwin in his 1859 book *On the Origin of Species*. *See* natural selection.

exaptation A trait that evolved from an earlier one that served a different function. Primitive wings may have initially enabled birds to regulate their temperature by trapping air for warmth. Over evolutionary time, these anatomical structures were *exapted* for flight. Because the ability to fly confers considerable survival benefits, elaborate wing structures specialized for flying gradually evolved.

expectancy Used synonymously with expectation. A tendency to anticipate based on prior context. There has been considerable research on the emotional, cognitive, and neurological effects of expectancy fulfillment (when an expectation is met) and expectancy violation (when a surprising event occurs) in musical contexts. Expectancy violations in music are often studied to understand how the brain processes musical syntax.

experimental method The use of controlled experiments for examining a phenomenon. A researcher typically manipulates an *independent variable* and makes observations using a *dependent variable*. In principle, a true experiment allows researchers to draw causal connections between independent and dependent variables. For example, an experiment in which tempo is the independent variable and reading comprehension is the dependent variable might reveal that increases in the tempo of background music will *cause* a reduction in reading comprehension.

explicit memory The conscious form of intentional recollection of previous experiences and information. Contrasted with the implicit, unconscious, nonintentional form of memory.

expressive aphasia A neurological disorder that causes a complete or partial loss of the ability to speak. Also known as Broca's aphasia. Contrast with receptive aphasia.

faster uphill rule The tendency for performers to increase tempo during passages that are ascending in pitch. It is one of the rules in the rule system developed by Johan Sundberg and his colleagues in Sweden, as part of their analysis-by-synthesis approach to the study of performance expression.

formant The distinguishing or meaningful frequency components of human speech and of singing. An intensity peak in an acoustic frequency spectrum.

Fourier analysis Named after Joseph Fourier. The decomposition of a function in terms of a sum of sinusoidal functions of different frequencies that can be recombined to obtain the original function. The recombination process is called Fourier synthesis. Using Fourier analysis, any complex tone in music can be decomposed into a set of individual frequency components. These include a fundamental frequency and a number of overtones. Individual frequency components of a complex sound are called *partials* or, in the case of complex *periodic* tones, *harmonics*.

frequency Rate of occurrence or rate of repetition. Frequency is measured in hertz (Hz), where 1 Hz is defined as a single cycle per second. Frequencies that are audible to the human ear (frequencies roughly between about 20 Hz and 20,000 Hz) are often called audio frequencies. *Compare* pitch.

fugue In music, a style of contrapuntal composition or technique of composition for a fixed number of parts or "voices" in a vocal or instrumental work. The form reached ultimate maturity in the works of Johann Sebastian Bach.

functional magnetic resonance imaging (fMRI) The use of MRI during cognitive or physical activity to measure the hemodynamic response related to neural activity in the brain or spinal cord. One of the most recently developed forms of neuroimaging.

functional music A generic name given to commercial closed-circuit or restricted-broadcast music whose purpose is to achieve specific goals, such as enhancing worker productivity in office and industrial establishments. The best-known functional music is Muzak—a Seattle-based company founded in 1936.

fundamental frequency The main frequency component of a complex harmonic or pseudo-harmonic tone; the basic cycle of repetition for a periodic waveform. The fundamental frequency is commonly (although not always) associated with the perceived pitch of a tone.

fusion The process by which simultaneous combinations of sounds (e.g., individual frequencies) are heard as a unified sound.

gap-fill melodies Melodies characterized by a large interval that is followed by one or more notes that fall between the first and second pitch of that large interval. Examples include "Over the Rainbow," "My Bonny," and "Blue Skies."

genome The genome of an organism is its whole hereditary information encoded in the DNA. The genome sequence for any organism requires the DNA sequences for each of the chromosomes in an organism to be determined.

grammar Grammar is traditionally defined as the set of rules that govern the use of language, but it can also be applied to music and other complex behaviors and communication systems (e.g., dance, gesture). The set of rules governing a specific musical idiom is the grammar of that idiom. For example, rules of harmony and counterpoint in Western tonal music describe how tones and chords are formed and put together to make larger units. The study of grammar includes a number of subfields such as syntax.

grooming A social activity that involves removing parasites from another individual. Grooming provides a means by which animals bond and reinforce social structures, family links, and relationships. Also used as a form of reconciliation and means of conflict resolution in some species.

habituation The process of decreasing responsiveness to a recurring stimulus. The simplest form of learning. Habituation is known to depend on four factors: (a) the rate of stimulus repetition, (b) the regularity of repetition, (c) the magnitude of the stimulus, and (d) the history of past cycles of habituation and spontaneous recovery.

hair cells The specialized receptors of hearing found in the cochlea of the inner ear. When they are moved the hair cells translate the mechanical stimulation into an electrical nerve impulse. *See* cochlea.

harmonic Adjective: The relationship between two frequencies such that one frequency is an integer multiple of the other (e.g., the frequencies 101 Hz and 303 Hz are harmonically related because $101 \times 3 = 303$).

Noun: Harmonically related (or nearly harmonically related) frequencies are called harmonics. Harmonics are of special interest because of some unique auditory properties. Many natural vibrators oscillate such that they produce several harmonics simultaneously. For example, if the first harmonic (or fundamental) of some complex tone is of frequency 200 Hz, subsequent harmonics might be of frequencies 400, 600, 800, 1,000, 1,200 Hz, and so on—called the harmonic series.

harmonic charge One of the rules of the rule system devised by Johan Sundberg and his colleagues for the automatic performance of music. A concept reflecting the remarkableness of chord in its harmonic context. The weighted sum of the chord tones' melodic charges, using the root of the main chord of the key as the reference.

harmonic series Any numerical sequence of ascending frequencies where successive numbers are integral multiples or share a large common divisor. For example, the sequence 100, 200, 300, 400,…represents a harmonic series, as does 29, 58, 87, 116,…. The sequence 500, 700, 930, 1,190…is not a harmonic series, and 100, 150, 200, 250,…is considered an incomplete harmonic series because of the missing first harmonic component (50). The frequency components of naturally occurring complex tones often conform to the harmonic series.

hemispheric dominance Implicating one hemisphere more than another.

hemodynamic/metabolic techniques Recording changes in blood flow and blood oxygenation in the brain (collectively known as hemodynamics). Closely linked to neural activity.

hertz The unit of frequency, defined as the number of cycles or complete oscillations per second. The unit is named after the German scientist Heinrich Hertz. It is abbreviated using an uppercase initial letter (Hz) and is written in full using a lowercase initial letter (hertz).

Heschel's Gyrus An area of the brain. Specifically, the convolutions that run transversely on the surface of the temporal lobe, border on the lateral fissure, and are separated by the transverse temporal sulci.

hominids Any member of the biological family *Hominidae* that includes the extinct and extant humans, chimpanzees, gorillas, and orangutans (the "great apes"). Scientists widely regard central eastern Africa as the founding site of humans and the *Hominidae* tree.

Homo habilis A species of the genus *Homo* thought to have descended from a species of *australopithecine* hominid. *Homo habilis* was less similar to modern humans than other species in the genus *Homo*, and may have been the first species of the genus to appear. They were short and had long arms compared to modern humans.

Homo neanderthalensis A species of the genus *Homo*. They inhabited Europe and parts of western and central Asia. They went extinct between 33,000 and 24,000 years ago, and it is believed that their population was roughly 10,000 individuals. Neanderthal fossils have been found in Germany, Israel, Spain, Italy, England, and elsewhere. One view is that modern humans displaced Neanderthals about 45,000 years ago, although their fate is the subject of debate.

Homo sapiens Modern humans are members of the *Homo sapiens* species. The words *Homo sapiens* translates roughly to "wise human." There are two subspecies of *Homo sapiens*: *Homo sapiens sapiens*, and *Homo sapiens idaltu*. The latter subspecies is extinct. *Homo sapiens sapiens* appeared in the fossil record in Africa about 130,000 years ago.

imperfect consonances In music theory, those intervals that are neither perfect nor dissonant. Specifically, the intervals of the major and minor third, the major and minor sixth, and their compound equivalents (major and minor tenths, etc.). Imperfect consonances typically exhibit low tonal fusion and low sensory dissonance.

implicit knowledge Tacit knowing that is wholly or partly inexplicable. Knowing more than we can tell.

implicit memory The implicit, unconscious, nonintentional form of memory. Contrasted with the conscious form of intentional recollection of previous experiences and information.

infant-directed speech (IDS) Baby talk, motherese, or parentese. A nonstandard form of speech used by adults in talking to toddlers and infants. Usually delivered with a cooing pattern of intonation and high in pitch, with more pronounced *glissando* variations than in normal speech.

information-processing paradigm An approach within cognitive psychology to the goal of understanding human thinking that arose in the 1940s and 1950s. Cognition is seen as essentially computational in nature, with mind being the software and the brain the hardware. Closely allied to cognitivism in psychology and functionalism in philosophy.

inharmonic A partial is considered inharmonic when its frequency is not an integer multiple of a given fundamental frequency. Two- and three-dimensional vibrators (such as plates, drum heads, bells, and gongs) typically produce inharmonic partials. Inharmonic is used both as an adjective and as a noun. *Compare* harmonic.

inharmonicity Partial components of a complex tone may be characterized according to the degree to which their frequencies conform with the harmonic series of overtones. Partials that vaguely correspond are called pseudo-harmonics; partials that are clearly different are called inharmonics. Inharmonicity is a descriptive term applied to the cumulative effect of inharmonic components—the greater the inharmonicity, the greater the "clangorousness" of the sound.

innate Cognitive and perceptual tendencies that are seen as hard-wired. Knowledge not obtained from experience and the senses.

inner ear One of three conceptual anatomical divisions for the organ of hearing, including also the outer ear and the middle ear. The inner ear consists of a snail-shaped, fluid-filled bony structure also known as the cochlea. The cochlea receives vibrations conveyed from the small bones of the middle ear and the resulting neural impulses are communicated to the auditory nerve.

interval The distance between two pitches, usually identified by either the ratio of two frequencies or according to the diatonic/chromatic interval system of traditional Western music theory.

in utero Within the uterus or womb.

James–Lange theory A theory of emotion that argues that emotional stimuli engender physiological responses, and that emotions arise from the experience of these physiological states. For example, the James–Lange theory claims that one feels sad because one is crying—in contrast to the view that one cries because one feels sad.

key A concept describing the organization of a passage of music. A sense of key is determined by the establishment of two features: a scale and a tonal center. The tonal center is the note that functions as a point of maximum stability and minimum tension. It is often the most commonly occurring note in the music, and is often found at the beginning and ending of the music. *See* tonality.

klezmer A genre of secular (nonliturgical) Jewish music developed by musicians called *kleyzmorim* or *kleyzmerim*. Drawing on a devotional and musical legacy extending from Biblical times and continuing to evolve. A repertoire of Yiddish dance songs for weddings and other celebrations. Easily identifiable by expressive melodies, reminiscent of the human voice, complete with laughter and weeping.

Krumhansl and Kessler key profiles Carol Krumhansl and Edward Kessler used the probe tone technique to study the nature of tonality. Krumhansl and Kessler (1982) played a key-defining context consisting of an ascending (major or harmonic minor) scale, or a key-defining chord progression. After each repetition of the key-defining passage, a different tone was played and listeners were asked to judge how well the tone fit. They found a distinctive and stable pattern of response for the major and minor keys. In both modes, the tonic pitch was rated most highly, and nonscale tones were rated the lowest. More specifically, a four-level hierarchy was evident for both the major and minor keys: (a) the most important pitch is the tonic, followed by (b) the remaining tones of the tonic triad (i.e., dominant and mediant pitches), followed by (c) the other notes belonging to the scale, followed by (d) the nonscale tones.

lateralization Implicating one hemisphere more than another. For most right-handed people, verbal and rhythmic skills are predominantly processed in the left hemisphere. It should be emphasized that most activities implicate at least some of the left and right hemisphere at the same time.

leitmotif A leading motive or recurring melodic theme associated with a particular character, place, or thing in an opera or film score (see Richard Wagner's *Ring* cycle or the Imperial March in *Star Wars*). Often a short melody or a chord progression.

lobectomy The surgical removal of a lobe of an organ such as the brain or lung. Lobectomies are performed to prevent the spread of cancer or to control seizures (e.g., from epilepsy). Frontal lobectomy is the removal of a portion of a frontal lobe.

logarithmic A scale of measurement that uses the logarithm of a physical quantity instead of the quantity itself. A logarithm of a given number to a given base is the power to which you need to raise the base to get the number. For example, the logarithm of 16 to the base 4 is 2, because 4 raised to the power of 2 is 16.

longitudinal fissure The deep cleft separating the two hemispheres of the cerebrum. Bridged by the corpus callosum and the hippocampal commissure.

loudness The subjective psychological correlate of amplitude or sound intensity. Perceived loudness depends on many factors, including frequency, timbre, amplitude, duration, and so on. To a certain degree perceived loudness is also dependent on experience and learning.

magnetoencephalography (MEG) An imaging technique used to detect electromagnetic fields produced by electrical activity in the brain. *See* electroencephalography (EEG).

masking The difficulty or impossibility of hearing one sound due to the presence of another sound. Masking often results when a loud (masker) sound occurs concurrently with a quieter (masked) sound. Masking may even occur when the masker and masked sounds do not sound concurrently: If the masking sound occurs after the masked sound in time, the effect is known as backward masking; when a masking sound appears prior to the masked sound it is called forward masking.

melodic arch A marked tendency for melodic phrases to (on average) rise and then fall in pitch over the course of the phrase.

melodic charge One of the rules of the rule system devised by Johan Sundberg and his colleagues for the automatic performance of music. The rule of melodic charge acts to increase the intensity, interonset interval, and vibrato (if applicable) of notes that have relatively high tension with respect to the current scale, with greater degrees of tension associated with greater increases in these variables.

mental representation A construct in cognition to describe the storage in the mind or brain of information-bearing structures such as thoughts, concepts, percepts, ideas, impressions, notions, rules, schemas, and images.

meter The measurement of music into measures of stressed and unstressed beats. Indicated in Western music notation by a symbol called a time signature.

middle ear One of three conceptual anatomical divisions for the organ of hearing, including also the outer ear and the inner ear. The air-filled ear cavity located behind the eardrum or tympanic membrane. The middle ear contains three small bones, ossicles, that connect the tympanic membrane to the oval window of the cochlea. The cavity can be vented to the outside world via the eustachian tube.

millisecond Unit of time equivalent to one thousandth of a second.

modularity thesis In cognitive science, the idea that significant parts of the mind, such as perceptual and linguistic processes, are made up of input systems that operate independently from one another and from the central processing part of the mind. This independence means that modules are restricted by the types of information that they can consult—a property known as *information encapsulation*. For example, in the Muller–Lyer illusion, two lines appear to be different lengths even if the perceiver is aware that they are the same length. According to Fodor, this disconnection suggests visual perception operates independently of mental processes.

mood A background feeling that extends over a length of time. Unlike emotions, moods often arise with no specific cause or origin, although they can be associated with general environmental factors such as the weather, lighting conditions, and background music. Examples of moods include feeling tired, grumpy, agitated, contented, or energized. Moods are accessible to introspection so we can describe our moods. Mood regulation (i.e., changing or enhancing moods) is possibly the most common use of recorded or broadcast music. *See* affect, emotion.

morphology The study of shape and form. Used in linguistics (structure and content of word forms), biology (shape and form of organisms), architecture (shape and form of buildings), and many other fields.

multisensory Involving more than one sense modality.

musical dissonance The quality of dissonance that cannot be explained by psychoacoustic factors and is dependent on historical and cultural factors. Whereas simultaneous combinations of tones are needed to generate sensory dissonance (roughness and other sensory interactions), musical dissonance can be experienced even for unaccompanied tones in a melody, if those tones are perceived to be musically unstable with respect to the musical context. Whereas sensory dissonance is detected by infants and remains relatively consistent throughout development, sensitivity to musical dissonance is dependent on knowledge and experience, and can evolve across the life span.

musical surface The foreground or "shallow" aspects of a musical passage represented by the full set of individual notes. Contrasted with deep structure, which represents the essence or skeleton of the music and excludes, for example, ornamental notes. Identification of deep structure is not always obvious, however, and requires a music analysis that aims to reveal hierarchical relationships among pitches (e.g., Schenkerian analysis).

music therapy The use of music by a trained professional to achieve therapeutic goals. May be used for individuals with special needs, as in using rhythmic exercises for the physical rehabilitation of stroke victims.

musilanguage A possible precursor to both language and music systems that may have been used for emotional communication. Proposed by Steven Brown in his influential model of music evolution.

Muzak A company founded in 1936 to provide commercial functional music. Its products include Muzak for workplaces, airports, and elevators. May also be used in a derogatory sense to describe generic, derivative, or repetitive music.

nativism The view that humans are born or hardwired with certain abilities or dispositions, such that most aspects of behavior or mental activity are natural rather than learned. In contrast to empiricism, the "blank slate" or *tabula rasa* view.

natural selection The process by which heritable traits that favor survival become more prevalent and traits that do not favor survival become less prevalent over successive generations. The process leads to adaptations that enable organisms to cope with specific environments, and can eventually lead to the emergence of new species. *See* evolution.

neonate An infant or human child at the youngest stage of life before walking or talking.

nontonal Music that has no specific key center.

norepinephrine One of the neurotransmitters in the central nervous and sympathetic nervous systems. As a stress hormone, it affects parts of the brain where attention and responding actions are controlled. Along with epinephrine, norepinephrine underlies the fight-or-flight response.

octave A musical term denoting an interval of pitch between two pitches whose frequencies are related in the approximate ratio of 2:1. Because exact octaves are not always precisely related by a 2:1 frequency ratio, psychoacousticians have also defined the octave as the pitch interval between two tones such that one tone is perceived as duplicating the basic musical import of the other tone at the nearest possible higher or lower pitch.

orienting response Moving one's head (or eyes) in the direction of a stimulus.

outer ear One of three conceptual anatomical divisions for the organ of hearing, including also the middle ear and the inner ear. The outer ear consists of the exterior ear or pinna, plus the tube-shaped ear canal. The outer ear terminates at the eardrum or tympanic membrane.

overtone Any simple sine tone (not necessarily harmonic) that exists above a fundamental frequency and that fuses with other components to form a single complex tone; any partial that occurs above the perceived pitch of a complex tone. Contrast with undertone. The term *overtone* has frequently been used interchangeably with harmonic—meaning a simple frequency component of a complex tone that is an integer multiple of some given fundamental frequency. The fundamental frequency (or simply fundamental) is also called the first harmonic, but is not called an overtone. The second harmonic is referred to as the first overtone, the third harmonic is called the second overtone, and so on.

P300 A feature found in the auditory evoked potential as measured in an EEG. When a sound is heard, the near simultaneous firing of thousands of neurons can be recorded. The first positive peak in the EEG is referred to as P1; the first negative trough in the EEG is referred to as N1. The third positive peak (P3) occurs roughly 300 msec after the onset of the sound. P3 has been shown to correlate with important subjective phenomena.

pant hooting A vocalization used by chimpanzees to express excitement. It begins with low-pitched hoots that make a transition into quicker, higher pitched, in-and-out pants that climax loudly.

partial Any simple sine tone component that fuses perceptually with other components to form a complex tone. Partials need not be harmonics and may occur either above or below the fundamental frequency. Harmonics, overtones, undertones, and inharmonics are all types of partials.

particulate principle A property of complex systems such as chemistry, language, genetics, and music, whereby simple elements are combined to form complex structures.

payola An illegal marketing practice whereby record companies pay (or otherwise induce) radio announcers to broadcast the songs of their artists beyond what would normally be scheduled. The term has come to refer to any secret payment made to cast a product in a positive light.

perception The process by which sensations are assembled into a mental representation of the external world.

perfect consonances In music theory, the intervals of the unison (P1), fourth (P4), and fifth (P5), plus their compound equivalents (octave, twelfth, etc.). Perfect consonances typically exhibit high tonal fusion and low sensory dissonance.

perfect fifth The musical interval formed by pitches with fundamental frequencies related by the ratio 3:2. It is a valuable interval in song development and Western tuning systems, and is part of all major and minor chords in root position. Its inversion is the perfect fourth.

perfect pitch *See* absolute pitch.

period The elapsed time between the beginning and end of a single cycle of a periodic waveform. The period of a sound is inversely proportional to its frequency.

periodic Any simple or complex function is described as periodic if it has an identifiable cycle of identical repetition. When the rate of recurrence or frequency of repetition lies within the range of human hearing, the resulting sound will convey a sense of pitch. (Note: All pitched sounds are not necessarily periodic, and only periodic sounds that lie in the audible range are pitched.) Complex periodic functions may be analyzed into simple periodic components by the process of Fourier analysis. Functions that are not periodic are referred to as aperiodic or nonperiodic.

periodic motion Motion that repeats itself. Periodic sound waves produce pitch sensations.

periodic waveform The shape and form of a waveform (like a sine wave) in a medium. The Fourier series describes the decomposition of periodic waveforms so that any periodic waveform can be formed by the sum of a fundamental component and harmonic components.

peripheral nervous system (PNS) The part of the nervous system that extends outside the brain and spinal cord (i.e., the central nervous system) to serve the limbs and organs. It is divided into the somatic and the autonomic nervous systems.

phase The current position in any cyclical pattern, such as a sound wave. The phase of an individual sine tone is not perceivable as a sound quality, but the overall intensity of frequency combinations can be affected by the relative phase of those frequencies. When two sine tones that have been combined are in phase, their waveforms will reinforce each other, increasing the overall intensity of the signal; when they are out of phase, the waveforms cancel each other out, reducing or even eliminating the intensity of the signal.

phoneme The smallest speech sound in language that distinguishes meaning, such as the /b/ sound in *book* or the /c/ sound in *cook*.

pianissimo (*pp*) A dynamic marking or directive for a musician to perform a certain passage very softly.

pitch The psychological quality of periodic sounds that extends from low to high (pitch height). Pitch is a psychological attribute that is related to the fundamental frequency of a complex periodic tone (expressed in hertz, or Hz). The relation between pitch and frequency is logarithmic. For example, given a tone with a fundamental frequency at 200 Hz, the next three octaves above will have fundamental frequencies at 400, 800, and 1,600 Hz. That is, equivalent perceptual intervals (an octave) are associated with equivalent frequency *ratios* (2:1). Many psychological models of pitch acknowledge that pitch height is only one of several dimensions of pitch perception.

pitch chroma A music-theoretic term equivalent to *pitch class*. It refers to a musical note (e.g., C, F, G) regardless of the octave in which that note occurs. That is, notes separated by an octave belong to the same pitch class. Pitch chroma may be represented as the "circular" dimension of pitch by which tones an octave apart may be deemed to be interchangeable. The concept of pitch chroma rests on the assumption that notes separated by an octave are functionally equivalent.

pitch class A music-theoretic term equivalent to *pitch chroma*. Notes separated by an octave have the same pitch class.

pitch height The psychological dimension of pitch that varies from low to high. The pitch height of any complex tone increases as fundamental frequency increases. Two tones may share the same pitch chroma (e.g., both C#), but differ in their perceived height (e.g., C#4 vs. C#5). *See* pitch.

plagal cadence A chord progression in which the subdominant chord is followed by the tonic.

positron emission tomography (PET) A technique for imaging the brain or other parts of the body. A short-lived radioactive tracer isotope is first injected into the subject (usually blood circulation). After a waiting period in which the metabolically active molecule becomes concentrated in tissues of interest (i.e., those associated with greater concentrations of blood), the research subject or patient is placed in the image scanner.

premotor area The motor cortex of the frontal lobe immediately in front of the precentral gyrus.

primary auditory cortex Located in the temporal lobe on the edge of the lateral fissure, it analyzes sound input from receptors in the ear.

probe-tone technique A technique by which a listener's musical experience can be probed at a particular moment in time. A musical context is presented—such as several chords or the initial notes of a melody. Following the context, a single tone or chord is played, and the listener is asked to judge the tone or chord according to some criterion. Often, the listener is asked to judge how well the tone or chord "fits" with the preceding musical context. The contextual passage is then repeated and a different probe tone or chord is played. Following each presentation, the listener is asked to judge how well the new tone or chord fits with the preceding context. In probe-tone experiments, a dozen or more repetitions of the contextual passage may be presented—each followed by a different probe. In this way, a detailed picture can be assembled concerning the listener's musical judgment at that moment. In some cases, exhaustive experiments are carried out to trace the changes in the listener's experience as the music progresses. For example, the first three notes of a melody may be played, followed by a probe tone. This procedure is repeated until a large number of continuation tones have been probed. Then the first four notes of the melody are played, again followed by one of several probe tones. This procedure continues for the first five notes, six notes, and so on. The probe-tone technique has been used to trace in detail such phenomena as how a modulating chord progression begins to evoke a different tonal center. *See also* Krumhansl and Kessler key profiles.

prosody Those features of spoken language that pertain to the quality or character of the voice, and that often convey emotional or intentional cues as well as lexical and grammatical aspects of language. Prosodic elements are usually considered to include variations in the pitch, amplitude, and tempo of the speech. Prosodic features include raising the pitch of the voice to express surprise, signal uncertainty, or designate a question; lowering the pitch of the voice to stress significant words or convey seriousness of purpose; increasing the amplitude to signal anger; decreasing the amplitude to suggest intimacy; increasing the tempo to convey excitement; or decreasing the tempo to imply lethargy or depression; and so on. Prosody is often characterized as "the music of speech."

protomusical behaviors Refers to the view that music developed from earlier or "proto" musical behaviors that arose in temporally organized interactions between ancestral mothers and their infants. These components gradually became music when early humans developed ceremonial ritual.

prototype A stimulus is prototypic when it is perceived as a good representative of a certain class of stimuli. For many people, robins and sparrows are prototypic birds, whereas ostriches, falcons, and pigeons are not prototypic birds. Compared with nonprototypic stimuli, prototypic stimuli are more easily learned, remembered, and recalled. When presented with a sequence of stimuli (e.g., a list of birds), individuals are more likely to recall the presence of a prototypic stimulus, are more likely to (falsely) report that an absent prototype was present, and are more likely to (falsely) report that a present nonprototype was absent. In addition, people are likely to judge that a nonprototypic stimulus is more similar to a prototypic stimulus than vice versa. For example, people tend to judge the color pink as being similar to red; however, people tend to judge the color red as being less similar to pink.

psychoacoustics Sensory and perceptual responses to sound. One aim of psychoacoustic research is to elucidate mechanisms by which the auditory system processes acoustical properties.

pure tone *See* sine tone.

Pythagorean tuning An ancient system of musical tuning that involves progressively tuning a perfect fifth above the current tone (3:2 ratio). Each tone around the circle of fifths is progressively tuned, along with its octave equivalents, until the cycle is complete and the starting point is reached. Unfortunately, to complete the cycle some degree of mistuning is required. The degree of mistuning is known as the Pythagorean comma. Although the tuning system is attributed to Pythagoras, its use has been documented as long ago as 3500 B.C. Today's tuning system, called equal temperament, avoids the musical problems associated with the Pythagorean comma.

raga In Indian music, a series of five or more musical notes on which a melody is based. Different ragas may be played at different times of the day.

rasa Among other meanings, an emotion inspired in an audience by a performer.

reductional structure *See* Schenkerian analysis.

relative pitch The ability to perceive and remember pitch relations. Sensitivity to relative pitch allows us to recognize a melody at different overall pitch heights. For example, we can recognize the song "Happy Birthday" whether it is sung in a high-pitched voice or a low-pitched voice, because the pitch relationships remain the same. Usually contrasted with absolute or perfect pitch, which is the ability to remember or label isolated pitches over long periods of time.

resection A surgical procedure to remove tissue or part or all of an organ.

resonance The acoustic disposition of physical bodies and enclosures to promote energy at one or more frequencies or bands of frequencies. The resonance characteristics of bodies (e.g., violins or oboes) are important features by which listeners are able to identify these instruments.

rhythm The temporal structure of music, speech, movement, and other phenomena. In Lerdahl and Jackendoff's *Generative Theory of Tonal Music* (GTTM), rhythm is conceived in terms of a distinction between metrical and grouping structure. *Metrical structure* refers to a regular hierarchical pattern of recurring accents. *Grouping structure* reflects a recursive segmentation of music into progressively larger units. Grouping boundaries need not align with metrical accents, so the combination of meter and grouping can generate a complex network of overlapping structures that are collectively experienced as the rhythm.

ritard/ritardandi (*rit*) Gradually decreasing tempo. Slowing down the pace of a music performance. Often introduced by performers at the end of phrases (to mark phrase boundaries), musical sections, and especially at the end of pieces to signal closure and finality.

scale The set of notes that represent a musical composition, and from which most or all tones in the music are drawn. In Western music, the most common scale is called the major diatonic scale (doh, re, mi, fa, sol, la, ti, doh). The scale is an abstraction in the sense that music may suggest a certain scale (e.g., major) even when not all of the scale notes are used in the music, and even when certain nonscale (nondiatonic) notes are used. Simple folk melodies usually adhere strictly to the use of scale notes only. Most classical music contains some nonscale notes, although they occur less frequently than scale notes.

schema (plural, schemata or schemas) A mental preconception of the normal course of events. Schemas may be viewed as mental templates or scenarios that influence how an individual perceives and interprets current events. Schemas are learned through previous experiences in like situations, and give rise to expectations.

schematic expectation An expectation that arises due to the existence of a mental schema.

Schenkerian analysis A method of music analysis based on the theories of Heinrich Schenker. A major aim of a Schenkerian analysis is to illustrate hierarchical relationships among pitches in music. This is achieved by differentiating structural notes from nonstructural notes (e.g., passing notes, ornamental notes) so as to give rise to reductions of the music. Using this technique, music can be progressively reduced until deep, background, or fundamental structure is revealed. Unreduced music is also called the *surface* or *foreground*.

selective impairment An impairment that is specific to a particular domain such as the ability to recognize words or familiar melodies. Focal brain damage (damage to specific areas) may give rise to selective impairments, whereas diffuse brain damage (damage that extends across several areas of the brain) may give rise to wide-ranging impairments.

sensory dissonance Dissonance or "roughness" between simultaneous tones that can be explained by sensory factors. Contrasted with *musical* dissonance, which is dependent on one's knowledge and experience. Maximum sensory dissonance arises between two pure tones when their points of maximum excitation on the basilar membrane of the cochlea are separated by roughly 0.4 millimeters (or 40% of a critical band). The unpleasantness drops to zero as the two tones approach unison. Unpleasantness also drops to a minimum as the frequency difference between the pure tones exceeds a critical band. The overall sensory dissonance for any sonority is the aggregate sum of the interactions between all of the concurrent partials.

sensory transduction The process by which a chemical or physical stimulus is converted or transduced by sensory receptors into an electrical signal.

serialism A posttonal method of composition in which various musical elements (like pitch, rhythm, dynamics, and tone color) are ordered according to a fixed series. It was introduced as an alternative to Western tonal structure, but has not enjoyed widespread success among audiences.

sexual dimorphism The systematic difference in form or behavior between individuals of different sex in the same species, as in size, color, and the presence or absence of parts of the body.

Shepard illusion The illusion of constantly increasing or decreasing pitch. *See* circular tones.

Shepard tone *See* circular tones.

simultaneous tones Tones played at the same time, as in a chord.

sine tone A single audible frequency, also known as a pure tone or simple tone in contrast to a complex tone. Sine tones are often described as "dull" sounding.

sine wave The waveform of a sine tone.

sinusoidal Pertaining to a sine wave or sine tone.

staccato A style of playing notes in an abrupt, detached, separated, distinct manner. As opposed to legato.

stream The auditory experience of a "line of sound." The mental image evoked when successive sounds appear to originate from the same sound-generating source or activity. Most monophonic melodies are experienced as a single stream. Polyphonic music tends to evoke multiple concurrent streams.

subcortical Anatomical term designating areas of the brain located below the cortex. Spots of gray matter (called nuclei) are found at various points throughout the central (white) region of the brain. These points of gray matter are typical examples of subcortical structures.

synesthesia A neurologically based phenomenon in which stimulation of one sensory or cognitive pathway leads to automatic, involuntary experiences in other sensory modalities. In color synesthesia, letters or numbers may be perceived as inherently colored.

tactus A Renaissance term for a beat. In current usage, the tactus refers to the perceived pulse of the music, usually indicated by the rate at which individuals naturally tap their feet to music. The tactus is not always predictable from the meter, because some individuals tap their feet on every other major division of the bar, or twice per major division of the bar. Thus, each individual has his or her own tactus for a given piece of music.

tempo The speed of a performance or composition. In Western music tempo is conventionally measured in beats per minute.

temporal resolution The precision of a measurement with respect to time.

temporo-parietal The temporal and parietal lobes of the cerebral hemisphere. A temporo-parietal stroke is one in which areas of the brain are affected in both regions.

tessitura The range of pitches used in a composition, instrument, or voice.

theme The subject or musical basis on which a composition is built. Usually consisting of a recognizable melody, characteristic rhythm, or both.

theory of mind (ToM) Proposed as a cognitive capacity in humans and other animals: the ability to attribute mental states such as beliefs, desires, emotions, and knowledge to oneself and others and to recognize that others have mental states that are different from one's own. The phrase can also refer to a particular theory about the mind, but its current use most often connotes a cognitive capacity.

timbre (Pronounced tam-bur.) Timbre, tone color or tone quality are catch-all terms that denote those properties of a sound—other than pitch and loudness—that combine to produce an overall auditory identity or character. The notion of timbre is closely associated with the identifiability or distinguishability of a sound, or class of sounds. Musicians will thus speak of the timbre of a violin, or the class of brassy timbres.

tonal fusion The propensity for two or more tones to fuse and sound as a single tone. Tonal fusion typically arises when the fundamental frequencies for the tones are related by simple integer ratios—and so are consistent with a possible harmonic series. In musical contexts, tonal fusion is strongest for the unison interval (e.g., two guitars playing middle C at the same time). Tonal fusion is next most likely at the interval of an octave, followed by the perfect fifth. Formerly, it was thought that tonal fusion contributed to the consonance of a sound. However, current evidence for this view is mixed.

tonal hierarchy See Krumhansl and Kessler key profiles.

tonality The quality of music that involves the use of a key or keys. The perception of key in Western tonal music involves sensitivity to a complex system of relationships among tones and chords. Two structures describe the representations that guide the perception of key. The first references relationships among tones within a key, and the second references key relationships. First, a musical key involves a collection of tones (called pitch classes) and a hierarchy of functions of tones. The most familiar collection outlining a musical key is the major scale (doh-re-mi-fah-sol-la-ti). Within this scale, the first note doh is said to have the most important function. It is called the tonic or tonal center, and has been likened to a cognitive referent, or prototypic element. Other pitches have subordinate functions; the next most important is the fifth note of the scale, sol, the next is the third note mi, followed by the remaining scale notes. Notes that are not in the scale (called nondiatonic tones) are least important in the hierarchy of tone functions.

The second principal structure deals with key relationships. Each of the 12 chromatic tones may function as the tonic of a key. Thus, there are 24 possible keys: 12 major and 12 minor keys. Key relationships are often described by the circle of fifths, with key distance defined by the number of steps on the cycle. Thus, the key of C is most closely related (least distant) to the neighboring keys of G and F, one step clockwise and counterclockwise on the cycle, respectively. Neighboring keys share all but one scale tone of their respective major scales; the number of tones shared between keys decreases as the distance in steps between keys increases.

tone deafness *See* amusia.

tonic The first note of the scale, or doh. Chords built from the tonic (doh, mi, sol) play an important role in cadences (harmonic transitions that signal an endpoint in the music). In a perfect cadence (which strongly suggests an ending), the dominant chord is followed by a tonic chord.

top-down Used to refer to knowledge-driven psychological phenomena.

traveling wave A disturbance that propagates through space and time. Traveling waves involve the transfer of energy from one point to the next, causing a temporary displacement of the particles of the medium, often with little or no permanent displacement of those particles.

valence The dimension of affect that extends from positive to negative. Joy is an emotion that has high positive valence, and grief is an emotion that has high negative valence.

vibrato A type of pitch variation, commonly found in instrumental and vocal performance, that adds warmth or emotional intensity to a given sound. Vibrato can be described as fast or slow, shallow or deep.

waveform The specific shape or contour of a single cycle or a periodic sound function as represented by a two-dimensional graph. Waveforms other than sine waves are considered complex, as they contain more than one simple frequency component (*see* Fourier analysis). The shape of the waveform is partly dependent on the harmonic content of the sound—hence, waveform is sometimes erroneously equated with timbre.

Wernicke's area That part of the cortex on the posterior section of the superior temporal gyrus, encircling the auditory cortex, on the Sylvian fissure (where the temporal lobe and parietal lobe meet). Located in the left hemisphere, which is specialized for language skills. Occlusion of the middle cerebral artery as in a stroke can affect proper functioning of this area.

zoomusicology The study of similarities between music and animal sounds.

References

Abler, W. (1989). On the particulate principle of self-diversifying systems. *Journal of Social and Biological Structures, 12*, 1–13.

Abrams, R. M. (1995). Some aspects of the fetal sound environment. In I. Deliège & J. A. Sloboda (Eds.), *Perception and cognition of music* (pp. 83–101). Hove, UK: Psychology Press.

Adler, M. (1985). Stardom and talent. *American Economic Review, 75*(1), 208–212.

Aiello, R., & Williamon, A. (2002). Memory. In R. Parncutt & G. E. McPherson (Eds.), *The science and psychology of music performance* (pp. 167–181). Oxford, UK: Oxford University Press.

Albert, M. L., Sparks, R. W., & Helm, N. A. (1973). Melodic intonation therapy for aphasia. *Archives of Neurology, 29*, 130–131.

Albinoni, T. G. (1981). Adagio in G minor for organ and strings [Recorded by I Solisti Veneti, conducted by C. Scimone]. On *Albinoni's adagios* [CD]. UK: Warner Classics. (1996)

Allen, D. (1967). Octave discriminability of musical and non-musical subjects. *Psychonomic Science, 7*, 421–422.

Amaducci, L., Grassi, E., & Boller, F. (2002). Maurice Ravel and right-hemisphere musical creativity: Influence of disease on his last musical works? *European Journal of Neurology, 9*(1), 75–82.

Anvari, S., Trainor, L. J., Woodside, J., & Levy, B. A. (2002). Relations among musical skills, phonological processing, and early reading ability in preschool children. *Journal of Experimental Child Psychology, 83*, 111–130.

Areni, C. S., & Kim, D. (1993). The influence of background music on shopping behavior: Classical versus top-forty music in a wine store. *Advances in Consumer Research, 20*, 336–340.

Ashby, F. G., Isen, A. M., & Turken, A. U. (1999). A neuropsychological theory of positive affect and its influence on cognition. *Psychological Review, 106*, 529–550.

Ashley, R. (2002). Do[n't] change a hair for me: The art of jazz rubato. *Music Perception, 19*, 311–332.

Astington, J. W., & Baird, J. A. (2005). Introduction: Why language matters. In J. W. Ashington & J. A. Baird (Eds.), *Why language matters for theory of mind* (pp. 3–25). Oxford. UK: Oxford University Press.

Astington, J. W., & Jenkins, J. M. (1999). A longitudinal study of the relation between language and theory-of-mind development. *Developmental Psychology, 35*(5), 1311–1320.

Auhagen, W., & Vos, P. G. (2000). Experimental methods in tonality induction research: A review. *Music Perception, 17*, 417–436.

Ayotte, J., Peretz, I., & Hyde, K. (2002). Congenital amusia: A group study of adults afflicted with a music-specific disorder. *Brain, 125*, 238–251.

Ayotte, J., Peretz, I., Rousseau, I., Bard, C., & Bojanowski, M. (2000). Patterns of music agnosia associated with middle cerebral artery infarcts. *Brain, 123*, 1926–1938.

Baharloo, S., Service, S. K., Risch, N., Gitschier, J., & Freimer N. B. (2000). Familial aggregation of absolute pitch. *American Journal of Human Genetics, 67*, 755–758.

Balkwill, L.-L., & Thompson, W. F. (1999). A cross-cultural investigation of the perception of emotion in music: Psychophysical and cultural cues. *Music Perception, 17*, 43–64.

Balkwill, L.-L., Thompson, W. F., & Matsunaga, R. (2004). Recognition of emotion in Japanese, Western, and Hindustani music by Japanese listeners. *Japanese Psychological Research, 46*(4), 337–349.

Balzano, G. J. (1980). The group-theoretic description of 12-fold and microtonal pitch systems. *Computer Music Journal, 4*, 66–84.

Barlow, J. S. (1969). Some observations on the electrophysiology of timing in the nervous system. *Electroencephalography and Clinical Neurophysiology, 27*, 545.

Baron-Cohen, S. (1999). The evolution of a theory of mind. In M. C. Corballis & S. E. G. Lea (Eds.), *The descent of mind: Psychological perspectives on hominid evolution* (pp. 261–277). Oxford, UK: Oxford University Press.

Beal, A. L. (1985). The skill of recognizing musical structures. *Memory & Cognition, 13*, 405–412.

Becker, J. (2001). Anthropological perspectives on music and emotion. In P. N. Juslin & J. A. Sloboda (Eds.), *Music and emotion: Theory and research* (pp. 135–160). Oxford, UK: Oxford University Press.

Bergee, M. J. (1989). An objectively constructed rating scale for euphonium and tuba music performance. *Dialogue in Instrumental Music Education, 13*, 65–86.

Bergee, M. J. (1992). A comparison of faculty, peer, and self-evaluations of applied brass jury performances. *Journal of Research in Music Education, 41*(1), 19–27.

Bergeson, T. R., & Trehub, S. E. (2002). Absolute pitch and tempo in mothers' songs to infants. *Psychological Science, 13*, 71–74.

Bergeson, T. R., & Trehub, S. E. (2006). Infants' perception of rhythmic patterns. *Music Perception, 23*, 345–360.

Berlyne, D. E. (1967). Arousal and reinforcement. In D. Levine (Ed.), *Nebraska symposium on motivation: Vol. 15. Current theory & research in motivation* (pp. 1–110). Lincoln: University of Nebraska Press.

Berlyne, D. E. (1970). Novelty, complexity, and hedonic value. *Perception and Psychophysics, 8*, 279–286.

Berlyne, D. E. (1971). *Aesthetics and psychobiology*. New York: Appleton Century Crofts.

Bever, T., & Chiarello, R. (1974). Cerebral dominance in musicians and non-musicians. *Science, 185*, 537–539.

Bharucha, J. J., Curtis, M., & Paroo, K. (2006). The varieties of musical experience. *Cognition, 100*, 131–173.

Bharucha, J. J., & Pryor, J. H. (1986). Disrupting the isochrony underlying rhythm: An asymmetry in discrimination. *Perception and Psychophysics, 40*, 137–141.

Bickerton, D. (2001). Linguists play catchup with evolution. *Journal of Linguistics, 37*, 581–591.

Bigand, E. (1990). Abstraction of two forms of underlying structure in a tonal melody. *Psychology of Music, 18*, 45–59.

Blacking, J. (1973). *How musical is man?* Seattle: University of Washington Press.

Blood, A. J., & Zatorre, R. J. (2001). Intensely pleasurable responses to music correlate with activity in brain regions implicated in reward and emotion. *Proceedings of the National Academy of Sciences, 98*, 11818–11823.

Blumenfeld, L. (1993). *Voices of forgotten worlds: Traditional music of indigenous people*. New York: Ellipsis Arts.

Bolinger, D. (1978). Intonation across languages. In J. Greenberg (Ed.), *Universals in human language: Vol II. Phonology* (pp. 471–524). Palo Alto, CA: Stanford University Press.

Bolinger, D. (1986). *Intonation and its parts*. Palo Alto, CA: Stanford University Press.

Boltz, M., & Jones, M. R. (1986). Does rule recursion make melodies easier to reproduce? If not, what does? *Cognitive Psychology, 18*, 389–431.

Borod, J., Pick, L. H., Hall, S., Sliwinski, M., Madigan, N., Obler, L. K., et al. (2000). Relationship among facial, prosodic, and lexical channels of emotional perceptual processing. *Cognition and Emotion, 14*, 193–211.

Bregman, A. S. (1990). *Auditory scene analysis*. Cambridge, MA: MIT Press.

Brown, S. (2000). The "musilanguage" model of music evolution. In N. L. Wallin, B. Merker, & S. Brown (Eds.), *The origins of music* (pp. 271–300). Cambridge, MA: MIT Press.

Browne, R. (1981). Tonal implications of the diatonic set. *In Theory Only, 5*, 3–21.

Bruner, G. C. (1990). Music, mood, and marketing. *Journal of Marketing, 54*(4), 94–104.

Brust, J. C. (2003). Music and the neurologist: A historical perspective. In I. Peretz & R. J. Zatorre (Eds.), *The cognitive neuroscience of music* (pp. 181–191). Oxford, UK: Oxford University Press.

Bryden, M. P., Ley, R. G., & Sugarman, J. H. (1982). A left-ear advantage for identifying the emotional quality of tonal sequences. *Neuropsychologia, 20,* 83–87.

Budd, M. (1985). *Music and the emotions.* London: Routledge & Kegan Paul.

Buelow, G. G. (1980). Rhetoric and music. In S. Sadie (Ed.), *New Grove dictionary of music and musicians* (Vol. 15, p. 793). London: Macmillan.

Bunt, L., & Pavlicevic, M. (2001). Music and emotion: Perspectives from music therapy. In P. N. Juslin & J. A. Sloboda (Eds.), *Music and emotion: Theory and research* (pp. 181–204). Oxford, UK: Oxford University Press.

Burns, E. M. (1999). Intervals, scales, and tuning. In D. Deutsch (Ed.), *The psychology of music* (2nd ed., pp. 215–264). San Diego, CA: Academic.

Burns, J. K. (2004). An evolutionary theory of schizophrenia: Cortical connectivity, metarepresentation and the social brain. *Behavioral and Brain Sciences, 27,* 831–855.

Butler, D. (1989). Describing the perception of tonality in music: A critique of the tonal hierarchy theory and a proposal for a theory of intervallic rivalry. *Music Perception, 6,* 219–242.

Butzlaff, R. (2000). Can music be used to teach reading? *Journal of Aesthetic Education, 34*(3–4), 167–178.

Cadalbert, A., Landis, T., Regard, M., & Graves, R. E. (1994). Singing with and without words: Hemispheric asymmetries in motor control. *Journal of Clinical and Experimental Neuropsychology, 16*(5), 664–670.

Campbell, D. T. (1974). Evolutionary epistemology. In P. A. Schilpp (Ed.), *The philosophy of Karl Popper* (Vol. 1, pp. 413–463). La Salle, IL: Open Court.

Cerulo, K. A. (1984). Social disruption and its effects on music: An empirical analysis. *Social Forces, 62,* 885–904.

Chabris, C. F. (1999). Prelude or requiem for the "Mozart effect"? *Nature, 400,* 826.

Chan, A. S., Ho, Y. C., & Cheung, M. C. (1998). Music training improves verbal memory. *Nature, 396,* 128–129.

Churchland, P. S. (1986). *Neurophilosophy.* Cambridge, MA: MIT Press.

Clarke, E. F. (1982). Timing in the performance of Erik Satie's "Vexations." *Acta Psychologica, 50,* 1–19.

Clarke, E. F. (1985). Some aspects of rhythm and expression in performances of Erik Satie's "Gnossienne No. 5." *Music Perception, 2,* 299–328.

Cohen, A. (2001). Music as a source of emotion in film. In P. N. Juslin & J. A. Sloboda (Eds.), *Music and emotion* (pp. 249–272). Oxford, UK: Oxford University Press.

Collins, D. (2005). A synthesis process model of creative thinking in music composition. *Psychology of Music, 33,* 193–216.

Cook, N. (1987). The perception of large-scale tonal closure. *Music Perception, 5,* 197–206.

Cook, N. (1990). *Music, imagination, and culture.* Oxford, UK: Clarendon.

Cook, N. (2003). Music as performance. In M. Clayton, T. Herbert, & R. Middleton (Eds.), *The cultural study of music: A critical introduction* (pp. 204–214). London: Routledge.

Cooke, D. (1959). *The language of music.* London: Oxford University Press.

Cooper, R. P., & Aslin, R. N. (1990). Preference for infant-directed speech in the first month after birth. *Child Development, 61,* 1584–1595.

Costa-Giomi, E. (1999). The effects of three years of piano instruction on children's cognitive development. *Journal of Research in Music Education, 47*(3), 198–212.

Cronin, C. (1998). Concepts of melodic similarity in music-copyright infringement suits. In W. B. Hewlett & E. Selfridge-Field (Eds.), *Melodic similarity: Concepts, procedures, applications* (pp. 187–210). Cambridge, MA: MIT Press.

Cross, I. (1997). Pitch schemata. In I. Deliège & J. A. Sloboda (Eds.), *Perception and cognition of music* (pp. 353–386). Hove, UK: Psychology Press.

Cross, I. (1998). Music and science: Three views. *Revue Belge de Musicologie, 52,* 207–214.

Cross, I. (2003a). Music and biocultural evolution. In M. Clayton, T. Herbert, & R. Middleton (Eds.), *The cultural study of music: A critical introduction* (pp. 19–30). London: Routledge.

Cross, I. (2003b). Music and evolution: Consequences and causes. *Contemporary Music Review, 22*(3), 79–89.

Cross, I. (2007). Music and cognitive evolution. In R. Dunbar & L. Barrett (Eds.), *OUP handbook of evolutionary psychology* (pp. 649–667). Oxford, UK: Oxford University Press.

Crowder, R. G. (1984). Perception of the major/minor distinction: I. Historical and theoretical foundations. *Psychomusicology, 4,* 3–12.

Crowder, R. G. (1989). Imagery for musical timbre. *Journal of Experimental Psychology: Human Perception and Performance, 15,* 472–478.

Crowder, R. G. (1993). Auditory memory. In S. McAdams & E. Bigand (Eds.), *Thinking in sound: The cognitive psychology of human audition* (pp. 113–145). Oxford, UK: Oxford University Press/Clarendon.

Crowder, R. G., Reznick, J. S., & Rosenkrantz, S. L. (1991). Perception of the major/minor distinction: V. Preferences among infants. *Bulletin of the Psychonomic Society, 29,* 187–188.

Cuddy, L. L., & Badertscher, B. (1987). Recovery of the tonal hierarchy: Some comparisons across age and levels of musical experience. *Perception & Psychophysics, 41,* 609–620.

Cuddy, L. L., Balkwill, L.-L., Peretz, I., & Holden, R. (2005). Musical difficulties are rare: A study of "tone deafness" among university students. *Annals of the New York Academy of Sciences, 1060,* 311–324.

Cuddy, L. L., Cohen, A. J., & Mewhort, D. J. K. (1981). Perception of structure in short melodic sequences. *Journal of Experimental Psychology: Human Perception and Performance, 7,* 869–883.

Cuddy, L. L., & Duffin, J. (2005). Music, memory, and Alzheimer's disease: Is music recognition spared in dementia, and how can it be assessed? *Medical Hypotheses, 64,* 229–235.

Cuddy, L. L., & Thompson, W. F. (1992). Asymmetry of perceived key movement in chorale sequences: Converging evidence from a probe-tone investigation. *Psychological Research, 54,* 51–59.

Cybulska, E (1997). Bolero unravelled. A case of musical perseveration. *Psychiatric Bulletin, 21,* 576–577.

Cziko, G. (1995). *Without miracles: Universal selection and the second Darwinian revolution.* Cambridge, MA: MIT Press.

Damasio, A. R. (1994). *Descartes' error: Emotion, reason, and the human brain.* New York: Avon Books.

Darwin C. (1871). *The descent of man and selection in relation to sex.* London: John Murray.

Darwin, C. (1872). *Expression of the emotions in man and animals.* London: John Murray.

Darwin, C. J., Turvey, M. T., & Crowder, R. G. (1972). An auditory analogue of the Sperling partial report procedure: Evidence for brief auditory storage. *Cognitive Psychology, 3,* 255–267.

Davidson, J. W. (1993). Visual perception of performance manner in the movements of solo musicians. *Psychology of Music, 21,* 103–113.

Davidson, J. W., & Correia, J. S. (2002). Body movement. In R. Parncutt & G. E. McPherson (Eds.), *The science and psychology of music performance* (pp. 237–253). New York: Oxford University Press.

Davies, S. (2001). Philosophical perspectives on music's expressiveness. In P. N. Juslin & J. A. Sloboda (Eds.), *Music and emotion: Theory and research* (pp. 23–44). Oxford, UK: Oxford University Press.

Davis, M. (1994). Folk music psychology. *The Psychologist, 7,* 537.

Dawkins, R. (1999). *The selfish gene* (2nd ed.). Oxford, UK: Oxford University Press.

DeCasper, A. J., & Prescott, P. A. (1984). Human newborns' perception of male voices: Preference, discrimination, and reinforcing value. *Developmental Psychobiology, 17,* 481–491.

Deliège, I. (1987). Grouping conditions in listening to music: An approach to Lerdahl & Jackendoff's grouping preference rules. *Music Perception, 4,* 325–360.

Dennett, D. C. (1995). *Darwin's dangerous idea: Evolution and the meanings of life.* New York: Simon & Schuster.

DeNora, T. (2000). *Music in everyday life.* Cambridge, UK: Cambridge University Press.

DeNora, T. (2001). Aesthetic agency and musical practice: new directions in the sociology of music and emotion. In P. N. Juslin & J. A. Sloboda (Eds.), *Music and emotion: Theory and research* (pp. 161–180). Oxford: Oxford University Press.

D'Errico, F., Henshilwood, C., Lawson, G., Vanhaeren, M., Tillier, A-M., Soressi, M., et al. (2003). Archaeological evidence for the emergence of language, symbolism, and music—An alternative multidisciplinary perspective. *Journal of World Prehistory, 17*(1), 1–70.

Desain, P. (1992). A (de)composable theory of rhythm perception. *Music Perception, 9,* 439–454.

Deutsch, D. (1975). Musical illusions. *Scientific American, 233,* 92–104.

Deutsch, D. (1980). The processing of structured and unstructured tonal sequences. *Perception and Psychophysics, 28,* 381–389.

Deutsch, D. (1999). The processing of pitch combinations. In D. Deutsch (Ed.), *The psychology of music* (2nd ed., pp. 349–412). New York: Academic.

Dewey, J. (1934). *Art as experience.* New York: Minton, Balch.

DeWitt, L. A., & Crowder, R. G. (1987). Tonal fusion of consonant musical intervals: The oomph in Stumpf. *Perception & Psychophysics, 41,* 73–84.

Diallo, Y., & Hall, M. (1989). *The healing drum: African wisdom techniques.* Rochester, VT: Destiny.

Dibben, N. (1994). The cognitive reality of hierarchic structure in tonal and atonal music. *Music Perception, 12,* 1–25.

Di Carlo, N. S., & Guaitella, I. (2004). Facial expressions of emotion in speech and singing. *Semiotica, 149*(1–4), 37–55.

Di Pietro, M., Laganaro, M., Leemann, B., & Schnider, A. (2004). Receptive amusia: Temporal auditory processing deficit in a professional musician following a left temporo-parietal lesion. *Neuropsychologia, 42,* 868–877.

Dissanayake, E. (2000). Antecedents of the temporal arts in early mother–infant interactions. In N. L. Wallin, B. Merker, & S. Brown (Eds.), *The origins of music* (pp. 388–410). Cambridge, MA: MIT Press.

Douglas, S., & Willatts, P. (1994). The relationship between musical ability and literacy skills. *Journal of Research in Reading, 17*(2), 99–107.

Duerksen, G. L. (1972). Some effects of expectation on evaluation of recorded musical performance. *Journal of Research in Music Education, 20,* 268–272.

Duke, R. A., Flowers, P. J., & Wolfe, D. E. (1997). Children who study piano with excellent teachers in the United States. *Bulletin of the Council for Research in Music Education, 132,* 51–84.

Dunbar, R. (1996). *Grooming, gossip, and the evolution of language.* London: Faber & Faber.

Durr, W., & Gerstenberg, W. (1980). Rhythm. In S. Sadie (Ed.), *New Grove dictionary of music and musicians* (Vol. 15, pp. 804–824). London: Macmillan.

Dyson, M. C., & Watkins, A. J. (1984). A figural approach to the role of melodic contour in melody recognition. *Perception & Psychophysics, 35,* 477–488.

Easterbrook, J. A. (1959). The effect of emotion on cue utilization and the organization of behavior. *Psychological Review, 66,* 183–201.

Edmonds, E. M., & Smith, M. E. (1923). The phenomenological description of musical intervals. *American Journal of Psychology, 34,* 287–291.

Ekman, P. (1992a). Are there basic emotions? *Psychological Review, 99,* 550–553.

Ekman, P. (1992b). An argument for basic emotions. *Cognition and Emotion, 6,* 169–200.

Ekman, P., & Davidson, R. (1994). *The nature of emotion: Fundamental questions.* New York: Oxford University Press.

Ekman, P., & Friesen, W. V. (1981). The repertoire of nonverbal behaviour. In A. Kenson (Ed.), *Nonverbal communication, interaction, and gesture* (pp. 57–106). The Hague, The Netherlands: Mouton.

Ericsson, K. A., Krampe, R., & Tesch-Römer, C. (1993). The rule of deliberate practice in the acquisition of expert performance. *Psychological Review, 100*, 363–406.

Essens, P. J. (1995). Structuring temporal sequences: Comparison of models and factors of complexity. *Perception and Psychophysics, 57*, 519–532.

Fachner, J. (2003). Jazz improvisation and a social pharmacology of music. *Music Therapy Today, 4*(3), 1–26.

Feld, S. (1990). *Sound and sentiment: Birds, weeping, poetics, and song in Kaluli experience* (2nd ed.). Philadelphia: University of Pennsylvania Press.

Fernald, A. (1985). Four-month-olds prefer to listen to motherese. *Infant Behavior and Development, 8*, 181–195.

Fernald, A., Taeschner, T., Dunn, J., Papousek, M., Boysson-Bardies, B. de, & Fukui, I. (1989). A cross-language study of prosodic modifications in mothers' and fathers' speech to preverbal infants. *Journal of Child Language, 16*, 477–501.

Fifer, W. P., & Moon, C. (1988). Auditory experience in the fetus. In W. P. Smotherman & S. R. Robinson (Eds.), *Behaviour of the fetus* (pp. 175–188). Telford, UK: Caldwell.

Fiske, H. E. (1978). *The effect of a training procedure in music performance evaluation on judge reliability.* Brantford: Ontario Educational Research Council Report.

Flores, R. G., & Ginsburgh, V. A. (1996). The Queen Elisabeth musical competition: How fair is the final ranking? *The Statistician, 45*(1), 97–104.

Flores-Gutierrez, E. O., Diaz, J. L., Barrios, F. A., Favila-Humara, R., Guevara, M. A., Del Rio-Portilla, Y., et al. (2007). Metabolic and electric brain patterns during pleasant and unpleasant emotions induced by music masterpieces. *International Journal of Psychophysiology, 65*, 69–84.

Fodor, J. (1980). Fixation of belief and concept acquisition. In M. Piatelli-Palmarini (Ed.), *Language and learning* (pp. 143–149). London: Routledge & Kegan Paul.

Fraisse, P. (1982). Rhythm and tempo. In D. Deutch (Ed.), *The psychology of music* (2nd ed., pp. 149–180). New York: Academic.

Freeman, W. J. (2000). A neurobiological role of music in social bonding. In N. Wallin, B. Merkur, & S. Brown (Eds.), *The origins of music* (pp. 411–424). Cambridge MA: MIT Press.

Friberg, A., Bresin, R., & Sundberg, J. (2006). Overview of the KTH rule system for music performance. *Advances in Cognitive Psychology, 2*, 145–161.

Gabriel, C. (1978). An experimental study of Deryck Cooke's theory of music and meaning. *Psychology of Music, 6*, 13–20.

Gabrielsson, A. (1973a). Similarity ratings and dimension analysis of auditory rhythm patterns: I. *Scandinavian Journal of Psychology, 14*, 138–160.

Gabrielsson, A. (1973b). Similarity ratings and dimension analysis of auditory rhythm patterns: II. *Scandinavian Journal of Psychology, 14*, 161–176.

Gabrielsson, A. (1974). Performance of rhythmic patterns. *Scandinavian Journal of Psychology, 15*, 63–72.

Gabrielsson, A. (1987). Once again: The theme from Mozart's piano sonata in A major (k. 331). In A. Gabrielsson (Ed.), *Action and perception in rhythm and music* (pp. 81–103). Stockholm: Royal Swedish Academy of Music.

Gabrielsson, A., & Juslin, P. N. (1996). Emotional expression in music performance: Between the performer's intention and the listener's experience. *Psychology of Music, 24*, 68–91.

Gardiner, M. F., Fox, A., Knowles, F., & Jeffrey, D. (1996). Learning improved by arts training. *Nature, 381*, 284.

Geissmann, T. (2000). Gibbon songs and human music from an evolutionary perspective. In N. Wallin, B. Merker, & S. Brown (Eds.), *The origins of music* (pp. 103–123). Cambridge, MA: MIT Press.

Gembris, H., & Davidson, J. W. (2002) Environmental influences. In R. Parncutt & G. E. McPherson (Eds.), *The science and psychology of music performance* (pp. 17–30). New York: Oxford University Press.

Geoghegan, N., & Mitchelmore, M. (1996). Possible effects of early childhood music on mathematical achievement. *Journal for Australian Research in Early Childhood Education, 1*, 57–64.

Ghiselin, B. (Ed.). (1955). *The creative process.* Berkeley: University of California Press.

Gjerdingen, R. (2002). The psychology of music. In T. Christensen (Ed.), *The Cambridge history of Western music theory* (pp. 956–981). Cambridge, UK: Cambridge University Press.

Goldstein, A. (1980). Thrills in response to music and other stimuli. *Physiological Psychology, 8,* 126–129.

Goleman, D. (1995). *Emotional intelligence.* New York: Bantam Books.

Gosselin, N., Peretz, I., Johnsen, E., & Adolphs, R. (2007). Amygdala damage impairs emotion recognition from music. *Neuropsychologia, 45,* 236–244.

Gosselin, N., Peretz, I., Noulhiane, M., Hasboun, D., Beckett, C., Baulac, M., et al. (2005). Impaired recognition of scary music following unilateral temporal lobe excision. *Brain, 128,* 628–640.

Gould, G. (1962, February). Let's ban applause! *Musical America, 70,* 10–11, 38.

Gould, S. J., & Vrba, E. S. (1982). Exaptation—A missing term in the science of form. *Paleobiology, 8,* 4–5.

Gregory, R. L. (1981). *Mind in science.* London: Weidenfeld & Nicholson.

Grey, J. A. (1990). Brain systems that mediate both emotion and cognition. *Cognition and Emotion, 4,* 269–288.

Grey, J. M. (1977). Multidimensional perceptual scaling of musical timbres. *Journal of the Acoustical Society of America, 61,* 1270–1277.

Griffiths, T. D., Rees, A., Witton, C., Cross, P. M., Shakir, R. A., & Green, G. G. (1997). Spatial and temporal auditory processing deficits following right hemisphere infarction. *Brain, 120,* 785–794.

Gromko, J. E., & Poorman, A. S. (1998). The effect of music training on preschoolers' spatial-tempo-ral task performance. *Journal of Research in Music Education, 46*(2), 173–181.

Hajda, J. M., Kendall, R. A., Carterette, E. C., & Harshberger, M. L. (1997). Methodological issues in timbre research. In I. Deliège & J. Sloboda (Eds.), *Perception and cognition of music* (pp. 253–306). East Sussex, UK: Psychology Press.

Hall, M. D., Pastore, R. E., Acker, B. E., & Huang, W. (2000). Evidence for auditory feature integration with spatially distributed items. *Perception and Psychophysics, 62,* 1243–1257.

Hall, M. D., & Weiberg, K. (2003). Illusory conjunctions of musical pitch and timbre. *Acoustics Research Letters Online, 4*(3), 65–70.

Halpern, A. R. (1989). Memory for the absolute pitch of familiar songs. *Memory & Cognition, 17,* 572–581.

Halpern, A. R., & Zatorre, R. J. (1999). When that tune runs through your head: A PET investigation of auditory imagery for familiar melodies. *Cerebral Cortex, 9,* 697–704.

Handel, S. (1989). *Listening.* Cambridge, MA: MIT Press.

Hannon E. E., & Johnson, S. P. (2005). Infants use meter to categorize rhythms and melodies: Implications for musical structure learning. *Cognitive Psychology, 50,* 354–377.

Hannon, E. E., & Trainor, L. J. (2007). Music acquisition: Effects of enculturation and formal training on development. *Trends in Cognitive Sciences, 11,* 466–472.

Hannon, E. E., & Trehub, S. E. (2005a). Metrical categories in infancy and adulthood. *Psychological Science, 16,* 48–55.

Hannon, E. E., & Trehub, S. E. (2005b). Tuning in to rhythms: Infants learn more readily than adults. *Proceedings of the National Academy of Sciences of the USA, 102,* 12639–12643.

Healy, E. C., Mallard, A. R., III, & Adams, M. R. (1976). Factors contributing to the reduction of stuttering during singing. *Journal of Speech and Hearing Research, 19,* 475–480.

Helmholtz, H. von (1954). *On the sensations of tone as a physiological basis for the theory of music* (A. J. Ellis,

Ed. & Trans.). New York: Dover. (Original work published 1863)

Henderson, M. T. (1936). Rhythmic organization in artistic piano performance. In C. E. Seashore (Ed.), *Objective analysis of musical performance* (Vol. 4, pp. 281–305). Iowa City: University of Iowa Press.

Hetland, L. (2000). Learning to make music enhances spatial reasoning. *Journal of Aesthetic Education, 34*(3–4), 179–238.

Hevner, K. (1935a). The affective character of the major and minor modes in music. *American Journal of Psychology, 47,* 103–118.

Hevner, K. (1935b). Expression in music: A discussion of experimental studies and theories. *Psychological Review, 42,* 186–204.

Hevner, K. (1936). Experimental studies of the elements of expression in music. *American Journal of Psychology, 48,* 246–268.

Hevner, K. (1937). The affective value of pitch and tempo in music. *American Journal of Psychology, 49,* 621–630.

Ho, Y. C., Cheung, M. C., & Chan, A. S. (2003). Music training improves verbal but not visual memory: Cross-sectional and longitudinal explorations in children. *Neuropsychology, 17,* 439–450.

Holden, C. (1994). Smart music. *Science, 266,* 968.

Holleran, S., Jones, M. R., & Butler, D. (1995). Perceiving implied harmony: The role of melodic and harmonic context. *Journal of Experimental Psychology: Learning, Memory and Cognition, 21,* 737–753.

Honing, H. (2005). Is there a perception-based alternative to kinematic models of tempo rubato? *Music Perception, 23,* 79–85.

Hubel, D. H., & Wiesel, T. N. (1968). Receptive fields and functional architecture of monkey striate cortex. *Journal of Physiology, 195,* 215–243.

Humboldt, W. von (1972). *Linguistic variability and intellectual development* (G. C. Buck & F. A. Raven, Trans.). Philadelphia: University of Pennsylvania Press. (Original work published 1836)

Huron, D. (1991a). The avoidance of part-crossing in polyphonic music: Perceptual evidence and musical practice. *Music Perception, 9,* 93–104.

Huron, D. (1991b). Tonal consonance versus tonal fusion in polyphonic sonorities. *Music Perception, 9,* 135–154.

Huron, D. (2001a). Is music an evolutionary adaptation? *Annals of the New York Academy of Sciences, 930,* 43–61.

Huron, D. (2001b). Tone and voice: A derivation of the rules of voice-leading from perceptual principles. *Music Perception, 19*(1), 1–64.

Huron, D. (2006). *Sweet anticipation: Music and the psychology of expectation.* Cambridge, MA: MIT Press.

Husain, G., Thompson, W. F., & Schellenberg, E. G. (2002). Effects of musical tempo and mode on arousal, mood, and spatial abilities. *Music Perception, 20,* 149–169.

Ilie, G., & Thompson, W. F. (2006). A comparison of acoustic cues in music and speech for three dimensions of affect. *Music Perception, 23,* 319–329.

Isen, A. M. (1999). Positive affect. In T. Dalgleish & M. Power (Eds.), *The handbook of cognition and emotion* (pp. 521–539). New York: Wiley.

Iverson, P. (1995). Auditory stream segregation by musical timbre: Effects of static and dynamic acoustic attributes. *Journal of Experimental Psychology: Human Perception and Performance, 21,* 751–763.

Iverson, P., & Krumhansl, C. L. (1993). Isolating the dynamic attributes of musical timbre. *Journal of the Acoustical Society of America, 94,* 2595–2603.

Jakobson, L. S., Cuddy, L. L., & Kilgour, A. R. (2003). Time tagging: A key to musicians' superior memory. *Music Perception, 20,* 307–313.

James, W. (1880). Great men, great thoughts, and the environment. *Atlantic Monthly, 46,* 441–459.

James, W. (1890). *The principles of psychology* (2 vols.). New York: Holt.

Johnson, W. F., Emde, R. N., Scherer, K. R., & Klinnert, M. D. (1986). Recognition of emotion from vocal cues. *Archives of General Psychiatry, 43,* 280–283.

Jones, M. R., & Boltz, M. (1989). Dynamic attention and responses to time. *Psychological Review, 96,* 459–491.

Jones, M. R., Boltz, M., & Kidd, G. (1982). Controlled attending as a function of melodic and temporal context. *Perception & Psychophysics, 32,* 211–218.

Joseph, R. (1988). The right cerebral hemisphere: Emotion, music, visual-spatial skills, body image, dreams, and awareness. *Journal of Clinical Psychology, 44,* 630–673.

Jourdain, R. (1997). *Music, the brain and ecstasy: How music captures our imagination.* New York: Morrow.

Juslin, P. N. (1997). Emotional communication and music performance: A functionalist perspective and some data. *Music Perception, 14,* 383–418.

Juslin, P. N. (2001). Communicating emotion in music performance: A review and a theoretical framework. In P. N. Juslin, & J. A. Sloboda (Eds.), *Music and emotion: Theory and research* (pp. 309–337). New York: Oxford University Press.

Juslin, P. N. (2007). *Emotional responses to music.* In S. Hallam, I. Cross, & M. Thaut (Eds.), *Oxford handbook of music psychology.* New York: Oxford University Press.

Juslin, P. N., Friberg, A., & Bresin, R. (2002). Towards a computational model of expression in performance: The GERM model. *Musicae Scientiae,* 63–122.

Juslin, P. N., & Laukka, P. (2003). Communication of emotions in vocal expression and music performance: Different channels, same code? *Psychological Bulletin, 129,* 770–814.

Juslin, P. N., & Sloboda, J. A. (Eds.). (2001). *Music and emotion: Theory and research.* Oxford, UK: Oxford University Press.

Juslin, P. N., & Sloboda, J. A. (Eds.). (in press). *Handbook of music and emotion: Theory, research, applications.* New York: Oxford University Press.

Juslin, P. N., & Västfjäll, D. (in press). Emotional responses to music: The need to consider underlying mechanisms. *Behavioral and Brain Sciences.*

Justus, T., & Hutsler, J. J. (2005). Fundamental issues in the evolutionary psychology of music: Assessing innateness and domain specificity. *Music Perception, 23,* 1–27.

Kallman, H. J. (1982). Octave equivalence as measured by similarity ratings. *Perception & Psychophysics, 32,* 37–49.

Kartomi, M. J. (1980). Musical strata in Sumatra, Java, and Bali. In E. May (Ed.), *Musics of many cultures* (pp. 111–133). Berkeley: University of California Press.

Kastner, M. P., & Crowder, R. G. (1990). Perception of the major/minor distinction: IV. Emotional connotations in young children. *Music Perception, 8,* 189–202.

Keller, P. (1999). Attending in complex musical interactions: The adaptive dual role of meter. *Australian Journal of Psychology, 51,* 166–175.

Kendall, R. A., & Carterette, E. C. (1990). The communication of musical expression. *Music Perception, 8,* 129–164.

Kenny, D. T., & Osborne, M. S. (2006). Music performance anxiety: New insights from young musicians. *Advances in Cognitive Psychology, 2* 103–112.

Kiang, N. Y. S., et al. (1965). *Discharge patterns of single nerve fibers in the cat's auditory nerve.* Cambridge, MA: MIT Press.

Kilgour, A. R., Jakobson, L. S., & Cuddy, L. L. (2000). Music training and rate of presentation as mediators of text and song recall. *Memory and Cognition, 28,* 700–710.

Kimura, D. (1967). Functional asymmetry of the brain in dichotic listening. *Cortex, 3,* 163–178.

Kivy, P. (1980). *The corded shell: Reflections on musical expression.* Princeton, NJ: Princeton University Press.

Koelsch, S. (2005). Neural substrates of processing syntax and semantics in music. *Current Opinion in Neurobiology, 15,* 1–6.

Koelsch, S. (2006). Significance of Broca's area and ventral premotor cortex for music-syntactic processing. *Cortex, 42,* 518–520.

Koelsch, S., & Siebel, W. A. (2005). Towards a neural basis of music perception. *Trends in Cognitive Sciences, 9,* 578–584.

Koester, L. S., & Farley, F. H. (1982). Psychophysiological characteristics and school performance of children in open and traditional classrooms. *Journal of Educational Psychology, 74,* 254–263.

Kolb, B., & Whishaw, I. Q. (1990). *Fundamentals of human neuropsychology.* New York: Freeman.

Kovacs, M., & Beck, A. T. (1977). An empirical clinical approach toward a definition of childhood depression. In J. G. Schulterbrandt & A. Raskin (Eds.), *Depression in childhood: Diagnosis, treatment, and conceptual models* (pp. 1–25). New York: Raven.

Kronman, U., & Sundberg, J. (1987). Is the musical ritard an allusion to physical motion? In A. Gabrielsson (Ed.), *Action and perception in rhythm and music* (pp. 57–68). Stockholm: Royal Swedish Academy of Music.

Krumhansl, C. L. (1979). The psychological representation of musical pitch in a tonal context. *Cognitive Psychology, 11,* 346–374.

Krumhansl, C. L. (1990). *Cognitive foundations of musical pitch.* Oxford, UK: Oxford University Press.

Krumhansl, C. L. (1991). Memory for musical surface. *Memory & Cognition, 19,* 401–411.

Krumhansl, C. L. (1997). An exploratory study of musical emotions and psychophysiology. *Canadian Journal of Experimental Psychology, 51*(4), 336–352.

Krumhansl, C. L. (2000). Rhythm and pitch in music cognition. *Psychological Bulletin, 126,* 159–179.

Krumhansl, C. L. (2002). Music: A link between cognition and emotion. *Current Directions in Psychological Science, 11,* 45–50.

Krumhansl, C. L., & Iverson, P. (1992). Perceptual interactions between musical pitch and timbre. *Journal of Experimental Psychology: Human Perception and Performance, 18,* 739–751.

Krumhansl, C. L., & Jusczyk, P. W. (1990). Infants' perception of phrase structure in music. *Psychological Science, 1,* 70–73.

Krumhansl, C. L., & Keil, F. C. (1982). Acquisition of the hierarchy of tonal functions in music. *Memory & Cognition, 10,* 243–251.

Krumhansl, C. L., & Kessler, E. (1982). Tracing the dynamic changes in perceived tonal organization in a spatial representation of musical keys. *Psychological Review, 89,* 334–368.

Krumhansl, C. L., & Schenck, D. L. (1997). Can dance reflect the structural and expressive qualities of music? A perceptual experiment on Balanchine's choreography of Mozart's Divertimento No. 15. *Musicae Scientiae, 1,* 63–85.

Krumhansl, C. L., & Shepard, R. N. (1979). Quantification of the hierarchy of tonal functions within a diatonic context. *Journal of Experimental Psychology: Human Perception and Performance, 5,* 579–594.

Kubrick, S. (director). (1968). *2001: A space odyssey* [Motion picture]. Los Angeles: MGM.

Kunej, D., & Turk, I. (2000). New perspectives on the beginning of music: Archeological and musicological analysis of a Middle Paleolithic bone "flute." In B. Merker, N. L. Wallin, & S. Brown (Eds.), *The origins of music* (pp. 235–268). Cambridge, MA: MIT Press.

Kurosawa, K., & Davidson, J. W. (2005). Nonverbal behaviours in popular music performance: A case study of The Corrs. *Musicae Scientiae, 9,* 111–133.

Lamb, S. J., & Gregory, A. H. (1993). The relationship between music and reading in beginning readers. *Educational Psychology, 13,* 19–27.

Langer, S. K. (1957). *Philosophy in a new key* (3rd ed.). New York: New American Library.

Large, E. W., & Jones, M. R. (1999). The dynamics of attending: How we track time-varying events. *Psychological Review, 106,* 119–159.

Large, E. W, Palmer, C., & Pollack, J. B. (1995). Reduced memory representations for music. *Cognitive Science, 19,* 53–96.

Lazarus, R. S. (1982). Thoughts on the relations between emotions and cognition. *American Psychologist, 37,* 1019–1024.

Lecanuet, J.-P. (1996). Prenatal auditory experience. In I. Deliège & J. Sloboda (Eds.), *Musical begin-*

nings (pp. 3–34). Oxford, UK: Oxford University Press.

Leman, M. (2000). An auditory model of the role of short-term memory in probe-tone ratings. *Music Perception, 17,* 481–510.

Leng, X., Shaw, G. L., & Wright, E. L. (1990). Coding of musical structure and the trion model of cortex. *Music Perception, 8,* 49–62.

Lerdahl, F. (1987). Timbral hierarchies. *Contemporary Music Review, 1*(3–4), 135–160.

Lerdahl, F. (1988). Cognitive constraints on compositional systems. In J. A. Sloboda (Ed.), *Generative processes in music: Psychology of performance, improvisation, and composition* (pp. 231–259). Oxford, UK: Clarendon.

Lerdahl, F., & Jackendoff, R. (1983). *A generative theory of tonal music.* Cambridge, MA: MIT Press.

Levi-Strauss, C. (1969). *The raw and the cooked* (J. and D. Weightman, trans.). London: Jonathan Cape (Original work published 1964).

Levitin, D. J. (1994). Absolute memory for musical pitch: Evidence from the production of learned melodies. *Perception & Psychophysics, 56,* 414–423.

Levitin, D. J., & Bellugi, U. (1998). Musical abilities in individuals with Williams Syndrome. *Music Perception, 15,* 357–389.

Levitin, D. J., & Cook, P. R. (1996). Memory for musical tempo: Additional evidence that auditory memory is absolute. *Perception & Psychophysics, 58,* 927–935.

Levitin, D. J., & Cuddy, L. L. (2004). Editorial: Introduction to the Angel of Death project. *Music Perception, 22,* 167–170.

Levitin, D. J., & Rogers, S. E. (2005). Absolute pitch: Perception, coding, and controversies. *Trends in Cognitive Science, 9,* 26–33.

Limb, C. J., Kemeny, S., Ortigoza, E. B., Rouhani, S., & Braun, A. R. (2006). Left hemispheric lateralization of brain activity during passive rhythm perception in musicians. *The Anatomical Record Part A: Discoveries in Molecular, Cellular, and Evolutionary Biology, 288,* 382–389.

Livingstone, S. R., & Thompson, W. F. (2006). Multimodal affective interaction: A comment on musical origins. *Music Perception, 24*(1), 89–94.

Livingstone, S. R., & Thompson, W. F. (in press). The emergence of music from the theory of mind. *Musicae Scientiae.*

Luria, A. R., Tsvetkova, L. S., & Futer, D. S. (1965). Aphasia in a composer (VG Shebalin). *Journal of Neurological Sciences, 2,* 288–292.

Lyons, W. (1980). *Emotion.* Cambridge, UK: Cambridge University Press.

Mâche, F. (2001). The necessity of and problems with a universal musicology. In N. L. Wallin, B. Merker, & S. Brown (Eds.), *The origins of music* (pp. 473–479). Cambridge, MA: MIT Press.

Maess, B., Koelsch, S., Gunter, T. C., & Friederici, A. D. (2001). Musical syntax is processed in Broca's area: An MEG study. *Nature Neuroscience, 4,* 540–545.

Mandler, G. (1984). *Mind and body: Psychology of emotion and stress.* New York: Norton.

Marin, O. S. M., & Perry, D. W. (1999). Neurological aspects of music perception and performance. In D. Deutsch (Ed.), *The psychology of music* (2nd ed., pp. 453–477). San Diego, CA: Academic.

Mathews, M. (1999). The ear and how it works. In P. R. Cook (Ed.), *Music cognition and computerized sound: An introduction to psychoacoustics* (pp. 1–10). Cambridge, MA: MIT Press.

Mayer, J. D., & Salovey, P. (1997). What is emotional intelligence? In P. Salovey & D. Sluyter (Eds.), *Emotional development and emotional intelligence: Educational implications* (pp. 3–31). New York: Basic Books.

McAdams, S. (2004a). Problem solving strategies in music composition: A case study. *Music Perception, 21,* 391–429.

McAdams, S. (2004b). Prolog. *Music Perception, 22,* 171–172.

McDermott, J., & Hauser, M. (2005). The origins of music: Innateness, uniqueness, and evolution. *Music Perception, 23,* 29–59.

McNair, D. M., Lorr, M., & Droppleman, L. F. (1992). *The profile of mood states*. San Diego, CA: EDITS/ Educational and Industrial Testing Service.

McPherson, G. E. (1993). Factors and abilities influencing the development of visual, aural and creative performance skills in music and their educational implications. *Dissertation Abstracts International, 54/04-A, 1277*. (UMI No. 9317278)

McPherson, G. E., & Thompson, W. F. (1998). Assessing music performance: Issues and influences. *Research Studies in Music Education, 10*, 12–24.

Meister, I. G., Krings, T., Foltys, H, Boroojerdi, B., Müller, M., Töpper, R., et al. (2004). Playing piano in the mind—An fMRI study on music imagery and performance in pianists. *Cognitive Brain Research, 19*, 219–228.

Menon, V., & Levitin, D. J. (2005). The rewards of music listening: Response and physiological connectivity of the mesolimbic system. *Neuroimage, 28*, 175–184.

Merriam, A. P. (1964). *The anthropology of music*. Chicago: Northwestern University Press.

Meyer, L. B. (1956). *Emotion and meaning in music*. Chicago: University of Chicago Press.

Meyer, L. B. (1973). *Explaining music: Essays and explorations*. Chicago: University of Chicago Press.

Meyer, L. B. (1989). *Style and music: Theory, history, and ideology*. Philadelphia: University of Pennsylvania Press.

Miller, G. A. (1956). The magical number seven, plus or minus two: Some limits on our capacity for processing information. *Psychological Review, 63*, 81–97.

Miller, G. F. (2000). Evolution of human music through sexual selection. In N. L. Wallin, B. Merker, & S. Brown (Eds.), *The origins of music* (pp. 329–360). Cambridge, MA: MIT Press.

Milliman, R. E. (1982). Using background music to affect the behavior of supermarket shoppers. *Journal of Marketing, 46*, 86–91.

Milner, B. (1962). Laterality effects in audition. In V. B. Mountcastle (Ed.), *Interhemispheric relations and cerebral dominance* (pp. 177–195). Baltimore: Johns Hopkins University Press.

Miyazaki, K. (1993). Absolute pitch as an inability: Identification of musical intervals in a tonal context. *Music Perception, 11*, 55–72.

Miyazaki, K. (2004). Recognition of transposed melodies by absolute-pitch possessors. *Japanese Psychological Research, 46*, 270–282.

Monahan, C. B., & Carterette, E. C. (1985). Pitch and duration as determinants of musical space. *Music Perception, 3*, 1–32.

Morrison, S. J. (1994). Music students and academic growth. *Music Educators Journal, 81*(2), 33–36.

Morton, D. (1976). *The traditional music of Thailand*. Los Angeles: University of California Press.

Morton, J. B., & Trehub, S. E. (2001). Children's understanding of emotion in speech. *Child Development, 72*, 834–843.

Mozart, W. A. (1985). Sonata for two pianos in D major. K 448 (K. 3375a) [Recorded by M. Parahia & R. Lupu]. On *Music for piano, four hands* [CD]. London: Sony Classical. (1992)

Murray, I. R., & Arnott, J. L. (1993). Toward the simulation of emotion in synthetic speech: A review of the literature on human vocal emotion. *Journal of the Acoustical Society of America, 93*, 1097–1108.

Nantais, K. M., & Schellenberg, E. G. (1999). The Mozart effect: An artifact of preference. *Psychological Science, 10*, 370–373.

Narmour, E. (1990). *The analysis and cognition of basic melodic structures*. Chicago: University of Chicago Press.

Nattiez, J.-J. (1987). *Music and discourse: Toward a semiology of music* (Carolyn Abbate, trans). Princeton, NJ: Princeton University Press.

NBC News (Producer). (1994, September 1). *Dateline NBC*. Livingston, NJ: Burrelle's Information Services.

Nilsonne, A., & Sundberg, J. (1985). Differences in ability of musicians and nonmusicians to judge emotional state from the fundamental frequency of voice samples. *Music Perception, 2*, 507–516.

Nkeita, J. H. K. (1988). *The music of Africa*. London: Gollanz.

O'Hanlon, J. F. (1981). Boredom: Practical consequences and a theory. *Acta Psychologica, 49,* 53–82.

Oram, N., & Cuddy, L. L. (1995). Responsiveness of Western adults to pitch-distributional information in melodic sequences. *Psychological Research, 57,* 103–118.

Overy, K. (2002). *Dyslexia and music: From timing deficits to music intervention.* Unpublished doctoral dissertation, University of Sheffield, Sheffield, UK.

Palmer, C. (1989). Mapping musical thought to musical performance. *Journal of Experimental Psychology: Human Perception and Performance, 15,* 331–346.

Palmer, C. (2005). Time course of retrieval and movement preparation in music performance. *Annals of the New York Academy of Sciences, 1060,* 360–367.

Palmer, C., & Kelly, M. C. (1992). Linguistic prosody and musical meter in song. *Journal of Memory and Language, 31,* 515–542.

Palmer, C., & Krumhansl, C. L. (1987a). Independent temporal and pitch structures in determination of musical phrases. *Journal of Experimental Psychology: Human Perception & Performance, 13,* 116–126.

Palmer, C., & Krumhansl, C. L. (1987b). Pitch and temporal contributions to musical phrase perception. *Perception & Psychophysics, 41,* 116–126.

Palmer, C., & Pfordresher, P. Q. (2003). Incremental planning in sequence production. *Psychological Review, 110,* 683–712.

Palmer, C., & van de Sande, C. (1993). Units of knowledge in music performance. *Journal of Experimental Psychology: Learning, Memory, and Cognition, 19,* 457–470.

Pantev, C., Oostenveld, R., Engelien, A., Ross, B., Roberts, L. E., & Hoke, M. (1998). Increased auditory cortical representation in musicians. *Nature, 392,* 811–814.

Parncutt, R. (1994). A perceptual model of pulse salience and metrical accent in musical rhythms. *Music Perception, 11,* 409–464.

Parncutt, R. (2006). Prenatal development. In G. E. McPherson (Ed.), *The child as musician* (pp. 1–31). Oxford, UK: Oxford University Press.

Parsons, L. M. (2001). Exploring the functional neuroanatomy of music performance, perception, and comprehension. *Annals of the New York Academy of Sciences, 930,* 211–225.

Patel A. D. (2003). Language, music, syntax and the brain. *Nature Neuroscience, 6,* 674–681.

Patel, A. D. (2008). *Music, language, and the brain.* New York: Oxford University Press.

Patel, A. D., & Daniele, J. R. (2003). An empirical comparison of rhythm in language and music. *Cognition, 87,* B35–B45.

Patel, A. D., Foxton, J. M., & Griffiths, T. D. (2005). Musically tone-deaf individuals have difficulty discriminating intonation contours extracted from speech. *Brain and Cognition, 59,* 310–313.

Patel, A. D., Iverson, J. R., & Rosenberg, J. C. (2004). Comparing the rhythm and melody of speech and music: The case of British English and French. *Journal of the Acoustical Society of America, 119,* 3034–3047.

Patel, A. D., Peretz, I., Tramo, M., & Labrecque, R. (1998). Processing prosodic and music patterns: A neuropsychological investigation. *Brain and Language, 61,* 123–144.

Pearce, M. T., Meredith, D., & Wiggins, G. A. (2002). Motivations and methodologies for automation of the compositions process. *Musicae Scientiae, 6,* 119–147.

Peretz, I. (1993). Auditory atonality for melodies. *Cognitive Neuropsychology, 10,* 21–56.

Peretz, I. (1996). Can we lose memories for music? The case of music agnosia in a nonmusician. *Journal of Cognitive Neurosciences, 8,* 481–496.

Peretz, I. (2001). Brain specialization for music: New evidence from congenital amusia. *Annals of the New York Academy of Sciences, 930,* 153–165.

Peretz, I. (2002). Brain specialization for music. *Neuroscientist, 8,* 372–380.

Peretz, I. (2006). The nature of music from a biological perspective. *Cognition, 100,* 1–32.

Peretz, I., & Babai, M. (1992). The role of contour and intervals in the recognition of melody parts:

Evidence from cerebral asymmetries in musicians. *Neuropsychologia, 30,* 277–292.

Peretz, I., & Gagnon, L. (1999). Dissociation between recognition and emotional judgment for melodies. *Neurocase, 5,* 21–30.

Peretz, I., Gagnon, L., Hébert, S. & Macoir, J. (2004). Singing in the brain: Insights from cognitive neuropsychology. *Music Perception, 21*(3), 373–390.

Peretz, I., Gaudreau, D., & Bonnel, A.-M. (1998). Exposure effects on music preference and recognition. *Memory and Cognition, 26,* 884–902.

Peretz, I., Kolinski, R., Tramo, M., Labrecque, R., Hublet, C., Demeurisse, G., et al. (1994). Functional dissociations following bilateral lesions of auditory cortex. *Brain, 117,* 1283–1302.

Peretz, I., & Kolinsky, R. (1993). Boundaries of separability between melody and rhythm in music discrimination: A neuropsychological perspective. *Quarterly Journal of Experimental Psychology, 46A,* 301–325.

Peretz, I., & Morais, J. (1989). Music and modularity. *Contemporary Music Review, 4,* 277–291.

Peretz, I., & Zatorre, R. J. (Eds.). (2001). *The biological foundations of music* (Annals of the New York Academy of Sciences, Vol. 930). New York: New York Academy of Sciences.

Peretz, I., & Zatorre, R. J. (2005). Brain organization for music processing. *Annual Review of Psychology, 56,* 89–114.

Phillips-Silver, J., & Trainor, L. J. (2005) Feeling the beat: Movement influences infant rhythm perception. *Science, 308,* 1430.

Pierce, J. (1999). Sound waves and sine waves. In P. R. Cook (Ed.), *Music cognition and computerized sound: An introduction to psychoacoustics* (pp. 37–56). Cambridge, MA: MIT Press.

Pinker, S. (1997). *How the mind works.* New York: Norton.

Piston, W. (1962). *Harmony* (3rd ed.). New York: Norton. (Original work published 1941)

Plantinga, J., & Trainor, L. J. (2005). Memory for melody: Infants use a relative pitch code. *Cognition, 98,* 1–11.

Platel, H., Price, C., Baron, J. C., Wise, R., Lambert, J., Frackowiak, R. S., et al. (1997). The structural components of music perception: A functional anatomical study. *Brain, 120,* 229–243.

Plomp, R., & Levelt, W. J. M. (1965). Tonal consonance and critical bandwidth. *Journal of the Acoustical Society of America, 37,* 548–560.

Pressing, J. (1984). Cognitive processes in improvisation. In W. R. Crozier & A. J. Chapman (Eds.), *Cognitive processes in the perception of art* (pp. 345–363). Amsterdam: Elsevier Science.

Pressing, J. (1988). Improvisation: Methods and models. In J. A. Sloboda (Ed.), *Generative processes in music: The psychology of performance, improvisation, and composition* (pp. 129–178). Oxford, UK: Clarendon.

Pressnitzer, D., McAdams, S., Winsberg, S., & Fineberg, J. (2000). Perception of musical tension for nontonal orchestral timbres and its relation to psychoacoustic roughness. *Perception & Psychophysics, 62,* 66–80.

Querleu, C., Lefebvre, C., Titran, M., Renard, X., Morillion, M., & Crepin, G. (1984). Réactivité du nouveauné de moins de deux heures de vie à la voix maternelle [Reactivity to the maternal voice by a two-hour old newborn]. *Journal de gynecologie, obstetrique et biologie de la reproduction, 13,* 125–134.

Quian Quiroga, R., Reddy, L., Kreiman, G., Koch, C., & Fried, I. (2005). Invariant visual representation by single neurons in the human brain. *Nature, 435,* 1102–1107.

Radvansky, G. A., Fleming, K. J., & Simmons, J. A. (1995). Timbre reliance in nonmusicians' and musicians' memory for melodies. *Music Perception, 13,* 127–140.

Raffman, D. (1993). *Language, music, and mind.* Cambridge, MA: MIT Press.

Rasch, R. A. (1979). Synchronization in performed ensemble music. *Acustica, 43,* 121–131.

Rauscher, F. H., Shaw, G. L., & Ky, K. N. (1993). Music and spatial task performance. *Nature, 365,* 611.

Rauscher, F. H., Shaw, G. L., Levine, L. J., Wright, E. L., Dennis, W. R., & Newcomb, R. L. (1997). Music training causes long-term enhancement of preschool children's spatial-temporal reasoning. *Neurological Research, 19,* 1–8.

Rauscher, F. H., & Zupan, M. (2000). Classroom keyboard instruction improves kindergarten children's spatial-temporal performance: A field experiment. *Early Childhood Research Quarterly, 15,* 215–228.

Repp, B. H., & Knoblich, G. (2007). Action can affect auditory perception. *Psychological Science, 18,* 6–7.

Resnicow, J. E., Salovey, P., & Repp, B. H. (2004). Is recognition of emotion in music performance an aspect of emotional intelligence? *Music Perception, 22,* 145–158.

Reynolds, R. (2001). *The Angel of Death,* for piano solo, chamber orchestra, and computer-processed sound. New York: C. F. Peters.

Reynolds, R. (2004). Compositional strategies in *The Angel of Death* for piano, chamber orchestra, and computer-processed sound. *Music Perception, 22,* 173–205.

Rigg, M. G. (1964). The mood effects of music: A comparison of data from earlier investigations. *Journal of Psychology, 58,* 427–438.

Robinson, K., & Patterson, R. D. (1995). The duration required to identify an instrument, the octave, or the pitch chroma of a musical note. *Music Perception, 13,* 1–15.

Roederer, J. G. (1984). The search for a survival value of music. *Music Perception, 1,* 350–356.

Russo, F. A., & Thompson, W. F. (2005a). An interval size illusion: Extra pitch influences on the perceived size of melodic intervals. *Perception & Psychophysics, 67(4),* 559–568.

Russo, F. A., & Thompson, W. F. (2005b). The subjective size of melodic intervals over a two-octave range. *Psychonomic Bulletin and Review, 12,* 1068–1075.

Sacks, O. (2007). *Musicophilia: Tales of music and the brain.* New York: Picador.

Saffran, J. R. (2003). Absolute pitch in infancy and adulthood: The role of tonal structure. *Developmental Science, 6,* 37–45.

Saffran, J. R., & Griepentrog, G. J. (2001). Absolute pitch in infant auditory learning: Evidence for developmental reorganization. *Developmental Psychology, 37,* 74–85.

Saffran, J. R., Loman, M. M., & Robertson, R. R. W. (2000). Infant memory for musical experiences. *Cognition, 77,* B15–B23.

Said, E. W. (1992). *Musical elaborations.* London: Vintage.

Salovey, P., & Grewal, D. (2005). The science of emotional intelligence. *Current Directions in Psychological Science, 14,* 281–285.

Sarason, I. G. (1980). *Test anxiety: Theory, research, and applications.* Hillsdale, NJ: Erlbaum.

Schacter, D. L. (1987). Implicit memory: History and current status. *Journal of Experimental Psychology: Learning, Memory, & Cognition, 13,* 501–518.

Schellenberg, E. G. (1997). Simplifying the implication-realization model of melodic expectancy. *Music Perception, 14,* 295–318.

Schellenberg, E. G. (2000). Music and nonmusical abilities. *Annals of the New York Academy of Sciences, 930,* 355–371.

Schellenberg, E. G. (2004). Music lessons enhance I.Q. *Psychological Science, 15,* 511–514.

Schellenberg, E. G. (2005). Music and cognitive abilities. *Current Directions in Psychological Science, 14,* 322–325.

Schellenberg, E. G., Bigand, E., Poulin, B., Garnier, C., & Stevens, C. (2005). Children's implicit knowledge of harmony in western music. *Developmental Science, 8,* 551–566.

Schellenberg, E. G., Iverson, P., & McKinnon, M. C. (1999). Name that tune: Identifying popular recordings from brief excerpts. *Psychonomic Bulletin & Review, 6,* 641–646.

Schellenberg, E. G., Krysciak, A., & Campbell, R. J. (2000). Perceiving emotion in melody: Effects of pitch and rhythm. *Music Perception, 18,* 155–172.

Schellenberg, E. G., & Trainor, L. J. (1996). Sensory consonance and the perceptual similarity of complex-tone harmonic intervals: Tests of adult and infant listeners. *Journal of the Acoustical Society of America, 100,* 3321–3328.

Schellenberg, E. G., & Trehub, S. E. (1994). Frequency ratios and the perception of tone patterns. *Psychonomic Bulletin & Review, 1,* 191–201.

Schellenberg, E. G., & Trehub, S. E. (1996a). Children's discrimination of melodic intervals. *Developmental Psychology, 32,* 1039–1050.

Schellenberg, E. G., & Trehub, S. E. (1996b). Natural intervals in music: A perspective from infant listeners. *Psychological Science, 7,* 272–277.

Schellenberg, E. G., & Trehub, S. E. (1999). Culture-general and culture-specific factors in the discrimination of melodies. *Journal of Experimental Child Psychology, 74,* 107–127.

Schellenberg, E. G., & Trehub, S. E. (2003). Accurate pitch memory is widespread. *Psychological Science, 14,* 262–266.

Schenker, H. (1954). *Harmony* (O. Jonas, Ed., & E. M. Borgese, Trans.). Chicago: University of Chicago Press.

Schlaug, G., Janke, L., Huang, Y., & Steinmetz, H. (1995). In vivo evidence of structural brain asymmetry in musicians. *Science, 267,* 699–701.

Schneider, P., Scherg, M., Dosch, H. G., Specht, H. J., Gutschalk, A., & Rupp, A. (2002). Morphology of Heschl's gyrus reflects enhanced activation in the auditory cortex of musicians. *Nature Neuroscience, 5,* 688–694.

Schubert, E. (2001). Continuous measurement of self-report emotional response to music. In P. N. Juslin & J. A. Sloboda (Eds.), *Music and emotion: Theory and research* (pp. 393–414). Oxford, UK: Oxford University Press.

Schubert, E., & Stevens, C. (2006). The effect of implied harmony, contour and musical expertise on judgments of similarity of familiar melodies. *Journal of New Music Research, 35,* 161–174.

Schwarz, N., Bless, H., & Bohner, G. (1991). Mood and persuasion: Affective states influence the processing of persuasive communications. *Advances in Experimental Social Psychology, 24,* 161–199.

Senju, M., & Ohgushi, K. (1987). How are the player's ideas conveyed to the audience? *Music Perception, 4,* 311–323.

Sergeant, D. (1983). The octave: Percept or concept? *Psychology of Music, 11,* 3–18.

Shaffer, L. H. (1984). Timing in solo and duet piano performances. *Quarterly Journal of Experimental Psychology, 36A,* 577–595.

Shaffer, L. H., & Todd, N. P. (1987). The interpretive component in music performance. In A. Gabrielsson (Ed.), *Action and perception in rhythm and music* (pp. 139–152). Stockholm: Royal Swedish Academy of Music.

Shahin, A. J., Roberts, L. E., Pantev, C., Aziz, M., & Picton, T. W. (2007). Enhanced anterior-temporal processing for complex tones in musicians. *Clinical Neurophysiology, 118,* 209–220.

Shahin, A. J., Roberts, L. E., & Trainor, L. J. (2004). Enhancement of auditory cortical development by musical experience in children. *NeuroReport, 15,* 1917–1921.

Shapiro, B. E., & Danly, M. (1985). The role of the right hemisphere in the control of speech prosody in propositional and affective contexts. *Brain and Language, 1,* 111–139.

Shepard, R. N. (1964). Circularity in judgments of relative pitch. *Journal of the Acoustical Society of America, 36,* 2345–2353.

Shepard, R. N.(1982). Structural representations of musical pitch. In D. Deutsch (Ed.), *The psychology of music* (pp. 343–390). New York: Academic.

Shepard, R. N.(1999). Pitch perception and measurement. In P. R. Cook (Ed.), *Music, cognition, and computerized sound* (pp. 149–165). Cambridge, MA: MIT Press.

Shepard, R. N., & Jordan, D. C. (1984). Auditory illusions demonstrating that tones are assimilated to an internalized scale. *Science, 226,* 1333–1334.

Simonton, D. K. (1980). Thematic fame and melodic originality: A multivariate computer-content analysis. *Journal of Personality, 48,* 206–219.

Simonton, D. K. (1984). Melodic structure and note transition probabilities: A content analysis of 15,618 classical themes. *Psychology of Music, 12,* 3–16.

Simonton, D. K. (1993). Genius and chance: A Darwinian perspective. In J. Brockman (Ed.),

Creativity (pp. 176–201). New York: Simon & Schuster.

Simonton, D. K. (1997). Products, persons, and periods: A historiometric analysis of compositional creativity. In D. J. Hargreaves & A. C. North (Eds.). *The social psychology of music* (pp. 107–122). Oxford, UK: Oxford University Press.

Skinner, B. F. (1969). *Contingencies of reinforcement: A theoretical analysis.* New York: Appleton-Century-Crofts.

Slawson, A. W. (1968). Vowel quality and musical timbre as functions of spectrum envelope and fundamental frequency. *Journal of the Acoustical Society of America, 43,* 87–101.

Slawson, A. W. (1985). *Sound color.* Berkeley: University of California Press.

Slobin, M. (1993). *Subcultural sounds: Micromusics of the West.* Hanover, NH: University Press of New England.

Sloboda, J. A. (1985). *The musical mind: The cognitive psychology of music.* Oxford, UK: Oxford University Press.

Sloboda, J. A. (1991). Music structure and emotional response: Some empirical findings. *Psychology of Music, 19,* 110–120.

Sloboda, J. A. (2000). Individual differences in music performance. *Trends in Cognitive Sciences, 4,* 397–403.

Sloboda, J. A. (2004). *Exploring the musical mind.* Oxford, UK: Oxford University Press.

Sloboda, J. A., Davidson, J. W., & Howe, M. J. A. (1994). Is everyone musical? *The Psychologist, 7,* 349–354.

Sloboda, J. A., Davidson, J. W., Howe, M. J. A., & Moore, D. C. (1996). The role of practice in the development of performing musicians. *British Journal of Psychology, 87,* 287–309.

Snyder, B. (2000). *Music and memory.* Cambridge, MA: MIT Press.

Standley, J. M., & Hughes, J. E. (1997). Evaluation of an early intervention music curriculum for enhancing prereading/writing skills. *Music Therapy Perspectives, 15,* 79–85.

Steele, K. M., Bass, K. E., & Crook, M. D. (1999). The mystery of the Mozart effect: Failure to replicate. *Psychological Science, 10,* 366–369.

Steele, K. M., Dalla Bella, S., Peretz, I., Dunlop, T., Dawe, L. A., Humphrey, G. K., et al. (1999). Prelude or requiem for the "Mozart effect"? *Nature, 400,* 827.

Stewart, L., & Walsh, V. (2005). Infant learning: Music and the baby brain. *Current Biology, 15,* 882–884.

Studdert-Kennedy, M. (2000). Evolutionary implications of the particulate principle: Imitation and the dissociation of phonetic from semantic function. In C. Knight, M. Studdert-Kennedy, & J. R. Hurford (Eds.), *The evolutionary emergence of language: Social function and the origins of linguistic form* (pp. 161–176). Cambridge, UK: Cambridge University Press.

Sundberg, J. (1999). The perception of singing. In D. Deutsch (Ed.). *The psychology of music* (2nd ed., pp. 171–214). New York: Academic.

Sundberg, J., Askenfelt, A., &, Frydén, L. (1983). Musical performance: A synthesis-by-rule approach. *Computer Music Journal, 7,* 37–43.

Sundberg, J., & Verillo, V. (1980). On the anatomy of the ritard: A study of timing in music. *Journal of the Acoustical Society of America, 68,* 772–779.

Takasaka, Y. (1985). Expectancy-related cerebral potentials associated with voluntary time estimation and omitted stimulus. *Folia Psychiatrica et Neurologica Japonica, 19,* 251–268.

Takeuchi, A. H., & Hulse, S. H. (1993). Absolute pitch. *Psychological Bulletin, 113,* 345–361.

Tchaikovsky, M. (ed.) (2004). *The life and letters of Peter Ilich Tchaikovsky.* Honolulu, HI: University Press of the Pacific.

Terhardt, E., & Seewann, M. (1983). Aural key identification and its relationship to absolute pitch. *Music Perception, 1,* 63–83.

Terwogt, M., & van Grinsven, F. (1991). Musical expression of moodstates. *Psychology of Music, 19,* 99–109.

Thayer, J. F., & Levenson, R. W. (1983). Effects of music on psychophysiological responses to a stressful film. *Psychomusicology, 3,* 44–52.

Thompson, W. F. (1993). Modeling perceived relationships between melody, harmony, and key. *Perception and Psychophysics, 53,* 13–24.

Thompson, W. F. (1994). Sensitivity to combinations of musical parameters: Pitch and duration, and pitch pattern with durational pattern. *Perception & Psychophysics, 56*(3), 363–374.

Thompson, W. F. (1996). A review and empirical assessment of Eugene Narmour's *The analysis and cognition of basic melodic structures* (1990) and *The analysis and cognition of melodic complexity* (1992). *Journal of the American Musicological Society, 49* (1), 127–145.

Thompson, W. F., & Balkwill, L.-L. (2006). Decoding speech prosody in five languages. *Semiotica, 158*(1–4), 407–424.

Thompson, W. F., & Balkwill, L-L. (in press). Music and emotion: Cross-cultural similarities and differences. In P. N. Juslin & J. A. Sloboda (Eds.), *Handbook of music and emotion.* Oxford, UK: Oxford University Press.

Thompson, W. F., Balkwill, L.-L., & Vernescu, R. (2000). Expectancies generated by recent exposure to melodic sequences. *Memory & Cognition, 28,* 547–555.

Thompson, W. F., & Cuddy, L. L. (1989). Sensitivity to key change in chorale sequences: A comparison of single voices and four-voice harmony. *Music Perception, 7,* 151–168.

Thompson, W. F., & Cuddy, L. L. (1992). Perceived key movement in four-voice harmony and single voices. *Music Perception, 9,* 427–438.

Thompson, W. F., & Cuddy, L. L. (1997). Music performance and the perception of key. *Journal of Experimental Psychology: Human Perception and Performance, 23,* 116–135.

Thompson, W. F., Dalla Bella, S., & Keller, P. E. (2006). Music performance. *Advances in Cognitive Psychology, 2,* 99–102.

Thompson, W. F., Diamond, C. T. P., & Balkwill, L.-L. (1998). The adjudication of six performances of a Chopin etude: A study of expert knowledge. *Psychology of Music, 26,* 154–174.

Thompson, W. F., Graham, P., & Russo, F. A. (2005). Seeing music performance: Visual influences on perception and experience. *Semiotica, 156*(1–4), 177–201.

Thompson, W. F., & Robitaille, B. (1992). Can composers express emotions through music? *Empirical Studies of the Arts, 10*(1), 79–89.

Thompson, W. F., & Russo, F. A. (2004). The attribution of meaning and emotion to song lyrics. *Polskie Forum Psychologiczne, 9,* 51–62.

Thompson, W. F., & Russo, F. A. (2007). Facing the music. *Psychological Science, 18,* 756–757.

Thompson, W. F., Russo, F. A., & Quinto, L. (in press). Audiovisual integration of emotional cues in song. *Cognition and Emotion.*

Thompson, W. F., & Schellenberg, G. (2006). Listening to music. In R. Colwell (Ed.), *MENC handbook of music cognition & development* (pp. 72–123). Oxford, UK: Oxford University Press.

Thompson, W. F., Schellenberg, E. G., & Husain, G. (2001). Arousal, mood, and the Mozart effect. *Psychological Science, 12,* 248–251.

Thompson, W. F., Schellenberg, E. G., & Husain, G. (2004). Decoding speech prosody: Do music lessons help? *Emotion, 4,* 46–64.

Thompson, W. F., & Stainton, M. (1998). Expectancy in Bohemian folksong melodies: Evaluation of implicative principles for implicative and closural intervals. *Music Perception, 15,* 231–252.

Thompson, W. F., Sundberg, J., Friberg, A., & Frydén, L. (1989). The use of rules for expression in the performance of melodies. *Psychology of Music, 17,* 63–82.

Tillman, B., Bharucha, J. J., & Bigand, E. (2000). Implicit learning of tonality: A self-organizing approach. *Psychological Review, 107,* 885–913.

Tillmann, B., Peretz, I., Bigand, E., & Gosselin, N. (2007). Harmonic priming in an amusic patient: The power of implicit tasks. *Cognitive Neuropsychology, 24*, 603–622.

Todd, N. P. (1985). A model of expressive timing in tonal music. *Music Perception, 3*, 33–58.

Tomasello, M. (2003). The key is social cognition. In D. Gentner & S. Goldin-Meadow (Eds.), *Language in mind: Advances in the study of language and thought* (pp. 47–58). London: MIT Press.

Toynbee, J. (2000). *Making popular music: Musicians, creativity, institutions.* London: Arnold.

Toynbee, J. (2003). Music, culture and creativity. In R. Middleton, M. Clayton, & T. Herbert (Eds.), *The cultural study of music* (pp. 102–112). Maidenhead, UK: Open University Press.

Trainor, L. J., & Heinmiller, B. M. (1998). The development of evaluative responses to music: Infants prefer to listen to consonance over dissonance. *Infant Behavior and Development, 21*, 77–88.

Trainor, L. J., McDonald, K. L., & Alain, C. (2002). Automatic and controlled processing of melodic contour and interval information measured by electrical brain activity. *Journal of Cognitive Neuroscience, 14*, 430–442.

Trainor, L. J., & Trehub, S. E. (1992). A comparison of infants' and adults' sensitivity to Western musical structure. *Journal of Experimental: Human Perception and Performance, 18*, 394–402.

Trainor, L. J., & Trehub, S. E. (1994). Key membership and implied harmony in Western tonal music: Developmental perspectives. *Perception & Psychophysics, 56*, 125–132.

Trehub, S. E., Schellenberg, E. G., & Hill, D. S. (1997). The origins of music perception and cognition: A developmental perspective. In I. Deliège & J. A. Sloboda (Eds.), *Perception and cognition of music* (pp 103–128). East Sussex, UK: Psychology Press.

Trehub, S. E., Schellenberg, E. G., & Kamenetsky, S. B. (1999). Infants' and adults' perception of scale structure. *Journal of Experimental Psychology: Human Perception and Performance, 25*, 965–975.

Treisman, A. (1986). Features and objects in visual processing. *Scientific American, 254*(11), 114–125.

Treisman, A., & Gelade, G. (1980). A feature integration theory of attention. *Cognitive Psychology, 12*, 97–136.

Treisman, A., & Schmidt, H. (1982). Illusory conjunctions in the perception of objects. *Cognitive Psychology, 14*, 107–141.

Trevarthen, C. (1999). Musicality and the intrinsic motive pulse: Evidence from human psychobiology and infant communication. *Musicae Scientiae*, 155–215.

Trimmer, C. G., & Cuddy L. L. (in press). Emotional intelligence, not music training, predicts recognition of emotional speech prosody. *Emotion.*

van Noorden, L. P. A. S. (1975). *Temporal coherence in the perception of tone sequences.* Eindhoven, The Netherlands: Druk vam Voorschoten.

Van Lacker, D., & Sidtis, J. J. (1992). The identification of affective-prosodic stimuli by left-and right-hemisphere-damaged subjects: All errors are not created equal. *Journal of Speech and Hearing Research, 35*, 963–970.

Vaughn, K. (2000). Music and mathematics: Modest support for the oft-claimed relationship. *Journal of Aesthetic Education, 34*(3–4), 149–166.

Vines, B. W., Krumhansl, C. L., Wanderley, M. M., & Levitin, D. J. (2005). Cross-modal interactions in the perception of musical performance. *Cognition, 101*, 80–113.

von Hippel, P. (2000). Redefining pitch proximity: Tessitura and mobility as constraints on melodic intervals. *Music Perception, 17*, 315–327.

von Hippel, P., & Huron, D. (2000). Why do skips precede reversals? The effect of tessitura on melodic structure. *Music Perception, 18*, 59–85.

Vos, P. G. (1978). *Identification of meter in music* (Internal Rep. No. 78 ON 06). Nijmegen, The Netherlands: University of Nijmegen.

Vos, P. G. (2000). Tonality induction: Theoretical problems and dilemmas. *Music Perception, 17*, 403–416.

Wechsler, D. (1991). *Wechsler intelligence scale for children* (3rd ed.). San Antonio, TX: Psychological Corporation.

White, R. K. (1931). The versatility of genius. *Journal of Social Psychology, 2*, 460–489.

Whitehead, B. J. (2001). The effect of music-intensive intervention on mathematics scores of middle and high school students. Unpublished doctoral dissertation, Capella University. *Dissertations Abstracts International, 62*(08), 2710A.

Whitfield, I. C., & Evans, E. F. (1965). Responses of auditory cortical neurons to stimuli of changing frequency. *Journal of Neurophysiology, 28,* 655–672.

Winner, E., & Cooper, M. (2000). Mute those claims: No evidence (yet) for a causal link between arts study and academic achievement. *Journal of Aesthetic Education, 34*(3–4), 11–75.

Winner, E., & von Karolyi, C. (1998). Artistry and aphasia. In M. T. Sarno (Ed.), *Acquired aphasia* (3rd ed., pp. 375–411). New York: Academic.

Winter, N. (1993). Music performance assessment: A study of the effects of training and experience on the criteria used by music examiners. *International Journal of Music Education, 22,* 34–39.

Wright, J. K., & Bregman, A. S. (1987). Auditory stream segregation and the control of dissonance in polyphonic music. *Contemporary Music Review, 2,* 63–92.

Yerkes, R. M., & Dodson, J. D. (1908). The relationship of strength of stimulus to rapidity of habit formation. *Journal of Comparative and Neurological Psychology, 18,* 459–482.

Zajonc, R. B. (1980). Feeling and thinking: Preferences need no inferences. *American Psychologist, 35,* 151–175.

Zajonc, R. B. (1984). On the primacy of affect. *American Psychologist, 39,* 117–123.

Zatorre, R. J. (2005). Music, the food of neuroscience? *Nature, 434,* 312–315.

Zatorre, R. J., & Belin, P. (2001). Spectral and temporal processing in human auditory cortex. *Cerebral Cortex, 11,* 946–953.

Zatorre, R. J., Evans, A. C., & Meyer, E. (1994). Neural mechanisms underlying melodic perception and memory for pitch. *Journal of Neuroscience, 14,* 1908–1919.

Zatorre, R. J., Evans, A. C., Meyer, E., & Gjedde, A. (1992). Lateralization of phonetic and pitch processing in speech perception. *Science, 256,* 846–849.

Zatorre, R., & Peretz, I. (Eds.). (2001). *Biological foundations of music.* New York: New York Academy of Sciences.

Zatorre, R. J., & Peretz, I. (2004). Brain organization for music processing. *Annual Review of Psychology, 56,* 89–114.

Zentner, M. R., & Kagan, J. (1996). Perception of music by infants. *Nature, 383,* 29.

Author Index

Subject Index